WITHDRAWN

Esprit
de
Law

Esprit
de
Law

ANTHONY NICHOLSON

Wolfe Publishing Limited
10 Earlham Street   London WC2

ISBN 7234 0497 6

© 1973 Anthony Nicholson
© 1973 Wolfe Publishing Limited

Printed in Great Britain by
Oxley Press Limited, Edinburgh and London

Contents

Contents

Preface

'GOD FORBID that it should be imagined that an attorney, or a counsel, or even a judge is bound to know all the law,' said Chief Justice Abbott in *Montriou* v. *Jeffreys* (1825) 2 C. & P. 113. This is probably why every law book has a Preface full of excuses. The author explains that the mistakes are his own, and that the law is as stated, but only up to a certain date.

This is an attempt to avoid the effect of *De La Bere* v. *Pearson Ltd.* (1908) 1. K.B. 280 where some publishers were held negligent and made to pay damages for bad advice given in a readers' service of their periodical. Such a verdict is even more likely since the House of Lords invented 'negligent misinformation' in *Hedley Byrne & Co. Ltd.* v. *Heller & Partners Ltd.* (1964) A.C. 465. Legal writers try to show good faith by listing all the good lawyers who have checked the proofs and made 'helpful suggestions'. Then they put the blame for the Index on some newly called young woman barrister. That is the one bit the author really should write.

This book follows precedent only to a limited extent. It has similarities to other law books, such as footnote references, but it is inaccurate to the point of distortion. Anyone who takes the slightest notice of it deserves all he gets. It is also very unfair, but the lawyers and the law cannot complain about that—though

> '*The law was not made for the lawyers,*
> *The lawyers were made for the law.*'

If anyone wants to know some law, he can look into *Halsbury's Laws of England*, which claims to set it all out. The footnotes on most of its pages are longer than the text. A man once suggested that a short Act of Parliament should be passed declaring:

> '*The law of England shall from henceforth be as set out in the* Laws of England *by the Earl of Halsbury, 3rd Edition, except that the footnotes thereto shall be of no effect.*'

It would be quite a good idea, except that the Explanatory Memorandum to the Act would be about fifty volumes. Law makes much of itself. The sources are so voluminous. They are also copyright. Reproductions of a substantial kind without permission, would be breaches of copyright. When, as in this book, the references are neither substantial nor accurate, there is of course, no infringement.

Strict literal accuracy is not of course, necessary in any book about the law of England. It is in fact, most unhelpful. For instance, a deed showing title to land has long been called by lawyers, a 'conveyance'. It is exhaustively defined in the *Law of Property Act, 1925 S. 205 (1)*. For generations, lawyers have spoken of a person who buys a piece of land as 'taking a conveyance' of it. When the *Theft Act, 1968* was being drafted, the draftsman wanted to coin a phrase to cover unauthorised taking away of motor vehicles, vessels or aircraft. He hit upon the idea of creating an offence called 'taking a conveyance'.

For exposition of the language of the Statutes, and other official documents one has to resort to the reports of the judgments of the judges, and to the text books. By great good fortune, the transcripts of what the judges actually say are sent back to them to correct before they are printed. When actually speaking, they often confuse the plaintiff with the defendant, or say something unintelligible.

The main sufferers from extempore judgments are newspaper reporters.

Reporters in the High Court used to be trained in the belief that the best stories did not report what a judge said, but what he meant. They were told equally frequently that it was not for them to decide what the old fool meant but just to write down what he said. Neither of these tasks is easy. In the result a newspaper report of a lawsuit often contains more of the reporter's decision than the judge's.

This is no bad thing. It creates a wide public interest and some knowledge of the law. The knowledge is seldom accurate. But any attempt to state any proposition of English law succinctly and without qualification is doomed to the same fate. Consequently judgments distinguishing lawsuits from precedents proliferate. This necessitates more law books. The publishers observe with equanimity their rapid obsolescence and the merry ringing of the cash registers as the new editions sell out.

The profession must keep up to date. Incomplete, impractical, incomprehensible a law book may be, but it must be up to date. The Man in the Clapham Omnibus requires no such thing. He wishes to be informed about the law in the manner to which he is accustomed. This book is for him. It needs no supplements or further editions, and is unlikely to have any. It has no foreword by a distinguished judge endorsing it. This book is for the ignorant.

They are, after all, the people for whom the law exists. As Lord Atkin explained:

> *'The fact is that there is not and never has been a presumption that everyone knows the law. There is the rule that ignorance of the law does not excuse, a maxim of very different scope and application.'*
>
> **Evans v. Bartlam (1937) A.C. 473.**

The Origins Of English Justice

'A page of history is worth a volume of logic.'
Justice Oliver Wendell Holmes in *New York*
***Trust Co.* v. *Eisner, 256 U.S.*

THERE IS NOTHING funny about the law. It is so serious that anyone who makes fun of it risks falling foul of it. The fellow who 'ject un brickbat' at a judge had his throwing hand cut off. He could have learned to throw left-handed, of course. Like nasty medicine it can be good for you in small doses, but taken to excess it makes you sick. It has to be restrictive because it is protecting freedom. How could freedom survive if everyone could do as he liked?

Sir Robert Peel invented policemen in 1829, and a great many people disapproved. It would interfere with their freedom, they said. Peel thought that 'the freedom to be robbed was not worth having'. Now that more of us have enough to be worth robbing, we see the point. Most laws do not seem worthwhile for a century or so.

Since Peel's time, the police have become synonymous in some quarters with the word 'Law'. Neither the vernacular nor the social standards of those people command acceptance in the most polite society, but there is unquestionably a subliminal image of a policeman conjured up on hearing the word. However natural, it is extremely narrow-minded because the great bulk of law has nothing to do with policemen and existed before them. Motoring apart, the criminal law affects a small and not very select class, but occupies a disproportionate amount of attention. For instance, the question whether murder should be punished by death can only affect the 100 people who are on average convicted of murder each year, and many of them were unlikely to hang even before 1958. Divorce, hire purchase restrictions or death duties are important to much wider classes of the population. Changes in these laws excite little reaction. The victims of violent criminals can get compensation from a fund only seven years old and still not properly constituted by Act of Parliament whilst Parliamentarians parade their consciences over the murderers.

13

The idea of The King's Peace, or Law and Order as it is now called at Party Conferences, developed in the two centuries following the Conquest. The legal system relied for its law on that which had prevailed in ecclesiastical, seignorial and governmental councils. Men did what their forefathers had done because they could not, for the most part, think of anything better to do. The great 'lawgiver' was the Second Henry. Indeed, he probably wrote the 'obscure and disorderly book' entitled The Laws of Henry the First.

There was no 'official' law enforcement agency. Whoever wanted to prosecute someone went ahead and did it. In theory, that is still the law in England but not in Scotland. The practical problem was that even if you were strong enough and well enough armed to get your prisoner to court, the chap who ran the court might turn out to be a pal of his. You could be lucky to get away with your neck. By his Assize of Clarendon, Henry introduced a system by which twelve men from each Hundred or district 'presented' for punishment in court before the King's judges 'On Circuit' round the country, those of their neighbours who had committed crimes. Vandals were rounded up by a Posse when the Hue and Cry was raised. Except that the police had replaced the posse, this remarkable system has endured little altered to the present day. The sending of Commissioners to hold Assizes throughout the kingdom has only just been reformed. The *Courts Act, 1971,* has merged Assizes and Quarter Sessions into Crown Courts, for easier administration.

Modern conditions make it difficult for the jurors to know all the criminals. Accordingly instead of sending them straight to the Ordeal by Hot Iron, the jurors have to be told why they should declare the accused guilty because the testimony of witnesses does not always make it clear. This process of instructing juries has been a closed shop of the legal profession for several centuries. The jurors, for their part, keep their reasons for their verdicts as secret now as they did 700 years ago. The ordeal was banned by the Lateran Council in 1215. The next Vatican Council was in 1961. That perhaps helps to explain why the law of England changed very little in the meantime.

Naturally, the procedures of the various tribunals over the years varied quite considerably. Inquisition, Impeachment, Torture and Trial by Battle all had their adherents. (This last was hastily abolished in 1819 when Thistlewood, the revolutionary traitor, challenged the Home Secretary to single combat.) However, a favourite early procedure was the employment of Compurgators or 'Oath-helpers'. The more people a party could get to swear in support of his case, the more sure he was to gain the verdict. The principle survived and merged with a rather revolutionary change in the 19th Century.

Until the *Evidence Act, 1851,* no one with an interest in the case as plaintiff or defendant was permitted to testify in his own behalf. The Common Law insisted that the principal parties were much too involved for their sworn evidence to be trustworthy. It will be remembered, for instance, that neither Mrs Bardell nor Mr Pickwick gave evidence in the celebrated breach of promise case. (Dickens was a solicitor's clerk, shorthand reporter and journalist before the Act.) By 1898 reform was so great that the privilege of giving sworn evidence in their own defence was conferred upon felons. They were technically not guilty until verdict anyway, and a rather large number used to get off without the benefit of testimony or counsel. Many lived to regret the great social advance, and not a few died because of it.

This is the system in daily use at the Old Bailey and the other superior courts where the tribunal in criminal cases consists of a judge of law and a fact-finding jury of 12 men and women who qualify for service as occasional judges by occupation of all but the most sordid of housing accommodation. The virtues of this ancient constitutional tribunal are extolled by lawyers and politicians alike. Mr Heath is so keen on it that he promises we can keep it as members of the Common Market. It is hardly ever used now in civil cases, and only in the most serious fraction of criminal cases. About 40 per cent of those tried by juries are let off and the others all appeal. Consequently the lawyers who engage in such work are very busy. It might have been true some years ago to say that 'crime does not pay'. Since the improvement in availability and payment for legal aid its accuracy is highly questionable. Lawyers and criminals are doing quite well. There are plans afoot to make some of the latter automatically bankrupt on conviction, which of course can already be done by any creditor who thinks it worth the expense. Accountants and lawyers are the only people who profit from Bankruptcy.

However, it would be quite wrong to suppose that those lawyers with vested interests in the expansion of crime (detected, of course), are either the best or the most numerous. They are outnumbered by the conveyancers and probate specialists, the insurance claim and commercial experts, the town and country planners and those in local authorities and hosts of others. To see how all these developed we have continually to return to the Middle Ages.

The King, as head of the Government, always had an officer in the county called the Sheriff, but local government was pretty much up to the feudal lords. The system of Justices of the Peace was introduced early in the 14th Century (earlier than the Act of 1361 popularly supposed to have introduced them), because there was, as usual, a crime wave on. Those of them who were not feudal lords, were their friends and neighbours helping them out. Controversy exists nowadays about whether JPs should be paid. In fact, they once were but they were done out of it. They did not mind because it kept the job select. The part they were paid for was adjudicating at the Quarter Sessions. There, they tried capital offences, of which there were a large number, e.g. stealing something worth £2. The Duke of Clarence and his County Justices once indicted, tried, convicted and hanged a woman all in one day at the Warwickshire Sessions. There was a complaint in Parliament, but nothing came of it. Delay is the only thing in the processes of law that seems to upset people. JPs now sit with the Circuit Judges. The extension of the jurisdiction of Quarter Session in 1968 so that under legally qualified chairmen they could try all but the most serious crimes was regarded as a great step forward in their responsibility. Presumably, it is safe to let them loose again now that hanging has been abolished.

Lord Darling, a great crime judge, once remarked that Quarter Sessions was where young barristers learned their trade 'by giving lessons in the law of the land to those who administer the one by virtue of owning the other'. For the Justices were the local government right up to the *County Councils Act* of 1888. Then they got on to the County Councils as well as the bench. Thus they still are the local government. The last century saw the feudal lords and their relatives shove up to make room for the wealthy manufacturers. For all their social superiority to Trade, most of the post-Reformation nobility had been enriched by it. A bigger gap, more quickly bridged, was when those classes were joined in public administration and judgment by the town councillors and trades unionists of the proletarian establishment. They got along splendidly together because privilege creates fraternity just as adversity does.

Of course they do not actually run the local government any more than the Government runs the country. They do what the officials advise except in odd cases where either it seems all right to let them or they get the bit between their teeth. When they are good they are very good. But their stupidity can be quite disastrous. Some of them gave custody of an eight-month-old baby girl to her foreign father who had never seen her. They had not the common sense to stay the order until an appeal was heard. (*Desramault* v. *Desramault, 1971.*) The child was taken to France where the legal struggles for physical possession of her have already been through more processes than would have been possible here and can quite well last until the child is grown up. This ineffable conviction of their own infallibility is common among the authoritarian classes of England.

That poses the question, are untrained lay magistrates fit to exercise legal jurisdiction? Chief Justice Scrope, in the time of Edward III thought not, but Parliament favoured them. Consequently they have done it for six centuries. Whether they put down or nearly caused a revolution at the beginning of the last is a debatable question. The Peterloo Massacre of 1819 was instigated by a bumptious magistrate who ordered mounted yeomanry to charge with drawn sabres on a peaceful meeting. In 1828 Henry Brougham said they were 'the worst constituted tribunal on the face of the Earth'. Their great virtue is their cheapness. Beggars cannot be choosers and if the nation will not pay for trained justice it must put up with free justice. Oddly enough, the idea behind appointing them was to get revenue for the Exchequer from fines. Miss Bertha Putnam, who devoted thirty years to research into the subject wrote, 'Profits of justice, not justice, were the essential consideration'. (*Proceedings before the Justices of the Peace in the 14th and 15th Centuries, Edward III to Richard III, 1938, p. xli.*) It could hardly have been appreciated at the time how successful they would be with the advent of the motor car—though parking meters are even more efficient.

The people of the class from whom the Justices were drawn had need of lawyers for other purposes such as penning the muniments of title to lands, and advising them on an infinite variety of legal relationships. Of course, all their relatives employed equally astute lawyers, and this taught them all to distrust lawyers. They still do, but they make an exception for their Clerks, whom they feel, often correctly, are on their side. This makes the other lawyers distrust the Clerks. In the result, to appear before magistrates represented by a lawyer is a decided disadvantage, if not a confession of guilt. Nowadays, however, the poor can get Legal Aid and so have that disadvantage either free or at small cost. It might benefit them little but it enures to the benefit of the lawyers. This is a social service and much is made these days of the enormous improvements in our lives which they have wrought.

This, however, is a benefit capable of exaggeration. Nine centuries separate the defeat of Harold at Hastings and the victory of Harold Wilson at the hustings in 1964. The period saw infinite change in the minutiae of the laws of the British Islands, true. But there has been little alteration in the ideas underlying the system, and even less in the romantic euphoria with which it is regarded by those subject to it.

For example, the first major governmental act of William the Norman was to send Commissioners round the kingdom making the Domesday survey. It took 20 years, but laid the foundation for our social development. Cribbed no doubt from the census of Caesar Augustus which figures so prominently in the life of Christ (William's brother was a Bishop) it was a masterpiece of bureaucratic counter espionage. The governors knew all about the governed. The King could therefore rule, and exploit anyone by rearranging ownership of land. Those who owned no land were serfs.

17

These truths were self-evident to Mr Wilson who lost no time in emulating the Bastard. The introduction of Crownhold Land administered by a Land Commission was the natural extension of the peculiar feudalism which William imported. It would be quite wrong to think that Mr Wilson was the first man to think of it in 900 years. Hundreds thought of it, but he achieved it. It has been done away with, of course, but it can be brought back in an improved form just as Development Charges were reincarnated as Betterment Levy. He turned Crownhold from a theory into a law. Not an immutable natural law like Boyle's Law which is the same for everyone. A law which is a political weapon. Such developments are very gratifying to conscientious lawyers. They like life to fit their theories.

One theory which obtains in all the seats of learning is that most of English law grew out of the survival-agriculture based social system of the Middle Ages. That is perfectly true, of course, but it needs elaboration if it is to serve as a scholarly theory. Then it can be used to explain history and so justify political change. Take this land law idea. Its basic postulate is that no-one in Britain 'owns' land except the Crown, i.e. the Queen in her capacity as Head of State. Everyone else 'holds' land as a subject, and 'ownership' is automatically under the law concentrated in the Head of State. The mediaeval kings might well have thought along those lines. But their subjects, the great magnates thought they owned their land. They cannot be blamed for their ignorance. The 18th-Century jurists had not yet invented the theory.

Their entirely comprehensible ignorance was no doubt at the root of the unconstitutional behaviour of the Barons at Runnymede in 1215. Magna Carta was quite plainly executed under duress. By our standards of law today that would render it void. It can, however, be reconciled to the constitutional theory quite simply by accepting that John was a tyrant. The Barons were consequently not traitors but merely honest men, asserting their right to 'freedom under the law'. If not a paradox that is a contradiction, but it endures as a constitutional principle which we now call 'The Rule of Law'.

There are bits of the Great Charter still unrepealed, though the *Statute Laws (Repeal) Act, 1969* has not left much. It traditionally represents, with the *Revolutionary Settlement of 1689* (another illegal plot), that vague conception beloved of the demagogue, 'the ancient rights and liberties of the English people'. In truth, adult suffrage from the age of 21 has existed only since 1928. Women could not vote at all until 1920. Secret ballot suffrage from a majority of householders is just under a century old. Our real political history is compressed into the present century, and depends on property rights as much as ever.

However, just as the Barons withstood a tyrant in 1215, the television licence holders of 1970 destroyed the power of Harold Wilson. They, the privileged class at that time might not have known what they wanted but they knew whom they did not want. This is the cardinal principle of law. To paraphrase Professor Paton (*Jurisprudence, 2nd Edn. 1951 p. 6*) Law is the imposition of the will of a political superior over a political inferior.

In England the philosophy of law has never been deeply studied. The judges and anyone else who wielded even for a brief, inglorious spell the power of judgment, seldom had qualms about abstract right and wrong. Their criteria were those ideas of right and wrong which had been so regarded for a long time by their side. This discipline had clearly very little to do with justice, which is a virtue, and not a science. It had even less to do with science. More than anything, it seems to stem from prejudice.

This kind of law cannot have the simple, permanent inflexibility of a law of Nature. It is no credit to Boyle that gases expand when heated. It just happens and it does not change. The laws by which men live are not like that. Diligent philosophy has nevertheless contrived to make of law itself a science. But this is no ordinary science with immutable laws waiting only to be discovered.

This jurisprudence is the science which seeks to marry up all the ideas of all law into a scientific, rational, logical whole. Its development has suffered many setbacks. Jeremy Bentham, for instance, worked hard on an analysis of the law of England in the hope that it would lead to it being reduced to a comprehensible, logical code. His *Limits of Jurisprudence Defined*, though written in 1782 was not discovered until 1945 in a cupboard at London University. Whether our law would now be much different had someone cleared cupboards out better is doubtful. After all, the Benthamite school of lawyers and philosophers developed without it. And other writers wrote books with similar titles.

Nowadays we kid ourselves that we are rationalising laws at a great rate. This adds to the complexity of studying the law and adds a new dimension to the romantic and fascinating uncertainty of it. By the time you have learned a bit of law, it might have been altered, often by some little publicised measure. Perhaps therefore the most important date in legal history is 1474 when William Caxton set up his printing press at the sign of the Red Pale at Westminster. Much of the early printing was of law books. The Office of King's Printer was always profitable, but never more so than now. Not only are more laws printed than ever before, but each has to have an Explanatory Memorandum for, as was said of the classical mortgage of real property, they cannot be understood by the light of Nature alone. They are much dearer than they used to be as well.

It might therefore seem odd that experts commonly refer to English law as being largely unwritten. It refers to case law and it is not literally true. What it means is that what is written because it is mere reportage from ancient and uncertain sources is difficult to understand. The problem is to isolate and analyse principles. Many of these are so obvious that it does not matter at all where they came from. The Law of the Saxons, for instance, provided for *wergild* ('man-price') to be paid to the kin of a dead man by his slayer. *Bot* was the name they gave to compensation for other wrongs. The thing which killed a man was forfeit as a *deodand,* a law which was invoked last in the 19th Century with a claim to forfeit a railway engine which had killed four men. At four separate inquests in 1840 the juries held the same engine deodand. However, in *R.* v. *Eastern Counties Railway (1842 10 M. & W.)* Lord Abinger held that the Crown was entitled to four separate engines, or their value. Curiously, a generation earlier, Lord Ellenborough had ruled that a wrongful death conferred no right to compensation on widows and children (*Baker* v. *Bolton (1808) 1 Campbell's Reports 493*). Lord Campbell managed to secure the passing of the first Fatal Accidents Act in 1846, the year that deodands were abolished. Otherwise, who knows, we still might have had to pay off the widow from the salvage of a killer's car.

According to the Laws of Alfred, a man carrying a spear must hold it level on his shoulder to avoid liability if someone else ran on to the point. If he held it in such a way that we would say he was negligent the spear carrier had to pay *wer* if the other person should die. Learned professors can demonstrate clearly that the action for damages for negligence is a recent development in our law. That simply shows that the Saxons did not call it negligence. They had little refinement about their laws, and we have improved a great deal on them—usually to the disadvantage of the injured person. But one principle is as strong now as ever. A Thegn's *wer* was six times as much as a common man's. Now it can easily be ten times as expensive to maim one man rather than another. And it is often cheaper to kill than to maim (*Wise* v. *Kaye, 1938*).

Henri Poincaré called sociology 'the science with the greatest number of methods and the least results'. But that distinction belonged to law long before sociology was anything more than an exploitation of history. Neither is, of course, anything more than an exploitation of history. However, the saying is particularly true of law because no other science affords so many ways of killing the cat.

Ranulf de Glanvill, who in 1185 published the first book of

English law, tells us that then it did not trouble itself much with 'private agreements'. But this was only the law of the King's court. You could have quite a nice little dispute over a private agreement in the Consistory Court of the Chancellor of the Diocese, or the court of the Steward of the Manor or a Pie Powder Court at a Fair, if you were a merchant. Some of the local courts which grew up between then and now like the Bristol Tolzey Court and the Liverpool Court of Passage were still in business until 1st January, 1972. They were on the same level as County Courts, but some had larger jurisdictions, particularly for the disputes in the trades indigenous to the areas they served. There are no privately owned courts any more. They were all nationalised centuries ago. Only the names survived.

This did not happen overnight, but it happened for a good reason. The Kings found out that people would pay fees to have their disputes settled by the Royal Judges who were a much better class of fellow than your stewards and that sort, who quite naturally favoured their lord and his mates. This independence was the foundation of the economic success both of the English Government and of the legal profession and they have to this day prospered out of the misfortunes of their countrymen.

The way a dispute would come before the court of the King was that his Chancellor's clerks would issue in his name a Writ of Right to authorise an inquiry by a judge into a man's entitlement to land. It was in Latin and said:

'The King to the Sheriff, Greeting, Order John of Salisbury to give possession of the Manor of Nonsuch to Richard or appear in Court and shew cause why he should not.'

Naturally, the first word after 'Greeting' was 'Praecipe'. It would be followed by different words as the different remedies the suitors claimed grew more various, but the word for 'Order' was always there, directing some official to get the parties into court for the dispute. A High Court Writ of summons differs little. Quintin, Baron Hailsham in the name of the Queen orders the defendant to 'enter an appearance' usually within 14 days.* This only requires taking or posting a form to an office. It is remarkably similar to the Middle Ages, save that from the time of entering an appearance it could well be many months, or years, before the dispute is actually tried.

Standard forms of writ were in early days issued by the clerks in the Royal Chancery. Nowadays you buy a printed writ form from a law stationer and fill in what you want. In the old days if you used

---

* Since 1st February, 1972.

the wrong form of writ you lost your case. Even now you cannot just get any remedy you want by asking for it on the form. It has to be legally recognised. The strictly technical system of pleading was abolished by the *Common Law Procedure Act, 1852*. In the County Courts today, however, the form used to start an action is called a 'Praecipe', not a writ. If you use the buff-coloured (ordinary action) one when you should have used the pink (default action) one, the judge or registrar might cause you all sorts of difficulties. You could even lose your case. Not, of course, because the rigid formalism of the old Common Law clasps us still within its shackles. Because it causes much unnecessary work and confusion among the Civil Servants in the Court Office. 'The Forms of Action we have buried', wrote Frederic William Maitland, greatest of legal historians, in 1907, 'but they rule us from their graves'.

The modern law of contract—those 'private agreements' once so little considered—actually traces back in the technical form we know it now to a case decided by Mr Justice Sharshulle in 1338, which can be found in the Year Book of that date. The Romans and others all had laws of contract, of course, and so had we. This, however, marked the Genesis of the modern doctrine that there must be 'consideration' to make an agreement made informally enforceable in court. Now, of course, we have to get rid of it because they do not have it in Europe.

Like all great lawsuits it was brought by a lawyer. Like most lawyer's actions, it was a claim for fees. The defence was that the contract of employment was not recorded in a deed under seal.

> *'If one were to count simply of a grant of a debt, he would not be received without a specialty (deed). But here you have his service for his allowance of which knowledge may be had, and you have* quid pro quo.'

Thus developed the fundamental rule of the British law. Whatever happens the lawyer must be paid. It was not, however, until the 20th Century that Parliament was constrained to create a special fund for the payment of lawyers and the long-standing feud between the lawyers and the Executive is directly traceable to this deficiency. Whilst only the wealthy could afford law, the lawyers and the judges recruited from their ranks were antagonistic to politicians and officials.

Now that the legally aided poor are able to litigate, and have become the most numerous class of litigant, the Establishment ranks have closed against them. This is most regrettable. The French jurist Montesquieu wrote a book in 1748 in which he showed that the separate functions of the governing powers in a civilised state were those of the Executive, the Administration and the Judiciary.

He said that if any two or more of the powers became allied or dominated by one head, the result must be tyranny. He held up Britain as the perfection of freedom under this system. It was not true, but we were enormously flattered, and the fiction has persisted to the present that the Separation of Powers is the bulwark of our liberty.

Lord Chief Justice Hewart, who held sway from 1922 to 1939 actually published a book whilst in office, called *The New Despotism* in which he gave full freedom to his well known hatred of Civil Servants. People are constantly taking up the topic as if it was something new and clever. But every history book is full of unjust judges, and tyrannous rulers. However, what has emerged out of the philosophy of law is the treatment of all 'rights' as analogous to contractual rights in the final analysis. The lawyers recognised this much earlier than the sociologists, but that is not to be wondered at because sociologists are mostly non-practising academic lawyers living on public salaries or grants, and the High Street practitioners are always way ahead of the professors among their dreaming spires. It is important to understand it because a legal right has to be justified by this curious form of logic whenever as often happens, its existence is denied.

Now ever since men began making bargains what the jurists call *concensus ad idem* it has been necessary for the formation of a legally binding contract. This meant a 'Meeting of minds'—agreement over the terms of the contract. Contracts are often called 'agreements' —tenancy agreements, hire-purchase agreements. Many are commonly called contracts—insurance contract, contract of employment. The majority of these nowadays are on printed forms. The man or woman who wants the goods or the job or the insurance signs on the dotted line and is bound by so doing to honour the contract or take the consequences the law applies.

If he wishes to be not bound by a certain term of the agreement he is of course completely free to refuse, and the other contracting party is equally free to refuse to accommodate him. If he needs the goods, or the insurance, or the job—say to earn his living or to put his car lawfully on the road he may take what is offered or leave it and to go without. Meeting of minds there may be, but not from free choice.

The reasoning of the lawyers was like this. In the Middle Ages there existed a Writ of Praecipe for a Debt of Record. A debt of record is most often created by a decision of a court that money is due and owing, say, for damages for repairs and injuries after a motor car crash. This is called a judgment debt. If the debtor does not pay, his goods can be seized, his bank account frozen, he can be bankrupted or the creditor can have it deducted from the debtor's

23

wages. For centuries it was possible to cast the debtor into prison, but this was done away with in August, 1971, except for maintenance arrears. What is important to realise is that a debt of record is created without agreement of the debtor. Quite often, he emphatically disagrees with its creation. The disagreement is of course the trial of the case and the 'contract of record' in legal parlance, is created by the judgment.

There is nothing quintessentially different in imposing terms on a man by process of law or by economic or social necessity. There can therefore be nothing incongruous about calling that which is forced upon a man against his will a contract. Consequently, the description by Mr Harold Wilson of the condition of a member of our present society as a party to 'the Social Contract' is most apposite. You pay your Social Security premiums or go to prison; likewise your Income Tax, or Capital Gains Tax. You can be prosecuted for unpaid rates even though the dustmen will not come up the lane to empty your bin.

You might not agree in words, oral or written, to these sanctions. But you do agree by implication, by your conduct in remaining here to live instead of going somewhere else. It is of course a *non sequitur*. You remain here because you cannot afford to go elsewhere. The only reason tax havens exist to provide cheap living is because very few people are rich enough to be able to live in them. The theorist argues that the fact that you pay rather than go to prison predicates that you accept the obligation. This is another *non sequitur*. You accept social obligations but not precisely those your political superiors choose to impose upon you. Your remedy is to go into politics and become a political superior. You might get the rate of Income Tax changed or the Resale Price Maintenance Act repealed. Unless and until you do, we all have to obey the law as it is.

But the lawyers helped their clients accused of wrongs against private persons or the Crown to escape liability by insisting on hair splitting technicality. On the private dispute side this was made easier by the writ system operated by the clerks in the Chancery. They were fairly hidebound, and would only seal writs complaining of well recognised causes of action like trespass by breaking down a man's fence. In early times if the wrongdoer merely threw rubbish over the fence so that the plaintiff's cow choked on it and died, there was nothing he could do about it. Nowadays, he will probably be unable to find who did it, and still be unable to do anything about it.

However, this state of the law was altered by Edward I, known as 'the English Justinian' though in fact he was French. By the Statute of Westminster II 1285 the clerks of the Chancery were authorised to seal writs alleging damage caused in ways other than those alleged in the established writs. The Act is sometimes called *In Consimili Casu* meaning 'in like case' and the kind of blameworthy act that was covered by them was therefore said to be an 'action upon the case'. It differed from a trespass because no compensation would be awarded unless some actual loss was proved in an Action on the Case, but damage was taken for granted in trespass.

An early writ in case might go like this:

> '*The King to the Sheriff, Greeting, If John shall make you secure, etc. then put William under gages and safe pledges that he appear before our Justices at Westminster on the morrow of all Souls to show wherefore the said William fixed a certain nail in one foot of a certain horse of the said John at Lambeth by which it became putrid so that the same horse for a long time could not work and he the said John during that time lost the benefit of his horse aforesaid to the damage of the said John and against our peace*
>
> And have, etc. Witness Etc.

Nowadays that would be a pretty ordinary statement of claim in a breach of contract case. But nobody then bothered much about whether a contract had been made. Rights were implied without agreement in certain fairly obvious cases according to the usage of society.

It has been learnedly contended that the Second Statute of Westminster did not start all this at all, but that it began with an Ordinance of Simon de Montfort's Parliament. It might very well be so. That does not matter: what does matter is that every system of law develops means of imposing duties upon people for the governance of their society collectively and the settlement of their disputes individually. The precise details of the rights, duties and remedies at a given time, when compared, reveal substantial differences, the virtues and benefits of which are accorded totally disproportionate importance by Reformers. Reformers are often politicians on the make. Their traditional opponents are lawyers on the make.

Thus in the study of English Law it is not only a fascinating mental exercise to discover what was the law of the Middle Ages and its language, it is a practical necessity. For to a very great extent it is our present law.

It is however, very helpful to recall that, as Maitland pointed out, the mediaeval Writ of Trespass was the 'fertile mother of actions'. We realise that what we now classify as crimes—wrongs punishable by the State, from murder to riding a bike without lights—have the same roots as wrongs requiring mere compensation such as running someone over, or prevention, such as nuisance by a noisy radio. Running people over is still, of course, a crime. The difference which seven centuries of jurisprudence has made is that originally a person was not guilty of trespass unless he did the wrong act intentionally. Now, however unintentionally you run someone over, you can be imprisoned for dangerous driving and made to pay compensation as well.

The history of our law is not merely a catalogue of compromise to overcome social disorder, however. Whilst the simple old principles have been perpetuated, they have also been distorted and confused to cope with change. It is possible with considerable expenditure of scholarship to trace such laws back through history, and that is really what the study of the Common Law and the system of Equity does. However, the eternal conflict between the lawyers who say what the law is, and Government who says what it ought to be, has resulted in the old customary law being overlaid by a multitude of statutes, most of which with great abruptness, change old laws or invent new ones. Whilst it is true that the lawful interpretation of these decrees is left to the judges the actual implementation of the great majority is in the hands of Government servants or agents. Some have been trained as lawyers, but most of them have not that disadvantage. They pass under the collective title of 'Officials' a term never defined in our law, even in the *Officia Secrets Acts, 1911–39.* So insecure and illusory is the power of our legal governors, however, that these creatures wield great power by reason of their permanence.

This has gone on for a long time, of course. The Council who sat in the Star Chamber were not all lawyers. They were bishops and noblemen and self-made entrepreneurs, who were all officials. Many of them were trained in the law and those who were not realised the importance of having on their side the best legal brains. They called them King's Counsel because they were retained to present the King's (or the Queen's) cases in the Star Chamber. The Monarch signed Letters Patent declaring that they were learned in the law. Nowadays they have to pay for the scrivenery of the Letters Patent and they have no guarantee of employment because the Star Chamber was abolished in 1641. Some people think it has been replaced by more modern tribunals, but that is very little help to these people distinguished by their gowns of Silk, because many of those tribunals dispense altogether with the services of lawyers.

But Star Chamber and the Council of the North and the Court of High Commission were founded upon a proposition which Governments at least find essential to civilisation. Those officials knew that they had to reduce the nation to order after the anarchy of the Wars of the Roses, and they knew they could not manage that by having fair trials. They knew the people with whom they dealt were guilty—in their eyes if in no one else's. What they had to do was convict them, whatever the law was. If it did not permit of convicting them, then new laws would have to be invented which did. Once convict them with some colour of legality, and they could kill or maim the worst, and make the rich ones pay huge fines which would at once profit the King and break their economic power. It is hardly to be supposed that such a policy would not commend itself to politicians, and it has been widely emulated abroad, e.g. South Africa, Dominica, and behind the Iron Curtain.

'The criminal law,' declares Russell on *Crime* (*1964 Edition, Vol. 2, p. 200*), 'is an instrument of government'. Is, not was. Star Chamber invented the crimes of conspiracy and seditious libel and other misdemeanours too sophisticated to develop by Common Law from the mere pursuit of cutpurses. They are with us still, together with improved crimes for which there is no defence. And not only in the substantive law did those Prerogative courts improve our law. The main aspects of the procedure of the Star Chamber are supposed to be employed no longer. The one which is admitted on all hands to survive is the use of affidavits, instead of oral evidence given from the witness box. It is convenient to reduce it to a written statement sworn to be true. It is used mainly in the Chancery Division, where suitors are much too busy and important to be able to go to court personally for every hearing. It is making strides elsewhere, particularly in the Divorce Courts. It is not clear whether it was Lord Justice Bowen or Lord Justice Chitty who said, 'Truth will out, even in an affidavit'. But it shows that the late Victorian judges were acutely conscious of the advantages of the system.

In the Star Chamber, of course the prosecution never showed the accused the affidavits condemning him—at least until he had confessed. This might have been because some of the signatures were a bit shaky after the torturers had finished with the witnesses. That is an aspect of procedure no longer widely employed, though it is true to say that witnesses are very often worse treated than criminals. They are required to give up their time, and lose wages, and hang about until they are wanted for much longer than the time they spend in the witness box. Then one side tells them not to bother with this and that and the other side calls them liars. They can be imprisoned for contempt of court if they do not turn up, or even if they do, and are cheeky. However, they are seldom tortured, and in truth, they seldom were in private litigation. It was only in affairs of State that officials felt duty bound to go that far.

Star Chamber procedure at the hearing was inquisitorial, like the French. Our modern procedure of having two teams of lawyers umpired by a judge owes more perhaps to cricket than to legal history. (Cricket scores are the one irrelevance which can be introduced in practically any court without risk of a contempt charge.)

27

The procedure was for the accused to be brought before the Council (with or without chains depending as the officials wanted him to turn his coat or not) but he was not asked whether he was guilty or not. He was asked straight out, why he did it and who helped. If he started lying about being innocent, he was told that the affidavits proved otherwise. If he kept on, they pulled his tongue out. This is the bit that we have done away with. In most other respects, the procedure is used to some extent. We have enormous respect for the legal wisdom of Sir Edward Coke, who was a Star Chamber prosecutor, and is often held up as the great champion of our constitutional liberty.

Keeping order in the courts is more difficult than it was then, but on balance the lawyers prefer it as it is now. The longer-winded modern procedure is acceptable because since late Victorian times, lawyers have been paid by the day. Contrary to popular prejudice, the 'refresher fee' which is supposed to make litigation go on too long, is a recent innovation. It is, of course, a foundation of justice because the accusatorial procedure could never be operated without it. It is noteworthy that in Spain, Haiti and other totalitarian countries where the inquisitorial system prevails, the lawyers are often poor, unless they work for the government.

There was very little development of the law except those Tudor innovations, between the Middle Ages and the middle of the 19th Century. This was of course, because nothing much happened during that period, anyway. The population at the end of the 18th Century was about the same as the present in Greater London, and they could not have many road accidents, because few people went anywhere, and when they did, they walked. They could not have factory accidents without factories. If you took away from the High Court and the County Courts and all the criminal courts the work arising from road and factory accidents alone, you would have a couple of hundred unemployed judges on your hands.

By a happy coincidence, the first case raising the idea of employers' liability happened to be a road accident case as well. This was decided in Hilary Term, 1837 in the Exchequer Chamber. The young Victoria was just on the throne and the Chief Baron of the Court of Exchequer was Lord Abinger, master of a great estate and splendid household at Inverlochy Castle, with many servants.

The plaintiff, one Priestley, was the servant of the defendant, Mr Fowler, a butcher. The jury at the Lincoln Assizes had awarded him £100 damages for a broken thigh. He had been, said the declaration, 'desired and directed to go with certain goods of his master in a certain van, overloaded and out of repair, and was thrown with violence to the ground thereby.' The report in *3 Meeson & Welsby p. 1*, does not say so, but actually a wheel came off the van.

28

Lord Abinger referred to the total absence of precedent for a claim by a servant against his master arising out of that 'mere relation'. No contract to carry him safely and therefore no duty could be implied on the part of the master to cause his servant to be safely and securely carried, or to make the master liable for any vice or imperfection, unknown to the master, in the carriage or the mode of loading or conducting it, he said.

Because there was no precedent, the court had to decide the case on general principles, and it was pretty clear where Abinger's general principles lie. If the master was liable, the principle would carry 'us' to an 'alarming extent', he said. It would make them liable for the negligence of all their 'inferior agents' which injured mere servants. Domestics were in those days the most numerous class of employed people.

> 'The master, for example, would be liable to the servant for the negligence of the chambermaid, for putting him into a damp bed; for that of the upholsterer for sending in a crazy bedstead, whereby he was made to fall down while asleep and injure himself; for the negligence of the cook in not cleaning properly the copper vessels used in the kitchen; of the butcher in supplying the family with meat of a quality injurious to the health; of the builder, for a defect in the foundation of the house, whereby it fell, and injured both the master and the servant by the ruins . . .
>
> The inconvenience, not to say the absurdity of these consequences, afford sufficient argument against the application of this principle . . .'

Absurd or not, it has come to pass. Of course the butcher and the builder and the upholsterer would not be the servants of the master at all. But nevertheless the case founded the principle of particular duties arising from the relation of master and servant and developed another curious principle which lasted until 1948. It also expressed a prejudice the essence of 'Contributory negligence'.

> 'The plaintiff must have known as well as his master, and probably better, whether the van was sufficient; whether it was overloaded, and whether it was likely to carry him safely.'

It is simply the question of whose fault caused the injury. But that was not the principle for which the case is famous.

> 'To allow this sort of action to prevail would be an encouragement to the servant to omit that diligence and caution which he is in duty bound to exercise on the behalf of his master, to protect him against the misconduct or negligence of others who serve him, and which diligence and caution, while they protect the master, are a much better security against any injury the servant may sustain by the negligence of others engaged under the same master, than any recourse against his master for damages could possibly afford.'

29

Since 1948, an injured workman or the widow and orphans of one who was killed at work, can recover damages even though he was 'in common employment' with a workmate whose negligence caused the injury. And the fact that the injured man was partly to blame does not destroy all his rights to damages.

But no accident lawyer can afford to forget about the doctrine of common employment any more than a conveyancer can afford to forget that the land law was very much altered 50 years ago. As recently as 8th November, 1971, there was a case in the Court of Appeal about Workmen's Compensation, which was abolished in 1949. An engine driver called John Knipe fell down some defective steps at the British Railways depot at Whitehaven in March, 1948, and received workmen's compensation. In 1957 his injuries were found to be much worse than a mere 'strain'. On his Union's advice he treated it as a workmen's compensation case until he was offered an unacceptable lump sum settlement in 1968. He only found out then that the *Workmen's Compensation Act, 1925 s. 29.* (since repealed) had given him an option whether to take the compensation or sue the Railways Board for damages. Since he did not know of the choice, his acceptance of the compensation in 1948 was not an exercise of the option.

Even though his claim was time-barred he was permitted to bring it under a provision of the Limitation Act, 1963 (which Lord Justice Sachs said was regrettably difficult to interpret). The judge had awarded him damages of £2,134, with interest since March, 1948, and the Court of Appeal said he was right to do so.

It is not the mere possibility of a case like Mr Knipe's coming his way which demands that the lawyer steep himself in antiquity. The reasoning of the law has changed little, though the attitudes of the judiciary have had to change considerably.

Mr Mather of South Shields, for instance, is described in the reports (*10 Exch. 261*) trying a pair of horses for the first time in double harness, and they did not like it. They knocked a Miss Holmes down. Said Baron Bramwell:

'The driver is absolutely free from all blame in the matter. Not only does he not do anything wrong, but he endeavours to do what is best to be done under the circumstances. The misfortune happens through the horses being so startled by the barking of a dog that they run away with the groom and the defendant who is sitting beside him. Now if the plaintiff under such circumstances can bring an action, I really cannot see she should not bring an action because a splash of mud, in the ordinary course of driving, was thrown upon her dress, or got into her eye and so injured it.

For the convenience of mankind in carrying out the affairs of life,

30

people as they go along the roads must expect, or put up with, such mischief as reasonable care on the part of others cannot avoid.'

That last paragraph is the law to this day. However, a hapless motorist could never excuse himself by saying that his car ran away with him. And he would be liable for prosecution for driving without reasonable consideration (*Road Traffic Act, 1960 s. 3.*) if he splashed mud on a lady's dress or in her eye. But the give and take of road use in common with everyone else is a principle of the law.

Holmes v. *Mather* is history, of course, being the first recorded instance of the 'Dog Defence' which is extremely common among people who do not want to lose their licences or whose insurance companies are in liquidation. Sometimes the cause of the accident is a cat or a woman with an umbrella dashing into the road. Ingenious examples are wasps stinging the driver, or birds flying in through the window. The defence works best for important public figures suffering the indignity of being prosecuted for some driving mishap, and really has no place at all in an analysis of the nature of legal wrongs.

But it goes without saying that *Holmes* v. *Mather* is explicable simply on the basis that the defendant was a gentleman. Had he been a common carter or a sporting butcher, the injured lady would no doubt have won. But, of course, gentlemen could not be expected to pay for their horses taking fright.

It took the invention of the motor car to give pedestrians any 'legal rights'.

31

Capital Men Of Business

*'If a man wrote that all lawyers were thieves, no
particular lawyer could sue him. . .'*

        Mr Justice Willes in *Eastwood* v. *Holmes*
        (1858) 1 F. & F., p. 349.

THE NOTEPAPER of most solicitors nowadays bears a discreet
intimation, that their offices are 'closed Saturdays' except, in some
instances 'by prior appointment'. The state of the nation is no doubt
due to the 40 hour week. Lawyers always have observed short
hours to the public. The clerks in *Pickwick Papers* got to the office
at half past nine in days when weavers threw the shuttle for twelve
hours.

> *'Seven hours to law*
> *To soothing slumber seven*
> *Ten to the world allot,*
> *And all to Heaven.'*

was the advice of Sir William Jones to budding lawyers, improving
a little on Sir Edward Coke who recommended only six hours a day
to 'law's grave study'.

Long and diligent application to business is however, the classic
foundation of success. The famous solicitor, Charles Russell, when
practising in Norfolk Street off the Strand kept open on Saturdays—
at least in 1895. The Marquess of Queensberry, author of the Rules
of Boxing, was walking the street looking for what the lower orders
call 'a good brief'. Mr Russell's was the only open door, and thus
he secured the retainer to defend the Marquess on the charge of
uttering a criminal libel on Mr Oscar Wilde. That led, as we all know,
to *The Trials of Oscar Wilde*, *The Ballad of Reading Gaol*, much
literature, and incidentally other litigation, including a copyright
action over the rival films about Wilde's trial 60-odd years later
which took seven years to come to trial. There may well be more,
and it is all due to Saturday opening.

I doubt if Saturday opening is discussed at the Law Society's
School of Law. Solicitors detest it, for it is spent entirely on dis-
abusing clients of the lies told by estate agents. The saga itself

teaches far more about solicitors than mere business hours. For example, the Marquess already had a solicitor when he was arrested. Some people, the rich and titled, are born with solicitors. Others acquire solicitors, frequently on the recommendation of a building society manager or an estate agent. (Estate agents' daughters often marry solicitors.) Yet other people have solicitors thrust upon them, e.g. persons accused of crime who ask for Legal Aid.

The Marquess's solicitor had refused to act for him in this case because he had broken bread with Oscar Wilde and could not bring himself to conduct a case in which Wilde would be attacked. That sort of scruple is the difference between the right sort of solicitor and the wrong sort. In those days, too, 'criminal work' was abhorred by the right sort. And of course, solicitors are perfectly entitled to refuse to conduct business. Barristers cannot refuse briefs in the courts where they affect to practise. But the initial relationship between solicitor and client is a perfectly simple contract. The relationship between the barristers and their clients, professional and lay, is exotically complicated.

Solicitors are quite socially acceptable now. In the 15th Century the profession was 'the refuge of the profligate'. They get into Public Relations with the non-practising barristers nowadays. The procurers of business who acted as go-betweens for barristers and lay clients, and carried on business in the Inns of Court were called attorneys for ages. It was on the Chancery side that they were called 'solicitors'. Until about 1840 the better sort wielded their power through The Society of Gentlemen Practisers in the Courts of Law and Equity. This explains better than any other treatise that whatever kind of law you ever had to have in England, there was a monopolist with a franchise for charging you money to get it.

The important word is 'practisers' a much better word than the pompous modern 'practitioner'. Few people until the late 19th Century actually studied the Law. All the eminent lawyers read classics and history at Oxford and Cambridge. The Vinerian Chair at Oxford was a sinecure, and the study of Law was *infra dig*. Things have changed now, but not much. The rebellious students of the Inns of Court complain about the lecture facilities being inadequate, and the solicitors complain about having to send their articled clerks to law school when they could be earning money typing land transfers. Solicitors are still for the most part very suspicious about learning lots of law. It is more important for a young fellow to learn to get some money on account from an embryo client before wasting time on his troubles.

An old clerk wrote that he once prepared a large volume of 'Instructions to Counsel' for Otto Danckwerts KC (father of Lord Justice Danckwerts) terminating with the two important

questions arising in the matter. The resulting Opinion of Counsel
read as follows:

> '*1. Yes.*
> *2. No.*
>
> *O.D.*'

For a very long time, solicitors knew better than to ask for more.
When Lord Chancellor Jowitt was at the Bar, he was often taken to
task by the conscientious Samuel for the same approach, scribbling
on the backsheet: 'Not a chance, W.J.'

Jowitt used apparently to reply that he was perfectly willing to give
all his reasons for his advice, 'But not for two pounds, four shillings
and sixpence'.

The difference between barristers and solicitors, of course, is that
barristers do not work for vulgar profit but accept honoraria for
performing the duties of their rank and station, whilst solicitors
contract with clients to perform services and can (and often do) sue
for their fees. This also makes them liable at law for professional
negligence, and sometimes when such actions are brought against
them, the duties of a solicitor are held by judges to be very onerous
indeed. But no such duties arise unless there is a specific retainer.
If a solicitor is acting for you on the purchase of a flat, and on the
side, so to speak, you ask for and receive a bit of advice on how to
resist your wife's extortionate demands for maintenance (as alimony
is now called) you cannot sue the solicitor for negligence. He was
retained for the conveyancing job. It is, of course, otherwise if he
was retained for both the conveyance and the 'matrimonial affairs'.

The theory is that solicitors have a wide general knowledge of
law and like Messrs Dodson & Fogg, are 'capital men of business'.
They are by law the only people allowed to charge money for
preparing instruments of transfer of title to property or to commence
proceedings on behalf of other people, and conduct them in the courts.
These two monopolies are seen by the more ignorant writers in the
newspapers as twin, similar restrictive practices, and violently
assailed by solicitors and barristers who do not 'practise' but shine
their seats in professorial chairs. They are in fact extremely dissimilar.

However efficient a Probate Department is, it can never get a
recommendation from a satisfied client. He who gives the instructions and foots the bill unfortunately cannot be present at the time
his solicitor's labours bear fruit. There will, however, be a host of
disappointed friends and relatives present all implacably convinced
that the solicitor is not only incompetent but probably fraudulent
as well. As to the first, the attorney can afford to be light hearted,
for since they have not retained him it would be very difficult to sue
him (but not impossible). Consequently solicitors who deal in

conveyancing and probate are jolly, extrovert men, who go out to business lunches and meet people and form companies for builders and manufacturers and make a great deal of money, not from soliciting, but from the ordinary processes of the employment of wealth which lawyers hardly understand.

The litigation solicitor is a different creature altogether. Rather he is two different creatures depending on whether he carries out divorce business or proper litigation. Divorce work is largely bedside manner. There are some solicitors in London and the larger cities who did a fair amount of it before it became fashionable during the War. No doubt they are descended from the Proctors who did the soliciting from Doctors Commons in the days when matrimonial causes were available only to the wealthy, in the Ecclesiastical Courts. Then as now, practice was much more important than Law.

It does not need a lawyer to write:

> '*Dear Sir, we have been consulted by your wife in connection with her matrimonial affairs. It appears that you have treated her with cruelty so that she is extremely nervous and in fear of you, and have seriously neglected her and the children of the family so far as finance is concerned. Unless we hear from you within three days that you are prepared to leave the matrimonial home and provide acceptable sums of maintenance we shall have no alternative but to apply to Court for an Injunction and an Order forthwith.*'

Lord Justice Sachs said in the Court of Appeal in early 1971 that injunctions to exclude husbands from their homes are granted much more easily now than a few years ago—when they were in the hands of High Court Judges and not the County Court Judges who make most of them now. They are often, said the Lord Justice— with a great deal of divorce experience behind him—tactical manoeuvres.

No Act of Parliament says that a court shall have power to make such injunctions. They are made every day, and quite often men who break them are sent to prison for contempt of court. Bold counsel successfully contended (in *Montgomery* v. *Montgomery* (*1965*) *P. 46*) that the *Judicature Act* of 1925 only permitted injunctions to be given in support of legal rights, and that consequently a husband who was tenant or owner of a matrimonial home could not be excluded—his legal right being stronger than the wife's. But the 'inherent jurisdiction of the court' has prevailed over that little difficulty and nowadays injunctions will be granted when a wife is entitled in the eyes of the court to return to the home and feels she could not if the husband is there.

Those who practise in divorce knew it would come right all

along. 'The life of the law has not been logic; it has been experience', said Justice Oliver Wendell Holmes.

This is not to say that solicitors do not turn to barristers in divorce matters. Even though divorce in the County Courts since 1968 has meant that they can do it all themselves in undefended suits, they still employ the Bar for most of the work. It is not merely the superior expertise of counsel. They are often cheaper than the six or seven guineas an hour at which even a suburban solicitor values his time.

Thus there is very little change in the old order of solicitors procuring business—but without actually 'soliciting' it, which is unethical—processing it through the formal stages with the assistance of their clerks, and taking the prepared 'case' to counsel for advice and advocacy. Even if they did not want the advice they had to have the advocacy because of the Bar's monopoly of the right of audience in all the 'Superior' Courts—which the solicitors have been trying unsuccessfully to break for a century and a half.

Once the profession of attorney became respectable, it was inevitable that some of them would think they were better advocates than the barristers. No doubt some of them are. But in the main the old florid style of address in court has largely died. The ininterred corpse is to be found in the Magistrates' Courts in the persons of seedy solicitors who once saw Marshall Hall in action. Not that a childhood glimpse of a great advocate is a bad start in the profession. Norman Birkett's genius was thus inspired—but his inspiration was Sir Edward Clarke, KC which may account for him becoming a Lord Justice of Appeal whilst the emulators of Marshall Hall succeed more modestly.

The real work of the litigation solicitor, interviewing witnesses and getting together the documentary evidence sounds much easier than it is in fact. Conveyancing, after all, is the mere manufacturing of evidence. After 20 years the fact that a bit of paper has a bit of wax or plastic on it 'proves' that a particular bit of land up to some measured point or distinguishing mark, is owned by someone, or was owned by someone until—as is proved by another such bit of paper—someone else bought it or had it left or given to them.

Anyone who manufactures evidence in anticipation of a forth-coming lawsuit, however, can be imprisoned for life if convicted of forgery. The same fate awaits anyone convicted of forging a will—but since the author thereof is the only likely witness of what he actually put into it, will forging is much safer than other kinds of forgery. No doubt as some clerk chooses letters from a file to be included in 'agreed bundle of documents' for a lawsuit, he entertains gradiose visions of himself using the vital document as Sir Charles Russell QC (later Lord Russell of Killowen) used once in cross-examining the wretched journalist Richard Pigott before the Parnell Commission. No doubt the possibility that any piece of correspondence might prove vital inspires them to make a dozen copies each of all those letters which read:

> *'Thank you for your letter of the 14th ultimo upon which we are taking our Client's instructions and will write to you again in early course.'*

Certain it is that the Xerox machine has made a greater revolution in the practise of the law than anything to come out of Parliament in the past three centuries.

Because a remarkable few have done very well at the Bar and on the Bench after starting as solicitors' clerks or solicitors it is easy to believe the reformers who want a common training for all lawyers, and abolition of the present distinction between the advocates of the higher courts and the backroom boys in their law firms. Until recently it was difficult to transfer from one branch of the profession to the other. You were not allowed to earn money at either during the long transition. After five years' experience in practice, it is now easier to transfer, but the problems of earning money during the transition are similar. The real difficulty about practising the law at all has been to stay alive whilst getting started, and this has tended to restrict the career to those who have someone to support them until their late twenties. It is remarkable that anyone so blessed should develop any taste for industry at all. And by the time a young solicitor discovers that he should have been a barrister because he likes the sound of his own voice, he has formed such an appetite for good living that he cannot afford to make the change.

However, the old rigid distinction is becoming blurred. Consider the career of the man to whom Russell entrusted the defence of the Marquess of Queensberry. He was Sir Edward Carson, newly appointed Queen's Counsel in England after having been Solicitor-General in Ireland. Traditionally, the incumbent of that office is called 'The Solicitor' (in court 'Mr Solicitor') but he never is a solicitor. When Carson started at the Irish Bar he worked a great deal at 'fair rent' cases after the Land League had imposed that system on the absentee landlords of that united and subject nation. Nowadays, the fair rent scheme which protects the industrial proletariat of Britain against the rapacity of landlords is administered by Rent Tribunals, and they are protected from eviction in the County Courts. Solicitors do a great deal of such work in both *fori*.

How unjust therefore, that even under the *Courts Act, 1971*, the highest judicial offices are closed to solicitors. Lord Goodman disapproves very strongly, and he is of course, a solicitor. Lord Hailsham does not agree that there is any injustice, and he is the Lord

Chancellor of England. He explains that it is extremely simple for a solicitor to become a judge of the highest courts in the land. All he has to do is to become a barrister, and then get himself chosen by the Lord Chancellor.

It is entirely wrong to suppose that the idea is to keep the judge-ships in the hands of Oxonians and Cantabrians who went to the Bar as a kind of preparatory penance before assuming a safe seat in Parliament. It is a mere accident of social history that whilst barristers nearly all knew each other at the Varsity, solicitors seldom know anyone except other solicitors and estate agents. The truth is that lawyer-fathers often make one child a solicitor and the other a barrister. This explains how some barristers continue to be briefed by solicitors in spite of their manifest ineptitude.

When Wilde learned that he was to be cross-examined by his old classmate of Trinity (Dublin) he delivered the famous:

'No doubt he will do it with all the bitterness of an old friend,'

They never were friends, actually. It is important to understand what led to the Trials of Oscar Wilde. The Marquess, disliking the association between his son Lord Alfred Douglas and Wilde, delivered at Wilde's club his calling card endorsed 'to Oscar Wilde, posing as a sodomite'. The porter saw the words, but had no idea what they meant. He put the card into an envelope, and Wilde did not get it for a week. Like the impulsive fool he was, Wilde went to his solicitor. Like the impulsive fool *he* was, he advised a prosecution.

Undoubtedly, he knew some law. The uncomprehended sight of the words by the porter did not amount to sufficient publication to a third person to found a civil action for damages for libel. But that was not necessary for a criminal prosecution for libel, for ever since the Star Chamber invented it, the crime is committed by publication to the victim if it would lead to a breach of the peace. However likely it was that Queensberry would thump Wilde, the converse was remote, to say the least. This demonstrates just what a farcical anachronism is the crime of libel, and it remains the same today.

As the considerable literature upon it shows, from the dock at the Old Bailey, Queensberry ruined Wilde. The playwright made a laughing stock of Carson at first, but thereby revealed his own personality. 'Did you kiss him?' demanded Carson. 'Oh, dear no. He was a peculiarly plain boy.' sounds clever, years later, but it led to the charge being dropped. Hours later, according to John Betjeman:

'. . . *the door of the bedroom swung open*
And TWO PLAIN CLOTHES POLICEMEN came in:
Mr Woilde, we 'ave come for to take yew

39

Where felons and criminals dwell:
We must ask yew tew leave with us quoitly
For this is the Cadogan Hotel.'

The moral is clear. Do not, even if your solicitor says you should, sue or prosecute anyone. Should, however, you be sued or prosecuted, find yourself a good solicitor (you cannot go directly to a barrister without the intervention of a solicitor). It is as well to retain one who opens on Saturdays. At least you will not have to lose time from work to consult him, which will be about the only economy you can make. (Russell's success was not due entirely to this practice, laudables though it is. His father was the Lord Chief Justice.)

Carson became Solicitor-General of England a little later, and it fell to him to introduce the *Public Executor and Trustee Bill*, which passed into law in 1906.

> 'There is no greater loss caused to poor people than by the want of someone whom they can absolutely trust in the settlement of their affairs. The number of letters I have received bringing before me cases of the most harrowing character where money has been altogether wasted either in costs or by misappropriation struck me as altogether pathetic.'

That was not quite right then, for the *Larceny Act, 1904* had been passed to make it a crime to misappropriate moneys being kept for someone else and which had not been specifically allocated to a purpose. The Common Law was far too primitive to make a crime of mere utilisation by a professional man of funds in his hands.

This Public Trustee Bill had been put forward a few times, but the attorneys had always lobbied against it, insisting that their members were perfectly capable of managing estates great and small. Carson saw that as a pretty insidious practice. Whenever a man went to a solicitor to make a will, the lawyer was bound to ask who was to be executor or trustee. Quite often the man would not know, and in the privacy of the office, what more natural than that the lawyer should say, 'Shall I?' Carson told the House of Commons:

> 'I remember one case in which an ex-President of the Incorporated Law Society and Chairman of the Disciplinary Committee of that Society had been for 25 years insolvent although he held the highest position in his possession. In every will and settlement that came into his office he put himself in as trustee and for 25 years he lived in luxury on the misappropriation of trust moneys.'

'Trust accounts' is perhaps the most difficult part of the solicitor's training. The penalties for incompetence let alone criminality, are severe. And yet 15 years ago a fraudulent solicitor died insolvent and short of half a million pounds of his clients' money.

The grave injustice under which solicitors labour is the constantly repeated slander that they really do nothing at all to earn their fees on the sales of houses. Since 1804 they have been the only people allowed by law to draw documents of transfer of ownership of property for other people in return for money. They are allowed to do so for a fee which increases as the value of the property increases.* The popular press has instilled into the public the notion that this is really money for old rope. Now here is a curious thing. The Conscience of the Nation delights in pop-singers, interior decorators, and women's hairdressers making lots of money. They all supply services with which a large number of people can and do supply themselves. Many of them do it just as incompetently, tastelessly and even dangerously as the do-it-yourselfers.

There is no law against a man or woman doing his or her own conveyancing. Anyone who thinks there is nothing to it can buy a paperback guide and get on with it. They may very well find that the registered conveyancing system is pretty straightforward, and that they can manage a transfer pretty well. They might even manage an unregistered transaction. If they try either with the aid of this book they will probably end up in the Bankruptcy Court. It is perfectly possible to do that after a property deal even if you have a solicitor acting for you. But if it is caused by his incompetence and not yours you have two chances of getting your money back—his insurers and the Law Society's compensation fund.

The only person to treat the knockers with the contempt they deserve is the gentleman who carries on business as a do-it-yourself garage proprietor. He makes large profits by having on hand expert mechanics who can get the customers out of trouble when they have messed their jobs up. Some bright solicitor might well start a rescue service for do-it-yourself conveyancers.

I once knew a chap who, when he could not make his motor bike go, would push it to a main road and sit down to wait until an A.A. or R.A.C. patrol came along. When he bought a car, he could not push it so far. In the mid-Sixties, Mr Sidney Carter started up in Harrow, and later nationalised, his Home Owners' Society and precipitated a public relations crisis for solicitors. Some admitted that estate agents could fill in printed forms and thus take a lot of the trouble out of conveyancing. This is perfectly true, but they and their staffs have no greater reputation for competence than solicitors and their staffs, and a rather lower one for honesty. The reason for the statutory monopoly in the first place was to keep the spivs out of the trade.

Mr Carter was prosecuted in 1964 for both unlawfully acting as a

---

* In April 1972 the scale of fees was abolished in the interests of healthy competition. Now they can charge what they like.

solicitor when he was not and for carrying out conveyancing work for gain. The first conviction was sustained on Appeal, but the Queen's Bench Divisional Court teased the 'junior branch of the profession' rather badly by holding that only the actual instrument of transfer need be prepared by a solicitor—anyone could make out the ancillary documents for gain without committing an offence.

If that had been a Machiavellian plot designed to inveigle un-suspecting home conveyancers to get into deep water, it could hardly have been surpassed. Anyone with any conveyancing knowledge at all knows that the actual deed of transfer by which the mystic process is consummated is common form claptrap. The real work is in all the preliminary inquiries, settling boundary and planning problems, putting off the other side because the new house is not ready, and all the other things. But solicitors went in for a lot of heart searching. Some of them were rather ashamed of getting a minimum fee, or a scale fee for a simple job. Newspapers and politicians joined in, venting their long-standing hatred of the lawyers.

Desperate measures were called for, and a ginger group of solicitors formed the British Legal Association. It was soon scoring telling blows against the critics by pointing out that in fact solicitors actually charged much less than commercial concerns for handling other people's business. Before long it was convincing itself, if not everyone else, that solicitors really should have much higher fees for convey-ancing work.

In November, 1971, the settlement was announced of an action by the Law Society against Mr Carter. He agreed to drop his activities. The Law Society's spokesman pointed out that people saved little by having the services of his association for much of the ordinary run of registered conveyancing.

Solicitors are not just Volvo-driving Establishment figures. There is a lot of adrenalin used up in soliciting. Oh, they do conform. They have all the trappings of bourgeois acceptability, and indulge in little tricks like using a favoured given name with an initial before it. Herbert Rowse Armstrong used to do that, and he was a Free-mason, Conservative, Clerk to the Justices at Hay on Wye. He was 'a capital man of business'. The clerks to Messrs Dodson & Fogg would have been proud to serve him. He had joined Mr Cheese as managing clerk, and then risen to the rank of major—in a staff job— during the First War. He returned to Hay and succeeded to the practice on the untimely death of Mr Cheese. Personal tragedy then afflicted him and his devoted wife was removed to an asylum. He took her back home though she was very ill and a month later she died. No one was surprised when he took a well earned rest in Italy and Malta. He was also all set to find renewed happiness with another lady when a vexatious conveyancing problem presented itself.

He was acting for the vendor of the Velinewydd Estate, and completion was due on the 2nd January, 1920. He had received the deposit, a large sum, as stakeholder. With all his various troubles, the transaction was still uncompleted in August, 1921. It was then that the purchasers instructed another solicitor in the town, Mr Oswald Martin, to get the matter hurried up. Mr Martin demanded completion of the sale or the return of the deposit. They had a friendly meeting, but nothing concrete transpired. Mr Martin served notice rescinding the contract and demanding his client's money back. Mr Armstrong asked Mr Martin to tea. He went on 26th October, 1921. They sat down. Mr Armstrong handed him a buttered scone. 'Excuse fingers,' he said. Mr Martin hardly gave it a thought at the time. Later that evening, Mr Martin became very ill. He called Dr Hincks. As soon as Dr Hincks visited him, Mr Armstrong called at the surgery to ask how Mr Martin was.

Mr Martin was very ill, but as he began to recover, he thought of the way Major Armstrong insisted so often that he come to eat tea. And he thought of the unsolicited gift through the post of a box of chocolates a few weeks earlier. Neither he nor his wife had any of them but their dinner guests who did had been very ill. Now, Mr Martin's father-in-law was the chemist in Hay-on-Wye, and naturally visited his son-in-law who in a rather unprofessional fashion began to expound uncharitable thoughts about Major Armstrong, thinking that his reasons for delaying on the Velinewydd transaction might be that he had got the deposit money mixed up with his own.

Mr Davies recalled that Major Armstrong was a rather persistent purchaser over the two previous years of substantial quantities first of a weedkiller containing arsenic, and then of neat white arsenic, which he said he would work up into weedkiller himself. Some of these purchases were in mid-winter, when there was little weed growth, and anyway, Major Armstrong's garden was overgrown with weeds. Mr Martin recovered somewhat and went back to business, and it was naturally not long before he met Major Armstrong again, who said:

'It may seem a curious thing to say, but you will have another attack soon.'

That was not all he said, of course. He said all the usual pleasantries, and he also invited him to come to tea again. And just as he had done before, he invited him again, and again. Mr Martin had considerable difficulty in putting off the assiduous solicitor.

He had taken the trouble of acquainting the Director of Public

Prosecutions, Sir Archibald Bodkin, and there were two Scotland Yard officers in the town, making stealthy inquiries at night. On Old Year's day, 1921, they arrested Major Armstrong and charged him with attempting to murder Mr Martin. He said in answer to the charge, 'I am innocent'. One of the Justices of the Peace said:

> 'That is good enough for us. Until he says something to the contrary, we will believe nothing else, no matter what evidence is dug up.'

What was dug up was Mrs Armstrong, the best preserved corpse the forensic scientist had ever seen—she was so full of arsenic.

Vice Chancellor Malins would no doubt have regarded his behaviour as contempt of court. He thought that throwing a brother solicitor out of one's office whence he had come to inspect some documents as ordered by the court was contempt. Lord Justice Mellish and his brethren in the Court of Appeal reversed the decision, saying it really came to this:

> '. . . That whenever the solicitors . . . or the clerks to solicitors in an action happen to meet each other . . . and one or other loses his temper . . . that is contempt of court.'
>
> **Re Clements, and the Republic of Costa Rica v. Erlanger (1877) 46 L.J. Ch. 375.**

Much more recently, efforts have been made to commit to prison solicitors who wrote letters threatening legal action in protection of what they conceived to be their clients' rights in industrial property—namely trade marks. But the judge said they need not bother to bring their overnight bags when the hearing was adjourned, an indication that Malins's standard of behaviour no longer applies.

These are only some of the dangers besetting the paths of solicitors in the enjoyment of their other monopoly: that of issuing proceedings and conducting litigation for other people for gain. There is here a long-standing tradition to be explained. This tradition has it that there is no money to be made out of litigation work, and that the conveyancing charges are the subsidy which enables the solicitor to provide for the public the expertly-managed access to the seat of justice which is every man's birthright, at the most reasonable expense. To those to whom this is not immediately apparent, I can only say that it is a statement about the economics of the law. Sir Oscar Hobson, the doyen of City Editors until the early Sixties, had a theory that economics is a basically simple subject. The simple basic fact about solicitors is that a time and motion man could justify a suburban solicitor charging about £8 an hour for his services. Very few ordinary people—and quite a few extraordinary ones—either can or will pay such sums. The only way a solicitor can survive therefore, is by getting someone else to pay his client's bill.

This apparent paradox, when clearly understood, explains all there is to understand about solicitors, and their public image. They have offices in High Streets and they deal with the public. People who wish to keep their driving licences so that they can continue to participate in the carnage on our roads, engage solicitors to represent them. This homely example is not far-fetched. A great many people employ a solicitor for the first time on such an occasion. They are often able to contemplate that luxury because the insurance policy they must have in order to be lawfully on the road provides that the insurers will undertake their defence in proceedings in the magistrates' courts and have them represented in any proceedings for damages (claimed by them or someone else). Already, therefore, someone else—the insurer—is paying the client's bill.

When there is any remote chance of such a thing being done, the solicitor will demand that the costs should be paid from public funds—actual prosecutors have no money with which to pay costs, in the ordinary way. Solicitors acting for people accused of crime are often paid from public moneys under the Poor Prisoners Defence Regulations or, since 1950, in whole or in part by the Exchequer through the Law Society which administers the civil Legal Aid scheme. In all of these cases, the solicitor must try to ensure that his client wins to the extent that the other side pays the costs. Even in those rare cases where the client is not entitled to be sponsored in his cause by a trade union, insurance concern or the legal aid funds, the solicitor has to try to get the opponents reduced to such disadvantage in law and fact that they will agree or be ordered to pay his clients bill.

So much for ordinary litigation and crime. In trust and probate work, all the solicitors for all the beneficiaries conspire together to have all the costs paid out of the estate or trust fund. This sometimes has the unfortunate result of leaving nothing for the beneficiaries, but at least they often find that out for nothing.

In conveyancing, of course, the ordinary commercial rule applies as strongly as in any other beneficial transaction like buying securities, works of art, antiques, or motor cars. The one with the whip hand has his costs paid by the supplicant. The building society therefore has its costs paid by the borrower; the hire-purchase company likewise. These conditions are always inserted in the contract documents. The lessor has his costs paid by the tenant under similar provisions. There is no general rule of law requiring this to be done. The lenders just do not lend, nor the landlords let, unless and until the economically weaker party agrees to their terms. Their solicitors are therefore getting other people to pay their

45

clients' bills. Owners of patents and copyrights emulate this thrifty example.

It therefore follows that the person who invariably has to pay not only his own costs but those of other parties as well, is the buyer or renter of property.

Not that this can possibly be apostrophised as unjust. Landed property, for instance, increases in value in some parts of Britain by 10 per cent a year. Many investments not only produce income but enjoy capital growth. Some, like many consumer durable goods, depreciate rather rapidly, but that is not the fault of solicitors. There is, as yet, no charitable institution which will pay solicitors their reasonable charges on behalf of purchasers of property. No Member of Parliament has yet been inspired to suggest a legislative remedy for this injustice. Since institutions are notoriously more reliable debtors than companies and individuals the legal profession would no doubt welcome some such provision, but in its absence they must do the best they can. They must charge what they do for conveyancing, and the public must not be surprised if in these inflationary days, those charges increase. Solicitors have to pay girls £20 or so a week to sit and chat between breaks for coffee and lunch (with vouchers). Those girls are difficult to get in solicitors' offices which do not normally boast sports grounds, social clubs, staff dances, and so on.

For it must be realised that solicitors are only labourers in the vineyard. Just as the original labourers who endured the heat of the day received each one penny, so did those who arrived at the seventh hour. By the same precedent, a solicitor gets less money for doing the same work on the purchase of a cheap house than he would have got if it had been dearer. This is of course a most unjust penalty on the solicitor whose clients cannot afford expensive houses. No doubt the British Legal Association will put this forward if another Remuneration Order is discussed. The Law Society will really have to pull up its collective socks if they do. The Prices and Incomes Board reported in 1968 that solicitors obtained 55 per cent of their income from conveyancing. This is a lower percentage, so far as can be ascertained, than when the monopoly of preparing instruments of transfer was first granted by Parliament in 1804. Solicitors are therefore actually worse off than they were nearly 170 years ago.

And what about the solicitor who has not even seen a conveyance for 30 years? There are several such. To outward appearances, he makes a living from crime and divorce—the same clients provide both. He is a little unusual, it must be confessed. For one thing, the typewriting in his office is excellent. It is said that when someone goes into his office and wants a conveyancing job or a will drawn he speaks to them along these lines:

> *'I am sorry, but I do not transact that sort of business. I should not be very good at it if I tried. You should be well served if you go along the street to Messrs. ——.'*

There are solicitors who regard such conduct as dubious. Where, one might wonder, does he get 55 per cent of his income?

Now some solicitors are simply good-hearted chaps who cannot turn away a client in need. They are consumed with a responsibility to be all kinds of lawyers to all sorts of client. When my father-in-law was young, his Commandant in the Church Lads Brigade was a solicitor. Nothing very grand, just an assistant in one of those City firms which spend all their time on ship-charter and marine insurance work. His enduring passions, outside the Church Lads Brigade, were Lay-time and General Average. Father-in-law, however, asked the Commandant to undertake the conveyance of a country bungalow in the days when manorial tenures still existed. Totally ignorant of rural title-abstracting he may have been, but he had enough *nousse* to employ a local solicitor as his agent just as he would have done for protesting a Bill of Exchange in Hong Kong. Forty years on, Father-in-law retired north of the Trent. The erstwhile Commandant was long where the Church Lads go to, and his firm did not really want to tackle this piece of business. But the new senior partner reminded himself that Father-in-law was, after all, an old client, and that they were, after all, his solicitors! They employed local agents again. Father-in-law was highly delighted with the service he received on both occasions, and swears he will never go elsewhere. He will have cost them a few quid by the time his will is proved. He is no doubt being subsidised by some Greek shipowner's charter party work, which accounts for 99 per cent of their income.

Solicitors have a valid complaint that the judges who criticise them—and thus afford newspaper ammunition for their critics—do not understand the difficulties under which they labour. This is because judges usually begin as barristers. Many judges of the High Court, including the Lord Chief Justice of England, Lord Widgery, were solicitors before they were barristers, but they are regarded more as renegades than heroes by the general body of local Law Society members. It must be confessed that the majority of the Bar have little opportunity to see solicitors in their lairs. The etiquette rules forbid it except in cases of dire necessity, such as a long conference with a pregnant divorce client in Oswestry. There was a scheme, apparently not terribly well supported, by which budding barristers during their student days could work for six months in a solicitor's office. I knew a man who attended on the first day to be informed by the solicitor that 'Courtesy and efficiency are our

47

watchwords here'. There was then shown in a shabby lady clutching an affidavit which she had to swear, for the gentleman was a Commissioner for Oaths, as well as being a Solicitor of the Supreme Court.

'Certainly, Madam,' he intoned. 'Hold the book in your right hand and repeat the words on the card after me:

'*I swear by almighty God that the contents of this my affidavit are the truth, the whole truth and nothing but the truth.*'

Thank you. That will be five shillings, please.'

As she left with his signature still wet upon the paper, the attorney turned to the fledgling barrister and said: 'That is what I mean, young man.'

He then restored the Concise Oxford Dictionary to his bookshelf and dismissed the pupil from his presence.

When the statute *44 Geo. III c. 98* first granted the conveyancing monopoly to solicitors, many of the standard forms of words used in deeds, of settlement, conveyance, assignment, and in wills and commercial documents had to be written out in full, by 'law writers' who charged by length like typing agencies do now. The actual composers of the muniments, conveyancing counsel, equity draftsmen and solicitors themselves, also charged on that basis. Dickens describes the ink and drink sodden existence of the law-writers. What they did, 'engrossing' on to parchment is now done by typing on heavy 'judicature' paper, but many common form provisions are left out, their effect being implied by Act of Parliament or Common Law or Equity. In property transfer work the registration system has done away even with much of that, and after registration the old deeds can be made into lampshades. Registered transfers are effected on buff coloured forms which look like job sheets in a run-down factory, and are often filled in in smudgy Biro by Comprehensively-educated junior clerks. The profession is a little shamefaced about this, and the fixed fees for registered conveyancing were only two-thirds of those fixed for unregistered work.

But to concentrate on such things overlooks entirely that there is a great deal more to the conduct of a conveyancing transaction than merely preparing the transfer. One hundred and fifty years ago a solicitor had to be able to pick out flaws in a title. For although the Real Property Commissioners of 1829 considered the English Land Law perfect, the multiplicity of feudal interests made the highly technical business of understanding deeds treacherous. Nowadays, this has largely simplified, and the difficulties are more in the financing and contract stages, heavily overlaid with planning and local by-law requirements, to say nothing of taxation and the rights of married women. Where a purchaser is having a loan from a

Building Society lower fees are charged for the work in connection with the mortgage because of course it is a common, printed form. Any borrower who objects to any of its provisions, as he is perfectly entitled to do, has a simple remedy. He can borrow his house price somewhere else. Approving the mortgage is therefore simple. It is often asked why should the seller's solicitor have to deduce title to the buyer's and the buyers to the mortgagee's. Why cannot the seller's solicitor's researches satisfy both the others? Of course they do in the long run, but the buyer has to satisfy the lender, because he is the borrower. Lenders take a much more sanguine view of things than people who are selling. If, for instance, a compulsory purchase order is made on a house whilst a lot of money is still owing on the mortgage, the lenders will have to rely on the borrower's ability to pay the balance from his earnings, or other assets. Building society managers and solicitors are much less optimistic much more cautious than estate agents and property owners. What you actually get for the fee on a conveyance of unregistered land (which includes buildings) is the security of the solicitor being insured against negligence liability and the Law Society's Compensation Fund for worse disasters. It is about £67.50 on a £5,000 purchase.

These safeguards, and the skill and knowledge of the solicitor and his staff, of course, are what you get in any transaction in which you employ him. He stands a very good chance of ducking liability for negligence if he took the advice of competent counsel over any awkward stage of the transaction. All the protagonists of fusion of the two branches of the profession—and they include many solicitors and barristers—overlook the enormous protection against claims by ill-affected laymen which this affords. The people who know most about the law of England, the judges and the civil servants who advise the Government, know perfectly well that the law is quite uncertain in its incidence in a great many common cases. But this defect is virtually insignificant beside the enormous difficulty under which most litigants labour. I refer to the unshakeable conviction of most disputants that their version of what happened is absolutely correct. Even if it is, it by no means follows that the judge, jury or official who forms the relevant tribunal will accept it. A solicitor may do a client the greatest service by telling him he has no case.

The legal profession collectively holds itself out as competent to conduct such business. But very few solicitors are argumentative. One was held negligent by a High Court judge a few years back for not persuading a client out of an unwise investment. Solicitors often have clients with funds available for investment, but they are not investment consultants. This particular man tried to caution the lady but she was infatuated and would not heed his advice. The judge

49

thought he should have put it more strongly.

It might be the very best thing for a solicitor to tell a client 'Don't do that', but plenty of people want to do as they wish and for the solicitor to protect them from the consequences of their folly. The solicitor, if he cannot make them do what is best, at least deserves his hire for mitigating the effect of their stupidity. Not that some solicitors cannot put things strongly. One was strongly assailed by an heiress for 'letting' her father make a will which put strict controls on her handling of a large inheritance. She declared that she would take independent advice and upset the will, so that she could inherit free of the restrictions under the intestacy law.

> '*You are perfectly entitled to try,*' *he said.* '*I shall of course have to be the person you sue, as trustee and executor, and also because I drew up the will. And I shall have to go into the witness box and tell the Court exactly what your father told me about you and why he wanted the restrictions.*'

She called him a blackmailer but she did not sue. Very gradually, the law makes life easier for incompetent solicitors. Before 1926, to miss out the word 'simple' in a conveyance or a will could have drastic results. The technical term for an everlasting freehold is a 'fee simple'. Everyone understood that in the 14th Century. If the term employed was just 'fee' the interest transferred by the deed was a mere life interest. To someone who had paid for a heritable estate this was a nasty shock but there was no getting round it. *Re Ethel & Mitchell's & Butler's Contract (1901) Ch. 945.*

The simple answer (no pun) was for the deeds to be very carefully read before they were executed and delivered. Since the introduction of dictating machines and temporary typists the examination of documents has become more important still, but unhappily it is possible to find deeds delivered and relied upon in disputes which have important bits left out. A remarkable attempt to overcome this involves the employment of the office photocopying machine to make a draft by fitting cards from a set printed with precedents together. The names, addresses and prices and other details can then be typed in on the photograph and it can be re-photographed ready for signature. It is less laborious than copying from a precedent book and there is less likelihood (so the salesmen claim) of missing something out, because there might be a gap.

Imagine the results of inadvertently inserting the wrong card into a frame. Something similar occurred in a dispute over a shop, which halfway through seemed to turn into a garage. The opposing side construed it as meaning that the shop had a garage attached, and denied that. The original draftsman, without bothering to check up, filed a rejoinder insisting that it had a garage. His opponent rang him up and when he realised what a fool he had been they had lunch together and settled the dispute. Both clients were delighted with the expert resolution of the differences.

The 'bumbling attorney's clerk' is now a legal fiction. He has become 'an employee no longer with us'. When as often occurs the clanger is dropped in some matter of which a partner should have had, or did have, charge, the blame has to be laid on 'an assistant solicitor (or junior partner) now no longer with us'. This conjures up a vision of a vast transient population circulating through solicitors' offices all over the country, each moving on from catastrophe to catastrophe. This is probably the source of the great statistic bandied about a few years ago that there were eleven jobs awaiting for any newly admitted solicitor. The question is, of course, which eleven jobs?

The prospect of being 'salaried partner, prospect of full partnership' with a drunken old lunatic in a seedy backstreet compares ill with the lure of being an 'assistant solicitor' in one of those great London offices with a staff of four hundred where the large corps of highly specialised partners keep in touch through the radio telephones in their limousines.

The statistics about the volume of work in the High Court can be very misleading. Of the million or so writs issued each year nowadays, most will be for simple money claims which will not be defended, and will have the judgments rubber stamped. No barrister will get anything out of that work, but most of it will bring in a few pounds to a solicitor. A much larger volume of their work will not be concerned with any court at all. When there is a dispute fought out in court, the solicitor must charge for it on the basis of running his office and paying the staff, and so unless the amount in dispute is considerable, the costs are bound to appear disproportionate. There is nothing new in this. In the legal year commencing 1881 there were only 714 Common Law Actions actually tried in the High Court (which then had 18 judges). In 554 of them, the verdict was for less than £200. Nowadays the County Courts can try a case involving up to £750 (soon to be £1,000) and you cannot recover the High Court scale of costs if the amount of the judgment is under £375. The correspondents to *The Times* all made the point that the costs in a dispute might well exceed the amount recovered. It was far more likely to be true then than it is today. But the answer is to provide a small debt court, not reduce solicitors to beggary. Since quite minor injuries and commercial disputes can involve four figures, the costs ratio is much lower.

Consequently, solicitors collectively feel that the public has very little to complain about, whilst on the contrary, they are themselves hard done by. Although Mr Carter is no longer active,

Do-it-Yourself conveyancing groups are still in business, insidiously advertising cheaper work. The 20,000 solicitors in the High Streets of England can hold off that challenge, but the more idealistic and political are very disappointed because the highest judicial offices are not open to them.

In the Courts Bill debate in the Lords, Lord Chancellor Hailsham said:

> 'Lord Goodman referred to the fact that solicitors were eligible for the paid employment of chairmen and deputy chairmen of Quarter Sessions. I wonder if your Lordships really would have gathered ... that that power has existed for thirty years. And how many people do you think have been appointed in that time? Two.
>
> 'The fact of the matter ... is that they are far too prosperous ... if a senior partner in a first-class solicitors' office, who is the head of a really big business with, I suppose, an invested capital of £500,000, is so full of public zeal that he wants to become a County Court Judge or its equivalent, then all I can say is that he needs his head examined.'

The very best thing that has happened to solicitors for some time was the abolition by the *Criminal Law Act, 1967, Section 13 (1)*. of the crimes of maintenance and champerty together with challenging to fight, eavesdropping, being a common barrator (trouble maker) common scold or common night walker. The latter offence no doubt explains the terminological similarity in the descriptions of solicitors and prostitutes. *Section 14* abolished civil liability for maintenance and champerty.

Now champerty was bringing an action for someone on terms that you got a share or commission of the proceeds. Maintenance included champerty, for that was helping, usually financially, in the bringing of an action in which you had no interest. After all, the Legal Aid fund was maintaining actions left, right and centre, and it hardly seemed right to call it wrong. In scattered cases over the past century, maintenance was held not to vitiate cases where plaintiffs were helped out of a sense of duty or charity, and this even extended to a newspaper. However, solicitors who operated on a commission were liable to suffer from champerty. The result would be that a litigant would win against a defendant, who would then sue the champertous solicitor for the amount he had thus lost—damages, costs and interest.

This was nonsensical when it was considered that there is no legal obstacle to the speculative or contingent fee: pay nothing if you lose, £x if you win. Champerty can still be the subject of an action where the grounds for it arose before 1st January, 1968. There are six years in which to sue, and no such action could be started after 31st December, 1973.

Of course, the only people who need the assistance of champerty or the speculative fee these days are those too well-off for Legal Aid, unaided by a trade union or insurance company. The contingent fee operates abroad. It may be just what is needed to make the Law a growth industry.

Champions Of Liberty

'I have found in my experience that there is one panacea which heals every sore in litigation, and that is costs.'

Lord Justice Bowen in *Cropper* v. *Smith (1884)*
26 Ch. D.

ONE HOT afternoon, in the old days when Ireland was ruled from Westminster, the last of the Serjeants-at-Law, the great A. M. Sullivan, KC was arguing a case at the Law Courts in The Strand. It was a tiresome point about an Irish family dispute and a judge tried to cut short the flow of that mellifluous brogue, with 'Brother, have your clients not heard of the maxim, *De Minimis Non Curat Lex?*'

'My Lord', retorted The Serjeant, 'in the bogs of Connemara, they speak of little else.'

He was never elevated to the Bench. But that would not be because of his capacity for back answers. In his day, the great advocate was a man apart, in the tradition of Cicero. When Erskine took the brief to defend Tom Paine for writing *The Rights of Man* in 1792, it cost him his job as Attorney-General to the Prince of Wales. When any counsel was inhibited from appearing for anyone in the court where he daily sits, he said, 'the liberties of England are at an end'.

The Defence of Liberties tradition is still endorsed by the General Council of the Bar, with the added qualification that counsel is only bound to accept a brief in these courts in which he affects to practise, and when it is marked with a 'proper' fee. This more or less dates from Erskine's day. A few years later, Mr Gurney, the celebrated shorthand writer, was being congratulated upon the success of his son at the Bar—a considerable social jump.

'Yes,' said the proud father, 'he has taken up the sedition line, and I hope he makes a fortune at it.'

For the next century, no one thought there was anything wrong in making a fortune at the Bar. Before the First War, Carson could command 4,000 guineas on some briefs. Now that the opportunities have disappeared—for few lawyers are so eminent as to organise tax dodges for themselves—the self-appointed consciences of the Welfare State have created the impression that it is rather indecent even for barristers to make a living. Law is unquestionably expensive. The employment of counsel makes it more so. Luxuries often are expensive. Where this particular luxury is demanded by the law, it is widely condemned as a 'restrictive practice'. This modern term was originally coined to condemn the demarcation disputes of boiler-makers. Boilermakers and barristers have much in common. Many of each earn about £3,000 p.a. The basic rate for boilermakers is much less, of course, and barristers do not even have a basic rate.

According to *The Daily Telegraph* of 9th May, 1896, the Bar was 'the strongest trade union in the world'. Certainly in those days, when they earned any money at all, barristers earned a lot more than boilermakers. Whether the boilermakers appreciated that this was due to their closed shop, and were thus inspired to take the action which led to *Allen* v. *Flood in 1895*, is a fit subject for historical inquiry. Certain it is that the economic advance of boilermakers has not been equalled by that of barristers.

That case was perhaps the most important ever heard in the English courts, though one can hardly say that it was decided. It showed that the non-Parliamentary Common Law of England could handle the political conflict between labour and capital, if not better than Parliament, certainly not worse. The power of the Bar Council as a trade union is discounted nowadays by a great many barristers. They believe that it has failed to protect their economic position. Curiously enough, many of the boilermakers feel that way about their union, though it has ostensibly a better record of improvement of conditions of employment than the Bar Council.

The boilermakers who earn good wages are highly skilled special-ists engaged on construction and pipeline work, under difficult conditions. The barristers who make large incomes are often highly skilled specialists working under difficult conditions. But this has never stopped other people condemning the restrictive practices of boilermakers or barristers, which are essentially similar. What is the question of the right of audience for solicitors in the superior courts if it is not a demarcation dispute? The boilermakers' leaders have in the past decade managed to tone down these disputes because they are bad public relations.

The boilermakers' leaders might well have learned their politics from the leaders of the Bar. When Ted Hill virtually advertised in his union's journal that he was willing to serve wherever the Government would like him to, he was doing no more than many distinguished lawyers who have asked Lord Chancellors for judge-ships. Professor Laski wrote of one who asked for a vacancy in the House of Lords 'as coolly as you might ask for a book in a shop'.

56

His researches showed that half the Victorian judges had been MPs. This was no doubt in the mind of the elderly Silk who called on a Lord Chancellor with *The Times* obituary in his hand and said hopefully, 'Me next?' This trait is rumoured to affect only Tories with big majorities. The Labour judges seem to get on the Bench without appealling first to the electors.

Apart from the natural desire for recognition in an exacting profession, the Bench has the attraction of regular hours, sick pay and pension. Boilermakers regard these as the ordinary rights of workers. Barristers lack them, in common with other self-employed workers on 'The Lump'. They are popularly believed to make large incomes. But even before the salaries of High Court judges were raised in 1954 from £5,000 to £8,000 there were many for whom elevation to the Bench meant no drop in income. Those who should know better fostered the false impression.

'I do not like to disagree with my learned friend,' said an eminent QC, once in the Commercial Court. 'Why not?' beamed the judge. 'You've made a fortune at it.'

With increasing age, barristers earn more, boilermakers less. Just after the Second War, an unctuous solicitor remarked to the clerk to Sir Valentine Holmes KC, 'I suppose we shall see him on the Bench soon.'

'I don't pretend that things are all they might be,' was the grim reply, 'but they are not that bad yet.'

The great tradition of advocacy was still casting its mysterious spell over the paying customers. People who could afford to pay were willing to pay to get whom they wanted. The advocate kept a good proportion of what he was paid. An American insisted on Sir Patrick Hastings KC being briefed in a winding-up case in the Companies Court, in the late Twenties. His City solicitor advised against it, saying that he proposed to instruct Wilfrid Green KC (later Master of the Rolls, the senior judge in the Court of Appeal). The client insisted. Hastings was a legendary cross-examiner and must be briefed. It is remotely possible that someone might give oral evidence and be cross-examined in a winding up case, and that was enough for the client. Hastings sat imperturbably beside Greene against the unlikely contingency of it happening.

The real reason was that the client could tell his friends that he was represented by a famous advocate. Traces of this snobbery linger still, and there are some people such as pop-singers who can afford to indulge it.

Whether it increased the costs by a large proportion is doubtful. No doubt the fee was 'proper'—even large. But the fees of counsel seldom amount to anything like those of the solicitor, who has to pay high rent and operate an administrative machine employing typists and clerks. The separateness of the payment for counsel's services is a plank in the platform for those who want to fuse the profession, by permitting solicitors to appear in the superior courts, and barristers to become partners with them.

There is some vague belief that this will cut the cost of litigation, which, it is supposed, is a denial of justice. The political solicitors who favour fusion are not renowned for the generosity of their fees. The public relations is succeeding because the newspapers think all lawyers get too much, anyway—especially for conveyancing. And the mystique of the Great Advocate is nowhere near as strong as it was a generation ago. Though it is not dead.

A young barrister defended four lads accused of a burglarious joyride a few years ago. Three were acquitted, and quite naturally the father of the fourth assailed him bitterly outside the court for his incompetence, cowardice, stupidity and corruption in permitting the only innocent one to be convicted when the guilty had gone free. When the boy appealed, asserted the parent, he would have the services of Mr Sebag Shaw QC. From considerable personal experience in the dock at the Central Criminal Court, Old Bailey, that gentleman was firmly of opinion that Mr Shaw (now Mr Justice Shaw) took some beating.

'He could not keep you out of the nick,' retorted the barrister.

'What,' demanded the parent, 'has that got to do with it?'

And he was right. A criminal does not need to be acquitted to enjoy the cachet of having been defended by a distinguished counsel. Whereas formerly, large sums in uncertainly acquired money had to be expended on defence against false accusations by oppressively inclined police officers, it was made a public facility by the *Poor Prisoners' Defence Regulations 1933*. It is fair to say that they were not properly appreciated by the client class until after the Second War. Since by no stretch of imagination could they be called 'proper' fees they were not avidly competed for by the Bar, but rather accepted as a gesture towards out-of-pocket expenses, for performing the traditional duty to aid some underprivileged person in need of counsel.

Since 1960 they have been reasonable, and the disaffected in Parliament and out have been able to raise again the parrot cry that the lawyers make fortunes out of the misfortunes of others. So, it might be said, do doctors, but they have managed to set up the Emergency Ward Ten image. The publicity backlash, however, has had a most unfortunate effect. The Judiciary, who believe very little as a rule, have given some credence to the idea that vast sums are expended on the Employment of Counsel.

Their own experience at the Bar should disabuse them of the notion, but it is remarkable how quickly they forget the vicissitudes of advocacy, and become unsympathetic. Some become obsessed by the notion that counsel only wastes the court's time. A fluid style of questioning comes with practise on one's feet but it is easy for a man preoccupied with important points to create an unfavourable impression with a gauche question.

'Now, Mrs Jones,' said a Divorce Court practitioner, 'what about sexual intercourse?' meaning only to elicit her complaints about her husband's peculiarities.

'What, now?' she replied.

The judge blamed counsel, but it was not, technically a Leading Question, whatever a layman might have called it. The slightest things can set judges against counsel. One once suggested to Mr Justice Rigby Swift, who liked a couple of Scotches at lunchtime, that a particular step in the proceedings might be left until 'after the luncheon adjournment.'

'What the Court does between one and two o'clock is its own affair,' growled Rigby.

It is this judicial temperament which makes the Employment of Counsel, such a touchy question. It very often happens that an advocate has to ask for an adjournment, either before a trial starts or when it is in progress. The most usual reason is because some witness or some party to the proceedings is physically unable to be present to testify from the witness box.

The objection to such adjournments is that the other side have expended a large sum on having counsel there, but he cannot do what he is paid to. If it is for a future adjournment, then it is inferred (on no good grounds, quite often) that the opposing counsel have cases already booked for that date. Thus he will be unable to earn his vast fee and the client will be denied the Counsel of His Choice. From this it might be supposed that every practitioner at the Bar of England enjoys that confidence so well expressed by George Robey.

The Minister of Mirth was waiting in the wings at a gala performance, but the lady occupying the stage was taking an endless succession of encores.

'It is no good,' he drolled. 'You'll have to get Marshall Hall to get her off.'

Fifteen years ago, Lord Chief Justice Goddard granted an adjournment to a man who exercised everyone's personal right of audience in his own cause and demanded an adjournment so that the counsel of his choice could represent him. But the only people who can count on adjournments from most judges are the Prosecution—and then not because of the Convenience of Counsel, but because some prosecution witnesses are not available.

This is not to say that the Convenience of Counsel is never studied. If it suits the court, he can work wonders. If he is busy in the House of Lords, which takes precedence over any other tribunal, he might get an adjournment, but the usual remedy is to 'return' the brief to someone else. The main work of barristers' clerks is arranging cases so that their masters can be present to conduct the cases in which they are engaged. It was said of Lord Gardiner that when he was at the Bar he never returned a leading brief, and he believed the lists were never arranged for that to happen. This most singular good fortune must deserve a place in legal history.

Whether counsel is worthy of his hire is a matter which has always to be taken upon trust. There is no telling, quite often, what strange exigencies a case will assume. The nearest that any judge in England has ever come to a definition of fraud was in *Peek* v. *Derry (1889) 14 App. Cas. 337*. It is consequently a celebrated case.

> '*Fraud is proved when it is shown that a false representation has been made (1) knowingly or (2) without belief in its truth, or (3) recklessly, careless whether it be true or false.*'

said Lord Herschell.

Because this high standard of proof was not achieved, the plaintiff lost, and Parliament had to pass the *Directors' Liability Act* in the following year, holding company promoters and directors responsible for false prospectuses unless they reasonably believed them true. It is now contained in *s. 43* of the *Companies Act, 1948*. But *Peek* v. *Derry* very nearly foundered during the evidence of the plaintiff, Sir Henry Peek. Lord Justice Scrutton recalled that it was only by 'the most skilful management of counsel' that he could be induced to say that he relied on the misrepresentations. Skilful or not, he still lost.

It is trite that Leading Counsel are employed to ask Leading Questions. On the other hand there is a view held by many judges with good grounds that it is only if counsel gets hold of a very 'each-way' case in its early stages and devotes care and ingenuity to it that he can make much difference to the result. The attitude is only ever expressed after appointment to the Bench, never before.

It must have a grain of truth because even if counsel rarely win a case on their own authority, persuasion or learning, many disappointed litigants believe that they lose them because of their deficiencies.

There was in the old days an Old Bailey hack who like several others of his kind eked out a pathetic existence on Dock Briefs. The story is still told that when a prisoner asked for one and a judge asked the disengaged counsel to stand for him to make his selection, he said to the man in the dock: 'I am sorry, they are all we have in stock.' The usual function of these counsel was to tell the tale to try to keep the prisoner out of prison after he had pleaded guilty. This particular hack was so used to doing this that he did not appreciate that his client and the other prisoners had denied the charges, and that their counsel were arguing with the judge that there should be separate trials. When he was asked what he had to say, he burst out fretfully, because he had been trying for a long time to remember what to say:

> 'He is very good to his wife and rendered great assistance to the authorities during the Dartmoor Mutiny.'

History does not relate what happened to him, but there had to be a new jury and the trial began again because it was thus revealed that he had a criminal record.

To conduct a criminal defence without referring to the record the accused often requires 'skilful management'. Any suggestion that the accused is of good character when he is not or 'Such as to involve imputations on the character of the prosecutor or the witnesses for the prosecution' (*Criminal Evidence Act, 1898 s. 1.*) could lead to the prisoner's character being revealed.

Many an advocate has successfully walked this tightrope during the prosecution case to hear his client blithely recall to the court that something happened or that he met someone, 'While I was in prison'. Counsel who take advantage of the ignorance of parties and witnesses are despised. Considerably less charity is expended on the ignorance of counsel.

A pimply young man in a white nylon wig can console himself that the surest way to a great reputation at the Bar is to lose cases. Very few solicitors or clients give credit to their counsel when they win. The clients knew they were right all along. The newspaper quote 'I knew that British Justice would triumph in the end', is quite often uttered by someone with no merit in his cause, who has succeeded because of some technicality patiently insisted upon by his counsel. The solicitor will reflect that his preparatory work was so good that the case was won before it started. The tyro might well employ an evening looking up the historic cases in which Rufus Isaacs, KC appeared before becoming Marquess of Reading and Lord Chief Justice of England. He lost most of them.

It does not necessarily help a career at the Bar to be a Law Officer. Going into politics and failing to become a Law Officer can be even more disastrous. One Speaker of the House of Commons told a newly elected young barrister MP when he approached the Chair: 'You have come here too soon.' He was right. When he was not available to take briefs, the solicitors went elsewhere. What choice had they?

The 'Artificial Silk' system whereby a barrister elected to Parliament could virtually automatically become 'one of her Majesty's Counsel learned in the Law', was abolished in 1962. It was a kindness. Traditionally,

'A successful Silk has the income of a Prince and the life of a dog. An unsuccessful Silk has the life of a Prince and the income of a dog.'

That might have been all right in days when tax permitted modest private incomes to suffice. Not long after that reform a few people were to be observed in the locality of the Law Courts, wearing neckties bearing the *motif* 'QC' and anyone could have been forgiven for supposing that the elite had, as men so often do, adopted a modest form of self advertisement. It was, in truth, a somewhat immodest advertisement by a firm of wine merchants whose slogan was 'Quality Counts'. But, on reflection, that is not a bad principle upon which a man and his clerk should decide whether to be a Queen's Counsel.

When Henry McCardie's practice became too big for Birmingham he continued his success as a commercial specialist in London. When he became extremely busy he applied to Lord Chancellor Loreburn to be a QC. It was during one of Loreburn's slack spells for recommending Silk. The trouble is that a Junior Counsel has to tell all his more senior colleagues that he has applied. The word therefore got round about McCardie's claim. Solicitors naturally stopped sending him junior work—the preparation of the case papers and requests for initial advice—because they expected him to be promoted.

But time went by without any new grants of Silk being announced. Work slumped. McCardie could not tell the Lord Chancellor to hurry up, but he could withdraw his application. He did so, and announced to the profession why he had done so. Shortly afterwards, a list of new QCs was announced, and McCardie's name was added to it. But having withdrawn his application, McCardie was not going to be made Silk against his will. He refused to accept the patent, and remained a Junior until appointed to the High Court Bench.

His stirring example was emulated a few decades later by a gentleman in large practice who discovered after he had sent in his own application that several of his contemporary brethren had also applied. Realising that there would be many new silks competing for a comparatively small amount of heavy work, he elected to remain one of the correspondingly fewer heavy Juniors who coped with the even larger amount of smaller work. By all accounts he was well rewarded for his modesty and unselfishness.

Physical attributes are valuable at the Bar. Norman Birkett confessed that he took to it so that he could speak in public. He was famous for the persuasive beauty of his voice. But there was more to him than the way he spoke. He knew enough to say what was relevant and apt. He was one of the most successful advocates of the century. Nevertheless it was he who suffered the remark of Lord Justice Scrutton:

> '*There was also a third point, which Mr Norman Birkett said was difficult to express in words, but which, as he never made me understand what it was, I cannot deal with.*'
>
> **Tolley v. Fry (1930) 1 K.B. 467.**

A valuable characteristic is height. Many distinguished advocates have been substantially built. Vertical measurement is preferable to circumference. Some small men are brilliant, but they acquire distinction only in the profession. The public likes tall advocates. It puts a man on level terms with witnesses, jurors and judges, because courts are usually built so that they are artificially elevated above the well of court where the counsel stand. Sir Reginald Manningham-Buller QC (now Viscount Dilhorne) is a big man. In *Marten* v. *War Office* (*1960*), when he was Attorney-General, he cheerfully admitted that he had had nothing to do with 'restrictive covenants' affecting land since he was a student. Few small men would admit such a thing. They would sit up all night mugging up the relevant law. Then, tired and irritable, they would miss some ordinary little thing about admissibility of a bit of evidence and never get the chance to use their learning.

Physical limitations can be even more of a handicap. Mr Marven Everett QC and Mr Bernard Caulfield (now Mr Justice Caulfield) were once opposed in an accident case brought by Mr Everett's client—a charlady who hurt her back in the course of her work shifting a piano. The instrument was exhibited in court, and Mr Everett who is about six feet three and powerfully built applied a hand to show how extremely heavy and difficult to move it was. It appeared to move. It was no doubt on extremely efficient castors. Mr Caulfield, who is somewhat less than 'medium' in height and build was constrained nevertheless to show that it actually moved quite easily. But he could not shift it. No solicitor would dream of hawking a brief round the Temple for a counsel who could shift a piano, of course.

That is most certainly not what is meant by a 'strong' counsel. That means one sufficiently adroit and experienced not to be shut up and reduced to ineffectiveness by a 'strong' judge. (Who was probably himself a 'strong counsel'). A moment's reflection will reveal that quite stupid men can get reputations for strength simply because they will not shut up. Indeed a thick skin is a real asset at the Bar. And women are at no disadvantage when this particular virtue is called into play.

There is a distressing tendency nowadays in discussion of fusion of the Bar and the Soliciting Profession to refer to The Average Barrister. To the man in the street no barrister is average. Even the daily prints call them 'brilliant' when they name them as co-respondents. Even a barrister who never goes into court is expected to be brilliant about Protective Trusts or drainage. The natural conservatism of the profession discourages brilliance *inter sese* so to speak. It deplores the kind of thing Marshall Hall did on Armistice Day, 1923. He was busy at the Law Courts in the Strand losing a libel suit. When the maroons went off at 11 o'clock everyone stood for the Two Minutes' Silence, a custom now unhappily forgotten. When it was over he turned to the jury and said something like:

> '*Do not this lady's complaints seem trivial and empty when our minds are full of the great sacrifice . . .*'

His opponent was on his feet, outraged. But that is the kind of trick a great many people expect from counsel. It is given to few men or women to enjoy the absolute trust which some clients repose in advocates. The difference between solicitors and barristers is advocacy. There are barristers who never go into court, just as there are solicitors who are never out of the Magistrates' and the County Courts. But the public image of the barrister is as a jury swayer or one of the refined exponents of the 'sharp quillets of the law' in the highest tribunals. And even if they cannot win, there is a cachet all its own in having lost in spite of the efforts of a celebrated advocate. The pathetic news clippings of old lags are the criminal practitioner's prestige advertising.

The poor wretched journalist who with a clerk in the Probate Registry was imprisoned during the Thirties for a breach of the Official Secrets Acts by getting a look at a will before it was admitted to Probate met Lord Kylsant in prison. His Lordship was doing seven years because he knew that the shipping market moved in cycles of, ironically, seven years. He consequently put moneys to a special reserve so that he could feed the accounts of his company in lean years from the harvest of the fat years.

Since this involved cooking the books, he was imprisoned for fraud. Both cases were total travesties of justice, but even that rather unusual pair of criminals chatted in gaol about their advocate —Jowitt. It is only fair to say that Kylsant remarked with the greater *savoire faire* of the City man, 'He did not do either of us much good'.

This careless talk about Average Barristers is commonest when the topic is their remuneration or their negligence. Many earnest social consciences deplore the fact that because a barrister is not contractually employed for money, but merely paid an honorarium for his services in right of his rank, he cannot be held liable for negligence like a solicitor, doctor, lorry driver or hairdresser. This has been established, and generously extended to solicitors performing advocacy in the case brought by Mr Norbert Rondel, an ex-wrestler and associate of Mr Peter Rachman, against a barrister called Michael Worsley. Mr Rondel alleged that Mr Worsley was negligent in conducting his defence on a charge at the Old Bailey, by not asking certain questions. The case was appealed on the preliminary legal point whether an advocate can be held liable for negligence, and since he cannot, the merits of the action were never decided.

This is probably as well. There are certain duties of such an individual nature each time they are performed that they are incapable of assessment by measurement against other performances except when it is too late to do any good.

There was a new barrister feverishly reading Archbold's Criminal Pleading Evidence and Practice at the Old Bailey not long ago, who was told by a colleague:

'Put that away. You would not read the Rules of Association Football and then go to Highbury and demand to be made centre forward.'

Just as a footballer has a good game or a bad game, a brilliant advocate may have a good case or a bad case. He may very well refrain from putting searching questions because the admissions they will bring, whilst damaging the opposing witness, might damage his client. During the preliminary proceedings of the Kray case a woman witness was severely cross-questioned about her way of life, and when she was reduced to nervousness, she was asked why she had delayed so long before telling the police her story. She replied:

'Because I know what happens to people who talk.'

There are many solicitors who do not want the profession fused or barristers to have enforceable claims to payment. Some are people who represent criminals and who are prepared to mark generous fees on the briefs of barristers more for the look of it than from any firm intention to pay such a fee. The old rule that the fee came with the brief in case the client went inside has fallen into desuetude since Legal Aid came in. The authorities, of course, pay up when all the accounting is done. The welshers seldom get round to the accounting. There is not much of this, of course, because criminals have found that it is almost as well to lie about what money they have in order to get Legal Aid. The law requires that anyone accused of a serious offence shall have the assistance of a lawyer, for advice and advocacy. In a system which presumes innocence till guilt be proved, this is only just. But whatever criticisms the underground press and the National Council for Civil Liberties and similar social agencies might have, the fact does remain that quite a lot of people who are accused before the courts are criminals.

There is nothing really new in this payment and negligence controversy. Bill No. 18 of 1876 was 'A Bill to Enable Barristers-at-Law and Advocates to Recover their Fees and to Render them Liable to Persons Employing Them'.

This and later similar measures, were successfully resisted on the ground *inter alios* that they would turn the barrister into 'the mere mouthpiece of his client'. The contention was that being able to sue for unpaid fees would destroy the privileged class of advocates because they would not be able to 'fearlessly, openly and without dread assist the judges in their administration of justice' by means of that 'free expression of view and opinion which has been for centuries the pride and glory of the English Law and of our English Courts'.

Shortly put, it would make them afraid to offend the judges and their clients. Good counsel often have to do both. Poor counsel cannot help it. It is told of F. E. Smith (later Lord Chancellor Birkenhead) that when a judge reproved him for being rude he retorted: 'And so are you, and the difference between us is that I mean to be and you cannot help it'.

It is not to be recommended. It is even going a bit far for most counsel to emulate the man who was having a rough passage with Lord Chief Justice Goddard.

'With great respect, My Lord . . .' he kept repeating, 'With very great respect . . .'

Goddard growled, 'Never mind the respect,' because he had plenty of other things to do.

'Very well, My Lord. Without respect . . .'

Many good advocates are not extremely impressive at first glance. But they grow on you. Gerald Gardiner QC, as he was then, made an opening speech in the Electrical Trades Union 'Ballot Rigging' case which lasted more than a week. He hardly looked at a document. Such virtuoso performances depend upon 'getting up the case' beforehand so as to know what you are talking about. It takes much time and effort and this must be expended out of business hours, because successful counsel are in court then.

People who stayed at the same house parties as Carson at the height of his career noticed that however late they went to bed, there was always a light under his door. Reading stamina and a good memory are probably better equipment than analytical brilliance. Brass neck helps. One counsel was having a tiresome time with the judge at one of those County Courts where it is possible to see out of windows—a very distracting convenience. The judge had formulated the issue he was going to decide and kept nagging that there was a case on it. Through the window the advocate saw a railway yard, and a familiar coal-merchant's trade sign.

'Rickett and Cockerell, Your Honour', he suggested spitefully.

'Ah, that's the one. I'm much obliged to you.'

Brilliance can be a handicap in a legal career—especially at the beginning. Baby barristers are not expected to be brilliant but to know the practice. Since they have no experience, they never do.

One man was a First at Oxford. He read the Lives of the Chancellors and his thesis on Modern Equitable Remedies was hailed as a masterpiece.

His first brief was for the petitioning creditor seeking a compulsory winding up order against a company.

When the case was called on in the Companies Court, he stood up and said, 'My Lord, I appear for the petitioning creditor. The petition is founded upon a judgment debt of £998 12s 4d, including costs. There being no appearance by the company as far as I know, I ask for the usual compulsory order.' This formula is best learnt by heart. There are variations, but they are not important.

'What about the list?' said the judge and a man stood on his chair just below the Bench and passed a little bit of paper up to the judge.

'List? . . .' mumbled the bewildered First.

'I'm now told that the list is negative,' said the judge severely. Then he addressed the court at large. 'Is there any support or opposition for this petition?' As expected, no one answered. The list was only the list of other creditors who might take one side or the other and no one had bothered.

'Then,' said the First with great relief, 'I submit I am entitled to my order *ex debito justitiae*.'

'Rule Thirty-Three has not been complied with,' said the judge. 'The postal district is missing from the London Gazette notice. I cannot allow that. This must stand over for re-advertisement and it had better come on again in a fortnight.'

The culprit was the solicitor, or no doubt the 'bumbling attorney's clerk' who drafted or typed the advertisement for the London Gazette and the local paper in which the application to wind up the company appeared. But there is very little sympathy for advocates in the superior courts. (There is none at all in the lower courts.) A drunken solicitor used to relate of an old Chancery judge that he said, 'My court is no place for baby barristers to learn their trade.'

Hewart was cast in the same mould.

> *'Mr Meston puts his case, such as it is, very clearly. It really comes to this: that if this case were different from what it is, he might succeed; but as this case is what it is, this appeal must be dismissed.'*
>
> **Sidcup Building Estates v. Sider (1940) Traffic Cases 164.**

It used not to be uncommon to find that people with nothing better to do—both professional and lay—loitered in the courts hoping for a laugh at the discomfiture of some advocate. But only at the Central Criminal Court and when some High Court Case has attracted publicity is there much of a gallery nowadays. People prefer television forensics to the real thing. And the days are—one hopes—past when the virtually unemployed barristers hoping for a chance at a Dock Brief or a 'court legal aid' made a sycophantic claque for a judge with such patronage to bestow.

Knowing how to handle a judge is a quality much admired in the advocacy market, but it means different things in different circumstances. Sometimes it means craven obsequiousness. This is probably becoming less common with the entry into practice of a generation not conspicuous for its veneration of grey hairs or the personal qualities of any but its own members.

It requires experience to content oneself with saying to a judge reluctant to adopt one's contention of law:

> *'Very well, My Lord, decide the point against me and I will go to the Court of Appeal.'*

It is rather better manners to put it this way:

> *'I should prefer, My Lord, to develop the matter, as it may well be in certain circumstances that this case could go further.'*

An advocate knows he has rattled the judge when he says, 'I propose to put my reasons in writing and deliver judgment after a short adjournment, in case this matter should go further'.

These are the considerations reflected in 'the expense of employing counsel'. Solicitors' and barristers' clerks have a great deal of bedside manner over this.

> *'We will have that young man in Paper Buildings. He is just the fellow for this case—even if he costs five guineas,'*

says the solicitor. It was said of Lord Chancellor Maugham (brother of Somerset) that when he left the Chancery Bar for the Bench in the late Twenties, he was making £20,000 a year. Wilfrid Greene was said to make £40,000 or £50,000 p.a. It is also said that there are no fortunes made nowadays at the Bar. Sir Andrew Clark's daughter confessed a few years ago, 'By his own standards, my father is not a rich man'.

Retirement or elevation used to mean that all outstanding fees were tax-free, and successful men let their debts pile up. But, in a spiteful attack upon the smallest and most self-supporting of the professions, the Wilson Government in 1966 abolished that provision which created a sort of pension fund for barristers. The first to suffer under it was Mr Justice Eveleigh. Barristers cannot sell their good-will like other professional men. Only the last year's income is tax free now. There are about 120 lawyers in Parliament, but they seldom do very well in politics. Disraeli was a solicitor, and so was Lloyd George, and Asquith was the last barrister Premier. A lawyer on the make is better off out of politics than in, though of course a spell in politics increases pretensions to eminence as industry and intellect seldom can.

The man who wrote to *The Times* bitterly protesting that it cost him £1,000 to plead guilty to a serious offence was understandably biased against the expense of counsel. He could perfectly easily have pleaded guilty *gratis* and done quite well, for many judges are sorry for the mighty fallen. But because people trust the expertise not to say wizardry of some counsel, they speculate large sums on their chances of success. He paid £1,000 to try to avoid a long prison sentence, not to plead guilty. The two objectives are distinct.

A solicitor can successfully defend an action for professional negligence if he has taken the advice at the proper stage of counsel who affects to deal with the appropriate branch of the law, and he has acted on that advice.

Now this may appear to accord to counsel an eminence and learning totally unrequited. Upon this question, opinions differ. There does exist a class of sanguine individual who has discovered that if you keep your nose clean and go through the motions you get by unless you are dead unlucky. It is equally evident that the enforced idleness of early life at the Bar drives some of its members at any rate to read law books simply because they have nothing better to do.

It was written of Lord Goddard that he was sitting workless in chambers and started reading a law report he found in a drawer quite by chance when he was told that he was required to have a consultation, sometime later in the day. Having nothing better to do, he read on. When the client and solicitor finally arrived, the dilemma centred upon a question with which the report had dealt. His progress to the Bench, the Court of Appeal and to Lord Chief Justice was assured as soon as his obvious expertise came to light. I do not doubt that that is a perfectly true story. I have heard it from many sources, about Lord Evershed, Lord Birkenhead, and several

69

lesser lights, I am sure.

There is quite a lot of law about barristers. It can be found in *Volume 4* of the Third Edition of *Halsbury's Laws of England*, between *Bankruptcy* and *Bastardy*. According to the decision in *Messor* v. *Molyneux (1741) C.B.* barristers are esquires by rank. That puts them two steps up the feudal scale of precedence, but according to Wharton's *Law Lexicon*, they are still only level with doctors.

In practice, barristers are far worse off than doctors. Doctors either get £1.50 for each patient every year whether they treat him or not, or as much as they can get in fees for work outside general practice. Barristers can only earn by the latter method, and have not the soft option.

They can of course get jobs as company or government lawyers or anything else that is going but no one really thinks of those fellows as barristers. This is a little hard, for the Bar Association for Commerce and Industry, their trade union, did a survey a few years ago which showed that some of their members do quite well. The range of income possible they expressed to be between £800 a year and £30,000.

The rank or profession of barrister has existed for 600 years or so, and was quite well known to the public even before the Old Bailey staff started writing television plays about the drama, chivalry and social acceptibility of the profession. Unquestionably the job has tone. It is now more crowded than ever with about 2,500 practitioners in England and Wales. But its exclusiveness was the by-product of its basic weakness. This was the practical impossibility of making a living until you were fairly experienced and accomplished. It was difficult to become either without work. The training system prevented most beginners from discovering anything about the day to day work of a barrister.

The newly qualified barrister, having eaten dinner at modest cost in his Inn six times per term for twelve terms, and defeated the examiners in all subjects thus had to be able to afford to pay for chambers and clerking without having any income. During such time, he could watch, help, discuss with and generally 'devil for' more established colleagues until he began to attract work himself. The better the class of work he dealt in, the longer the wait.

Little learning is ever wasted. The head of a set of Chambers in the Temple used to affect a profound respect for the mysteries of the Chancery Division. He called himself a 'very Common Lawyer' and insisted that the only bit of Chancery drill he knew was that when in doubt one should 'undertake to keep accounts' since all property actions involved such things sooner or later.

A young man heard this joke several times over tea, and one day he was cast in at very short notice to hold a brief for one of several parties to an action in which an interlocutory application was being heard in Chancery. The client and his solicitors had been forced into the action in a great hurry and did not understand what they should do. The counsel had even less idea and listening to the succinct and expert resumé of the matter given by the applicant's counsel left him none the wiser. When the judge asked him, in common with all the other counsel, what he had to say, he had no idea, not having followed what the others said, and his mind was full of the fear of being arrested for contempt of court by making incomprehensible noises. He thought he might as well say, 'My Lord, we will keep accounts', as anything else, so he did.

'Well, in that case, if you keep all parties informed, the matter can stand over until the action is tried. Costs reserved,' said the judge pleasantly, and everyone went away quite happily with the day's work.

The solicitors were impressed, because apparently they had tried unsuccessfully to get the other solicitors to agree to some such thing. But the other solicitors would not commit themselves until they had been advised about it by their counsel. This gigantic chess game is the foundation of the axiom expressed by the elderly junior that, 'It is almost as difficult to get rid of solicitors as to get them.'

In 1766 the great Serjeant Davy said in open court that the ignorance of attorneys caused difficulties in cases. The Society of Gentlemen Practisers in the Courts of Law and Equity immediately resolved that its members would not brief him again. A few months later, he abjectly apologised. This power is still as strong as ever. It has all the force of an entrenched law. But the law does not in fact demand that a barrister shall only be instructed by a solicitor except on dock briefs and conveyancing and certain specialised advisory work. In *Doe. d. Bennett* v. *Hale* (*1850*) *15 Q.B. 171* the Court of Common Pleas held that the intervention of a solicitor was not required by law. Any barrister who departed from the convention would be disciplined by his Inn. If disbarred, he would not, of course, be able to practise in the courts.

'Counsel may not in general act without the intervention of a solicitor', state the Bar Council.

Fusion, of course, would merely make the advocate the court-room specialist of the firm from which he worked.

'In the United States, we recognise no distinction between barrister and solicitor; we are all barristers and solicitors by turn. One has but to frequent the courts to become convinced that, so long as the more than ten thousand members of the New York County Bar all avail themselves of their privilege to appear in court and try their own clients' cases, the great majority of the

71

trials will be poorly conducted, and much valuable time will be wasted.'

Francis L. Wellman. *The Art of Cross Examination.* **New York, 1903.**

Lord Chancellor Hailsham has in the debate on the Courts Bill given us his reasons for becoming a barrister rather than a solicitor.

'*My father was a barrister . . . I do not like writing letters, and solicitors do practically nothing else . . . I do not keep accounts, and solicitors have to keep not only one set of accounts but at least two; or they get turned out . . . and I cannot be trusted with my own money, let alone anybody else's . . .'*

What fusionists are really crying out for, of course, is their lost youth. The chance to make their choice again, solicitor or barrister, is what they really crave. What young men do not realise is that, as a great Victorian lawyer put it, they may have to 'quench their passions in Rating Appeals'. The romantic might despise such employment, but Lord Buckmaster pointed out that the *Rating and Valuation Apportionment Act, 1928* had provided 'the relief of a depressed profession' (*Moon* v. *L.C.C.* (*1931*) *A.C. 151.*). And Town Councils are better clients than thieves.

Depression struck again during the Fifties, but fortunately a crime wave began then which has continued practically unabated, and few barristers nowadays could claim as Sir Andrew Clark QC, then leader of the Chancery Bar, did not so very long ago when asked by a judge what procedure with regard to Legal Aid should be adopted, 'I cannot help your Lordship. I do not do Legal Aid cases, and I have never had Legal Aid.'

The Fund is a reliable client, and no slower than most others, in paying. While it exists, the Bar can continue to enjoy the independence of honorary remuneration. Many barristers would not bother to sue for fees if they could. Having seen the trouble their clients have in enforcing just debts, they probably would not think it worthwhile. Of that side of the law at least, their knowledge is not *de minimis*.

The Judgment Seat

*'If I am asked whether I have arrived at the meaning
of the words which Parliament intended, I say frankly
I have not the faintest idea.'*
Lord Justice Scrutton *(1928) 1. K.B. 566.*

IT IS TOLD of Sir Thomas Inskip KC the pre-war Attorney-General
that once when addressing the House of Lords he informed them
that roulette was a game played with cards. The Lord Chancellor
corrected him with a single five-letter word. This is a precedent not
followed by the large majority of judges, however great the temptation, and it must often be great. The *Act of Settlement, 1706*
provided that the judges hold office *dum se bene gesserint*, which
means 'whilst they remain of good behaviour' (and not, as some
believe, 'while they jolly well keep quiet'). They can only be sacked
by Address of both Houses of Parliament, a standard of unanimity
never in practice achieved. More than one discreet retirement has,
however, resulted from a word from the Lord Chancellor.

The Unjust Judge in *Luke 18:1–8* 'neither feared God nor respected
Man'. But there was a widow who kept coming to him, demanding,
'Protect me from my enemies'. For a while, he refused, but in the
end he said to himself, 'I will vindicate her or she will worry me to
death'. By the harsh Biblical criteria he was 'unrighteous'. That
word is most uncharitable. Any modern judge knows how tiresome
some litigants can be. When judges give way to the suitors before
them they are themselves subject to withering criticism by academic
lawyers and politicians.

It was Jesus who defined charity as the greatest of gifts, not his
Evangelists: they, noticeably St Paul, were a stern bunch. Most
ambitious politicians have a bit of St Paul about them. The communist Willie Gallacher was a fan of his. Critics of the judiciary
tend to be more evangelical than charitable. The approach of the
Unjust Judge is to be detected in many courts. It is merely the
judicial desire for a quiet life. Documentation is lacking to support
the story of a woman who threw a dead cat at a County Court judge.
He apparently contented himself with the admonition: 'I shall

commit you for contempt if you do that again'. She may have been a widow, but in recent years at any rate the ladies who have thrown books and tomatoes at the Court of Appeal have been spinsters of middle age. Judges cannot obey the Biblical injunction to 'judge not' and consequently they are themselves perpetually judged.

For a long time in our history there were not many judges. There were only 18 in the High Court in 1910. Now there are 90. Most of them did not have to decide questions of fact. That was done by juries in the courts of Common Law as well as the criminal courts. In Chancery there was often no dispute of fact, and so the main decision of fact by judges was by the Doctors in matrimonial and probate cases and the County Court judges when these courts started up in 1848. Modern judges must wish that they could do as was often done in the old Court of Chancery and have the evidence taken for them by an Examiner. For the supposedly dramatic process of examination and cross-examination of oral witnesses is often tedious. The tedium is exceeded only by the addresses of learned counsel. But if they try to cut through it, they earn the obloquy of the opinion makers.

The majority of the cases involve justice on only one side. When both sides are being entirely straightforward they usually stay out of court. Judges seldom say, as Lord Goddard, Chief Justice did:

> '*I hope counsel for the plaintiff will not think that I have been discourteous to him if I say that it seems to me that this is an obvious "try-on".*'
>
> **Hargreaves v. Bretherton (1958) 3 All E.R. 122.**

But they often think it. That judicial generation often dilated upon whether cases should have been brought. The present generation accept that the courts are open to all, like Tom Paine's White Horse Tavern. When they were open like the Ritz, judicial censure was the great deterrent to excessive litigiousness. Hardly surprisingly, the people of that time were infuriated by unworthy suitors subsidised by Legal Aid. They did not mind it during the War when it was a welfare service to enable servicemen and women to get divorces. But when it extended to practically all civil claims in 1950, they cried 'enough'.

> '*Do you and I subscribe for people who are not English to litigate, and do we pay for their litigation in English Courts?*'

demanded Mr Justice Hilbery of counsel in a dispute between two Iraqis, assisted by Legal Aid in 1953.

'Feather bedding' was a judicial phrase much in evidence during the Fifties. Often used in cases where workmen claimed damages for injuries alleged to be due to 'unsafe system of work'. The specific complaint was usually that the employer had left too much to the worker. In the old days a man who was partly to blame was legally entitled to nothing. Judges leaned over backwards to give sympathetic verdicts to injured men. When the law of contributory negligence was reformed in 1948 they could for the first time be fair. When someone was half to blame they could say so. They soon got used to it. They also said when a claimant was entirely to blame. And they did not see why the taxpayer should help people to bring hopeless cases.

The High Court judges of most junior rank only got £5,000 until 1954. They had not had a rise for 87 years. After tax some took home under £3,000 per annum. In 1950 Mr Justice Donovan and Mr Justice Lloyd Jacob asked Lord Chancellor Jowitt if they could go back to the Bar. Donovan, who had risen from being a clerk in the Inland Revenue to become a leading tax Silk, and Lloyd Jacob, the first specialist in patent and trade mark law to be made the special 'patent judge' had both more than £15,000 in practice.

Why should judges not feel narked at paying for other people's 'try-ons'? They were not often wealthy. The Bar was a 'depressed profession' in the early Fifties and anyone who went on the Bench for security quite naturally did not enjoy seeing his former colleagues well paid by the State for 'trying it on'. Mr Justice Stable remarked of an action by an aided customer against her hairdresser. 'It really has become a scandal.'

The certifying committees of solicitors and barristers were not properly used to the idea of allowing Legal Aid in those days. Some of them are probably more generous now; some less. The climate is in favour of giving a man his day in court. In most accident litigation, the bills are paid by insurers, or trades unions. When someone who is paying for his law is opposed by someone subsidised the judge is often inclined to believe that the fight is not fair.

A man who lets his house for a few months whilst he goes to work elsewhere can be put to grave expense by some tenant who can employ lawyers to make a technical filibuster over possession. The protections against Rachmanism are effective against decent people as well. Parliament can seldom legislate for the merits of all cases. When the judges expatiate on the merits they incur the obloquy of the Hampstead social pundits. When a divorce judge called the pop-singer Sandie Shaw 'a spoilt child' many people asked by what right he did it. But there was nothing new in it. Newspapers have been sold on such judicial utterances for generations.

From a page of the *Daily Telegraph* for 15th October, 1903, found behind a partition at home, I find that Sarah Ann Fells sued her husband Arthur for arrears of maintenance at the Whitechapel County Court. She said an order had been made at Oxford House,

75

Bethnal Green, but Judge Bacon told her that the social workers there had no power to make orders. It turned out that an agreement had been made, and the Judge accepted it, but remarked that 'Oxford House might be better employed than in separating husbands and wives'.

He was just as much entitled to say that as the critics of his latter day brother were to criticise judicial comment. It is perfectly valid for critics with esoteric knowledge to point out that often a judge's comments are necessary for elucidation and decision of the point in issue. But to go further and insist that a judge should make comments only when that is so, is to demand not perfection but deadly dullness.

How can the essential be separated from the not so essential? When Mr Justice McCardie ordered a co-respondent—a subaltern—to pay £250 damages to his mistress's husband—a colonel—he justified it thus:

> '*It may be that the co-respondent will say that he does not possess 250 shillings. It matters not. The law rightly says that a man cannot, because he is poor, escape from an award of damages in respect of a wrong which he has done . . . It may be that some will think that it would have been of greater dignity if the petitioning colonel had not insisted on his claim for damages . . . But the law provides that such damages can be claimed and I am bound to award them if asked.*'

Ewer v. Ewer and Charlton (36 T.L.R. 517).

Damages for adultery are abolished. But the uninsured driver must often be adjudged to pay thousands of pounds to his victims. Perhaps the judges' dislike of adultery damages led to their abolition. Perhaps their comments will lead to a reform of the insurance system so that insurance companies do not go broke and leave thousands of motorists without cover.

Of course, no one would want to shut the judges up completely. And once acknowledged that they have to say their piece it is rather difficult to stop them saying all of it. It is one thing to read a lot of papers in the quiet of chambers, and then make your mind up and commit your decision to paper. It is much harder to rationalise a decision *ex tempore* after days of dithering testimony. The temptation to dislike someone irritating or to discount a badly articulated point must be resisted. Those failings are conducive neither to reason nor reasonableness. And reasonableness—if not reason—is the very foundation of English law.

One of the Year Books of the reign of Henry VIII says that

> '*The law of England is the most reasonable thing in all the world.*'

That was a prophetic utterance, for more and more the canons of decision are expressed to involve an objective criterion which a mythical 'reasonable man' would observe in all his doings and sayings. A person to whom an offer is made must answer in a reasonable time. The length of notice given to a licensee or employee must be 'reasonable'. The manner in which a motor car is driven must be reasonable. The appointment of the non-driving Barbara Castle to be the Minister of Transport called up howls of derision. But no one ever objected to Mr Justice Havers trying a motoring case, and he was a non-driver.

Since motor accidents have assumed social seriousness instead of being rather a lark, motorists have developed a very critical mien. They often find that judges hold different views about proportions of wrongness and rightness not only to themselves but to each other.

When Lord Devlin drove out of a side road and collided with another car he leapt out and assured the lady driver, 'It was my fault'.

An anguished underwriting member of Lloyds wrote to *The Times* soon after, begging other motorists to eschew this example of chivalry. It might be all right for a Lord of Appeal to admit liability, he conceded (though he clearly had reservations), but the question of liability for accidents on the road is a technical business and drivers who from misguided courtesy assume blame should realise that their insurers might differ.

'Reasonableness' can therefore involve a great deal of money or inconvenience, and so calls for judgment of a rarely encountered quality.

And quite apart from knowing about reasonableness the judges are supposed to know some law as well.

For as Lord Justice Bucknill once pointed out, the so-called judge of a horse race is not a judge at all. He merely observes which beast passes the post first. The stewards decide whether it was eligible to run, or whether according to the rules it is the winner.

Unhappily, judicial eagerness to discover the multitudinous facets of information so necessary to exercise this function, makes judges appear sometimes to interfere. Mr Justice Paull, for instance was twice recently criticised by the Court of Appeal for asking too many questions in cases. This is not a new complaint against judges, and there are considerable numbers of statistics to support the critics. The staple doctrine on which these appeals rest is expressed by Lord Greene in the case of *Yuill* v. *Yuill* (1945) *P. 15.* Judges who take over the questioning from counsel:

*'descend into the arena and are liable to have their visions clouded
by the dust of the conflict.'*

What is usually forgotten is that the excessive questioning in that case was held not to justify a new trial. This is well known in some courts, mainly criminal, and the judges do the questioning unperturbed. Wise defenders seldom object, for jurors' respect for the opinions of judges often decreases in inverse proportion to their silence. If they feel he is just like one of them they will like him a great deal but his cleverness will not impress itself upon them.

A cab driver recently finished jury service once eulogised a chairman of Quarter Sessions to me in the most fulsome terms.

> '*He is a very fair man. He doesn't put up with any old buck from black fellows.*'

The best place for judicial questioning is in divorce cases, especially now that solicitors conduct undefended suits. Cruelty cases are often pleaded as long catalogues of maltreatment. The judge might merely ask the background to a couple of the most recent or worst. A couple more questions about the arrangements for the children and a painful episode is over.

There are many judges perfectly capable of sitting silent and straight faced whilst a pair of advocates go through all the drill of opening speech, examination and cross-examination of one side's witnesses, ditto for the other side, and two closing speeches.

Since its pay rises of the mid-Sixties the Bench has had a guilt complex about not wasting the taxpayer's valuable time. Not only their salaries come out of public funds, but a great deal of the remuneration of solicitors and barristers does as well, by way of Legal Aid. Quite often, therefore, they look at the papers before coming into court. In a civil claim for damages for an industrial injury, it seems eminently reasonable for a judge to say:

> '*I have read the Pleadings. It seems to me that the question is whether there should have been a lookout man to warn the crane driver that the Plaintiff was underneath before he lowered the locomotive on to him.*'

Nothing is more likely to infuriate the counsel who has swotted up the finer points of railway workshop practice, entirely overlooking the fact that the judge has conducted crane cases as counsel and tried them as a judge for about thirty years. They will appreciate the wisdom of Lord Greene, who in an address on The Judicial Office said that cases which appear to raise complicated questions of law really decide themselves once the facts are found and considered in relation to one another.

> '*A frequent source of judicial error—if I may permit myself the freedom to mention so unseemly a thing—is the application of a legal principle to facts insufficiently appreciated or imperfectly ascertained.*'

Mr Justice Ashworth once had before him a case in which a painter fell from a scaffold whilst working at Bush House, in the Strand. A plank was produced, and witnesses who had been factory inspectors for many years gave evidence about it. It was warped an inch and a quarter from the horizontal and one expert said that this was perfectly safe and acceptable, whilst the other, naturally, said that it was highly dangerous.

When the defendant's counsel was addressing the judge, the counsel for the plaintiff applied to him to permit more evidence to be called. A valuable witness had just been discovered at work elsewhere. After some discussion about the propriety of it, the witness was heard. He merely described his mate falling, which everyone knew he had done. Defendants' counsel was plainly wondering whether he should spend time in cross-examination but he asked what the witness did after his mate fell. After helping the ambulance men, he said, he went on with his work.

'On that plank,' said counsel triumphantly.

'Not a bit of it, do you think I'm daft? It was all ricketty and I chucked it out and put up a couple of new ones.'

As the awful realisation dawned that the experts had expended all their expertise on the wrong plank and that the right one would never be found, the judge took that decisive action for which the bench is renowned.

'I shall be in my room, and you can send for me when you have come to your arrangement,' he said. And they did.

Some judges were less accommodating about retiring to their rooms for settlements to be attempted. Mr Justice Glyn-Jones said that he did not mind doing it—he could always spend the time improving himself with the Law Quarterly Review. Mr Justice Roxburgh, on the other hand, in the same year (1959) grumbled that the main function of a judge had become:

> 'to sit in his private room for as long as counsel required to settle a case which if they had any consideration for the Court they would have settled at an earlier stage.'

Settlements at the door of court were condemned for all sorts of reasons. Plaintiffs who played up for it were avaricious. Defendants who did so were mean. Neither really holds water. If the briefs had been delivered to counsel the fees had been incurred anyway. Some desirable witness might not have been available, or even more likely, the true situation had only become clear at that late stage. It quite often happens that some perfect case has a catch in it.

Should it begin and the opening speech is over—sooner or later—the perfect ascertainment of facts can begin. 'Come into the witness box, Mr Boilermaker' invites the judge. The oath is then administered with greater or less solemnity. Some judges are more particular than others. Mr Justice Paull, for instance, is a stickler. No movement or noise is tolerated whilst the oath is administered. Considering that this boilermaker had probably never been in court in his life; that the layout and furniture, and the wigs and robes make a rather awe-inspiring scene, the effect of the oath ceremony is probably considerable.

A foolish woman member of the Magistrates' Association at their conference a year or so ago declared that the oath should be done away with because she and her colleagues knew that when someone had pleaded 'Not guilty' they were going to lie on oath, and it was therefore better from the religious viewpoint to do away with the oath.

What should really be abolished, of course, is not the oath, but lay magistrates. No doubt many people do lie on oath. The importance of it however is that it is a fixed or datum point after which everything that the witness says is taken seriously and subject to challenge. If it is shown to be incorrect, it might redound to the discredit of the speaker, or lead perhaps to a prosecution for perjury. Add these matters to the fact that there are many people left who do believe in the sanctity of the oath, and there seems every reason to retain it. It might not do much good when a person is convicted because some policeman bothered to charge him, but that is the fault not of the law but of the people entrusted with its adminstration.

'No doubt you will find this question offensive, but it is not intended to be. I must ask you if you have any religious belief involving an objection to taking an oath, or no religious belief at all,'

said Mr Justice Russell (as he then was) to a very strict Non-Conformist who wished to affirm. A wealthy Chinese was about to testify at the High Court and a fine china plate was taken to the court in case he needed it, together with a chicken. In one Oriental form of oath the plate is symbolically broken as would the witness's soul break if he did not tell the truth. In another form the chicken's neck is wrung as a kind of *memento mori* to the same effect. When the usher asked him what he wanted to do, he said, 'Actually, we Balliol men usually affirm'.

Judge Leon has pointed out that there never has been any law against witnesses sitting down, but that it is only recently has it become common. This is no doubt because of the influence of television showing American counsel perambulating round the well of the court in front of a witness chair. The reason for making people stand up was no doubt that it got their evidence over quicker because they were not comfortable. Many years ago the courts were in session much longer during the day and got through the evidence faster—especially in the criminal courts, where the excellent system prevailed of preventing the prisoner from testifying. This alone must have shortened matters by more than half.

Getting the whole story from someone is a long-winded business, particularly if the counsel is not permitted to ask 'leading questions' —which are questions calculated to indicate to the witness what answer he should give. Even 'What is your name?' could come into that category, but it is not a leading question. 'Your name is John Smith, isn't it?' is a leading question. In civil actions the system of pleading has removed the necessity for much laborious questioning because the admitted facts appear on these papers. It is now possible to make formal admissions in criminal proceedings in order to save questioning time, but the system is not much used. This is because many advocates have a touching belief in their own powers of cross-examination, and hope that the people they have to examine will be nervous, inarticulate and forgetful. In order to upset this ploy, judges interfere with questions in just the same way as they interfere to cut the cackle. And of course, by interfering, the judges give their own feelings away.

Now the whole business of judging involves the judge telling the world what he thinks of a case when he decides it. There would seem consequently to be no real objection to him giving his views at any earlier stage. But this, of course, indicates pre-judging, and the noun most commonly associated with that is prejudice. For some obscure reason, prejudice is widely regarded as unjudicial, and the judiciary are constantly accused of it by intellectual critics in the serious publications.

Not many judges bother to complain about bad cases being brought on Legal Aid, now. Most of them did a fair bit of Legal Aid work before elevation, and have not the same respect for the people who have to pay for their law that the previous generation of judges had. Mr Justice Vaizey was outraged to discover that two people enjoying Legal Aid for a dispute had a television set, 'obviously a luxury of an expensive kind', as late as 1957. What the Hampstead critics forget is that it is when a case is before a judge that the criticisms of it are most appropriate. The committees of solicitors and barristers who decide whether Legal Aid shall be granted must not pre-judge cases even if they are not sanguine about their chances of success. If the situation technically affords a claim or defence they must permit the assisted person to put it forward, contributing according to his ability as determined by the Ministry of Social Security. If it were otherwise, there would be no need for courts.

Doctor Samuel Johnson was asked how he could plead a bad cause, and replied rather typically that he did not know it was a bad cause until the judgment.

Some of the remarks made by judges are hurtful and avoidable. But they are required to state fully their reasons for coming to decisions of both fact and law. No one ever knows why juries make the decisions they do, and it is extremely difficult to upset a jury verdict. When two officials of the National Union of Teachers brought defamation proceedings against a member, and the jury gave him the verdict, the Court of Appeal was very sympathetic. They had been defamed but an English jury, not obviously perverse, had favoured the other side.

It is perhaps better that one responsible man should justify his findings than that a dozen amateurs should not, even if it does hurt some people's feelings. Curiously enough, though judges are criticised for uncalled-for remarks, lay magistrates who are often more bigoted and free with their censure, seldom endure reproof for their bad manners.

Most of the public seem highly delighted with judges who cut the cackle and come to the 'osses. There was one County Court judge who retired a few years ago who always politely proffered his 'system' for the use of advocates in hire purchase repossession cases. At the beginning of the action he would have the defendant sworn, and then ask him, 'When can they come for it, and how long do you need to pay?'

If the answer was, 'They can have it when they like. It's no use to me, and I don't see why I should pay because it does not work,' not only was it clear that there must be a full hearing of a defended action, but it emerged with more clarity than upon many learned pleadings, what the defence actually was.

Litigation in the County Courts is not well paid, and lawyers need quick wits to survive. The pressure of work often attenuates the full ceremonial opening speech, evidence of one side, cross-examination, evidence of the other and cross-examination, closing speeches and full scale judgment speech.

Counsel recently opened a County Court case under the *Married Women's Property Acts* with the words: 'This concerns a house which was conveyed into the names of the husband and wife jointly. . . .' The judge remarked 'Well, that's the end of the case isn't it?' The House of Lords had recently given exhaustive consideration to the proportions of the whole matrimonial property to which working wives can be entitled and gave great weight to the ostensible shares to be discovered from the deeds. This approach is what the Court of Appeal (in *Newgrosh* v. *Newgrosh in 1953*) called 'palm tree justice'.

Disappointed litigants, and disappointed lawyers, can always turn for criticism of this approach to the most overworked judicial pronouncement of the century.

In *R. v. Sussex Justices exparte McCarthy (1924) 1 K.B. 256 and 259*, the Queen's Bench Divisional Court quashed a motoring conviction because the Clerk to the Justices, a local solicitor, had retired with them during their deliberations in case they needed advice. In his private practice he was the solicitor for the other driver, who was of course, the principal prosecution witness. Said Hewart:

> '. . . *he scrupulously abstained from referring to the case in any way . . . But while that is so . . . it is not merely of some importance but is of fundamental importance that justice should not only be seen to be done but should manifestly and undoubtedly be seen to be done.*'

The manifest visibility of justice according to Hewart was never clearer than in the action for libel brought in 1935 by the Duchess of Marlborough against some newsagents who imported an American magazine called *Hooey*. It had in it a cartoon of two rose trees and was captioned 'We should not have planted the Duchess of Marlborough and the Rev. H. Robertson Page in the same bed'. Rosarians will know, of course, that there is a variety named after the Duchess and one called Rev. F. Page Roberts.

Hewart demanded of counsel for the plaintiff: 'Have you considered the wisdom of prosecuting in this case?' How on earth it could conceivably lead to a breach of the peace was not apparent. But in his private room he bullied the defendants into capitulation. Having got his way, he declared that the Duchess had 'acted with magnanimity towards the defendants. They were at her mercy'. Exactly whose mercy they were at is plain, but he took the opportunity of that sorry episode to deliver himself of one of the remarks for which he is also celebrated:

> '*Not the least mischief which is done by a publication of this kind is that it may tend to cast some discredit even upon journalism itself, a profession, which, as everyone knows, contains a great number of able and conscientious gentlemen.*'

The Press treasures that tribute from The Advocate on the Bench, who was himself a journalist in his early years. He was also counsel for Artemus Jones in the libel action which in the words of his successor, Lord Goddard, added 'a terror to authorship'. Having become Attorney-General, he had a kind of constitutional option on the job of Lord Chief Justice. His predecessor on appointment had to give the Government an undated letter of resignation, so that Hewart could take over. This he did at the Government reshuffle in 1922. Lord Trevethin read of his own resignation in *The Times*.

Just why the trial of a civil dispute between contractors, motor car drivers, shipowners or landowners should follow the procedure of a trial for felony or treason is not clear. Historically, there was little distinction between civil wrongs and crimes. It is changing now, and many English people are sorry to see it change. Every now and then the judges who run the Commercial List in the High Court announce that they are eager to try cases without pleadings and on agreed statements of facts. But still their main customers are shipowners and insurance companies. Other business men and lawyers do not seem interested in getting down to the meat of their disputes.

The Industrial Court does not look right, with ordinary looking men in lounge suits sitting only an inch or two higher than everyone else, being called 'Sir', instead of 'My Lord'. The English love a judge. Newspapers love to stick in a bit of background about the 'Red-robed Judge in a book-lined Court'. That is usually inserted in divorce reports by sub-editors who were not present, to give the reporter's bare account some verisimilitude. Very few of the Divorce Courts in London are book-lined. The Divorce judges wear black, or in the County Court, the navy-blue robe with purple swathe.

The attitude of the judges to the get-up varies. The 6th July, 1971, was very hot. Mr Justice Cusack was sitting in the Queen's Bench, wearing his wig, stiff collar, bands, gown and sash. A witness stepped into the box wearing an open-necked shirt, and was asked by counsel if he had forgotten his tie or could not wear one. Said the judge:

> '*I am not in the least bothered about that. He is much more sensibly dressed than I am.*'

Mr Justice Paull is another who, when witnesses hastily summoned came in their working clothes, waved away their apologies—'It was very kind of you to come at such short notice. You have been very helpful'.

A few days after Mr Justice Cusack's case, a witness wearing an open-neck shirt went into the box in the Divorce Court, before Judge Percy Rawlins. Said the judge:

> '*I cannot understand why solicitors don't advise their clients to dress properly before coming to Court.*'

Many of them do. I remember one who borrowed a collar and tie from a prisoner's friend at the Old Bailey so that the man should look a bit more respectable in the dock. The friend went home without his neckwear because the prisoner got five years.

Judges can be quite tough on counsel who are sartorially incomplete. 'I cannot see you, Mr So and So,' they say. The usual imperfection is the absence of a waistcoat. The invisibility of counsel also manifests itself when they speak whilst not actually in the benches reserved for them. This happens more often than one might imagine.

In the Companies Court on Monday mornings it is often physically impossible for the counsel engaged in a particular case to get into one of the rows of benches because so many barristers are there waiting for so many cases to come on. Each one lasts only a few minutes, but that is precisely why everyone has to be there waiting for it. Some counsel are concerned in more than one case.

It might appear to warrant an orderly queue outside a Registrar's office, but what is being done is a serious matter, winding up companies, or even more serious, trying to prevent them being wound up. This is the responsibility of judges of the High Court—although a little winding-up is done in County Courts. It is done in public because, 'Justice must not only be done but must manifestly be seen to be done,' a legal person is being doomed.

The complaint most often levelled against judges is that they have not made it patently clear that justice has been done. Judges are often sensitive men deeply wounded by criticism of their efforts to be reasonable. Because of the curious system we have, the criticisms are sometimes repeated and exacerbated by other judges in the Court of Appeal and then the only protection the judge has is the House of Lords in its judicial capacity. It is astonishing how often the House of Lords says that the Court of Appeal was wrong and that the trial judge was right. Very recently, the Court of Appeal has retaliated by saying that the House of Lords was wrong. *Broome* v. *Cassel (1971)*.

Since decisions of the highest courts govern the law to be applied in the lower courts, this could lead to confusion. Fortunately, that particular vice has characterised our law for sufficiently long to be regarded with equanimity by the profession, if not the public. What they don't know they won't grieve over. A few learned critics think two appeals is wrong because of the expense and uncertainty and would abolish the House of Lords as an appeal court. It was actually abolished by the *Judicature Act, 1873,* but the provision never became law, it was replaced instead with the *Appellate Jurisdiction Act, 1876.* It all came about because a lot of Victorians did not think much of the quality of the judges who decided appeals in the Lords. The 1876 Act was designed to improve the judicial quality. Thus the House of Lords is the best place to start an appraisal of the judiciary because it is supposed to be the best. The Act had to be passed because when Baron Parke was made a life peer so that he could act as a judicial member of the House of Lords, it was held, in the *Wensleydale Peerage Case (5 H.L.C.)* that he could not do so because a life peer was not then allowed to vote in that House.

Almost immediately, the superior intellects of the professional judges—as distinct from retired Lord Chancellors—made themselves felt. Reasonableness itself was soon commented upon by Lord Bramwell:

> *'I cannot understand how it could have been supposed necessary that it should have been referred to a judge to say whether an agreement between carriers, of whose business he knows nothing, and fishmongers, of whose business he equally knows nothing, is reasonable or not.'*
>
> ### *Manchester, Sheffield & Lincolnshire Railway* v. *Brown (1883) L.R. 8 A.C. 703.*

Fifty years later, Lord Macmillan was able to observe that 'there is no acquired learning, however seemingly remote from the profession, which a lawyer does not sooner or later have an opportunity of putting to practical use'.

Lord Justice Scrutton confessed once that:

> *'It is difficult to know what judges are allowed to know, though they are ridiculed if they pretend not to know.'*
>
> ### *Tolley* v. *Fry (1930) 1 K.B. 467.*

They are ridiculed because newspapers do not know the rule of evidence which limits judicial knowledge to particularly notorious general information, and requires everything else to be 'on the record' in evidence of some kind or another. Mr Justice Darling, as he was for so much of his long career, was renowned in those very papers as a wit. He once had to ask, 'Who is George Robey?' and Sir Patrick Hastings had to tell him: 'He is the Darling of the music halls'.

Darling's career spanned the difficult transition between the old law and the beginnings of our modern law. When he started at the Bar, Sir John Day was still going his circuit on horseback. Now, of course, the circuit system has been reformed by Dr Beeching, to whom it had to be left because only he knew which railway lines to Assize towns were going to be closed by the time the changes were made. Darling was a barrister of not very large practice. He spent his time in the House of Commons. He had been hard-up when young, but was made suddenly rich on the death of his uncle. Lord Chancellor Halsbury, even then a very old man, thought highly of his capacities, and he was made a Commissioner of Assize on his own circuit.

Modern crime required that experienced QCs were always being given the Commission to go off and try some long case which would obstruct the ordinary buisenss of an Assize. It led to the reform of the criminal courts on 1st January, 1971. But the Press at the turn of the century was collectively appalled at the idea that a politician and creature of the Government should also be acting as one of Her Majesty's judges.

The idea seemed to be that Darling was the link by which the judges, who as a class disliked the politicians intensely, should be brought under political control. It was this furore before he was made a judge which led to a celebrated contempt case after Darling actually left Parliament for the High Court Bench.

A Birmingham newspaper wrote of him in 1900 after he warned the Press about printing indecent evidence:

> '*No newspaper can exist except upon its merits, a condition from which the Bench, happily for Mr. Justice Darling, is exempt. There is not a journalist in Birmingham who has anything to learn from the impudent little man in horsehair, a microcosm of conceit and empty-headedness.*
>
> '*One is almost sorry that the Lord Chancellor had not another relative to provide for on the day that he selected a new judge from among the larrikins of the law. One of Mr. Justice Darling's biographers states that "an eccentric relative left him much money". That misguided testator spoiled a successful bus conductor.*'

No newspaper would dare to publish such a tirade nowadays. The Transport and General men on its payroll would walk out to a man because of the slight on 'bus conductors'.

Chairman of North London Quarter Sessions, Mr Reginald Seaton had to apologise to the Seamen's Union when he called some seamen the 'scum of the Earth'. The Birmingham editor, Mr Gray, was fined £100 which presumably left him feeling that the article was well worth it.

The fact is that judges were until recently rarities. Years of urging between 1868 and 1907 for the number of King's Bench judges to be increased finally succeeded when the establishment was raised by one. Three years later, another was added and then there were 17 in addition to the Lord Chief Justice.

And yet there was pressure, even in *The Times*, to enlarge the jurisdiction of the County Courts. This would have left only the bigger cases to the High Court and increased the exclusiveness of its judges. They did not need to have their exclusiveness increased. Wilde makes a young woman of the time to declare with great pride 'My father was a judge'. But when Lady Bracknell retorted, 'Of the County Court!' everyone in the house knew just what was meant. The High Court Bench then was a distinction, almost like a Dukedom. Now it is a responsible and highly skilled job, but not so august that Sir Henry Fisher did not feel constrained to give it up and take a job in the City.

It was a little curious that the heavy handed punishment of contempt of court should have been employed, in Mr Gray's case. Three years earlier the Judicial Committee of the Privy Council had decided a case in which contempt of court was alleged—though admittedly it came from the Caribbean Island of Grenada which, unlike now, had very little in common with Birmingham.

On that island there was a newspaper called *The Federalist* and in it appeared a letter signed 'Fair Play' with an address on the neighbouring island of St Vincent.

> '*Kindly grant me space in your unfettered and fearless journal to expose the scandalous state of things that has existed here since Mr. Geoffrey Peter St. Aubyn's appointment as acting Chief Justice in November last. The public career of this gentleman is interesting. A briefless barrister, unendowed with much brain, who religiously attended with his empty bag at the several courts of London in the forlorn hope of picking up a case, he after long weary years of waiting exchanged the law for the stage (being a good amateur actor) and tried to earn an honest penny by turning his undoubted histrionic talent into account.*

> '*In the meantime he had become an assiduous hanger-on at the Colonial Office and applied for every vacancy real or imagined that he heard of, and it was while he was "starring" in the provinces that in an evil moment for St. Vincent he was appointed police magistrate of the Kingstown district in May, 1891, at a salary of £450 a year.*'

It went on to list the sins of St Aubyn since he had become acting Chief Justice, particularly his treatment of a barrister, Charles John McLeod. The paper had an article about the St Vincent judiciary as well, which said that the public had no confidence in the previous Chief Justice and that 'Mr St Aubyn is reducing the judicial character to the level of a clown' and would 'prostitute one of the most sacred secular positions merely to gratify his venom and his spleen'.

Mr McLeod the barrister happened to be a correspondent of the paper on St Vincent and walked down to meet the ferry when the issue carrying these words was delivered. He took possession of his own copy and carried a few other copies to his friend the librarian. This, it was said when he was haled before St Aubyn, amounted to publication of the contempt though there was no evidence at all that he had any knowledge of its being in the paper. St Aubyn clearly believed he wrote it. The Privy Council allowed his appeal from the sentence of imprisonment which St Aubyn passed upon him.

'Committals for contempt of court by scandalising the court itself have become obsolete in this country.

'Courts are satisfied to leave to public opinion attacks or comments derogatory or scandalous to them.

'But it must be considered that in small colonies consisting principally of coloured populations, the enforcement in proper cases of committal for contempt of court or attacks upon the court may be absolutely necessary to preserve in such a community the dignity of and respect for the court.'

Lord Morris (1899) A.C.

It is a fact that since then no newspaperman has been committed to prison for libelling a judge after adjudication in a case. When Clifford Sharp, editor of the *New Statesman*, wrote in 1928 that the verdict against Dr Marie Stopes in her libel action against the *Morning Post* was a miscarriage of justice he added that anyone holding her views, could not hope for a fair hearing from Mr Justice Avory 'and there are so many Avorys'. The court said it was contumelious, because it imputed unfairness, but the apology was accepted and Mr Sharp merely had to pay the costs.

Avory was known as The Hanging Judge, a rather vinegary sort of chap who goes down in history as the author of:

'If history is to be made of the tittle-tattle of the Upper Tooting tea tables, you will no doubt consider whether it would not be better that history should not be made at all.'

By the mid-Thirties, Lord Hewart could say that 'His Majesty's judges are satisfied with the almost universal admiration in which they are held.'

Hewart was obsessed with the notion that the Civil Service was trying to turn the judges into office boys. This was merely another manifestation of pathological fear for judicial privilege dressed up as a concern for independence.

This has its roots in a theory of the French jurist Montesquieu who in the mid-18th Century wrote an analysis of what Dicey called in late Victorian days, The Rule of Law. In his Esprit de Lois, Montesquieu said that in Britain the Executive, and the Administration and the Judiciary were completely separate because any combination of any of them was bound to create tyranny. We were enormously flattered by this Theory of the Separation of Powers, which was even less true then than it is today. In the time of the early Stuarts Sir Edward Coke had insisted that the King and the Executive were subject to the Common Law. When he was Attorney-General to Elizabeth he supported the Crown, as a judge he defied Parliament and in and after retiring from Parliament, he supported its claims to sovereign power, even though in 1610 he had ruled that 'when an Act of Parliament is against common right or reason, or repugnant or impossible, the Common Law will control it'—Bonham's Case.

Judges still rail against the imposition of uniformity and the consequent destruction of independence and individuality but in fact they actually exercise power of determination of disputes over a much wider area of everyone's lives than they did even a few years ago. They still engage in a running war with the Government and Civil Service, even though Lord Parker did say once that the courts are the handmaiden of the Executive. They also give way to prejudice. But they usually decide individual cases on their particular facts as applied to disinterested canons of law. Steeped in the philosophy of expediency, the politicians and bureaucrats find this measure of objectivity incomprehensible, if not downright perverse.

The lower orders always have felt that the judiciary was merely the enforcement arm of the conspiracy between their betters and political masters. Professor Harold Laski said in evidence in his own libel action against the *Newark Advertiser* in 1946 that in political libel actions, at least down to 1924, London juries would award damages to Tory MPs but not to Labour men. He was quite careful to say it about juries—it was in one of his books—but it is quite common among leftist publicists to point to that case as one where Lord Chief Justice Goddard demonstrated political bias, as an instance of Tory sympathy among the judges. He had it all worked out that many judicial appointments were given to Tory MPs with safe seats. But the period of his statistics was mainly during Victoria's reign. In recent times a Socialist connection has been a good foundation for success in a legal career. Trades Unions are very good customers. And it is the venerable Marxist QC, D. N. Pritt, who tells the story of the County Court judge who confessed that he felt bound to give judgment for a person in a political dispute because he had a good case and there was no proof that he was a Communist.

Laski was prophetic if nothing else. He lost the case but, of course, no one really believed he was an advocate of violent revolution. Revolutionary he certainly was in his attitude to the judiciary. The letters he exchanged with Justice Oliver Wendell Holmes reveal that he considered the judges the biggest obstruction to proper legal education and understanding. He said that Augustine Birrel QC, the Liberal politician, told him, 'When I balance a law school against Grand Night at the Inner Temple, my stomach rebels against scholarship.'

The great judges of the last and early this century were men of education. They were classicists and historians from Oxford and Cambridge. Few of them believed that law was a fit subject for learning. When Lord Sankey became Lord Chancellor in the Labour Government in 1929, Laski tried to get him to make a Cambridge professor a judge, but the others soon put a stop to that. In their own way, the judges, few in number and poorly paid, imbued with Christian Principles, and Victorian Self Help attitudes, did a great deal to protect Britain from try-anything-once-fashions in social life, business and politics. Curiously reactionary though many of them were, others were not only enlightened but strong enough in intellect and character to advance the law and yet retain integrity and independence.

Lord Reading was unwise enough to speculate in Marconi shares, and one or two judges went ga-ga. But with the help of the daily papers they did establish an aura of quality. One Chancery judge in the Thirties used to give all his wards tea parties in his room at the Law Courts. Wards in those days were usually the children of the wealthy or at least the Upper Classes. In the late Fifties there began a great vogue for warding working-class girls—usually hairdressers' apprentices. Mr Justice Vaizey once remarked as he left his court, 'My wards think that if they become pregnant I'll have to let them marry. Well, I won't'.

Agonised women journalists complained about young lovers being subject to the rule of old Chancery judges, and they still do although the average age of the Chancery Bench is now about 20 years younger than 15 years ago. But sob sisters have not always realised that shotgun weddings do no one any good. For all its snobbery, the Judiciary knew this long before the agony columnists. A great deal of the mystique surrounding the judical office is founded in snobbery. Even now you can hear it said in winding-up cases that 'The court is not a debt-collecting agency'. In the strict theory of the law of bankruptcy and company liquidation, that is perfectly true. The idea is that because there is not enough to go round each creditor shall have a smaller slice of the cake—even though feeding the five thousand requires supernatural powers.

However, the public would like to know, if the courts are not debt collecting agencies, what are they? They know, of course, that they are imprisoning and divorcing agencies as well, but fines and maintenance orders look to the unlearned very much like debts. The distinction between the County Courts and the High Court really lies not so much in financial limits of jurisdiction but in the acceptance by the former that it is a debt collecting agency. In the Nineties apparently at least one County Court judge in Kent was quite happy to let debt collectors represent clients in his court. But he was forced to let solicitors take over and call the debt collectors as witnesses. Now, of course, the electricity boards, gas boards, local authorities and licensing authorities often send along officers who virtually act as witness-advocates in debt collecting. At least it saves the debtors the costs of lawyers. And there is no law in so many of the cases except that of supply and demand.

Not all judges are of the refined intellect which demands no more than some novel question of law to determine. Some are much happier—often because their experience fits them for it—to preside at criminal trials. Intellectuals are often scornful of the quality of justice in the criminal courts. The judges of the High Court only sit on the more serious cases on Assize and at the Old Bailey. Most criminal trials particularly in recent years, which were not disposed of before magistrates, were tried by Quarter Sessions with legally qualified chairmen. Now replaced by the Crown Courts, High Court judges on Circuit have to deal in pretty quick succession with people who plead guilty to the most serious crimes. Reformers point out that sentencing is a job for which judges are quite unfitted because they are not trained psychologists and social workers. They are not, but it is also the fact that however it turns out, the criminal law is not, theoretically, an institution operated for the benefit of the criminal classes. A progressive idea of a criminal trial appears to be one in which acquittal is guaranteed so that the leading actors therein can get back to unjust enrichment with the least possible loss of productivity.

Crime has become so sophisticated that what goes on at a trial often has little connection with reality. The jury need guidance, and the judge is all the guidance they have.

Mr Justice Stable attracted a storm of criticism a few years ago when he told a jury to disregard legal quibbles and give a verdict if they could for he had to leave the court building. (He was due at a dinner.) They were back in four minutes with a conviction— which did not survive the Court of Criminal Appeal.

Just why that should be regarded as reprehensible in a country which only a few years later introduced majority verdicts in criminal trials, is difficult to understand. The reason for starting majority decision was because it was considered wrong for one or two people to be able to hold up a verdict. But why should they be cranky and wrong? Might it not be that the minority are the conscientious intelligent ones who do not believe that 'He must have done it or the police would not have arrested him'?

About 40 per cent of people tried on indictment are acquitted. Technically, a prosecution should not be launched unless there is evidence capable of proving beyond reasonable doubt that the accused is guilty. Men with the authority of preventive detention behind them prefer trial by Red Judges, as those of the Queen's Bench are called.

On the Chancery side, there is no crime. An old joke says that Chancery judges try no one except counsel. The Queen's Bench judges have to suffer it like Sir Thomas More's hair shirt. Now that the death penalty has been abolished for arson in naval dockyards as well as murder, the only chance a judge is likely to get to sentence anyone to death is in case of a war and a traitor being caught. Litigation of all kinds has its booms and slumps. At present crime is the dominant market. Most of the other work in the Queen's Bench involves accidents either in industry or on the roads.

It might seem an appalling waste of intellect and legal knowledge to decide such a simple thing as which driver was to blame for a collision. Not only do untrained magistrates do it when policemen tell them to, but every one of us each mile we drive makes an unarguable judgment upon the quality of someone else's driving. It is, however, rather different seeing the bad driving from having to make up your mind who is describing it most accurately a couple of years afterwards. In most cases where there is cogent evidence, the question of liability is agreed. Then the judges have to calculate in money terms the value of the maiming. Reformers consider that this is not really work for judges. The recently retired Lord Chief Justice, Lord Parker, sees a system of insurance to compensate those injured in motor accidents irrespective of blame, as the coming thing.

When it shall come to pass, what shall we do with the surplus judges? Commercial men now favour arbitration of the contract disputes, because they can get it done cheaper, by being less formal over proof, and sending all the letters and statements to an arbitrator (often a QC) to decide a dispute in a report. Admittedly, cases often come before the judges where it is alleged that the arbitrator has gone wrong in law. There ought to be quite a future there for the judges.

They already have very few defended divorce cases to decide. The hope for judicial employment in years to come lies with crime, labour relations and foreign trade. These two latter are fields fertile for development in English law. At long last, some of the County Court judges are being elevated to the High Court.

Judges get pensions at the full rate, transmissible to their widows, if they survive 15 years in office. The most successful barrister has no pension save what he buys for himself by way of insurance. He cannot sell his practice, like a successful solicitor. His goodwill lasts only whilst he retains his faculties. Elevation to the Bench and retirement—which are not synonymous—used to enable barristers to collect all their outstanding fees free of income tax (if they could collect them at all; they cannot sue for them at law). Since 1966 they can collect what they are owed only in respect of their last year of practice tax free.

It is quite understandable that a man should want to finish his stint and qualify for the full pension. Since judges used not to be appointed until they were getting on, that made some of them very old. One High Court judge was extremely ancient but all efforts to retire him failed. The Lord Chancellor sent a diplomatic secretary to see him who laid it on very thick that he was giving too much of himself and really should not overdo it. The judge was greatly touched, and the Chancellor soon had from him a little note in which he said how much he valued the regard in which he was held. In the circumstances he felt able to resign as Chairman of his County Quarter Sessions but would be quite willing to sit as a Deputy Chairman whenever required, and that he looked forward to many more years at the Law Courts in The Strand.

But the judges now 'get their bottoms on the Consolidated Fund', as Sir Travers Humphreys put it, in their forties and fifties. They can finish their term well before they are 70. And the famous public school and Oxford or Cambridge backgrounds are no longer required.

Sir Terence Donovan was little known except as a Labour MP from 1945 who said:

> 'I ask myself why private enterprise can't give me a decent cup of tea or a sandwich on a railway station.'

Starting work in an Inland Revenue office in 1920 as a clerk, he read law for two hours every day. He was called to the Bar in 1924, but did not begin to practise until 1932. He specialised in tax law and took silk in 1945.

The great virtue claimed for our system—if such it can be called—of legal education and training is that in his early experience in the Magistrates', County and Coroners' Courts the advocate meets all kinds of people in all kinds of difficulties and learns to sift evidence and get a feel for situations. Lord Donovan had no such experience and he had none of the advantages of a superior university education —having been in the trenches at Passchendaele when he might have been there. As a King's Bench judge dealing with accidents and crime he was very sound. Although the Court of Criminal Appeal said that he was wrong to direct that it could be murder for 'Gypsy Jim' Smith to drive off with PC Leslie Meehan clinging to his car so that he was flung off and killed, the House of Lords said that Donovan was right. When he himself became a Law Lord he was plainly one whom his brethren regarded as a leader.

He was a great simplifier. For instance:

> 'At football matches, loud and pointed doubts are often expressed about a referee's ancestry, but this is not slander in the legal sense.'

No doubt when Nye Bevan introduced the Rent Tribunals made

up of non-lawyers with the words that they had 'as much right to say what is a reasonable rent as has the Lord Chancellor' he really meant that ordinary working-class people are quite capable of understanding laws. Some of them undoubtedly are. Whether all of them—or of any other class—are able or willing to work at it so as to become good at it is an entirely different question.

But they must never be too good at laying down the law. For our system of reform depends largely on their mistakes.

The main ground of appeal in criminal or civil cases is judicial error. Indeed, until late in the last century, appellate courts were called Courts of Error. Very often these errors are not the fault of the judge. Mr Justice Rigby Swift read to a jury in 1935 a passage out of *Archbold's Criminal Pleading Evidence and Practice* to the effect that if a person was proved to have killed someone else it was for him to prove that the killing was less than murder, that is either manslaughter or accident. The Court of Criminal Appeal agreed. But the House of Lords, in the only case where it saved a man from the gallows, quashed the conviction and put the 'Prosecutor's Bible' in the wrong.

One cannot help wondering how many people hanged as the result of the wrong version. Perfectly lawfully, of course.

The Law Givers

'*Forget about William III*'

      advice of Harold Wilson, M.P., to the Irish, 26th August, 1971.

WE BRITONS are firmly persuaded not only that we ought to be, but that we are in fact, governed by Law. The label given by Professor Albert Dicey to our philosophy—'The Rule of Law'—is now the greatest thing since sliced bread and the watchword of the United Nations. It commands the enthusiastic allegiance of all the countries of the world, especially those where the Government's grasp on power is precarious. Even more keen on the Rule of Law are the people in process of overthrowing governments.

In order to govern according to Law, a regime has to know what the Law is. It is quite often possible to refer to a document to discover the precise terms of the laws by which a state is to be governed. Such documents are called Constitutions. We have not got one.

What we do have is a collection of principles which are the foundations of our Constitution and several statutes, and rules of law less well articulated to fill in the details. These are all well known to the whole populace, in theory. Consequently, we British often take a stand on principle. John Hampden's celebrated resistance to the class-tax called Ship Money is the archetypal stand over principle. It is reported at *3, State Trials 825*. Everyone knows what 'a Village Hampden' is. It is immortalised in Gray's Elegy in a Country Churchyard. Unfortunately, the poem does not state exactly what the principle was. Thus very few people know what it was. It is, however, constantly and fervently invoked.

During the personal rule of Charles I, when even the Protestants of Northern Ireland complained about English tyranny, he decided to raise a tax by extending the levy of Ship Money all over England, though it was previously confined to coastal districts in wartime. It is now a principle of taxation that everyone should pay it, on all money over a certain level and the rich get allowances just like the poor. But people did not think that way in the 17th Century and John Hampden the wealthy landowner who was MP for Buckinghamshire when Parliament sat—which was not often—refused to pay £1 Ship Money. The case was heard by all twelve judges of the Exchequer Chamber, and they decided 7 to 5 that the King was right. They were, after all, his judges.

> '*I never heard or read that* lex *was* rex; *but it is common and most true that* rex *is* lex'

was Mr Justice Berkley's neat apophthegm. But his brother Vernon put it straight on the line:

> '*The King* pro bono publico *may charge his subjects for the safety and defence of the kingdom, notwithstanding any Act of Parliament, and a statute derogatory from the prerogative doth not bind the King and the King may dispense with any law in cases of necessity.*'

As it turned out, of course, Parliament dispensed with the King, but before it did it passed an Act—to which the King gave his Royal Assent on 7th August, 1641, reversing that judgment, and consequently, Hampden's fine. Now of course it may be the reason for his inspiring all the village Hampdens who take stand on principle over unjust library fines, and things of similar importance, that he made such a fuss over only £1.

That aspect is seldom mentioned, however, for ignorance of principles is not important. The important thing is the knowledge that should you want a principle you can always find one. You can find a principle of the English Constitution much more easily than you can find a law to support it. The Cabinet, for instance, rules according to Law. But there is no Act of Parliament which sets up the Cabinet, authorises its meetings, standing orders or powers. If Mr Heath's Ministry was defeated at a General Election, none of the Ministers would break the law by refusing to resign office. They could draw the salaries which they and their immediate predecessors have raised to such generous proportions until at the next Finance Bill Parliament refused to vote the money for them. Or, it may very well be that Her Majesty the Queen, acting on her prerogative, could give them all their cards. Which would look rather like what Charles I did.

The convention that the Queen will not refuse the Royal Assent to a Bill which has passed Parliament really means that a majority in the House of Commons is all the Constitution we have, said Mr Kenneth Pickthorn MP in Parliament in 1956 (*550 Commons Hansard Col. 1821*). Maybe so, but we have a lot of Constitutional Law. It broods over everything, omnipresent but largely ignored. Ulster, the Common Market, Rhodesia, the Industrial Relations Act are obvious applications. But there is nothing which cannot be fertile of a constitutional point.

Consider, for instance, the little known action of *Hall* v. *Hall*. Reported in only 21 lines of 'Our County Court Letter' in the *Solicitors' Journal* for 11th November, 1944. It was to all appearances a mere bagatelle. Miss Hall sued her brother for possession of 'Ashen Coppice', Dewchurch, at the Hereford County Court. There have been thousands of such cases. The title deeds showed that her father left it to her mother whose executrix she was. Her brother admitted all this but he did not want to get out. Most lawyers would have said he had no case. But he contended that the probate of their mother's will was invalid and so did not pass the house to his sister. Oh, it was verily his mother's will and testament. The invalidity was a point of pure law. The *Probate Act, 1857*, under which it was granted was at fault. It was assented to, by Queen Victoria, who was not the rightful Queen of England. The true succession to the Throne was through James Stuart.

As a matter of law, that argument is not without merit.

> '*Do not think I am arguing for the Jacobite cause. I am only endeavouring to show you how much purely legal strength that cause had.*'

Maitland. *Constitutional History of England, P. 285.*

He also pointed out that it was technically treason to put it forward. Since he was not put in the Tower, it seems safe to chance an explanation.

Mr Hall could not have made the best of his case, because His Honour Judge Roope Reeve, KC decided against him. Unfortunately, Mr Hall did not appeal. Whether he was overawed by two and a half centuries of usurped monarchical government, we shall never know. He could have begun by claiming that the Hereford County Court had no jurisdiction because the *County Courts Act, 1846*, by which such institutions were brought into being was also assented by Victoria. So, for that matter, were the Acts by which the Court of Appeal was created. On one point at least the judge was quite wrong in law, though no doubt quite right in prophesy, to hold against Mr Hall. His main ground of decision, prosaically enough, was that he did not feel able to ignore the fact that the Probate Act had been acted on by everyone for 87 years, and they all seemed to think it was all right. If, perchance, it was invalid, Parliament would simply pass an Act validating all the probates which had been invalidly granted since 1857. That was the voice of Pragmatism. When they act illegally—which is quite often—Governments bend the rules.

Their ability to do so, and the way it is done depend upon Parliament's sovereign powers. How it derives those powers is a long tale of history. The particular episodes can be convincingly employed to prove the rightness or wrongness of any dispute over the Constitution. There is now a movement afoot to lay down our basic Constitution, because we might need to refer to it when we are in the Common Market. All the other member countries have written constitutions and so we should write ours down, is the plausible argument. That is easier said than done. The commonest constitutional disputes result from people applying precisely the same facts, principles and reasoning to problems and arriving at opposite conclusions.

If a Commons majority can do what it wants, it follows that, however many political parties there are, there has to be a Majority and a Minority in Parliament.

History teaches us that the right to lay down the law was arrogated to themselves by our Kings in like manner to the other rulers of old. As Professor Hugh Trevor Roper has remarked, the precise date when one barbarian succeeded another on the banks of the Tagus is unimportant. It is sufficient to recall that by the time of Edward I we had a King, Lords and Commons comprising our Parliament. The King in Council governed. The Courts of Law, some operated by the Crown and some by great lords, resolved disputes. The King in Parliament made laws by Statute. The King in Council made laws called Ordinances. When Charles I tried to rule by what was in effect the latter method, a rebel majority in Parliament cut his head off, 30th January, 1649. No doubt this could be explained by a lawyer as an exercise of the right the Roman jurisprudences called *dominium*—the right to use, abuse or destroy.

No doubt they had firmly in mind the words of the author of 'Against Writers that Carp at Other Men's Books'.

> *'Treason doth never prosper; what's the Reason?*
> *For if it prosper, none dare call it Treason.'*
> **John Harington, 1561-1612.**

Whilst the rotted remains of the regicides were still on the gates of London after the Restoration, that remarkable man, Thomas Osborne, Earl of Danby replaced the Cabal of Cavaliers around the King with party politics organised on the basis of bribery. He actually founded the Tory Party. 'Tory' was the name of a tribe of bog-Irish bandits, which was attached to the politicians who stood for the Divine Right of hereditary monarchy. Danby himself was 'impeached' on the evidence of a letter he wrote trying to negotiate a secret peace in Europe. He was actually given away by Louis Quartorze. The letter itself is on view in the British Museum, not for its constitutional importance but because it has Charles II's initials on. He scribbled on it 'I approve of this letter. C.R.' As

Danby noted on it later 'This is the letter on which I was impeached, and which was signed by the King himself before I would write it. 23/5/1678'. That did not prevent him being imprisoned in the Tower.

This was the beginning of 'ministerial responsibility' which has caused several Ministerial resignations until lately. Like other constitutional conventions, however, it is by no means always observed. Where one Minister might have to resign, another might find support for an Act of Indemnity. *Danby's Case (1679) 11 St. Tr. 599* is no doubt constantly in the minds of politicians, but impeachment has fallen into desuetude. It has largely been replaced by inquiries by committees and tribunals, a process compendiously described in some quarters as 'whitewashing'. The first time a Select Committee was ever appointed, as a matter of incidental history, was in 1689 to investigate the war in Ireland. The latest tribunals, also appointed for that purpose, are presumably triumphs of hope over experience.

Understandably enough, Danby regretted having put his trust in a Prince. (*Psalms c xl vi 3*.) He it was who led the movement to invite William of Orange to come here and rule with James II's Protestant daughter, Mary. To that extent, he was still clinging to Divine Right, but he was also creating for us the problem of Ulster. He also created that situation which Mr Hall failed to develop to its logical conclusion in the Hereford County Court. For in July, 1688, James II dissolved Parliament and it was never again summoned by him. There was no Parliament in existence when William landed on 5th November, 1688. (Oddly enough, never commemorated like Independence Day or Bastille Day.)

James fled from London on 11th December, 1688, his legalistic mind seizing upon a cunning ploy. Passing over the Thames from Millbank to Vauxhall, he threw into the river the Great Seal of England, without which no valid Writs could be issued for the summoning of Parliament and therefore the government of the realm.

It was found again in the mud and the Convention called by William on the advice of an assembly of lords and commoners, declared that when he threw that Seal away, James 'abdicated'. It also declared, lamely, that he had broken 'fundamental laws'— it did not say which ones because it did not know. There was no blood on their hands, like there was on those of the murderers of Charles I. But those murderers were a validly called Parliament. The Convention and the assembly which preceded were mere unlawful assemblies, which set up an illegal regime. The Convention purported to declare itself a Parliament, but it was not called by a valid monarch. The writs issued by William and Mary for the

101

'Parliament' which met on 22nd March, 1690, were illegal. But we all regard the Bill of Rights which it accepted as a cornerstone of our freedom under the law. They provided, too, for the succession to the throne, but William and Mary produced no heir. The *Act of Settlement, 1700* became necessary, and it ordered that the succession should be through the aged Sophia, Electress of Hanover, granddaughter of James I. Not one but two Acts were deemed necessary even to make her a naturalised British subject.

It is perhaps no wonder that Chief Justice Holt was moved to remark in *City of London* v. *Wood (1701) 12 Mod. 669 & 687*:

> *'an Act of Parliament can do no wrong though it may do several things that look pretty odd.'*

Had Mr Hall pursued his case, the essential point would have turned out to be: granted that Parliament is sovereign and can make or unmake a king nevertheless the succession in 1689 was treasonable. An unlawfully summoned assembly is not a Parliament, and the products of its illegal acts cannot make it into one.

And in a most convincing way, Maitland condemns the Glorious Revolution. Of course, Public International Law is used to recognising revolutionary governments. In the Middle Ages, the great supra-national government of the Roman Catholic Church ruled Europe. The Kings and Princes and Grand Dukes exercised the sovereign powers of life and death over their own subjects. But the most absolute monarch dreaded excommunication or non-recognition by the Pope (either of them, at Rome or Avignon). People and kings alike said, though they may not have believed, that kings were invested with the power of ruling by God's will. Henry VIII was a great one for citing the law of God—usually drafted by his non-ecclesiastical Secretary, Thomas Cromwell. Charles I, when he tried to rule by Right Divine, was nearer to God than he thought.

And so just as the Revolutionary Settlement was recognised by other states, it was recognised here, but not at first by everyone. The Sun King financed James II and in March 1689 he landed in Ireland and called a Parliament—validly—in Dublin. Catholicism was established, but what was more to the purpose the Irish peers whose estates had been confiscated by Elizabeth I, James I and Cromwell were restored to their own. Then by the procedure of *Act of Attainder*—still theoretically open to Parliament to use—it condemned to death 2,500 Protestant gentry who refused to join him in recovering England.

The Sieges of Londonderry and Enniskillen where these Ulstermen held out against James are vividly commemorated to this day in those Marches honouring the Apprentice Boys of Derry which the Ulster government could or would not stop. They dared not surrender for fear that at least their gentlemanly leaders would suffer the barbaric punishment for treason. William III relieved them and won Ireland back for England in July, 1690, at the Battle of the Boyne. This is still being fought, although England has been trying to give Ireland back to the Irish for a century. It almost did it with a Home Rule Bill, the passage of which was prevented by the First World War. During the Ulster Crisis just before then, weapons for the Ulster Volunteers were smuggled into Ireland on a ship called the Mountjoy II (the first was the vessel which relieved Londonderry in 1690). They were bought with funds raised by Sir Edward Carson KC and other people of rank and station. When it was pointed out in the House of Commons that this sort of thing was treason, Carson replied, as befitted a former Law Officer of the Crown, who was to become Lord of Appeal, 'Does the right honourable gentlemen think I do not know that?' This is one of the rare cases of two politicians disputing a constitutional point but nevertheless agreeing about the law.

Later on, when Carson was a Law Lord, Asquith chatted with him about the great pressure exerted for him to prosecute Carson. But he doubted whether a jury would have convicted in Ulster. Carson said, 'I would have pleaded guilty'. But he qualified it by insisting that he would then have said that if fighting to remain a loyal subject of the Crown was treason, he then was guilty. 'That just shows how wise I was not to prosecute', said Asquith.

The division of Ireland has been legislated into English law by the *Ireland Act, 1949*, a remarkable statute which contradicts the principles of the English constitution and no doubt thereby helps to perpetuate the Apocalyptic life of that island. Eire declared itself a republic in 1948. From 1922 it had been a Free State and from 1932 enjoyed Dominion status.

In consequence, her citizens were British citizens, not by their own law, but by the law of England. The *British Nationality Act, 1948* enabled them to claim British nationality to be retained by people born in Eire before 1922 who were British subjects in 1948. The 1948 Act expressly declares that citizens of Eire are not aliens. Those born after 1949 are not British subjects unless they register. The *Commonwealth Immigrants Acts* have failed to prevent vast numbers of them establishing here, for they are not Commonwealth citizens. Their elected representatives here are sympathetic to Catholic opinion in Ireland.

At the same time, the *Ireland Act* states by *S. 1 (2)*:

> '*It is hereby declared that Northern Ireland remains part of His Majesty's dominions and of the United Kingdom, and it is hereby affirmed that in no event will Northern Ireland or any part thereof*

*cease to be a part of His Majesty's dominions and of the United
Kingdom without the consent of the Parliament of Northern
Ireland.'*

Now here is a constitutional curiosity. We have seen that Parliament
is sovereign and can re-generate itself after a Revolution. All our
history is full of the supreme legislative power of Parliament. Chief
Justice Herbert, who presided in *Godden* v. *Hales (1686) 11 St. Tr.
1165* was a creature of James II, but his decision is still law. Sir
Edmund Hales was made a colonel only to enable the King to test
the Test Act, by which Catholics were deprived of official positions.
The King claimed to have given him a 'dispensation' from taking
the Protestant oath.

> *'If an Act of Parliament had a clause in it that it should never be
> repealed yet without question, the same power that made it may
> repeal it,'*

said the judge.

The logic was undeniable, and the case is an authority to this day,
although the court was packed. It was the same kind of reasoning
as that which the County Court judge used in Miss Hall's little case.
It is the power by which the *War Damage Act, 1965* swept away any
rights which a subject had to be compensated by the Crown for
damage or destruction of his property by Crown authority under
war conditions (The House of Lords, in *Burmah Oil Co. Ltd.* v.
Lord Advocate (1965) A.C. 75 had ruled that the company was
entitled to compensation). And just as Parliament can sweep away
retrospectively rights that have long existed, it follows logically that
it cannot bind a future Parliament. That future Parliament could do
likewise, and sweep away any law that purported to bind it.

There can therefore be no 'entrenched' laws in England as there
are in, say, South Africa. The natural consequence is that the courts
can probably never do that which is done quite often in say, the
United States of America, and declare a statute illegal because it is
ultra vires Parliament or the Constitution. A regulation made under
statutory powers can be *ultra vires* if the statute did not enable it
to be made. But Parliament can pass what Acts it will.

Consequently the Ireland Act provision binding Westminster to
the wish of Stormont has no legal force.

> *'This must be taken to be an expression of present intention,
> which is not legally binding on Parliament.'*
>> **Professor O. Hood Phillips. *Constitutional and Adminis-
>> trative Law, 4th Edn., p. 63.***

Home Secretary, Reginald Maudling, said on 'Panorama' on
20th September, 1971, that that part of the Ireland Act was emphatic-

ally binding on the Government. However right he might be politically, as a proposition of law, that is rubbish.

Stormont, in theory at least, cannot tell the Parliament at Westminster what to do. Both Lord Justice Vaughan Williams and Lord Justice Harman have described Parliament as 'omnipotent', and of course, in 1707, by the Act of Union with Scotland, Parliament did away with itself and reconstituted itself as the Parliament of the United Kingdom. While it was about it, it created a new Great Seal for sealing writs calling Parliament. No doubt this was a concession to the symbolism of sovereignty started by Edward the Confessor, but it was also a convenient wriggle round that Seal of James's found near Vauxhall Bridge.

'Parliament has absolute sovereignty and can make new legal creatures if it likes,' said Lord Justice Scott in

National Union of General & Municipal Workers v. Gillian (1946) 1 K.B. 81.

It can un-make them, too. Notwithstanding the Ireland Act, it has put Stormont into suspended animation.

It can quite plainly take us into the Common Market. Rather more to the point is that at the time of our first real try to get in, Lord Dilhorne, then Lord Chancellor, advised the House of Lords (not just the judicial panel, the whole House) that Parliament's power to repeal the law which would bind us to the Rome Treaty could not be fettered, i.e. an avenue of escape remains open.

It is true that *Article 3* of the *Treaty of Rome* requires in *paragraph (h)* merely

'the approximation of their respective municipal law to the extent necessary for the functioning of the Common Market.'

of member states.

With all the authority of a former Minister of Agriculture and a member of Mr Wilson's Cabinet until 1970, Mr Fred Peart MP told the Co-operative Congress on the Common Market at The Festival Hall on 3rd September, 1971 that:

'Entry into Europe offers a fundamental challenge to British Sovereignty and to Parliament'.

Presumably under the doctrine of 'collective responsibility' he agreed with Lord Chancellor Gardiner when the White Paper on 'Legal and Constitutional Implications of the United Kingdom Membership of the European Communities' (*Cmnd. 3301*) was published in May, 1967 (our second try). That document mentioned that the novel features of the EEC treaties were the power of the Community institutions to issue subordinate instruments which might impose obligations on Member States or take effect directly as law within them, and the powers of the institutions to enforce much of this law.

Of course, those were the days when Mr Wilson 'would not take "no" for an answer' and was not trying to recover sovereign power. What *Article 189* of the *Rome Treaty* actually says is that

> '*the Council and the Commission shall adopt regulations and directives, make decisions and formulate recommendations or opinions.*
>
> *Regulations shall have a general application. They shall be binding in every respect and directly applicable in each Member State.*
>
> *Directives shall bind any Member State to which they are addressed, and to the result to be achieved, while leaving the domestic agencies a competence as to forms and means.*
>
> *Decisions shall be binding in every respect for the addressees named therein.*
>
> *Recommendations and opinions shall have no binding force.*'

Of course, the Treaty will not cover every facet of our lives. The fields of law which would be affected are really quite few. There is only the production and sale of food and everything else; transportation, taxation, employment and social security. Marriage and inheritance and trial by jury remain unaffected, Governments have assured us. Unless you get married frequently, are often left money, or frequently stand trial for indictable offences, you might regard this redeeming feature as making the best of things.

Neither that nor Mr Heath's 1971 White Paper dwelt on this sovereignty question. It is beyond doubt that Parliament has every right to take us in without a General Election or a referendum. It would not be such a blight on sovereignty if the Common Market Treaties were merely binding in International Law. The principles of International Law do not bind Parliament. There is plenty of authority for the proposition that International Law is part of English Law. But there is none to the effect that English Law is part of International Law. Looked at in this way, had Common Market Law been merely International Law any pro-Market Government* could have argued that we would not be joining it, but it would be joining us.

Lord Gardiner is to be congratulated on the way he tackled this question of sovereignty without actually giving the game away.

> '. . . *the legislation of the Parliament of the United Kingdom giving effect to that law would have to do so in such a way as to override existing national law so far as inconsistent with it.*

---

* And any Government can be pro-Market from time to time.

. . . It would also follow that within the fields occupied by the Community law Parliament would have to refrain from passing fresh legislation inconsistent with that law as for the time being in force.'

1967 Cmnd. 3301, para 23.

To the unsophisticated eye, that might read suspiciously as if they could tell us what to do. That of itself might appear to be a departure from our jealously guarded sovereignty. Not at all. Lord Gardiner continued:

'This would not however involve any constitutional innovation. Many of our treaty obligations already impose such restraints—for example, the Charter of the United Nations, the European Convention on Human Rights and GATT.'

The reference to the Convention on Human Rights was quite naturally in his mind. We ratified it in 1951, but did not accept the jurisdiction of the European Commission where people could take proceedings against us until 1966. And still the Convention has not been made legally binding in the United Kingdom. It is *binding in International Law—which is not binding.*

Exactly what sovereignty involves is simply expressed in the internal political sense. It is power. It probably means the same in International Law as well. Since however, the only practical application of International Law is in diplomacy, it is diplomatic not to emphasise the power angle.

A Sovereign State is often described as one having a definite geographical jurisdiction, governed by an 'independent' administration and occupied by a defined population capable of reproducing itself. Size is, according to one school of thought, irrelevant. They instance the Vatican City as one of the oldest established Sovereign States. And so it is. Its population of 3,000 celibate priests and nuns does not seem too keen on reproducing itself, but definitions tend to be elastic in this field of study.

One of our little-realised problems of International Law affects Ulster. Quite apart from anything else, there is a presumption of our law that a Statute will not offend against International Law. Now when Ireland was partitioned in 1922, the six counties were arbitrarily drawn into the Protestant pale by the decisions of David Lloyd George—who had a country solicitor's style with a compromise. Carson claimed that the nine counties were Protestant, Redmond the Irish Nationalist, would admit non-Papal superiority in only three. Result—The Six Counties. All the Irish were at that date British subjects, and capable of bringing others into the world. The strongest foundation in nationality law is the *jus sanguinis* by which a man takes the nationality of his parents. The capacity of the Irish to procreate has never been doubted.

It would also follow that these British subjects would owe allegiance to the British Crown. Indeed, during 1921 several Sinn Feiners were tried for treason in England for 'compassing and intending to levy war against the King'.

Their argument was that they were entitled to fight because the armistice agreed between Michael Collins and the British Military Commander on 11th July, 1921, was a tacit admission that a state of war had existed between England and the IRA before then. Intended, no doubt, to secure for them the recognition of Prisoners-of-War, that was virtually a confession of treason. Certainly one innocent man went to prison for ten years because he refused to recognise the court, and would not testify though he was not at the raid in Erskine Street, Manchester for which he was charged.

The 'dominion status' accorded to Eire from 1932 is a euphemism for a curious and uneasy acceptance of the fact that the Irish Sea is not very wide. But when Ireland declared itself a Republic in 1948 —although it had made its own nationality law in 1935 and taken part in the discussions which led to the *British Nationality Act* in 1948—it committed a somewhat surprising oversight if it can be taken to know about the definition of a Sovereign State.

It enacted its geographical limits as including the whole of Ireland.

Technically, therefore, it has made people like Dr Paisley subjects of Eire by incorporation of territory. When Tsaioseach Jack Lynch speaks of the desire for the unification of Ireland he speaks of something which in the law of the Republic of Ireland has already been achieved. One might think that a Queen's Counsel—they keep the old style even though they no longer have a Queen—might know that—particularly one of the Irish Bar.

If there is one thing fairly clear about sovereignty it is that two states find it difficult to exercise it over the same territory. For it means omnipotence, or freedom from external control, according to Dr George Schwarzenberger (*Manual of International Law 5th Edn. 1967*—before the Bogside Rising). The curious situation therefore presents itself that on paper at any rate, the British Government at Westminster, is bound to ask Stormont* before it can agree to what the Government of Eire have already done. But that Eire regards Stormont as an illegal organisation on its territory.

And by the simple fact of coming to live here untramelled by any laws, a large number of Irish are voting for Members of Parliament who favour the unification of Ireland in fact. Anyone of these is potentially one of the constituents of our internal and external

---

* Currently in mothballs.

sovereign power—a majority of the House of Commons. Which for the nonce is content to detain the Irish without trial on what Eire regards as Irish soil.

And a Member of Parliament is a representative, not a delegate. Once he is there, those who put him there cannot tell him what to do. Rather they can tell him, but there is no sanction by which they can make him do it. (To try is to commit a contempt of Parliament.) The only thing to do if you disagree strongly with the way the MPs are running things is to become one yourself. The money's not bad, either. Theoretically, at any rate, anyone can try.

Membership of the House of Commons is achieved by a process described as 'democracy'. It consists initially in a person being sufficiently autocratic to put himself or herself forward as worthy of the suffrages of his fellows. Henry V passed an Act which required MPs to live in their constituencies, but they very soon appreciated that it was not necessary to go that far to be a good Constituency Member, and the Act was repealed when it had long been obsolete, in 1774. Civil servants, servicemen, policemen, and other officials have to give up their positions if they are elected to Parliament. Anglican clergy, Catholic Priests and Scottish Presbyterians clergy are disqualified, but not clergy of the Welsh Church. There is a doctorate thesis in the constitutional privileges of the Welsh if only a non-Welshman could tackle it. Corrupt and illegal practices at elections also disqualify the practitioners for ten or five years respectively. Presumably by that time they are expected to have reformed, or at least to have become expert enough not to get caught. Women were made eligible in 1918. By that time it was a career, payment at the rate of £400 p.a. having begun in 1910. Trades unionists who regard the *Osborne Case* in 1910 as one of the high points of anti-union repression may not realise that it was because political levies were held illegal in that case that payments for MPs was introduced. The pay is now £3,250 salary, £750 expenses, plus travelling allowances (and due to go up).

Until the *Representation of the People Act, 1832*, the House of Commons was completely dominated by the borough mongers of the House of Lords. The great manufacturing districts like Manchester and Birmingham had no Members, whilst Cobbett's 'accursed hill' at Old Sarum was represented though a man had to be paid to live there to be the only elector. Now, of course, there is no such thing as a 'rotten borough', its place having been taken by the 'safe seat'. The *Parliamentary and Municipal Elections Act, 1872* introduced secret ballot papers for voting.

The right to vote belongs to people over 18 who are British subjects or Irish citizens. This results from *s. 2* of the *Ireland Act, 1949*. It gives citizens of a foreign power, many of whose subjects are making war on British troops and subjects in Northern Ireland, the right to live here and vote on matters which affect British relations with Ireland. In this case it is the English law which is Irish. Other aliens cannot vote, nor can lunatics or peers, except non-representative Irish peers.

A peer can disclaim his peerage to get into the Commons under the *Peerage Act, 1963*. Or a non-hereditary peer can become a member of the House of Lords for life under the *Life Peerages Act, 1958*, for which he can claim £4.75 day attendance expenses plus his travelling expenses. Parliament, like Tom Paine's White Horse tavern, is open to all. Once in, all one needs is the confidence of a majority of one's fellow members to be invited by the Queen to propose to her whom she should make into Ministers. The person to receive such an invitation is now officially recognised as Prime Minister. This is because the *Ministers of the Crown Act, 1937* used the title when specifying what his salary should be. It also recognised the Leader of his Majesty's Loyal Opposition. This label was actually a joke made by John Cam Hobhouse when the King was better supported by the Opposition than the Government. It is no joke nowadays.

This system of electoral government necessarily presupposes that there will be basically a two-party Parliament. No provision exists for the situation where those parties are divided vertically as well as horizontally as over Market entry. We have become very used to the idea that there are the Tory 'haves' and the Radical 'have nots' and that their inexorable conflict will go on and on. This was Marx's historical materialism. He did not envisage the kind of conflict that exists over the Common Market. He was, after all, a political refugee from the Germany of the Zollverein and firmly believed that the United States of America was the most fertile breeding ground for Communism.

We may have to realise that our ideas of the Constitution are no longer in tune with the demands upon our governmental system made by current conditions. If that should occur the enormous advantage of an unwritten Constitution in which no one is sure what the law is will be manifest. Influential people for the time being will then be able to explain that it is what they think it ought to be. If it was written down in plain language they would be embarassed by apparent contradictions.

A constitutional crisis would cast a great deal of responsibility on the Queen. It is an opinion widely held by scholars that the monarch is powerless. She must accept the advice of the Prime Minister to dissolve Parliament. He may wish to do so because he can no longer command the support of the Commons, or in order to strengthen his position with a General Election at a favourable time.

But as Professor Berriedale Keith pointed out:

'The right to a dissolution is not a right to a series of dissolutions'.
The British Cabinet System, 2nd Edn., p. 301.

What should happen, therefore, if a Prime Minister appealed to the country and could not get a working majority, is not necessarily that he should be given another throw of the dice forthwith, but that some other politician from his side of the House should be invited to form a Government. This is a topic discussed not in law books, but in memoirs of retired politicians. There is no Act of Parliament, nor rule of the Common Law about this Government-making. The authoritative writers do not even agree on whether there is a Convention of the Constitution, and if so, what it is.

Anathematical though a late 20th-Century Prime Minister might find it to have to concede defeat not foretold by the opinion polls, an improvement in politicians' prospects has undeniably occurred. The treadmill of memoir authorship is infinitely preferable to the Tower.

Once having acquired the privileges of Membership of Parliament the MP is a subject of the Law of Parliament. The privileges of Parliament are in truth the privileges of the constituents of the Members, essential for the discharge of their duties. They include, for example, the right to exclude all 'Strangers' from the Parliament House when the Members choose. Constituents are strangers.

Town Councils used to be able to do that.

'I cannot deduce any intention on the part of the Legislature that the public shall have a right to be admitted to the meetings',

said Mr Justice Kekewich in *Mason* v. *Tenby Corporation (1907) Ch.*

In 1960 the *Public Bodies (Admission to Meetings) Act* was passed. *Section 1* gave the public the right to be present at Council meetings —unless the Council choose to remove them by special resolution or going into committee.

When Parliament meets for a session which is not opened by the Queen it asserts its freedom of debate and action—which we can now familiarly call its 'sovereignty'—by having a first reading of a Bill for the Suppression of Clandestine Outlawries. According to Erskine May,* debate is out of order on this piece of business, which is why it has never been passed, and why it still serves its useful function a generation after the abolition of outlawry. The important principle, of course, is the freedom of debate, without which no one would ever emerge as a political leader, and so would not command a majority, which would be the end of the Constitution. And that would be the end of freedom.

---

* **Parliamentary Practice—the book of Parliament's own special laws.**

We are so free that imprisonment is illegal. Lord Atkin said so, and you cannot want a sounder opinion than that.

> '... *in English Law every imprisonment is* prima facie *unlawful* ...
> *it is for the person directing imprisonment to justify his act.*'
>
> **Liversidge v. Anderson (1942) A.C. 206.**

This might come as a surprise to all those people who are locked up by policemen, denied release on bail by magistrates, tried by judge and jury, and sentenced to stay in prisons run by the Home Office. Even for the imprisonment before conviction, they are not entitled to any compensation for loss of wages, damage to reputation, nor the costs of legal representation. They can get damages for malicious prosecution and false imprisonment against the police officers, if they can prove that they acted without having an honest case against them. This might at first appear to conflict with *Liversidge* v. *Anderson*, which says that the person doing the imprisoning has to justify the imprisonment. But to anyone who raised that case the judge would explain that the criminal trial was the justification, and that now the accused person has shown that the police and the courts were wrong in that trial, he must do it all over again in order to prove that not only had the prosecution no case, but that the officers who launched it knew they had none. In a police state, of course, you have no chance of challenging the authorities in that way.

You cannot sue the Justice of the Peace who issued the warrant for your arrest. (*Justices Protection Act, 1858*) Nor the policeman who executed it. (*Constables Protection Act, 1750*), Nor the magistrates who committed you for trial—even though there was no case in law against you. The key to this paradox is to be found in Magna Carta, or at least the confirmation of it by Henry III. No man shall be imprisoned except by 'due process of law'. This has several times been confirmed, notably by the *Petition of Right, 1628*, and the American television series, 'The Defenders', which has made 'due process' a catchphrase. The Common Law has long provided a quick, convenient remedy for anyone being unlawfully arrested without the authority of a warrant. He or she may use reasonable force in self-defence to prevent it. The large majority of people who avail themselves of this unquestioned legal right find themselves charged with assaulting police officers in the execution of their duty. (*Police Act, 1964, s. 54.*) The last Lord Chief Justice, Lord Parker, said that this was such a serious matter that the ordinary punishment must be prison. It is consequently perfectly possible to resist arrest for say, theft or indecent assault, and be acquitted of the charge, but to be sent to prison for assaulting the constable who was arresting you on the charge of which you were innocent.

For when a constable, with reasonable cause, suspects that an arrestable offence, as defined in the *Criminal Law Act, 1967*, has been committed, he may arrest without warrant anyone whom he, with reasonable cause, suspects to be guilty of the offence. He can also under similar conditions arrest anyone whom he suspects to be about to commit an arrestable offence. This much needed simplification of the law was enacted because the Common Law powers of arrest were uncertain and obscure, and the powers of arrest under a multitude of Acts of Parliament were even more so. Anyone who actually saw a felony being committed was entitled to arrest the felon, and the powers of constables and certain officials were extended by various Acts. But a constable is personally responsible for all the arresting he does. We do not have any wicked foreign impositions of authoritarian government here. When a constable arrests the wrong chap he carries the can for it. When his superior officer tells him to arrest the wrong chap, he still carries the can for it. This is a free country. And we retain the great advantage of citizen arrest, as well. For *s. 2* of the *Criminal Law Act* also provides that 'any person may arrest without warrant anyone who is or whom he, with reasonable cause, suspects to be in the act of committing an "arrestable offence" '. Just what an arrestable offence is involves detailed knowledge of many statutes. There is nowhere near enough room here to list them. It is mentioned here only to demonstrate that our Constitution creates no privileged class. Everyone has the right to arrest other people. Everyone has the right to be arrested himself. If policemen and magistrates have people arrested who should not be arrested, the law recognises that they have done something wrong. But it forgives them.

It is sometimes obvious that an arrest and subsequent imprisonment is sufficiently unusual to require investigation at judicial level. There is an ancient process to protect the freedom of the subject by application through the courts for the exercise of the Royal Prerogative to question the actions of the subjects who are imprisoning their fellows. The writ *Habeas Corpus ad Subjiciendum* first used in the time of Edward I was 'originally intended not to get people out of prison, but to put them in it' (*E. Jenks (1902) 18 L.Q.R. 64*). It commands someone having the custody of someone else's body to bring it before the Court. It says nothing about 'dead or alive'. It was the process by which the celebrated Mr Jackson was required to deliver up the person of his wife. But it was not the process used in *Liversidge* v. *Anderson*. Mr Liversidge (whose original name was Perlzweig) was detained during the Second World War under Defence Regulation 18B made under the *Emergency Powers (Defence) Act, 1939,* under which a lot of people were locked up, and provided full employment for a large number of Civil Servants working out which of them could safely be released. Mr Liversidge was locked up because the Home Secretary 'had reasonable cause to believe that he was a person of hostile associations'. While in Brixton Prison, he brought an action alleging false imprisonment, and the Home Secretary, Sir John Anderson, merely pleaded the detention order as justification. Liversidge asked for 'further and better particulars' of this defence—a process employed by lawyers to undermine and pin down the other side's case.

It therefore went to the House of Lords on the question whether the Minister could rely on the order as an exercise of the ministerial powers, or whether he had to justify it. Lord Atkin pointed out that the Regulation required the Minister to have reasonable cause for detaining people. It was not good enough for him merely to *think* he had reasonable cause. The other Law Lords all said he was wrong. The demands of those dark days in our history plainly overbore their devotion to the liberty of the subject. Atkin's is the currently accepted view. Lord Reid, in a 1964 case, called it, 'a very peculiar decision'. It might very well not be followed—unless there is another war. The Defence Regulations are no longer law.

Mr John Mathew, the Senior Treasury Counsel told the Jury in the Official Secrets case against the *Sunday Telegraph* over the Biafra Report:

'We do not have political trials here, thank God.'

That is not really right, even nowadays. Certainly within memory there have been some blatantly political cases. Many have had little enough effect, but that cannot be said of *Elias* v. *Passmore* (*1934*) *2 K.B. 164* which arose out of the arrest of the Communist Wal Hannington for an allegedly seditious speech in Trafalgar Square. He was arrested on a warrant at the office of an unemployed workers' organisation. The police illegally seized some papers there and used them as evidence to prosecute not only Hannington but the unfortunate Mr Elias. Mr Justice Horridge ruled that the papers were admissible in evidence at the trial even though Mr Elias was entitled to damages for the illegal taking of them, and also to have them returned to him after the trial was over. Their use in prosecuting him was lawful 'in the interests of the State'. Eminent lawyers have condemned the decision for nearly 40 years but no Government has attempted to overrule it by legislation.

It is a direct encouragement to unscrupulous officials to act in a high-handed way, and to steal material to which they have no legal right. Sedition was the all-embracing anti-establishment crime. What is now so earnestly legislated for, an incitement to racial hatred, could quite easily be indicted as sedition. It covers deeds, words, writings falling short of high treason but tending to excite

114

discontent or dissatisfaction, or ill will between different classes of the Queen's subjects, create public disturbance or civil war. And that is not all. Anything tending to cause hatred or contempt of the sovereign, the Government, the laws or the constitution, or to cause public disorder, unlawful associations, insurrections, breaches of the peace or forcible obstruction of the execution of the law. A seditious conspiracy can only exist when two or more people agree to do some such thing. The agreement is the crime and it is proved by some 'overt act'. But the necessity for there to be two conspirators does not demand proof that they should even have seen each other or have corresponded with each other. The prosecutions of Daniel O'Connell (*1844*) *11 Cl. & F. 155* and Charles Stuart Parnell (*1881*) *14 Cox. Crim. Cases. 508* establish that proposition and that the act conspired for can be quite lawful, but that it is still a crime if the means contemplated to achieve it are illegal.

Judges have according to Archbold, 'frequently deprecated' charging conspiracy where the real case is either some different crime, or there is evidence of the commission of the substantive offence. Every joint crime logically involves a precedent conspiracy even if only seconds before its commission. But conspiracy, being necessarily circumstantially proved, permits much more prejudicial evidence to be admitted than where distinct elements of substantive offences can be produced.

Conspiracy was developed by the Star Chamber, just as the crime of libel was. Until *Fox's Libel Act, 1792* juries were told by the judge whether something was libel or not, and only permitted to say whether the prisoner published it. One poor wretch whose only part was 'to clap down the Press' was convicted. But on the day Fox's Act passed, the gentry were quite convinced that the Paris Terror would extend forthwith to London. Sir Francis Burdett, the Radical, contributed to the law on this topic with his trials for libels. His case in *4 B. & Ald. 314* established that it is no defence to prove that the libel is true. *Lord Campbell's Act, 1843*, improved things for libellers by providing that it is a defence to prove that the publication of the libel is for the public good. The difficulties of showing the public benefit from an inflammatory outburst are considerable.

It must be confessed that sedition is not often invoked. But a man was convicted of 'insulting behaviour' whereby a breach of the peace was likely to be occasioned in 1960 outside the Red Chinese Embassy. He called out: 'Long live Chairman Mao'.

Quite how that can be considered insulting is not readily apparent, but a Stipendary Magistrate found no difficulty at all in holding the charge proved.

The enactment under which that charge is brought varies in individual cases. It can either be the *Metropolitan Police Act, 1839* or the *Public Order Act, 1936, S. 5.* There was a widely held opinion that the Public Order Act applies only to political incidents but Lord Parker disposed of that. It was certainly passed to outlaw the illegal drilling and political uniforms of the Blackshirts. But it has been employed against soccer hooligans more than any others in the past decade.

Libel prosecutions after the Napoleonic Wars were largely conducted by Prosecuting Societies who claimed merely to be protecting the populace from blasphemy and obscenity—usually Tom Paine's *Rights of Man.* These prosecutions are the foundation for the current radical assertion that obscenity prosecutions are in reality political. Richard Nevill, for instance, made this claim after the *Oz* trial in 1971. That was not a sedition case, but one under the *Obscene Publications Act, 1959.* There is something in it. The notion was first expressed by the 18th Century pornographer, Edmund Curl, who employed 20 writers to churn out his dirty books in Grub Street.

Crown Licensing of Printing expired in 1695 and the 'underground' printers found that the Stationers' Company men had legitimate publishing monopolised anyway. They turned therefore to pornography and found a ready market. Obscenity was then no crime.

In 1708, a judge dismissed a prosecution of *The Fifteen Plagues of a Maidenhead* saying:

> '*There is no law to punish it. I wish there was, but we cannot make law.*'

Read's Case, 11 Mod. Rep. 142.

But they had learnt how to make law by 1727. Edmund Curl was convicted of corrupting public morals (*2 Stra. 788*) by publishing *Venus in the Cloister or The Nun in Her Smock.*

In the *Ladies Directory* case in 1962 the Law Lords held that publishing a magazine of that name containing

> '*advertisements to induce readers thereof to resort to the said advertisers for the purpose of fornication and of taking part in or witnessing other disgusting and immoral acts and exhibitions with intent thereby to debauch and corrupt the morals as well as of youth as of divers liege subjects of our Lady the Queen and to raise and create in their minds inordinate and lustful desires*'

still exists.

This came as rather a surprise, for the 1959 Act had quite definitely stated that there were to be no prosecutions at Common Law for any offence of which the basis was that something was obscene. The law-making capacities of the judges had not diminished a bit in 250 years—at least as far as obscenity was concerned.

There had been an *Obscene Publications Act* in 1859 under which the Wolverhampton Magistrates in 1867 ordered the destruction of a shilling pamphlet called *The Confessional Unmasked Showing the Depravity of the Roman Priesthood, the Iniquity of the Confessional and the Questions put to Females in Confession.*

Henry Scott, the Protestant zealot who distributed it, succeeded before the Recorder in getting the destruction order revoked on the ground that his intention was not to corrupt morals but to expose Papists. On further appeal Chief Justice Cockburn ordered destruction and made the celebrated definition:

> '*The test of obscenity is whether the tendency of the matter . . . is to deprave and corrupt those whose minds are open to such immoral influences and into whose hands a publication of this sort may fall.*'

Charles Bradlaugh and Annie Besant were convicted in 1877 for a birth control pamphlet 40 years old at the time. Later the great circulating libraries practised a censorship based on fear of the Act. Thomas Hardy's books were denied circulation. Zola's novels were prosecuted for being 'French'. Havelock Ellis's publisher was prosecuted for his 'Sexual Inversion' in 1898 whereupon the Recorder of London congratulated him for pleading guilty. 'You might at the first outset have been gulled into the belief that somebody might say that this was a scientific work', he said. Wells, Shaw, Lawrence, Joyce were all called immoral soon after.

In 1954 the prurience broke out again and Swindon Magistrates ordered destruction of Boccaccio's *Decameron*, as other justices had done. Their order was, however, reversed in appeal.

Martin Secker and Warburg were prosecuted at the Old Bailey over *The Philanderer* in 1954 and Mr Justice Stable instructed the jury that Cockburn's definition was the law, adding:

> '*Throwing one's mind back over the ages, the only real guidance we get about how people thought and behaved is their contemporary literature.*
>
> '*It would not be much assistance, would it, if contrary to the fact we were led to suppose that in New York no unmarried woman or teenager has disabused her mind of the idea that babies are brought by storks, or are sometimes found in cabbage patches, or under gooseberry bushes?*
>
> '*Are we going to say in England that our contemporary literature is going to be measured by what is suitable for a 14 year old schoolgirl to read?*'

No one was really amazed at the acquittal. But it sparked a reforming move. In the capable hands of Roy Jenkins MP a vastly improved law began its journey to the Statute Book. In Committee he asked the Commissioner of the Metropolitan Police how he felt about literary merit and received the encouraging answer that so long as they could seize and destroy the hard-line porn—blue films and so on —they would not bother with the literature. By the time the Act began to work there was a new Commissioner.

Not that he can be blamed for the prosecution of *Lady Chatterley's Lover*. If anyone was responsible for that being prosecuted it was Penguin Books. Who could condemn the work of which an American reviewer wrote:

> '*Although written many years ago*, Lady Chatterley's Lover *has just been re-issued by Grove Press, and this fictional account of the day-by-day life of an English gamekeeper is still of considerable interest to outdoor-minded readers, as it contains many passages on pheasant raising, the apprehending of poachers, ways to control vermin, and other chores and duties of the profession of a game-keeper.*
>
> '*Unfortunately, one is obliged to wade through many pages of extraneous material in order to discover and savour these sidelights on the management of a Midland Shooting estate, and in this reviewer's opinion the book cannot take the place of J. R. Miller's* Practical Gamekeeping.'

It was not really surprising that District Judge O'Brien's acquittal of that work had been upheld on appeal. Nevertheless Mr Mervyn Griffith-Jones (as he was then) prosecuting at the Central Criminal Court asked the jury:

> '*Is this a book you would wish your wife or your servant to read?*'

Now the Jenkins Act had introduced the defence of literary merit. But Mr Justice Byrne ruled that the Act was so worded that the defence could not allege that they had no intention to deprave or corrupt. That would have been allowed on charge of obscene libel at Common Law. Nor could the literary experts testify whether publication was for the public good. Was it all a gigantic Parliamentary spoof? There was no need for fear. The jury acquitted.

But less worthy works were also exonerated. In *R.* v. *Clayton and Halsey* (*1963*) *1 Q.B. 163* counsel asked the officers of the obscene publications squad whether their feelings were affected by the photographs they bought from the defendants, and was told 'No'. Since the persons who might be depraved had to be those into whose hands the articles might come, the conviction was quashed. Members of Parliament were assured during the debates on the amending Bill that they were similarly 'vocationally immune'— though the House of Commons librarian keeps their modest collection of erotica under lock and key.

In *John Calder Publications Ltd.* v. *Powell* (*1965*) *1 Q.B. 509* the Court of Criminal Appeal ruled that the experts' evidence was not to be received on the question whether a publication was obscene. They were only to extol the 'public good' occurring from publications which were obscene. The *Oz* appeal was allowed because there were misdirections on the meaning of 'obscene' and on the possibility of aversion being created rather than depravity. But where are the politics? Mr Jenkins—in office—was glad that our society was permissive, but his Act has done no harm. Pornographers can still be prosecuted as they were two centuries ago, in spite of it. There is no censorship, ostensibly. A man publishes, and only if it is then shown that he should not have done so, is he damned. Of course, it can be pretty plain that a charge will be brought but that is not technically censorship. And it is not confined to obscenity.

Well, there is the prosecution of the Tory newspaper and politician over the Biafra Report. Begun under Labour it was prosecuted to acquittal under the Tories. Allegedly a breach of the Official Secrets Acts, it established that every secret had been published in the world's press long before.

Shortly after, a Labour MP was acquitted on Official Secrets charges. The Committee of 100 members went down under those Acts, too, for trespassing on airfields—and sundry breaches of the peace. But it is 45 years since the 'Red Conspiracy' was in the dock at the Old Bailey. The case, and the Zinoviev letter, probably brought down our first Labour Government in 1925. The prosecution rested on articles in the *Workers Weekly* urging soldiers not to shoot strikers. They were charged under the *Incitement to Mutiny Act, 1797*. Wal Hannington, Harry Pollitt, Bill Rust and Willie Gallacher got 12 months each and martyrdom.

When he fell out with Fleet Street over the D Notice Affair, Harold Wilson did not cause Official Secrets charges to be laid. A Parliamentary Commission vindicated the *Daily Express* over its disclosures that Government officials vetted cables. That did not stop him asking for Parliamentary censure.

That rather put Westminster out in the cold. In *Conway* v. *Rimmer* in 1968 Mr Jenkins as Home Secretary had objected to disclosure of police reports in an action against a police chief. The Court of Appeal had asserted power to override Ministerial objections in proper cases. This denied the Ministerial right upheld in the Thetis submarine disaster case in 1943 for the Government to refuse to make disclosures in Court.

With the courts taking a hard line and MPs making up their own minds what are Governments to do but legislate themselves more powers. They know best. Nye Bevan said that the Labour Government of 1945 would not tolerate judicial sabotage of the Socialist legislation. But in 1965 Parliament was having to pass an Act to take away rights that the courts had created. When the Law

Lords announced in 1966 that they would no longer be bound by their own decisions, Parliament must have got the wind up.

For judicial dissent is the great source of legal change. The reasoning and analysis of the judges often leads to different conclusions. Knowing this, lawyers and judges argue that the subject is entitled to certainty in the law laid down. Judges should strive for consistency and unanimity. The law should not be lightly discarded or altered. But that argument does not always succeed.

> '*It has been put forward in all the great cases which have been milestones of progress in our law, and it has always, or nearly always, been rejected.*
>
> '*If you read the great cases of Ashby* v. *White, Pasley* v. *Freeman, and Donoghue* v. *Stevenson you will find that in each of them the judges were divided in opinion. On the one side there were the timorous souls who were fearful of allowing a new cause of action. On the other side there were the bold spirits who were ready to allow it if justice so required.*'

Lord Denning was a member of the Court of Appeal when he said that (*1951*) *2 K.B. 164*. He is now Master of the Rolls and president of the Court of Appeal having in the meantime served in the House of Lords. But Lord Justice Asquith remarked in reply:

> '*I am not concerned with defending the existing state of the law or contending that it is strictly logical—it clearly is not. I am merely recording what I think it is. If this relegates me to the company of "timorous souls" I must face that consequence with such fortitude as I can command.*'

All Manner Of Persons

'The Man Friday, as we all know, was a respectable man.'

Chief Justice Denman in *Hoare* v. *Silverlock* (1848) 12 Q.B. 624.

LIEUTENANT COLONEL Alfred Daniel Wintle was a 'donkey walloper' or, more formally, a Dragoon. He made a profound impact upon the law, not least because he removed the trousers of a Brighton solicitor for the purpose of a horsewhipping. The consequent six months jankers permitted him to reflect upon the laws of England to such good effect that he personally conducted the legal argument in the inheritance dispute which provoked him to the assault, and finally won it in the House of Lords in 1959 (*Wintle* v. *Nye*).

He said afterwards that it was not until he got to the Lords that he was dealing with his own intellectual equals. Upon a facile interpretation, that might seem to be a claim to status. In the ordinary, everyday meaning of the word, no doubt it is. But in its legal application the word has a curious significance.

When Sir Henry Maine wrote (*Ancient Law*, p. 170)

'We may say that the movement of the progressive Societies has hitherto been a movement from Status to Contract'

he was constructing, in 1869, a formula to express the historical progress of Private Law, i.e. the rights and duties of ordinary individuals. It did not mean that he necessarily regarded England as a progressive society. But if 'persons' are to be the creatures who suffer the burdens and the benefits of law, one would expect that a scientific analysis of the law's application would define the persons on whom the laws operate. The law of England, however, takes it for granted that everyone knows what a person is. The *Interpretation Act* says that it includes companies, and consequently, it does, even though they have 'no body to be kicked nor soul to be damned'. This caused some odd quirks in the logic of the law. A company can be convicted of a conspiracy to cheat and defraud. But a man who is the life and soul of a one-man company cannot be convicted of conspiring with his company. It is these oddities and distinctions which make up status in the eyes of the law.

Colonel Wintle was a very good example of differences which might or might not affect status. As an army officer, he had a particular status. But not as a gentleman—the law of England does not regard that as a status at all. 'Gentleman is not a proper description in an affidavit', said Lord Justice Cotton in *Re. Orde (1883) 24 Ch. D. 271.*

Nevertheless when a solicitor cannot remember what his client's occupation is he often inserts into a deed that he is A Gentleman after his address. Colonel Wintle was abnormally proud of being English. He began his autobiography with a dissertation upon this inestimable advantage. Save that it protects one from the worst inconveniences of the Commonwealth Immigrants' Acts, that has very few advantages in law. It might be imagined that it automatically clothes one—willy nilly—with a 'personal law' which is English Law, but nationality alone does not do that. British nationality is a very curious legal conception indeed for by the *British Nationality Act, 1948* it was made to depend on 'citizenship' and any 'citizen' of the United Kingdom and the Commonwealth was given the status of a British subject.

Before then the matter was relatively uncomplicated, depending on nation of birth, parents' nationality, marriage, incorporation of territory, adoption, legitimation, acceptance of paternity or naturalisation. Wintle is again a good example. He was born in the Crimea, brought up in France and Germany. But he would have been English even had he not been of English parentage, because as a serving soldier he owed allegiance to the Crown, and that allegiance conferred nationality.

The doctrine of allegiance had inconvenient applications for William Joyce, 'Lord Haw Haw', who was actually an Irish-American but who travelled on a British passport obtained because of his Irish ancestry and thus had sufficient allegiance to the Crown to be hanged for treason. G.O. Slade KC (as he then was) asked him before his trial if he wished any jurors to be challenged, and explained that because of Haw Haw's Nazi connections he might think it wise to have any Jewish-looking people off the jury. It was further explained that seven challenges can be made without assigning a reason.

> '*If there are seven, why not leave them in the jury box, and I could cover my head and swear on the Old Testament,*'

he suggested.

Nationality and allegiance, clearly are too inconvenient bases for personal laws. English law therefore has had to seek others as well. For this personal law business is dominant in our lives. All our life is spent making relationships with everyone else. Marriage is an obvious example, and the change of status on marriage or divorce is a clear example. Bankruptcy is a change of status *qua* everyone else. The bankrupt cannot own property or a bank account. This is done for him by his Trustee. He commits a crime if he gets credit without telling the creditor he is an undischarged bankrupt. Marriage is a similarly limiting status because while married to one person you cannot marry someone else.

This conception of status was a great ornament of the Roman Law. A person's social position gave him privileges and liabilities under the law. The word status seldom appears in our law books but it would be wrong to suppose it has no importance in English law. The Common Law of England was exported to America with the Pilgrim Fathers, and is the foundation of their law. One of their jurists, Frederic Westlake, defined the notion of legal status with the question:

> *'What is Status except the sum of the particulars in which a person's condition differs from that of the normal person?'*

But that sounds uncomfortably like saying that anyone who has status must be abnormal. In fact the opposite is often true. A VIP may have great wealth, position and influence, but his legal status may be totally unremarkable, a mere normal person, married or not. A Civil Servant may give advice to the Cabinet which makes history. In the ordinary meaning his status is great. At one time, he could have sold the freehold of his position as a Government official on his retirement, having become rich on the perquisites while he held office. That is all over—ostensibly—since the 18th Century. A Civil Servant is so badly off for status that he can be sacked without notice and with no right to compensation in the courts even though he has been treated with gross injustice. The Crown can do no wrong to its servants. In law he is bereft of rights. In fact, he is safer than a highly paid company director, whose job, house and car might all disappear after a take-over and who will have to pay tax on his golden handshake, if he gets one. Yet neither the Civil Servant nor the Company director is regarded as having any special status in English law because of his work. The Civil Servant is subject to the *Official Secrets* Acts, and the director to the *Companies* Acts, but those liabilities are never called status in law books. It is very tempting to believe that English Law does not bother with status at all. The word appears only in three Acts of Parliament. It is sometimes used in its popular meaning by judges in their judgments, and it is used in its true legal signification in regard to marriage, illegitimacy, minority and inheritance.

This neglect of status is one of the reasons why Dean Roscoe Pound wrote in Professor Graveson's monograph on status in 1954 that there was no Public Law in the Common Law system. This appears to discount several centuries of torture and death for treason, sedition, heresy and other great crimes, but on reflection it is true. There is a cosy personality about the law of England. Robbers, rapists and roadhogs are all brought to justice in the name of The Queen. We don't refer to that clinical abstraction 'The State'. However many lanes and flyovers it has, we all travel The Queen's Highway. The Queen's Peace protects us all, and no one at all has the right to break it. The learned Dean founded Victorian legal theory on Immanuel Kant's definition of justice as the liberty of everyone limited only by the same liberty of everyone else.

But clear your mind of Kant. Personal law is changing fast, and so presumably it could not have been all that perfect. Since 1st January, 1970, illegitimate children have some limited rights of inheritance under *The Family Law Reform Act*. Progress in our society whittles away a stigmatised status which according to John Selden in his *Table Talk*, is based on a Biblical misconception:

> *"Tis sayd 23rd. Deut. 2. a Bastard shall not enter into the congregacon of the Lord even to the Tenth Generacon . . . he shall enter into the Church; the meaning of the phraze is, he shall not marry a Jewish woman. But upon this ground grossly mistaken. A Bastard at this day in the Church of Rome cannot take Orders . . . An Ammonite or a Moabite shall not enter into the congregacon of the Lord even to the Tenth Generacon. Now you know with the Jewes an Ammonite or a Moabite could never be a Preist (sic) because their Preists were borne and not made.'*

The Common Law, 'grossly mistaken', my foot. It regarded a bastard as *filius nullius*—'Nobody's baby' to protect the inheritance of a lawful wife and her legitimate first-born son, and the Devil take the father's indiscretions. I very much doubt whether the history books are right when they say the Barons at Merton in 1236 cried out with one voice *'Nolumus leges Angliae mutare'*. What the Clergy had asked them to do was to alter the custom of inheritance of land so that a child born before his parents married would be legitimated then. This was the Canon Law of Holy Church, observed in all Christendom except independent England. What they did say was no doubt, 'We shan't let the Bastards get away with that' since most of them owned their lands and castles by right of legitimate first-born male inheritance, if not by cutting someone's throat.

Be that as it may, they succeeded and it was not until the *Legitimacy Act, 1926* that *legitim per subsequens matrimonium* became the law of England. Even then, the child was not legitimated if either parent was married to someone else when he was born.

Not until 1959 did such children become legitimate on the eventual marriage of their fathers and mothers. By *Section 14* of *The Family Law Reform Act, 1969* illegitimate children and their parents can now succeed each other, on intestacy, but cannot participate in the intestacy of any other relatives. By *Section 15*, 'children' in a disposition now means illegitimate as well as legitimate children. Legitimated children have been able to claim since 1926 and adopted ones since 1958.

Profound changes in personal law, however, have affected the criminal law little. Status is unimportant whether a man commits murder or merely gets drunk in England. Rank, and therefore status, used to make quite a difference. The last Peer to be tried by the House of Lords, Lord de Clifford, was acquitted of manslaughter in 1935. This aristocratic privilege was abolished for the usual modern reason—it was expensive to organise trials by the Lords. (*Criminal Justice Act, 1948, s. 30.*) Peers are now tried in the ordinary courts like the rest of us—including foreigners—and quite often convicted. Not only do we punish foreigners for their crimes within our shores, but we give civil judgments against them—even sometimes when they are not here—and enforce those judgments against their property here. One way of enforcing a judgment is to make the debtor bankrupt and we oblige foreigners in that way. In that fashion they have a different status here from what they enjoy at home.

Such a thing involves no International Law. That is of two kinds. *Public International Law* governs the relation between nations, and therefore controls the status of diplomats. But they are the only foreigners who get any special privileges. *Private International Law* does not involve giving any favours to foreigners at all. It merely decides questions—usually of status in cases which have a foreign element. For foreign legal systems often treat status in different ways from us and we recognise those laws.

We do not recognise any special sorts of person except Heads of State and diplomats. It was, after all, as long ago as 1894 that Sir William Harcourt QC said 'We are all Socialists now' (and he became a Liberal Cabinet Minister). When Lord Mowbray invoked the ancient privilege of Peers to be immune from arrest for civil process—divorce proceedings—whilst Parliament was in session, there was quite a demand for the abolition of privilege.

Total equality is no doubt a good theoretical foundation for a system of law, but we have not got it. The Romans did very well with a graded structure—no status, no rights; some status, some rights; top status, do as you please. But even patrician status declined, and in its later years, Roman citizenship was given to all sorts of foreigners—including the Ancient British. That does seem to happen when you start mixing up nationality and citizenship. The foundation of their system, however, was theoretically good because they had the rightless ones, the slaves. Lots of these grew quite wealthy, but still had the status of slaves. In those conditions, however, it can't last.

We are persuaded, somewhat in the teeth of the evidence, that it did not even begin here. Less than a century ago, servants who broke their contracts were sent to prison under an Act of 1823. This squares ill with 'Britons never shall be slaves'. The foundation for this belief in its most often cited legal context appears to be more atmospheric than legal.

'This air is too pure for a slave to breathe, Let the black go free'

is attributed to Lord Mansfield, Chief Justice, in the case of Thomas Somersett, a slave chained in the hold of a ship moored in the Thames in 1772 (*20 State Trials 1*). Actually, he did not say it. It was said by counsel, Serjeant Davy. About that time, fashionable ladies kept little black slaves in splendid livery, and bought and sold them like pets, and apparently no one thought there was anything wrong with it. However, it emerged during the case that slavery was not possible under the law of England. Discussion turned upon the serfs, and the judge said that when the military tenures of land were abolished in 1660 there were only two of them left, anyway. They were actually villeins, not serfs; the distinction being that whilst technically tied to the soil, they were not in bondage. They were thus better off than labourers in tied cottages because they had security of occupation. They did not lose their homes if they lost their jobs with local landowners. Which is more than a farm labourer in a tied cottage can say today.

Being a service occupier of a dwelling-house is not technically considered a status in English Law, any more than being a council tenant is. Indeed, council tenants have no security of tenure under the *Rent Act, 1968*, though of course, they have much more actual security than most people because some councils do not turn them out even for appalling rent arrears and squalor.

Thus emerges the real characteristic of status in the context of legal philosophy. It subsists not in privileges or special rights, but in an absence of some rights. To get the best out of English law, one has to appreciate this and so turn disadvantages into advantages. This was superbly well done by Mr Gerald Gardiner QC (as he was then), as counsel for George Eastham the Newcastle footballer in the test case which resulted in the sale of footballers being declared repugnant to human rights, and the restrictions in their contracts therefore not legally binding. The judge was Mr Justice (now Lord) Wilberforce, scion of the slavery abolitionist, William Wilberforce.

Footballers are still sold, of course, but they are quite willing to be sold because the prices, as anyone on the terraces will tell you, are ridiculously inflated and they get a cut. Consequently, it is no longer degrading slavery. We have moved, as Sir Henry Maine said we would, from Status to Contract.

But that is only so far as work is concerned. In the home, slavery has been a bugbear. John Stuart Mill, also in 1869, wrote that there was then only one kind of slave known to our law—'the mistress of every house'. I prefer myself, the description of the status of women not so long ago given by Sir Percy Winfield, 'a rather barbarous hotchpot of humiliating disabilities and scandalous immunities' (*Law of Tort 4th Edn. p. 106*). The amazing thing is that the disabilities have diminished but the immunities multiplied at the present day. One hundred years of effort have been bent to remedying by law something which the law was powerless to control. Queen Victoria was agin it, of course. In a letter dated 29th May, 1870, she wrote:

> *'The Queen is most anxious to enlist everyone who can speak or write to join in checking this mad, wicked folly of "Women's Rights"* . . .
>
> *Lady —— ought to get a good whipping. It is a subject which makes the Queen so furious that she cannot contain herself. God created men and women different . . .'*

That does not pinpoint the question. Is Sex a Status? Victoria was Queen by inheritance, Act of State and religious ceremony. She could, had she wished, have abdicated. She was a wife by contract, religious sacrament and ceremony. She could not help being widowed —and so free to marry—but the termination of marriage by judicial divorce was a dozen years old when she wrote that letter, and Parliamentary dissolutions much older—especially for Queens. She was a woman and mother by the laws of Nature. Even the latter she could have controlled. Her womanhood was the only thing she was powerless to change. The great Status of being Queen of the Realm she could have altered with a stroke of the pen, as her great grandson was to prove in 1937.

Similarly, for non-Royals many of the incapacities creating status are quite arbitrary on their incidence. Until quite recently— the *Age of Marriage Act, 1929*—infant marriage was perfectly lawful after puberty which was normally 12 for a girl and 14 for a boy. But the Act made marriages under 16 void. The spirit of Romeo and Juliet is honoured in *Section 6 (2)* of the *Sexual Offences Act, 1956*, which provides that the offence of unlawful sexual intercourse with a girl between 13 and 16 is not committed where a marriage is invalid under *Section 2* of the *Marriage Act, 1949* and *Section 1* of the *1929 Act*, if the husband believes on reasonable grounds that the girl is legally his wife. She cannot actually be his wife because under 16 she has no capacity to marry. And there is also a defence for men under 24 for the offence of unlawful sexual intercourse (so long as he has not done it before) if he believed with reasonable cause that the girl was over 16. But there is no defence against this crime for older men—however loving and mutually desired—with a girl the day before she is 16, though she can legally marry the following day.

Until the *Family Law Reform Act, 1969* came into force a person actually reached an age the day before his birthday. Old cases showed that 'the law will make no fraction of a day' and were applied to enable the successors of an officer killed in France the day before his birthday to inherit through him from his father's estate (*(1918) 1 Ch 263*). Though no doubt a patriotic sympathy verdict it was founded in sound old law and just why it was altered is a bit of a mystery. By such totally arbitrary changes can the law of status alter. It would have been possible to defend a charge of intercourse the day before a girl's 16th birthday until 1st January, 1970, but no longer. Parliament may take the line that the law ought to be certain but in this case it was. The date of a marriage or an absolute decree of divorce determines a change of status. In the Bankruptcy Court the Registrar records in his book the very minute that a Receiving Order is pronounced. From that moment, the order will relate back to the act of bankruptcy and vest in the Official Receiver what the Debtor owned at that time.

This sort of consideration was just as important in former times. Until the *Forfeiture Act, 1870*, felons and traitors forfeited their lands and goods to the Crown upon conviction. Their lot was somewhat improved, and they might even manage to keep some of their ill-gotten gains, as the result of that Act. The status of felon was abolished by the *Criminal Law Act, 1967*, and now only traitors are affected by the status-changing provisions of the *Forfeiture Act*. They are considerable. Naval, military and civil offices, and pensions and superannuations of them cease unless within two months of conviction the traitor receives a Royal Free Pardon. He also becomes incapable of holding office for the future, or of being an MP or having a vote in England or Wales.

The 1870 Act provided that prisoners could not take legal action whilst under sentence. This protection of the helpless was removed by *Section 70* of the *Criminal Justice Act, 1948*, and they are now as free as anyone else to dissipate their fortunes—whether or not ill-gotten—in Jarndyce-like litigation. Several have turned this facility to account by bringing libel actions designed to vindicate them, but the only one which worked was that of Mr Alfie Hinds.

However, the *Civil Evidence Act, 1968* has put a stop to such libel suits. People serving sentence are not even 'convicts' any more since the *Criminal Justice Act, 1948.*

There would thus appear to have disappeared from the law of England any trace of complete rightlessness, for the most complete rightlessness formerly depended on criminality. Since the abolition of felony—and actually since the practical end of outlawry in 1869 —no class of rightless person exists in England. Even traitors after sentence are not outside the law and can use its processes (always assuming they survive. The death penalty has not been abolished for treason but this can only be committed while the nation is at war, though this can exist without formal declaration by 'levying war').

The little appreciated *Section 7 (5)* of the *Criminal Law Act, 1967* seems therefore to be just a tidying-up provision:

> '*There is hereby abolished so much of the punishment for any offence as consists in any general forfeiture of lands or goods and chattels or in being placed outside Her Majesty's protection or otherwise incapacitated to sue or be sued.*'

Now Parliament is presumed—aren't we all?—to know the law. This, it might be supposed, is a forgive and forget provision for the benefit of subversives, repentant or not. But by 1967 the only crimes apart from treason which could be punished by being put outside the protection of the Queen were those offences which amounted to *praemunire.*

This offence appears in the Index to the Latest (37th) Edition of *Archbold's Criminal Pleading, Evidence and Practice*, with the reference to Paragraph 3811. There is no such paragraph in the book. Earnest research prompts the suspicion that this is no mere printer's oversight. The punishment of *praemunire* involved a state of rightlessness closely akin to outlawry, which was finally abolished by the *Administration of Justice Act, 1938, Section 12.* There may yet be some outlaws lurking about who do not know of this amnesty. ('Lurking' is how the Bill of Middlesex described what outlaws do.) Now Part 1 of the Fourth Schedule to the 1967 Act states that the *Statute of Praemunire, 1392 (16 Ric. 2. c. 5.)* is repealed *in toto.* Maybe so, but of course, *praemunire* did not start with that Act. It was already well established. It began with the *Statute of Provisors, 1350.* Now, mysteriously enough, this Act is not to be found in *Halsbury's Statutes of England 5th Edition 1970*, and neither is any statute abolishing it. It looks very much as if the reformers have forgotten all about it and not repealed it.

Does this matter? Well, a provisor is a person who claimed a church living on the authority of the Pope. Gregory IX claimed to be entitled to appoint Rectors in no fewer than 300 English parishes, and the place was becoming overrun with Italians, and so Parliament put a stop to it. By great good fortune, a selection of highly Protestant statutes under the Tudors made provisory presentments void. But it looks very much as if provisors are still known to the law of England. Neither the status nor the punishment has been abolished. Some Archbishop refusing to consecrate a bishop nominated by the Queen on the advice of the Prime Minister might be convicted of it. It is not necessary to go that far. Anyone uttering words undermining the supremacy of either Church or Crown might find himself accused of it, if the prosecuting counsel was in the least diligent. This discovery will no doubt be a comfort to Dr Paisley and one trembles for *Private Eye*.

Now, should some apolitical Primate or some lesser seditionist suffer a praemunire how can he ever get back his rights? That is the relevance of this esoteric discourse in connection with the law of Status. Let us hope that *Section 7 (5)* of the 1967 Act would be generously construed to protect him. He would fortunately not be treated just like an outlaw, which is as well, for in 1938 we also abolished the Reversal of Outlawry. No doubt, theoretically, it would be open for him to get a Royal Free Pardon. Should all fail, he would, however, have the enormous status of being the only truly rightless person in England and Wales, which might afford him some little comfort.

It is important to notice that *Section 7 (5)* of the 1967 Act specifically preserves the right to sue and be sued, and in these days when the lawyers are under attack from all quarters for alleged restrictive practises that is something of a comfort. This is a right of all citizens, but *Section 51* of the *Judicature Act, 1925*, does provide that a person who keeps bringing groundless proceedings can be declared a Vexatious Litigant. He—or more often she—then has to get leave of the court to start proceedings. It is not, therefore, a total bar, and people hooked on litigation are not slow to make applications. Mercifully, the right of appeal against refusal was taken away in 1959.

Exactly what constitutes vexatious litigation is not easy to define. The Rules of the Supreme Court provide for striking out 'frivolous and vexatious' pleadings, but do not state exactly what such conduct consists in.

Any reference to a vexatious litigant is to invite an application for a writ for something or other. In 1964 the Co-operative Permanent Building Society appeared by counsel in the Court of Appeal to ask for an order restraining a vexatious litigant from making applications to them about some possession proceedings they were taking. Lord Denning, the Master of the Rolls, said that though the order was very unusual, it would be made. If it were broken the vexatious litigant would be liable to imprisonment or other punishment for contempt of court. There was, of course, no necessity for an application to proceed with the defence of proceedings, brought against the vexatious litigant by someone else. To someone who yearns for the thrill of litigation, this is better than nothing. But for the opponent, having to keep paying costs for representation on proceedings, it is no fun at all. Vexatious litigants can issue summonses in the Magistrates' Courts, but they tend to prefer the intellectual climate of the superior courts. They sometimes raise legal questions of a rewarding nature, but their opponents seldom relish the enjoyment of academic controversy.

Before Mr Radomir Pasic became a vexatious litigant he got off to a promising start by asking Mr Justice Roxburgh to conduct an action in Serbo-Croat. Since he made the request itself in Serbo-Croat, that learned judge was, for once, lost for an answer. He several times told an interpreter that he had no right of audience, being a Yugoslav lawyer and not an English barrister, but at length it emerged what Mr Pasic wanted. This was a declaration that he owned the Ploesti oilfield because he held some shares in an English company which he had inherited from his father, a former Rumanian Prime Minister. The likelihood of the Rumanian Government taking any notice of his rights was not great and the action never went its full course. Mr Pasic is now dead. However, his litigation brought to light the existence of a 14th Century Statute which requires proceedings to be conducted in English. The judge was nearly as disappointed as Pasic, because they discovered in the course of the argument that they could get on tolerably well together in French.

However, no one, then, by operation of law *simpliciter*, is unable to claim some rights, though rights may be in abeyance for a time. The disabilities or incapacities which we acknowledge are natural or supernatural—lunacy, infancy, marriage, Holy Orders and the peerage. As we shall see, the most important is marriage, because it affects so many other elements and incidents of status. The harsh doctrines we have adverted to begot even harsher. For instance, the injustices to the bastard created the illogical 'presumption of legitimacy' for a child born in wedlock.

> *'When he is born within espousals although he was begotten by another the law of this land will judge him* mulier *and by the law of Holy Church he is Bastard.'*

How many men's heirs were foisted upon them by cuckoldry will never be guessed at. On the other side of the coin, the father of an illegitimate child is not a 'parent', cannot prevent adoption of the child and is faced with great difficulties if he wishes to assert his 'rights' to take part in control of its upbringing. Adoption, though in fact common, was unknown to the Common Law. The *Adoption of Children Act, 1926,* showed once again that Parliament could do what Nature could not when it enabled the total dissolution, so far as law could, of any relationship between the real mother and child and created the totally unnatural one with the new parents, legitimating the child if necessary in the process. The adopted child could thus succeed to their estates, whilst they might have illegitimate issue who could not, without a specific gift by valid will.

The attitude of legal thought having been to ignore status and deal with circumstances as political or social pressure might demand, the legal personality of the unborn child was hardly considered until recently. A child is born alive when it is breathing through its lungs, without deriving its power of living through connection with its mother. If it has a separate existence, even though the umbilical cord still connects it with the mother, it is capable of being murdered. Killing a child in the womb was never murder by the Common Law and the *Infant Life Preservation Act, 1929,* was passed to punish it. Abortion is punished under the *Offences Against the Person Act, 1861,* and of course, can be perfectly legally performed with medical advice.

It might appear, therefore, that the unborn child has no existence and consequently no rights in the law. However, so far as the law of property was concerned, it was held in 1907 that a child in the womb was deemed to have been born at such time as was necessary for it to benefit—*Villar* v. *Gilbey (1907) A.C. 139.* Analogously, a child *en ventre sa mere* should be capable of being compensated for an injury it suffered in the womb. In an Irish case, a child was held unable to recover damages because the railway company did not know of its presence on the train within its mother when she was injured in the collision (*Walker* v. *G. N. Railways (1890) 28 L.R. Ir. 69*). But had it been a babe in arms it must have been entitled to damages. Where was the essential differences? In Canada, a child born with club feet after its mother was injured in a tram crash was compensated on the basis that once born alive it had all the rights it would have had if it had been alive at the time of the injury—*Montreal Tramways* v. *Leveille (1933) S.C.R. 456; 4. D.L.R. 337.*

The principle arose of course in the claims brought on behalf of the 'thalidomide babies'. This drug was used in preparations supplied to pregnant women and bristled with difficulties of law. A test case, *S.* v. *Distillers Co. (Biochemicals) Ltd. (1969) 113 S.J. 672* was compromised on terms that 40 per cent of the damages which were either agreed or assessed by the court would be paid and that all allegations of negligence in producing the drug would be withdrawn. An unborn child therefore can look forward to a six-to-four chance of establishing that it has a status under the law of England. A dead body, on the other hand, belongs to no one, though leaving it about the streets is indictable as a public nuisance—*R. v. Clarke, 15 Cox 171.* Between the two extremes, it is a person, and has status.

The incapacities creating advantages incidental to status are not confined to women. The incapacity for the formation of certain legal relationships of lunatics and drunks is well recognised. It is founded in the proposition that no true consent to contract or run risk can be present in an unsound mind, and the 'voluntary induced madness' as the 17th Century Chief Justice Hale defined drunkenness, is as much a defence to intention as involuntary insanity. Not that the commonly advanced defence of being too drunk to intend to kill or maim very often impresses juries. Nevertheless the principle appears in the *Sale of Goods Act, 1893 s. 2,* tempered with Victorian equity:

> '*Where necessaries are sold and delivered to a person who by reason of mental incapacity or drunkenness is incompetent to contract, he must pay a reasonable price therefor.*'

Now, insanity is a status clearly recognised by the law. Drunkenness has not achieved that distinction, although many more people get drunk than go mad. But the reasoning behind the enactment is not bedevilled by any philosophical considerations about legal capacity. In 1893, there were no licensed hours. A great many men were engaged on hot and dusty work in factory, foundry and field and drank large quantities of beer. Water supplies were not so well distributed as now and much water in piped systems was undrinkable. Beer was accordingly a 'necessity', and the brewers wanted paying for it. To have permitted the labouring man to escape payment of his score on a plea of intoxication would have undermined the finances of the Tory Party. The Act only declared what had long been the Common Law.

Now whilst it is true that a drunken person can ratify a contract when he regains sobriety, just as an insane person can ratify a transaction when he is again *compos mentis,* neither the British Working Man nor the ordinary sort of lunatic is that daft. Social conditions therefore forced the question of recovering payment for goods consumed to depend more on whether they were 'necessaries' than upon the status of the purchaser. Consequently, it dominated, as well, the legal liability of those persons whose disability was the status of infancy. Long described, as 'the pampered darlings of the law' people under 21 were equally long recognised to enjoy 'scandalous immunity' so long as they were lavish.

The unfortunate Mr Nash, a tailor of Savile Row, claimed £122 for clothes from a Cambridge undergraduate, but lost the suit. The account included eleven fancy waistcoats at two guineas a time which, with other items, were said by the judge not to be 'necessaries'. That young man, declared public policy, had to be protected from himself and his wanton waistcoat-buying propensities. One way to go about this work might have been to make him give the waistcoats back. But the *Infants' Relief Act, 1874,* a monument rather to Self Help than *laissez faire,* had made contracts of loan, account stated and contracts for goods other than necessaries, with infants, absolutely void. Such Draconian protection was not new; it merely reinforced the anxious care for those of tender years which characterised the Common Law.

Mr Justice Coleridge had earlier declared that diamonds and race horses were not necessaries even for the son of the richest man in the kingdom. He seems never to have considered what kind of friendship they could afford to girls, but this was before they themselves ceased to be chattels. This doctrine actually helped the tradespeople who were so unwise as to serve the *hoi polloi.* It taught them to overcharge the adult relatives of the younger set in order to underwrite their losses. On the other hand one really could not blame those shopkeepers, of whom Bonaparte said the nation was compromised, for co-operating with the mine and factory owners to pay the labouring sort of people in kind instead of money. No doubt some judges could have been found to say that bread and salt pork were not 'necessaries' for young proles.

At the ancient seats of learning the law was part of the curriculum if not a popular diversion. Quite apart from any really malicious desire to tuck-up the tradesmen, undergraduates liked having parties with expensive wines and exotic dishes even though their funds did not run to them. But their tutors instructed them in the law and they had it borne in upon them that to regale their friends with bangers and mash washed down wtih beer would court findings of necessity. Plover's eggs, smoked salmon, oysters and fine wines, not being necessaries, could be enjoyed *gratis.* John Maynard Keynes once said that his great regret was that he had not had champagne more often. Had he studied law instead of economics, he could have managed it.

Thus an infant with £500 a year for himself, when a working man raised a family on 18 shillings a week, got away with a pair of jewelled solitaires and an antique goblet (*Ryder* v. *Wombwell (1868) L.R. 4 Exch. 32*). But a young working lad had to pay for the bicycle he needed to get to work (*Clyde Cycle Co.* v. *Hargreaves (1898) 78 L.T. 296*). Where he went wrong was in aiming low. A carriage and four horses he could have had for nothing. Plainly they would not have been necessary for his 'station in life'. And there the theory of the law had to recognise that this principle was founded in status, after all. What determined whether something was a necessary was the social niche into which he fitted. And this was determined upon no classical Roman notions of status, but upon the popular conception of those Forsyte Saga days. 'Station in life' was not narrowly interpreted. Lord Cozens-Hardy, Master of the Rolls said that what was essential did not just cover bread and cheese and clothes; it included the other things in life and so some people might have more necessaries than others.

When young Gray bound himself apprentice to Mr Roberts, the billiards professional, to play exhibition matches on a world tour, he was held firmly to the bargain, for it was necessary to his education and ability to support himself that he be kept to the terms of his indenture. The educational atmosphere of a billiards saloon might not commend itself to Lady Plowden. For one thing, girls are seldom allowed in. But youth was less tenderly nurtured in life than in law ((*1913*) *1 K.B. 520*).

Matthew Bacon in his 'Abridgement' recognised that 'infancy is a personal privilege of which no one can take advantage but the infant himself'. In order to evade the law, the antagonists of infants often tried to sue them in tort, instead of in contract, for an infant is and always has been liable for civil wrongs independent of contract, such as running someone over. However, where the un-lawful act complained of was connected in any way with a contract, the law would not permit the injured person to get round it and hold the infant liable. A boy called Shiell fraudulently mis-stated his age to get credit of £400 for radio equipment, and the contractors, R. Leslie, Ltd. were prevented from getting back the money because that would have amounted to enforcing the contract. The fraud, though capable of being actionable alone, was tied up with the contract. Had he still got the actual goods in his possession, said the court, it would have made him hand them over. Had the actual coins and notes advanced still been in his possession, they would have made him hand them back. Restitution would have been different from repayment. But repayment would have meant en-forcing the contract, by giving a remedy for its breach. And the *Infants' Relief Act* forbade any sort of enforcement of such contract (*R. v. Shiell* (*1914*)).

In 1967, the Age of Majority Committee recommended abolishing the *Infants' Relief Act*. What was in fact done was to abolish infancy at 18. If it was an electoral carrot, it did not work. On the other hand, there was not a single protest march against the Family Law Reform Bill. It was seen, of course, as a reduction by three important years on the threshold of adulthood, of a disability. Very few of our hyperintelligent youngsters appreciated that it was three years loss of personal privilege. They were in the same euphoric state as the Child Crusaders seven centuries before and thought they had won a great right when in truth they had been saddled with an oppressive liability.

Certain it is that the directors of the finance houses mention the Labour Administration in their prayers when they reflect upon the legally enforceable agreements for record players and motor scooters and Lord knows what else which now repose in their files instead of the old ones 'guaranteed' by parents much less able to afford the payments than the principal debtors. Status is a balance sheet.

Infancy, like matrimony, is a status which has been described as 'dependent' not for the simple economic reason, but because the characteristics of the person depend on the status or characteristics of some other person. Much of one's law depends exclusively on where one lives.

> *'The law of England and of almost all civilised countries, ascribes to each individual at his birth two distinct legal estates . . . binding him by the tie of national allegiance and which may be called his political status; . . . the civil status is governed universally by one single principle, namely that of domicil . . . it is on this basis that the personal rights . . . his majority . . . his marriage, succession, testacy or intestacy, must depend.'*
>
> **Lord Westbury, *Le Mesurier* v. *Le Mesurier (1895) A.C. 517*.**

The important word is 'he'. *She* gets her domicil from him, and so do their children.

> *'By domicil we mean home, the permanent home, and if you do not understand your permanent home, I am afraid that no illustration drawn from foreign writers or foreign languages will very much help you to it.'*
>
> **Lord Cranworth, *Whicker* v. *Hume (1858) 7 H.L.C. 124*.**

With such statements of the law who needs any Act of Parliament to specify the details of the law of domicil? And there are none. Lord Denning thinks the domicil rules are 'the last barbarous relic of a wife's servitude'. He added in a later case:

> *'The tests of domicil are far too unsatisfactory. In order to find out a person's domicil you have to apply a lot of archaic rules. They ought to have been done away with long ago. But they still survive. Particularly the rule that a wife takes the domicil of her husband and the rule that a child takes the domicil of its father.'*
>
> **Re P (G.E.) an Infant (1965) Ch. 568.**

Unhappily, domicil is the basis of divorce law, and the law of

136

succession to movable property. It must be quite a nuisance not to be able to get a divorce or an inheritance when you need it. Your domicil is the state having a separate legal system—e.g. Scotland—in which you live, having in your mind the settled intention of staying there—so long as you are a man over 18 or an unmarried woman over 18. It sounds simple enough and so it is, but suppose you are a woman whose husband leaves you and goes to live in Switzerland, and then dies. Because it is his residence—which though similar is not the same in law as domicil—his estate may well not be saddled with heavy death duties. But it may also devolve on the persons entitled to it under Swiss law, which might not include the widow. Doubtless there is very little accidental about it, but it makes his wife unable to get reasonable provision out of his estate.

If my son marries under the age of 18, his wife would acquire my domicil. When they presented me with a grandchild, it, too, would have my domicil. If I retired to Majorca, they would all become domiciled in Majorca even though they had never left England. When the age of majority was 21, there were many people affected by retirements in this way. Fewer people are concerned now, since the reduction of majority. The Private International Law Committee in 1954 recommended changing the domicil rules, particularly to give separated women the ability to acquire a 'domicil of choice'. There are four kinds, origin, choice, or that imputed by 'operation of law', and 'dependent'. But, of course, the domicil of origin is dependent on the domicil of the father. A widow keeps the dependent domicil she got from her husband until she changes it by choice (*Re. Wallach. (1950) 1 All E.R. 199*). But in *Re. Scullard (1957) Ch. 107*, Mr Justice Danckwerts asked 'Why?'

The reason for these rules is the dependence of the laws of marriage and inheritance on the law of the ecclesiastical courts.

When the *Statute of Citations (23 Hen. VIII c. 9)* provided that no man could be 'cited out of the diocese' it was merely making the law of the land what was already the law of the Church, covering something which the temporal law did not provide for. It meant that you could only sue someone in the Bishop's Court for the diocese where he lived, in the kind of case which was brought there—like judicial separation, or for a will to be proved. (There is a similar principle in the County Courts. Actions can only be brought in the court for the area where the defendant lives or where the cause of the action arose). This principle is residence, not domicil. However, those courts not unnaturally with so rigid a local jurisdiction, refused to take any notice of decrees or orders of foreign courts. But they would recognise orders of courts of the state having a political and legal system of its own in which the suitor had a settled residence. This principle was an old one in the law of the

Church and the Civil law, dating back to the first Latin laws of the Salian Franks, which ran in all three parts of Gaul in the 8th Century, and then spread all over Christendom. When the Divorce Court was set up in 1857 it was ordered to act according to the previous principles and practice of the Ecclesiastical Courts, which rested their jurisdiction on domicil.

Thus as Maitland says, our modern law of marriage and will and inheritance is the result of the 'close and confused union between Church and State in the 10th Century'. However, the other States of Christendom have done without it for some time—mainly since the *Code Napoleon* of 1804 was imposed upon them. This replaces domicil with nationality. A French national can get a divorce in France, but a British national quite often cannot get one in England. Suppose he has become domiciled in Switzerland to dodge tax; he cannot come back here to get a divorce. He must hunt around for somewhere more pliable and his divorce might not be recognised here if he gets it. To adopt nationality as the basis in Britain would not make things as easy as it seems. By the British Nationality Act, 1948, every citizen of the United Kingdom, the Colonies and the Commonwealth is a British subject and so would be able to claim divorce in our courts. Since the courts would not be able to enforce their orders on people living overseas no doubt they would not give them relief.

Because women's domicil depends on that of their husbands, women whose husbands had deserted them and changed their domicil could not get divorces. The law was changed in 1949 to allow them to claim divorce if they were deserted here and after three years' residence. Domicil operates in curious ways to affect the marriage status, because it affects not only the ability to get divorced but whether a marriage abroad will be recognised here.

And it is totally unaffected by nationality. Just as an Englishman can become domiciled in the Bahamas or Basutoland, a Basuto can be domiciled here just like a Chinaman can. Then they can marry and have the marriage dissolved here. If however they are already divorced under foreign law, the questions may arise whether their status is recognised by English law.

Mr Hyde married his wife in Salt Lake City, Utah, U.S.A. at Brigham Young's Mormon Temple when they were still practising polygamy. He renounced that faith and returned to England, but his wife stayed in Utah and married again. In 1866, he sued for divorce on the ground of her adultery but Lord Penzance ruled that since the Mormon marriage was not recognised by English law—because it was potentially polygamous—there was nothing to dissolve (*Hyde* v. *Hyde & Woodmansee* (*1866*) *L.R. 1. P. & D. 130*). That case did not decide that the Mormon marriage was invalid. It

138

was perfectly valid in Utah; it was simply not recognised by the law of England. It is accordingly possible to have a foreign marriage which is not valid here, and one which though valid is not recognised here. It is consequently fairly easy to have two statuses at once by being married in one country and not in another. Lawyers call these 'limping marriages'.

It naturally follows that if a man cannot get a divorce here—because he is not domiciled here—he might go abroad and get a divorce which would not for some reason be recognised here. But an English domiciled person might find himself still married after a foreign divorce. This was the situation when Bertrand (later Earl) Russell got an American divorce in 1897 and remarried here, only to be imprisoned for bigamy, because the American decree was not recognised here.

A woman domiciled in England went through a ceremony of marriage with a Hindu domiciled in India, and then found out that he had a wife in India. She sued for a nullity decree on the ground that the marriage was bigamous and so void. However, by the law of India, his domicil, the husband was permitted to practise polygamy. Since his marriage in India was valid there, the second marriage here was bigamous, and void (*Baindail* v. *Baindail* (*1946*) *1 All E.R. 342; P. 122*). This appears at first to be the opposite of *Hyde* v. *Hyde*, but in law they are the same. The essence of Hyde's case was that he was domiciled in England. Because it was potentially polygamous, his marriage was not recognised. The court's refusal to recognise it depended on his domicil. Mr Baindail, on the other hand, enjoyed the personal status which permitted him to make a polygamous marriage in India which would be recognised here. But he could not make a polygamous marriage here because it is not permitted here. Consequently Commonwealth immigrants who have made valid and recognised polygamous marriages can claim Social Security here for all their wives.

The reason that divorce and validity of marriage are maintained on different bases was explained by Lord Justice James in *Niboyet* v. *Niboyet* (*1878*) *4 P.D. 1*. If the jurisdiction of the English court to try a nullity case depended on domicil, that would beg the question it had to decide. If it was valid, the wife had her husband's domicil; if not, she could well have some other. It can be quite difficult to prove that someone has a particular domicil, and therefore the status which depends upon it. Mr George Bowie left Glasgow in 1890 at the age of 45, to live in Liverpool. He persisted in calling himself a Glasgow man, but often declared that he would never again set foot there. He even arranged his own funeral to take place in Liverpool (at a date and time to be notified by someone else). The House of Lords decided that he remained a domiciled Scotsman

(*Ramsay* v. *Liverpool Royal Infirmary* (*1930*) *A.C. 588*). A man's motive, it had been judicially pointed out, might be different from his intention when he makes his home. Motive might be dictated by convenience whilst intention might never be fulfilled. The mere intention to follow the sun cannot give you the status of a Bahamas domicil. You must find the fare and actually get there before you can begin to acquire it, but once away from your domicil, the fact that you do not get back need not alter your domicil. A man went to Florence each year for his health and returned to England for the fine weather. He was held to have lost his English domicil (*Hoskins* v. *Matthews* (*1856*) *8 de G.M. & G. 13*).

A fugitive from justice or his creditors might well not change his domicil because he might not have the compelling intention to settle in his hideout. The point has not arisen in practice because such people rarely leave enough to litigate over and their successors equally rarely admit that they have what is left, or bring it back here where the losers might sue for it. Income tax and estate duty, however, often raise domicil and residence questions. The rule is that land here passes under our law and movable goods under the law of the domicil. But it is not very easy sometimes to decide where movables are. A share certificate, for instance, is evidence of ownership of shares, but it is not the shares. Where they 'are' will be decided according to the Private International Law of the owner's domicil. Unhappily, this subject is not a single unalterable code which applies to all the nations of the world. Its rules differ somewhat in each. In England, it is deceptively simple. All you do is to decide whether a point in a case has to depend on foreign law. Then you get some foreign lawyers to give expert evidence on what the foreign law is. If they disagree you decide which is right, then you know as a fact what is the foreign situation with regard to the situation or property in dispute. You then decide what is the effect of that in English law. The difficulty occurs when applying the foreign law. Does the law of the state concerned apply only its 'relevant' law to a case with a foreign element—*e.g.* its matrimonial or testamentary law? Or does it apply its whole law, including its Private International Law? This doctrine is called *renvoi* and can be entire or partial. The modern name for Private International Law is 'The Conflict of Laws'.

It is a somewhat sophisticated discipline, which English judges have reduced to simplicity.

> '*No country is bound to recognise the laws of a foreign state when they work injustice to its own subjects,*'
>
> **Lord Justice Cotton in *Sottomayer* v. *De Barros* (*1877*) 3 P.D. 7.**

> *'The courts of this country are not compelled to recognise a decree of a court of another country when it offends against our ideas of justice.'*
>
> **Lord Denning, Master of the Rolls, in** *Gray* **v.** *Formosa (1963) P. 259.*

This refusal to be put upon by foreigners is important in the English law of status. Companies being legal persons, have domicils and residences just like the rest of us. They are often called into existence just so that their domicil can be different from those of the people who created them. Accountants and experts in comparative tax systems anxiously preserve, not to say create, the evidence of what a company's domicil is because they know how problematic it can be. They conceive to be sheer busybodying the frame of mind revealed in:

> *'A company cannot eat or sleep, but it can keep house and do business. We ought, therefore, to see where it really keeps house and does business.'*
>
> **Lord Loreburn in** *De Beers Consolidated Mines Ltd.* **v.** *Howe (1906) A.C. 455.*

British Petroleum pays none of its tax to the British Exchequer although 37 per cent of its employees work here (Fabian Tract No. 409).

This is the sphere in which status will have its great renaissance. These artificial persons can have their status determined before conception; and have it altered when the chill wind of economic inconvenience is forecast by the watchers on the shores of the sea of opportunity. People with real status get very good at looking after it. During the financial depression in 1933 the salaries of some of the Government and civil servants were cut, and the judges pretty sharply told Lord Chancellor Sankey that they had been asking for a rise since 1878. One of the few pieces of legislation to have the word 'status' in the title—the *Status of Judges Bill*—was proposed to protect their pockets by requiring an address of both Houses of Parliament to cut their pay. It never passed, and they have done better since.

The limitations of the domicil doctrine affect only the personal law. Anyone living here can be sued for a debt, or a tort or a breach of contract, and a company registered abroad can be sued through its Principal Place of Business here. Whether it will have enough property here to satisfy the judgment is another matter. No writ or summons can be served on a defendant 'out of the jurisdiction'—i.e. abroad—without leave being given by the court. The court does not want to start anything it cannot finish. There are reciprocity treaties with many countries, enabling judgments to be enforced in neighbourly states, but only an optimist would call it easy. There is, of course, nothing to stop someone abroad suing someone resident here in our courts, and there are instances where someone abroad, sues someone else abroad, in our courts usually because they have contracted that English law shall apply to their bargains, e.g. Liberians and Greeks in shipping disputes. But they will usually have a 'place of business' and bank accounts here as well as elsewhere so the first essentials for litigation—money—are provided for. But Greek shipowners are often only represented by agents and their disappointed cruise customers find it arduous to take action in the Greek courts.

Sometimes the prosecution of an action here rests upon a fragile foundation, but it is done because our law is preferred to any other. Not long ago, Stephen Vicinczey, the Hungarian-born author who lives in Canada, brought an action for libel against the German magazine, *Stern*. He joined as defendants the Seymour Press, the English distributor of the magazine, who of course, in the eyes of the law of libel, published it here. He claimed to have been libelled in a review of his book 'In Praise of Older Women—The Amorous Recollections of Andreas Vajda'. Nearly two million copies of *Stern* are sold every week in Germany and Austria—and only about 8,000 a week here. After an 11-day trial, he was awarded damages of half a new penny and no costs.

Now residence is not a recognised status and the restrictions it imposes upon the traveller to the seat of justice are practical rather than theoretical. No doubt litigation across frontiers will be conducted with increased facility once we are in the Common Market. One of the practical safeguards which the law provides, if not for the litigant, for the lawyer, is the requirement of Security for the Costs. This is permission to proceed with an action, subject to depositing a sum of money to cover some at least of your opponents' costs if you lose. This was the Genesis of the troubles of Mr Moses Fairchild Gohoho. He was libelled in a Ghanaian newspaper, but since he was politically unpopular there at the time, chose to sue here, relying on publication in the few copies sent here to some advertising agents. They applied to the Court of Appeal for an order that he should give security for the costs of his appeal against an adverse decision. The Court ordered that he pay in £50 as such security. He then removed his coat and declared that he would come to the court every day. Then he took off his trousers and underpants. According to the law reporter of *The Times*:

'*At the Tipstaff's request, all present in Court left while several police officers assisted him in his task.*'

Mr Gohoho was removed to Brixton Prison for a week for

Contempt in the Face of the Court. Removal of trousers—those of an Officer of the Court or even your own—is not to be recommended as a means of calling attention to the justice of your cause. A person with few rights can have status according to law. But the removal of trousers is an indignity, and dignity is the distinction between legal status and ordinary status.

Ninety Per Cent Proof

'Young people are more apt to speak the truth than those who are grown cunning by age.'
Lord Hardwicke, L.C., in Bell v. Howard (1742) 9 Mod. 302.

DURING HIS EARLY DAYS in the Irish Courts, Carson once asked a witness what happened in his part of the country to people who told lies on oath. 'Their side usually wins, Your Honour', was the answer. It is, however, upon the fragile foundation of oral testimony that the Temple of Justice rests. Evidence is nothing but information offered to a tribunal in order that it may determine the facts of the situation into which it inquires. But there is a great distinction between the work of tribunals of inquiry, which are investigating a happening to find out what causes it, and courts, which decide disputes between two or more factions who each know perfectly well what caused the trouble, but want to blame someone else for it. Consequently, it is often said that tribunals of inquiry, Royal Commissions, and Select Committees and such institutions are not subject to the law of evidence.

This branch of our law is widely misunderstood, especially by lawyers, who frequently complain that it is designed to conceal the truth. This is because the distinction between information which is 'admissible' and that which is not is frequently obscure. Quite usually, too, evidence which is plainly receivable is practically useless to prove anything, but the courts do permit a great deal of inference from the information it receives. The law ducks all responsibility for accepting nonsensical information as 'proof' by leaving it to a jury when it can, saying that a judge must persuade himself that he is a jury when he sits alone, but must also explain himself so that other judges can say he was wrong. Most decisions of fact are left to the Justices of the Peace who are chosen from autocratic classes and are more convinced of their own infallibility than the Pope.

These expedients unfortunately have to be resorted to, for there is no legal proceeding at all that can take place without evidence. Very

145

often there is no dispute at all on the prime facts, but a profound disagreement about their effect in law. It is in this field perhaps that the confusion of evidence and inference is seen most distinctly.

> *'Can I, in the existing state of the law, infer that adultery occurred where the Respondent admits that the Woman Named slept in the bedroom where he slept, but both deny that adultery occurred?'*

asked Judge Leon of counsel in a divorce suit some years ago. The difficulty was heightened by the approach to proof of adultery adopted for a while—until overruled by the Court of Appeal—by Sir Jocelyn Simon when he was President of the Divorce Division. He thought that the 'criminal standard of proof' was necessary, i.e. proof 'beyond all reasonable doubt'. The standard of proof in civil cases is usually expressed to be 'on the balance of the probabilities'. The Court of Appeal said that the criminal standard did not apply to proof of adultery, but that it was a very serious matter and so required convincing proof. It says so about fraud and other questions which arise in serious cases in the civil courts. In *Hornal* v. *Neuberger Products Ltd.* (*1957*) *1. Q.B. 247*, it said that the more serious an allegation the more difficult it is to prove. But it never tells us exactly what 'proof' is, because of course, it can't.

This much abused and misunderstood phenomenon called 'proof' is used by lawyers in other senses than its obvious one, and that does not help to understand the matter. Lawyers speak of the paper on which the solicitor sets out in a brief to counsel what a witness is prepared to say in the witness box, as a 'proof of evidence'. It is of course, nothing of the kind. It proves nothing and certainly is not evidence. Evidence is of two kinds, sworn testimony, written or oral, and anything actually produced in court. Sometimes it is difficult to produce things in court and then the mountain in the person of the judge goes to Mahomet. This is called 'having a view', and some judges like doing it because they can smoke their pipes while they do so. It has the collateral advantage of showing very often that most of the witnesses have described the *locus in quo* totally inaccurately.

The trouble with litigation is that it is not simply a game between opposing sides referred by a judge. When a jury tries the facts, it often degenerates into that. But when the judge or magistrate has to decide the facts he quite often decides something which neither party is putting forward. The problems of the litigant are therefore not simply to make his version of the dispute acceptable, and to diminish the force of the other party's. It has to stop the court taking some different view of its own. It is perfectly possible for a set of facts to be incontrovertibly proved, but for the consequences flowing from them to be very different from what is contended for.

Lawyers understand this and because solicitors fear negligence claims and barristers are jealous of their reputations and thus their livelihood, they introduce not only the main facts but facts which tend to prove their version of the main facts. These facts are described technically as *'res gestae'*, or 'things which indicate'. It is quite common for litigation to be conducted entirely by reference to these indicia, which of course, prove very little in many cases. Lawyers, however, are necessary to be able to demonstrate that they are indeed receivable evidence, or *contra*, that they are not.

Of course, mere imperfection in a piece of evidence does not destroy its probative value. If that was not so, British Justice would not be the envy of the world. A little, imperfect thing might be very cogent proof. A man is serving 30 years in prison because there was a small smear of paint on the bottom of a pair of shoes at Leatherslade Farm after the Great Train Robbery. On the other hand there have been a great many cases where clear identification by eye witnesses was regarded by juries as insufficiently reliable to support convictions.

When John William Stupple was sued by an insurance company for £84,908 after a bank van raid, Mr Justice Paull said he thought that he was not rightly convicted, on the evidence which he had heard. Quite often, however, the surrounding circumstances of a decision convince the tribunal where another would decide the question differently.

When several people are tried together for a crime, the clearly proved guilt of some might carry over and serve to convict those against whom the case is much weaker. Some accused people strive desperately to be tried separately from their alleged confederates for this very reason.

The decisive power reposed in the jury is largely unappreciated.

'If I make a mistake, it can be corrected elsewhere. If you do, it cannot.'

said Mr Justice Devlin, in his charge to the jury on the trial of Dr John Bodkin Adams for murder. The acquittal was a triumph of reason over prejudice. How often it goes the wrong way in other cases we shall not know.

At the hearing of an application by a bookmaker for the renewal of his Betting Office Licence a few years ago, a disappointed punter opposed it on the ground that the bookie had refused to pay out on a winning bet—or rather series of bets, for it was a 'Yankee' or some similar chain of transactions by which any winnings on one bet go on to others as stakes. The multiplication of the odds by a succession of fortuitous forecasts had served to turn a stake of seven shillings and sixpence into something over £14,000. The turf accountant conceded that that was indeed the result of the transaction, but insisted that it was not valid—except to the extent of a couple of hundred pounds—because two of the races upon which constituent bets were placed were less than a quarter of an hour apart.

This circumstance of itself would not ordinarily invalidate a bet, but that particular betting shop's Rule Book provided that there would be a limit to what they would pay out on any multiple bets where the races were so close in time. The Rule Book also provided that these rules should apply to all bets struck in that shop. The ordinary law does not recognise betting transactions, but there is a limited remedy for a disappointed punter to oppose a licence to a Bookmaker with whose dealings he is dissatisfied. This punter alleged that the Rule Book did not apply because he had specifically requested the manager what would be the terms of his bet, and the Rule Book and the quarter-hour rule had not been mentioned in reply. The manager said that he was quite sure he had referred the gentleman to the Rule Book, and instanced as a supporting fact the circumstance that notices prominently displayed on the walls of the betting shop reminded patrons that the Rule Book governed all transactions. With that statement, the gambler profoundly disagreed, and it looked very much as if the Licensing Committee would have a serious dispute to resolve. But into their chamber came two men in overalls bearing a stud partition wall with frayed plaster edges where it had been rent from the premises to prove that fact. Firmly attached thereto with transparent adhesive plastic was such a notice, which anyone with moderately good eyesight could have read without glasses at three or four paces.

This appeared to satisfy the Committee that the manager was right and the punter mistaken, although he pointed out that it was much easier to stick a notice on a wall than to tear the wall out of the betting shop.

In *Archbold 37th Edition*, the index states 'Proof—See Evidence'. Nowhere under 'Evidence' does it claim to tell you where to find the meaning of 'Proof'. Burden of proof, yes, but no proof itself. The two things are quite different. The burden is merely the responsibility of achieving that undefined phenomenon. It is the function of a judge to decide for a jury whether certain facts are capable of being evidence to prove something. If there is no such evidence available, he must refuse to let them decide the case. For they are charged to decide the matter according to the evidence. In criminal cases the jury have to be satisfied of the guilt of an accused person 'beyond reasonable doubt'. Lord Chief Justice Goddard in *R. v. Summers (1952)* said:

148

The same criterion of proof applies to cases in the Magistrates' Courts. There is a body of opinion to the effect that the Justices and Stipendiary Magistrates in these courts regard the evidence of prosecution witnesses, particularly policemen, as incapable of controversion. This is only the notion that the prisoner would not be in the dock if he had not done it. If that view is held by any magistrate, he or she is breaking the oath which they all take on appointment to 'do right between all manner of persons'. Their venality is upon their consciences. There may well be retribution elsewhere, but there is none under the law of England.

Sergeant Arabin explained the position to an Old Bailey jury in 1835:

> *'. . . if he can show precisely at what moment it was done, and that the prisoner was not there when he did it, and if so he could not do it.'*
>
> **Arabiniana, cited in *Arabinesque-at-Law*, by Mr Justice Megarry.**

But he was, as usual, wrong: the prisoner need prove nothing. He often does prove a great deal. Many a weak prosecution case has been improved out of recognition by the insistence of the prisoner on his statutory right to testify. For the very appearance, demeanour, conduct of some people can persuade a tribunal about some fact without him saying a word.

There was a dispute about a piano in one of the South London County Courts not long ago. An auctioneer sued a bidder for the price of the instrument, but the defence was raised that delivery of the correct piano had not been made. A light coloured piano had been bought, and a dark one had been tendered and refused. There was a great deal of evidence about the different lot numbers and how the porter had clearly pointed to the right piano and then the porter was called into the witness box. As soon as he faced the judge, the case was decided, for the poor man was acutely cross-eyed. It is for such reasons as these that when a factual dispute is raised on an appeal, the Appeal judges so often shake their heads and remark, 'The judge saw the witnesses'.

The best comfort for anyone who has decisions to make is the attitude of the great Victorian Master of the Rolls, Sir George Jessel, 'I may be wrong. I sometimes am. But I never doubt'. Chancery judges, of course, have to feel as confident about their deductions as that because the facts in their cases are usually agreed, and it is only the inferences and the law that they can make mistakes about. The chances of being upset on appeal are therefore much stronger.

There is probably less truth and more distortion in a matrimonial dispute than in any other kind. Alibi witnesses in the trials of professional criminals are often speaking perfect truth about Harry Boy being indoors all evening watching the telly. The only trouble is that it is truth about a different evening, not the one on which the crime was committed. However, the evidence because what is being described is true, manages to convey intrinsic credibility, which is all that is demanded of it. This kind of testimony is therefore suspect among experienced criminal practitioners. The former Recorder of London, Sir Gerald Dodson, more than once summed up in these words:

> '*An alibi, Members of the Jury, is the best defence there is—if you believe it.*'

That is, actually, a wrong direction on the Burden of Proof, for the jury do not have to believe a word the accused says in order to acquit him.

> '*If at any period of a trial it was permissible for the Judge to rule that the prosecution had established its case and that the onus was shifted on the prisoner to prove that he was not guilty . . . it would be enabling the Judge to say that the jury must in law find the prisoner guilty, and so make the Judge decide the case and not the jury, which is not the Common Law . . .*'

> '*Throughout the web of the English Criminal Law one golden thread is always to be seen, that it is the duty of the prosecution to prove the prisoner's guilt . . .*'

> **Viscount Sankey, Lord Chancellor in *Woolmington* v. D.P.P. (1935) A.C. 462.**

That case of Reginald Woolmington was the only one in which a man was ever saved from the gallows by appealing to the House of Lords. He had shot his wife. He made three highly incriminating statements. The couple were on bad terms and parted. He sawed the barrels off a shotgun, loaded it, hid it, and then went to her. A neighbour heard him ask her to return, and the door slammed. Then the neighbour heard the shot. The jury had to infer whether he had a criminal intention when he pulled the trigger.

His defence was that he had no intention of killing his wife, merely to ask her to return to him. The gun went off by accident. Mr Justice Rigby Swift in his summing-up read the law from the current edition of Archbold's Criminal Pleading to the jury. It said that once the killing was proved, accident, necessity or some other excuse or justification had to be proved by the prisoner. The Court of Criminal Appeal said that this was right—and it was based on *Foster's Crown Law*, an authoritative work since 1762. But the

House of Lords said that it was wrong, and made innocence until guilt is proved the law as well as the popular impression.

The Woolmington doctrine gives way, of course, to the burden on the prisoner to prove insanity, and also to some statutory requirements expressly requiring the prisoner to prove something, such as that a car is licensed or insured when it is on a public road.

It is perhaps as well that prisoners do not have to prove themselves innocent because that would be even more difficult to do than for the Crown to prove them guilty. Not that the rigidity of the rules of evidence and heavy burden of proof are always demanded. It is perfectly possible for a person to be convicted of receiving stolen property (now part of the offence of handling stolen goods governed by *S. 22* of the *Theft Act, 1968*) without it ever being proved that the goods were stolen by distinct evidence. The circumstances in which the receiver has the goods in his possession may themselves 'prove' the goods are stolen.

People are convicted in this way, very often, on the authority of *R*. v. *Fuschillo* (*1940*) *27 Cr. App. R.* He had a much larger quantity of sugar than he could lawfully have obtained, in those days of stringent rationing, and a case from the First War showed that no direct evidence that the goods were stolen was needed. Quite often when the loser of the goods cannot be traced someone is convicted and sentenced under this doctrine. The usual defence is that the goods were in some way abandoned or obtained from someone untraceable. It is possible in all of these cases that they might not have been stolen at all.

One great advantage the prisoner does enjoy here over some other countries, such as France, is that the prisoner's character is not discussed during the trial unless he elects to bring it into controversy by claiming that he has a good character when he has not, or by attacking prosecution witnesses in such a way that he puts his own character in issue. The Continental idea is that the kind of man he is is relevant to assist in the decision whether he committed a crime. The English notion is that just because he did something else it does not mean he committed the crime charged. This makes the case of *John Straffen* (*1952*) *2 Q.B. 911* somewhat odd. He was charged with strangling a little girl in April, 1952. His confessions to two similar murders the previous year were received in evidence, not, said the court, to show that he was a 'professional strangler' but on the question of identity of the murderer of the 1952 victim.

The distinction between admitting evidence to identify a prisoner as the criminal, and excluding it when it only shows a tendency to commit certain offences might savour somewhat of casuistry, but in its anxious care to protect the prisoner from conviction in the absence of proof beyond reasonable doubt, the criminal law cannot overlook its responsibility to all the rest of us—any of whom might be next.

Juries are very often told, however, that they might like to consider the effect of the prisoner telling an untruth. The technical position is that a false statement made by an accused person before proceedings are begun, or to a policeman, may be corroboration of some necessary fact showing guilt but is not necessarily so. The modern leading case for that is *Credland* v. *Knowler 35 Cr. App. R. 48* decided by the Queen's Bench Divisional Court in 1951.

But that is a far cry from saying that anyone who tells lies must be guilty of the offence he is charged with. A great many people questioned in connection with offences tell lies. They tell them so that their wives will not find out where they have been and with whom, and to cover up for other people. They also tell them in the hope of being left alone, and because they do not want to 'shop' their friends. A man might well tell lies if he is guilty, but how lying can prove that he is, in fact, guilty is not clear. Nevertheless it is the last desperate resort of many a prosecutor. They sometimes run two steps into one, suggest that the accused is lying, must therefore be lying for a purpose, and try to 'prove' their case with the simple negative appeal of a complete *non sequitur.*

Judges do it as well. It is a misdirection for which a conviction will be quashed to tell a jury

> '. . . *he was fully entitled to refuse to answer questions; he has an absolute right to do that, and it is not to be held against him that he did that. But you might well think that, if a man is innocent, he would be anxious to answer all questions.*'
>
> **R. v. *Sullivan* (1966) 51 Cr. App R. 102.**

It is, however, perfectly all right for a judge to let a jury know that he does not think much of a defendant's story, so long as he makes it plain to them that it is up to them whether they believe it or not. A favourite form of direction is, 'He has to prove nothing'.

Judges and magistrates are not the only people gifted with capacity for conviction. Some jurors possess it to a remarkable degree. It was widely feared in the mid-Sixties, as the result of one or two 'nobbling' efforts that perversity in some jurors might be inspired by more than mere stubbornness. The great constitutional revolution of accepting majority verdicts was therefore enacted by the *Criminal Justice Act, 1967.* Many eminent judges opposed this reform, for unanimity of the jury has been a cornerstone of the 'innocence till proved guilty' idea. However, much of the rest of the Act was designed to save time and therefore money in the administration of justice; there was a big backlog of cases waiting to be tried and principle has so often before been sacrificed on the altar of expediency by politicians that there is every likelihood that it was done again. Not many people took it up as the Bill went through Parliament. There are not many votes in the criminal classes outside, and those inside are deprived of their votes *pro. tem.* by the *Representation of the People Act, 1949.*

Where one or two people on a jury stick out against unanimity, and cause disagreement, considerable public expense is incurred. The trial has to be had all over again. But to imagine that the dissidents are always fatheads trying to obstruct an obviously proper conviction is another *non sequitur.* They might well be the intelligent ones insisting that the case is not properly proved. Or they might equally be the only two who can see that the accused is guilty whilst the others are trying to spring him because of a successful smokescreen defence. However, the notion that the minority could be right seems not to have occurred to the legislators —even the Opposition.

Much the most difficult aspect of evidence is the analysis of it to indicate not only whether certain things happened, but how they happened and what ramifications the happenings had.

'Many good lawyers have failed completely as judges of the facts,'

said Lord Greene MR, addressing the Holdsworth Club in 1938. That has not prevented the fact-finding work of judges being much increased in the past generation. What has to be ascertained, he said, are the material facts, and this calls for an appreciation of what is material.

One would have thought that the essential prerequisite to deciding whether certain things have happened, and whether certain people did them, and what were the underlying reasons, would be to comprehend fairly clearly what actually occurred. The big difference between judges and jurors is that judges have to try to understand cases in case there is an appeal, whilst jurors do not have to understand a word.

Even if they are sufficiently conscientious to provide themselves with papers and pencils with which to make *aides memoires*—only very rarely furnished by the authorities—most jury boxes have no desk or shelf on which to write. Intelligent participation in the complexities of the forensic process by jurors has always been discouraged.

'Come awa' and let us hang these rascals,'

Lord Braxfield, the Lord Justice Clerk invited an Edinburgh jury in the 1790s.

The job of the jury was to spare the wretched from the law. Advocacy was consequently directed to whether what the prisoner did was reprehensible even though unlawful—moral rather than legal considerations. Much of it was therefore strictly irrelevant, but it did not prevent the drama of the trial court being a popular superstition and a free entertainment. Very gradually however there had developed among the judges a feeling that they should elucidate for the benefit of the jury.

When the Quarter Sessions came to be presided over by barristers there were some who developed the knack of saying all that had to be said—according to Archbold—in a smooth, easy, accurate, and totally unintelligible patter which, of course, looked absolutely right on the transcript of the shorthand note which the Appeal Judges saw. The fact that the jurors collectively or severally had not understood a word of it has never been a recognised ground of appeal. Nor would the English legal theory admit it.

Since the jurors are entirely unknown quantities all a judge has to do is to explain in language which he thinks ordinary people understand. But his ideas of what ordinary people understand and the capacity of that jury might be a long way apart.

Before the creation of the London Boroughs in 1965 there was a phenomenon known as a West Ham Jury at the Quarter Sessions holden for the County Borough of that name. These juries revealed a marked disinclination to convict dockers of anything. It was widely believed that no person accused of drunkenness in charge of a motor vehicle had ever been convicted there but this is totally untrue. A policeman who had been connected with the court for 30 years remembered both convictions.

One crime which no West Ham jury would tolerate was indecency —in whatever form it was charged and whether the accused was guilty or not. Since the catchment area for the jurors has been expanded to take in Woodford and Chingford, of course, radical changes have occurred. Many people accused of drinking and driving and of helping themselves to other peoples' goods are convicted, but some of the people accused of indecent practices are acquitted. Old West Ham jurors are very shocked at the onset of Permissiveness.

There is a body of reformist opinion which demands that 'complicated fraud cases' should be taken away from juries and entrusted to judges alone or in threes, or judges with technical assessors. In civil cases, the right to a jury for defamation, malicious prosecution and fraud cases can be denied where long and involved examination of accounts or documents is required. It would probably be a great benefit to sophisticated crooks. The conviction rate on complicated frauds is high. The jurors work either on the assumption that a rich man is no more likely to enter the kingdom of Heaven than a camel is to pass through the eye of a needle, or

154

more simply, that they would not be in the dock if they had not done it.

It must be confessed that some appeals in fraud cases succeed because the summing-up reveals that the judge did not understand the case, either. Very often the only people who understand the case are the accused and some of the counsel. Since the accused often keep the true state of affairs to themselves and let everyone else make the best guesses they can, the whole thing is often decided on the theories of the counsel and the judge as to what occurred. If the judge is demonstrably wrong the accused gets away with it— whether or not he was guilty.

The public are duly impressed by the enormous figures, but they do not want to know the minutiae of fraud cases. Dr Emil Savundra was not imprisoned for eight years because Fire Auto and Marine Insurance Co. Ltd. was liquidated, leaving 400,000 motorists un-insured. He was convicted for making a false statement in some accounts. That might have had little to do with the company's collapse. John Bloom was fined £30,000 for bad accountancy. The reason for the collapse of the Rolls Razor washing machine enterprise was that it did not sell enough washing machines at enough profit. However romantic the stories of great wealth, they rarely command much close attention.

The biggest financial collapse case of the century was undoubtedly the failure of Clarence Hatry's Drapery Trust group in 1929. A crash of £13,500,000 in those days was equivalent to about ten times the figure now, not just because money was worth more but because businesses were smaller. But although special seating arrangements were made at the Old Bailey in anticipation of a huge increase in spectators there was not even an increase in the usual line up for entry to the court. The public care little for lots of figures, whether or not they lie. The opening speech of Sir William Jowitt KC, the Attorney-General, who prosecuted, was acclaimed by the legal profession as a masterpiece. Who remembers him?

When the solicitor, Frederick Grunwald and the director of the State Building Society were on trial in 1960 everyone knew the vague background. The State's money had been used to buy shares and the share deals were directed in the end to a take-over for Lintang Investments Ltd. which controlled among other properties the 1,200 flats at Dolphin Square on the Thames bank in West London. Frederick Beney QC, a very fine advocate, then aged 76, was explaining to the jury that what was alleged to be criminal was the misuse of the money of the building society:

> *'If this was illegal—and Grunwald was not a director—. . . and you*
> *come to the conclusion that the motive underlying those responsible*

155

for this was to serve the interests of the State Building Society to the best of their ability . . .'

When Mr Justice Paull intervened:

'I shall direct the jury that that is not the right way to approach this problem. It is absolute nonsense. You cannot tell the jury that the best way to support someone is to commit illegal acts. It is quite nonsense.

'If what you say is right it would be a complete answer for every burglar to state that to commit burglary was the only way he could support his wife. That would be the answer for every criminal in the country. I shall direct the jury that if the directors of the State Building Society chose to use its money in a way that they knew was illegal which will bring benefit to themselves that is quite sufficient to support the charge of fraudulent conversion. Whether it will ultimately benefit the Society is neither here nor there. It is the same as an office boy who takes ten shillings out of the office till and puts it on a horse in the Derby saying "I know it will win, and when it wins I will put it back". That is fraudulent conversion.'

All absolutely right. But Beney's point was that Grunwald was not a director, and so, of course, could not actually move money out of the Society. Of course, he could convert it once it was out of their coffers. Whether sharp quillets of the law like this impress jurors is doubtful. But the elucidation that suggests that manipulating £3,205,000 to make a £7 million take-over bid is just the same as 'borrowing' the tea money gets home.

On 10th July, 1960, the judge apologised to Mr Beney for those sharp criticisms.

Many of the frauds reported in the Press as highly complicated and demanding quantities of papers for counsel which have to be delivered in vans are essentially simple. Local authorities are induced to lend money on mortgages by false statements about the ability of the borrower to repay, quite often. It is only another little step to make up a fictitious borrower. The great series of agricultural lime frauds in the early Sixties turned simply on whether the statements on the Ministry's forms were true. A two-thirds subsidy was paid of the price of the quantity of lime delivered. The only question therefore was how much lime was in fact delivered. If it was more or less what appeared on the form nothing was wrong. If the claim was exaggerated, was it done by mistake or dishonestly? Nevertheless one of the cases got into a dreadful muddle.

Sir James Fitzjames Stephen, the remarkable late Victorian judge and legal author, wrote leaders for the Pall Mall Gazette on the side. This connection with the world outside the law might have inspired his attitude to the inferences drawn in litigation:

156

'Proof is nothing more than a presumption of the highest order', Lord Erskine had said in the *Banbury Peerage Case* (reported in Mr Nicholas's work on Adulterine Bastardy).

The presumption of the legitimacy of a baby is perhaps the most powerful known to the law. It had to be rebutted by proof beyond reasonable doubt that a husband could not have begotten the child. Quite recently the disputes of gynaecologists threw the law into a considerable uncertainty. A gestation of 300 days or more was perfectly possible, said some. In *Preston-Jones* v. *Preston-Jones (1951) A.C. 391* the Law Lords agreed that they could take 'judicial notice' i.e. dispense with formal evidence of the fact that normal gestation is 270 or 280 days.

Section 26 of the *Family Law Reform Act, 1969*—no doubt to buttress the institution of marriage—enacted that the presumptions of legitimacy or of illegitimacy can be rebutted by that lesser standard of proof 'the balance of probabilities'. Whether the different standards of proof are any more helpful to the ordinary man than to Lord Goddard may be doubted.

Lord Coleridge dilated on the probative force of circumstance at the Newcastle Summer Assize of 1910.

> '*One may describe it as a network of facts cast round the accused man. That network may be a mere gossamer thread, as light and insubstantial as the air itself. It may vanish at a touch. It may be that, strong as it is in part, it leaves great gaps through which the accused is entitled to pass in safety. It may be so close, so stringent, so coherent, in its texture that no efforts on the part of the accused can break through. It may come to nothing—on the other hand it may be absolutely convincing. The law does not demand that you should act on certainties alone. In our lives, in our acts, in our own thoughts, we do not deal with certainties. We ought to act upon just and reasonable convictions founded on just and reasonable grounds. The law asks for no more and the law demands no less.*'

R. v. *Dickman.*

Baron Alderson thought that:

> '*It was necessary to warn the jury against the danger of being misled by a train of circumstantial evidence. The mind was apt to take a pleasure in adapting circumstances . . . even straining them a little if need be, to force them to form parts of one connected whole; and the more ingenious the mind of the individual, the more likely was it in considering such matters, to overreach and mislead itself, to supply some little link that is wanting, to take for granted*

157

some fact consistent with its previous theories and necessary to render them complete.'

R. v. Hodges (1838) 2 Lewin C.C. 227.

As might have been expected from Chief Justice Hewart, circumstantial evidence:

'of undesigned coincidence, is capable of proving a proposition with the accuracy of mathematics.'

R. v. Taylor and others (1928) 21 Cr. App. Rep. 20.

However, logical precision does not always result from mathematics. Lord Donovan said in a libel appeal that:

'it was plain that each one of the six witnesses had put two and two together and made it a good deal more than four'

Morgan v. Odhams Press Ltd. (1971) 2 All E.R. @ P. 1180.

Inference from facts must not be left to surmise, conjecture or guess, insisted Lord Justice Buckley (*(1911) 1 K.B. 988*).

How then could the Court of Appeal in Mrs Hough's libel action against the *Daily Express* in 1940 have held that she was libelled? The story in the paper said that all the fights in which Frank Hough boxed were anxiously watched by his 'wife'. But the lady was not his wife. His real wife claimed that that would make people think she was not his wife. The witnesses she called could hardly think that. They had danced at the wedding. Maybe, said the court, but other people might think so.

The inferential powers revealed by individual judges, and those expected of jurors are therefore infinite in their variety. But judges have to draw much more difficult inferences than jurors. Not only must their inferences stand the scrutiny of their elder brethren in the appellate courts, but they must deal effectively with the arguments of the counsel. And no hypothesis is too remote for some advocates. The late Mr Donald Bain QC, when Chancellor of the Ipswich Diocese in 1962 was hearing an application to move the valuable font from a little used church to another. In his judgment he acknowledged the force of the argument that if Britain entered the Common Market more trade might develop in the district, and the population would grow, and the church might be brought back into frequent use, and it would of course, need a font—its own font.

The Chancery Division is the place for deductive inference. There was a fashion for a long time of making the settlements of wealthy families dependent on the lives of members of the Royal Family. The law requires that a trust should take effect during a life in being and 21 years thereafter, and the value of naming a young member of the Royal Family is that future lawyers will have no difficulty in finding out whether the 'life' is in being or not because a death in the Royal Family always gets in the papers. At the turn of the century, the relevant lives were sometimes expressed to be 'the great grandchildren of Her Majesty Queen Victoria, now living'. That would, of course, keep the trust funds accumulating for many years. The only trouble was that when the Czar and his family were butchered at Ekaterinburg on the 16th July, 1918, his youngest daughter, the Princess Anastasia, might not have perished.* She might be alive today. Faced with this situation the judges can infer that she is dead or not as they please. *Re Dawson (1888) 39 Ch. D. 155* demonstrates their powers of inference in this connection. The trust was for a woman over 60, and then to her children who reached the age of 21—which they all had done already. However, the court ruled that the mother was still capable of having a child, who might die before 21 leaving however, a child of his or her own, who could not inherit within 21 years of his grandmother's death. The trust was therefore invalid. Professor Barton Leach in his book on *The Rule against Perpetuities P. 89* suggested that the world the judges live in is populated by fertile octogenarians. Evidence is therefore often given in such cases by doctors who declare that women don't have babies after menopause. Now that there are some women on the Bench perhaps 'judicial notice' will be taken of that. Where the trust deed was made after 1964, the *Perpetuities and Accumulations Act* of that year enables the judge to presume that a man cannot beget a child when he is under 14 and that a woman can only have children between the ages of 12 and 55. But the old law applies to pre-1964 trusts and evidence is necessary.

It is a good policy to have evidence of every possible point in any litigation in case the judge is not very observant in the 'judicial notice' field. If anyone should be sorry to see judges' general knowledge improving it is those journalists who delight in reporting their ignorance. But there is a distressing tendency now for judges to be 'with it'. Mr Justice Lawton even confessed not long ago 'I read the newspapers', and spoilt an illuminating explanation of exactly what counsel was talking about.

However the difficulties of Chancery judges are that they often have to infer what was meant in documents written by people who are dead. By the ordinary Canons of Construction, as the law professors grandly denominate the rules for working out what legal documents mean, in a proper document, such as an Act of Parliament, the rule is that the words must be given their plain ordinary meaning, and so as to avoid absurdity. This is called The Golden

---

* A B.B.C. T.V. feature in January, 1972, suggested that none of them died.

Rule, notwithstanding that there are no Golden Rules according to George Bernard Shaw.

Mr Justice Harman got the judges' own back on Shaw when he held in *(1951) 1 W.L.R. 729* that George Bernard Shaw's bequest by will of the income from his works for the research and development of 'the Proposed British Alphabet' of 40 letters was not a valid trust. It was, he said, the proceeds of the musicals and films based on 'Pygmalion' which had 'enabled the executor to get on terms with the existing death duties payable on the estate' which brought the interpretation of the will into practical politics.

> *'The Testator, whatever his other qualifications, was the master of a pellucid style, and the reader embarks on his will confident of finding no difficulty in understanding the objects which the Testator had in mind. This document, moreover, was evidently originally the work of a skilled equity draftsman.'*

Nevertheless the trusts were not enforceable. However, the more common failing is that a will is not sufficiently certain to be enforced. The intention to be collected is what the Testator meant. This may involve departure from the plain, ordinary meaning.

The Chancery judges can therefore allow themselves a bit of imaginative latitude when metaphysically 'sitting in the Testator's armchair when he made his will'. The chances of them being right every time are not good. Many troublesome testaments come into existence as Mr Justice Harman described:

> *'The Testator made his will by the expedient which so many testators adopt of buying a sixpenny form and filling it in . . . he no doubt thought he had done a good day's work, as for the legal profession, he had.'*

Professionally drafted wills do not always survive judicial scrutiny, particularly when subjected to expert destruction, from counsel retained by the people who would benefit from intestacy. A will which does not clearly indicate what is to be done with some or all of the estate can be declared invalid for uncertainty, and then the intestacy rules apply. Evidence of the Testator's intention is permitted in stringently controlled circumstances. It is seldom lacking. The number of people who can be called forward to testify in support of a hopeful friend or relative is often large. Take the simple case of a bequest: 'To my nephew, William'.*

However, equivocal references are now treated as latent ambiguities, at least in cases where beneficiaries have the same name. Quite patently, they are not.

---

* See page **403**.

If, therefore, evidence can be heard in court to help the judge decide which William is intended in the will when there is more than one William, is evidence received to fill in a name where the Testator left a blank? Decidedly not. (*Re. de Rosaz [1877] 2 P.D. 66.*) The rule is that will must speak from death, not that it can be contradicted by survivors. Although in the Middle Ages to die intestate was like dying unsanctified (and so go to Hell) the rules of intestacy now provide so generously for wives and relatives that a man's duty might easily be better done by distributing his estate without reference to his will. There must be thousands of wills which never come to light when people die. It is quite common for someone to make a will and leave it with a solicitor, or in a safe place, and then move away from the neighbourhood, and die some long time afterwards apparently intestate.

Much of the uncertainty in wills is caused by attempts to avoid taxes. Lawyers are the main beneficiaries from such instruments, for whether the Revenue or the relatives get the money, the costs will be paid from the estate. Most people litigate to spite the taxman. Much learning is necessary to make a good tax plan. Like every other testamentary disposition, it depends on the forecast of events which will happen being correct.

It must be quite maddening, for instance, for a rich man to settle all his fortune on his son as soon as he comes of age so as to get the maximum advantage in payment of Estate Duty—or even to give it all to his children so that he shall pay no duty if he survives seven years after the gift—and then for the youngster to die first. Think how often rich youngsters die in car and plane crashes. The father in such a case has no remedy at all even though he has been impoverished by the death of his 'successor'.

What more can a man do for someone, asked Dr Johnson, than to make a will in his favour and die on the spot?

It is very sound advice in those bank brochures, that you should make a will to prevent your nearest and dearest having problems 'should anything happen to you', and so that the Executor and Trustee Department's trade can be increased. Corporate executors have the great advantage of never dying themselves. The Public Trustee is similarly blessed. Solicitor executors are mortal, and when they die, their executor becomes your executor—and executor of all his other clients. Solicitors cannot be blamed for dying, of course, but they can be blamed for drawing invalid wills, and unhappily they sometimes do. But more often the will is not invalid—simply wrong. But it is the only evidence of what the Testator intended. No one can gainsay it. It is one of the few pieces of evidence someone is not permitted to contradict.

Feme et Baron*

'*Marriage is an institution. Who wants to live in an institution?*'

Groucho Marx.

FOR THE MAJOR part of our history, no ceremony was necessary for the celebration of a lawful marriage. The only reason for a ceremony becoming necessary was the convenience thereby afforded in the proof of status. The date and time of the ceremony determines the point in time after which sexual intercourse operates to establish a legal relationship. There are however, certain conditions precedent to the contract of marriage.

The first of these to be considered is an illustration of the distinction between man-made and natural law. The natural law is expressed in *Matthew 19: 4–6* and *Mark 10: 6–9*:

> '*He who made them from the beginning made them male and female.*'

Upon marriage, according to *Genesis 2: 24*:

> '. . . *a man shall leave father and mother and shall cleave to his wife, and they shall be two in one flesh.*'

Mr Justice McCardie pointed out that the actual joining was 'only occasional and of short duration' (*Gotliffe* v. *Edelston* [*1930*] *2 K.B. 378*). This might be thought a natural enough impression for a bachelor, although Lord Justice Scrutton once had occasion to point out that:

> '*For a gentleman who has never been married, the Learned Judge shows a considerable knowledge of ladies' underclothing.*'

Both Matthew and Mark had made it perfectly clear (at least in the Revised Standard Version, which may possibly benefit from hindsight) that:

> '. . . *the two shall become one so they are no longer two but one.*'

---

* Viner's and Bacon's *Abridgements* both put the man first in this title. However, I face facts and this is more polite.

This denies the natural sciences (biology and mathematics) but it is the foundation of the marriage law of England, and much of the rest of the world.

Mr Justice Ormrod, who, as the *Evening Standard* never fails to point out, is a doctor as well as a lawyer, stated the modern law of the marriage basis with his customary lucidity as recently as February, 1970. He was giving judgment upon 'the essentially pathetic but almost incredible' case of the 'marriage' between Arthur Cameron Corbett and April Ashley, who had a sex-change operation beforehand (*1970*) *2 All E.R. 33*).

April Ashley changed her name by deed poll, from George Jameson, and obtained a passport stating that she was female. Attempts to persuade a Superintendent Registrar to change her birth certificate had failed, but the Ministry of National Insurance treated her as a woman. The question for the court was whether she was a man or a woman.

> '*Since marriage is essentially a relationship between a man and a woman, the validity of the marriage in this case depends in my judgment on whether the Respondent is or is not a woman . . . My conclusion is that the Respondent is not a woman for the purposes of marriage but is a biological male and has been so since birth. It follows that the so-called marriage on 10th September, 1963 is void . . . Marriage is a relationship which depends on sex and not on gender.*'

And that was the second telling point. Marriage has depended on sex for centuries and still does. Given a man and a woman, it still needs sex. Sex after the ceremony, nowadays. Pre-marital sex is not sufficiently potent to carry over its legal effect to seal the ceremony. The doctrine of relation—back to the inception of the legal process, which holds sway in bankruptcy and kindred matters—is unknown in the law of marriage. This important principle was not decided until 1947.

However, the necessity of sex to create a valid marriage was a live controversy in the Middle Ages. Marriage was quite a sophisticated business by then. The theologian Peter Lombard insisted that it was the ceremony or solemn promise which actually made the marriage. *Concensus non concubitus facit matrimonium* was his doctrine, but it was not accepted. To this day, consummation is required. The way this came about is blamed on St Paul. Few texts have done more harm than 'It is better to marry than to burn' (*Corinthians 1:7:9*). It has supported the presumption of a legally binding marriage where there was no evidence at all of one ever having been contracted. The alternative for the ecclesiastical courts was to declare man and woman cohabiting mere fornicators, their issue bastards not entitled to inherit, the widow denied her sustenance in old age.

Thus was developed the concept of the English Common Law marriage, which by its own hypothesis was no marriage, but a union implied to defeat hellfire.

The modern translation of Corinthians does not say 'burn' but 'be aflame with passion'. This is capable of the interpretation that if you are not particularly passionate, you had better marry. This accords with the more modern tendency to regard marriage in the nature of a contract, but that is not free from difficulties in principle. A marriage has long been regarded as good consideration for a contract. Bargains such as 'If you marry me I will make a will in your favour' are long established. But the marriage as contract of itself has difficulties. What is the price? A contract without consideration has long been denied the force of law because it is *nudum pactum*. Marriage appears therefore to be the only nude pact valid in English law.

In 1765, Mr Justice Blackstone (*Commentaries Book 1, cap. 15 (1) p. 433*) wrote: 'Our law considers marriage in no other light than as a civil contract'. ('Civil' in this context refers to its jurisprudential character, rather than its manner of performance.) 'The holiness of the matrimonial state is left entirely to the ecclesiastical law,' he continued. But of course, the Ordinaries exercised temporal law. Their decrees of judicial separation and restitution of conjugal rights and alimony were not mere expressions of pious preference, but judgments enforceable between husband and wife.

The classical definition is that of Lord Stowell:

> '*It is a contract . . . which may take place to all intents and purposes, whenever two persons of different sexes engage, by mutual contracts to live together . . . A mere casual commerce, without the intention of co-habitation and bringing up of children, would not constitute marriage under any supposition . . .*'
>
> **Lindo v. Belisario (1795) 1. Hag. Con. 216 at 230.**

The bringing up of children (and even the conception and birth of them) is no longer essential to marriage. The House of Lords did away with those supposed requirements in 1947 (*Weatherley* v. *Weatherley [1947] A.C. 628; Baxter* v. *Baxter [1948] A.C. 274*). Until then, however,

> '. . . *the first cause and reason of matrimony ought to be the design of having an offspring; the second ought to be the avoiding of fornication*'

said Sir John Nicholl in *Greenstreet* v. *Cumyns [1812] 2 Hag. Con. 332*.)

There is nowadays a vicar who thinks he ought not to call upon brides and grooms to take each other until death do them part. It is at least arguable that if they do not, they will not be validly married. The Court of Appeal explained in *Nachimson* v. *Nachimson* (*1930*) *P. 217*, that the couple must intend when they marry that it should last for their lives—even though that might be a triumph of hope over expectation. Judicial divorce had been available for eight years when Lord Penzance said:

> '*I conceive that marriage, as understood in Christendom, may be defined as the voluntary union for life of one man and one woman to the exclusion of all others.*'
>
> **Hyde** v. **Hyde and Woodmansee (1866) L.R. 1 P. & D. 130.**

He was also aware that defects in the organs can prevent consummation; physiological ambiguities could have the same result. But he was stating the law, not making it. The law of marriage is not the only law which has its foundation in the religious regimen which became the Canon Law of Rome. Christianity became lawful in Rome—and therefore Britain—in 313 A.D. A few years later the Christians were putting the pagans to death (in spite of Constantine's Edict of Tolerance, 314 A.D.). From this time dates the white dress of the bride and the wedding breakfast. Formality has the great virtue of crystallising a relationship. Marriage creates a multitude of rights and liabilities. The lawyers, striving for definition of the precise instant at which a right comes into existence, look for the metamorphosis from one state to the next as the crystallographer watches for the first tiny precipitate. But none of these things is important until something goes wrong. Until then, validity is immaterial.

Ritual is a sentimental, emotional thing until the relationship is called in question. Thereafter it becomes vital. The absence of a white dress or the inadequacy of the wedding feast to this day excites condemnation among the relations, but neither amounts to a breach of the 'requirement of due form' which is the technical denomination of a ritual shortcoming sufficient to annul a marriage. The Romans did not have to bother about that sort of thing. Their *divortium* was a casual manifestation of the potent power of the head of the family. (They called it *patria potestas*.) A *paterfamilias* in the great days of Rome could have a wife, or a son, or his son's wife, put to death. He was considered a rarely charitable chap if he merely declared the marriage finished. Informal divorce, however, did not catch on. Informal marriage did. Nowadays in Britain there is more formality to drawing the dole than in a Register Office marriage. But beneath the disenchanting facade a great deal of form lies concealed, and much of it is very necessary for legal marriage. It is a long and devious story.

'With this ring I thee wed,' throws us back to the Anglo-Saxons living in marsh and forest, and very sensibly doing without judges and solicitors. Their government was effectively pursued through respect for the judgments of the heads of the families, backed when necessary by the muscular power of the sons and brothers-in-law. Similar sub-cultures are to be found in the Mediterranean Islands and the East End of London. (Indeed, most of the inhabitants of the Mediterranean Islands will soon live in the East End of London by virtue of the singularly inept immigration laws which have been made in the past ten years.)

The encouragement to marriage engendered by these means is regarded by the law nowadays as wrong, but oddly enough the first system of police in these islands was founded upon it. When a murderer was apprehended by the Saxon victim's kin they did not put him to death. They demanded from him *wergild*. (Claims for such compensation nowadays are addressed to the Criminal Injuries Compensation Board.) The taking of *wergild* was a very formal ceremony. Those present included the *bohr*—people willing to be sureties for the criminal meeting his obligations. The offender would give *wed*—a symbolic security of small value for his meeting his liability. After all, he would have to get in the harvest before he could make the first payment to the relatives for the maintenance of the widow and children. The usual form of *wed* was a finger-ring.

Thus did the atonement of the criminal become the gage of eternal fidelity between groom and bride. But it was only betrothal, a binding pledge to take the girl in marriage but not the marriage itself. It was a symbol, like the morning gift to the bride, but the bride-price was no symbol but a purchase of the girl from her family, upon her removal into the groom's protection and into his family. As the ages passed a much better scale of values developed by which a girl's father would pay a dowry to the groom to get rid of the girl. But these things in due time lost their legal significance although the ritual which surrounded them remains to us as important ceremonial in what Professor Maitland called the 'cabinet of antiquities which is the marriage service of the Established Church'. A modified version is required by the Marriage Act, 1949, in most marriages today.

But before that ceremony can have effect the conditions precedent must be observed, and not the least of them is that the parties shall not only be of different sexes and of the age of sixteen but that both shall be free to marry. Mrs Marie Therese Rachelle Messina, for instance, went through a ceremony of marriage with Eugenio Messina, whose activities as a whoremaster in London were the

Sunday morning reading of the 'Fifties.

He was at the time of the ceremony on his deathbed. When he expired he left a fortune of £800,000 to be administered by the courts of San Remo. Now Madame Messina was by birth Belgian. In 1954 she married in England a Mr William George Smith, whom she met a short time before that ceremony and had not seen since. Accordingly, the marriage to Mr Messina was 'attackable', as the lawyers say, because it could be contended that it was bigamous. Bigamy as a crime was only created by James I's act of 1603 for the protection of 'Honest Men's Sons'. But by the old Civil and Canon Law, imported into the law of England, a marriage contracted whilst one partner was already validly married has always been void.

In June 1970, Mme Messina obtained a *decree nisi* declaring that the 1954 ceremony was a nullity because she did not know that it was a wedding. The effect of that judgment would be to make the marriage to Eugenio valid for she would have been free to marry. However, before the decree was made absolute Eugenio's brother, Salvatore, opposed the making of the final decree, alleging that she had put up a false case. Mme Messina returned to the Divorce Court in London on the 12th January, 1971, to claim further that Mr Smith was himself already married when he 'married' her—and so could not validly marry, and so she was free to marry Eugenio.

Her counsel was Mrs Betty Knightly (in private life the President of the Married Women's Association whose membership does not include all those qualified). Said Mrs Knightly of Mme Messina, 'She does not know where she is'. The proposition would command sympathy in any forum, but Mr Justice Ormrod retorted, 'Do let us be realistic. She does not want to know where she is, but whether she is entitled to a lot of money.'

For such trenchant and lucid expressions of the principles of the law, the English Bench is justly celebrated. Of course, before these *rationes decidendorum* are enunciated, many months have to pass after the origination of a cause (which is the lawyer's name for a case in what A. P. Herbert rather quaintly dubbed the Wills, Wives and Wrecks Division of the High Court). When the final judgment was given in May, 1971, the marriage to Mr Smith was held to be valid after all, and so Mme Messina did not inherit the fortune. She was no doubt advised about the possibilities of appealing, and it may well be that the last has not been heard of the matter. A rather similar case in some ways was that of Richard de Anesty, in 1143. He claimed lands as the heir of his uncle, but Mabel of Francheville was in possession of them.

Then as now, it was considered that 'Possession is nine points of the law' (one of the few maxims which sounds better in English than in Latin, and is not true in either). King Stephen was then in

168

Normandy and in his day the Court of King's Bench had not been invented. Anyone who wanted a writ had to go to the King's actual Court or Household and ask one of the Chancellor's clerks for it. It was no doubt somewhat analogous to applying for Legal Aid under the 1949 Act, and waiting until the solicitor sends off the form and the officials process it through the usual channels. Quite probably the wheels could be oiled by a *douceur* to the clerk in those days, but the system has done away with all that sort of thing.

Richard was of course raising a Question of General Bastardy, which topic was within the jurisdiction of the Archbishop of Canterbury. This was one result of a deal done by William the Conqueror with the Church, the effect of which was to leave the ecclesiastical courts in business after he had nationalised the Government. The question of title to land was decided in the King's Court, but the relationship in the Church Court. It is perfectly possible to this day for the two questions to be decided in different divisions of the High Court.

Richard went to France for the necessary writ authorising him to refer the matter to the Archbishop, but the King had gone to Gascony for a war. Richard followed him, and incidentally had a stroke of luck. He found out that he required as well another order permitting the Archbishop to get on with the case even though there was a war on. This was a tradition of the Civil Service which has been perpetuated in the Lord Chancellor's branch down to our own times. No litigant need ever feel unwelcome in a court office. The staff are helpfulness itself. Summonses and motions of every description are there for the asking, and every 'step in the action' has its own rules, time limits, principles, penalties, and the possibility of appeals. Of course one no longer has to go to Gascony; the Divorce Registry is at Somerset House in the Strand, and in cathedral towns and other thickly populated centres are District Registries of the High Court and Divorce County Courts.

Back in London, Richard produced the orders to the Archbishop, who held ten hearings. Richard lost. A man of principle, he appealed. This entailed another trip to France for a Royal Licence to appeal to Rome before a Court of Delegates. (Henry VIII put a stop to all that. He started his own Courts of Delegates, each of whom had to be paid by the winner of the case afterwards. This lasted until Queen Victoria's time, and it was a useful law, because the litigant who could best afford the fees always won. In that respect at least the law was certain.)

Richard won with the Delegates, but Mabel appealed to the Pope, who nevertheless decided in Richard's favour. Armed with his Papal Rescript, Richard returned to England where the King's Justices gave him judgment to take the lands as rightful heir. The case settled a legal doctrine of international importance from that day forward. Mabel was declared bastard because the formal church marriage of which she was born was void. It was bigamous. Before it took place, her father had married another woman, not in church, but by a mere informal exchange of consenting words and performing the act of sex. The first great law book of the Angevin period, by Ranulf de Glanvill, published soon after shows that this principle of the informal but consummated marriage being strong enough to prevent a proper Church wedding was then the Canon Law and the marriage law not only of England but of all Christendom. This Roman Canon Law became at the Reformation 'the King's Ecclesiastical Laws' through the *Act of Submission, 1534.* (According to Sir Edward Coke in *Caudrey's Case (1591) 5 Coke's Reports 1a at 9a.*)

Richard of Anesty's Case was backed up by a decretal from Pope Alexander III to the Bishop of Norwich in the reign of the second Henry. The law of the Ecclesiastical Courts was kept alive by the *Matrimonial Causes Act, 1857 s. 22.* Our own law of marriage has changed quite a bit, but even now some odd informal customary marriage in a jurisdiction where such things are lawful could render null and void an English ceremony performed in Caxton Hall or Westminster Abbey.

When such questions arise it is usually because some ulterior reason has arisen, often a disputed inheritance. Usually the evidence of the capacities of the bride and groom and the due performance of the marriage ritual will conflict. This all began as the result of those Anglo-Saxon betrothals. At the Conquest the mass-priest was the honoured guest at most weddings, but no special ceremony was laid down, the only really reliable proof of consummation was the bride's pregnancy, which when you come to think of it, did not prove anything. But the doctrine evolved that if the betrothed couple had only promised that they would get married, they were not married unless and until they consummated the union. This was designated by the rising class of ecclesiastical lawyer, *sponsalia de futuro*—espousal by future words. However, if they declared themselves then and there married, they were lawfully wedded whether intercourse followed or not. This was the *sponsalia per verba de praesenti.*

According to Maitland, 'In the Middle Ages, marriages, or what looked like marriages, were exceedingly insecure. The union which had existed many years . . . might with fatal ease be proved adulterous and there would be hard swearing on both sides about "I will" and "I do".'

It was, of course, the way in which people got out of inconvenient marriages before divorce was invented. Archbishop Hubert Walter,

Henry III's great Justiciar, hit upon an idea to prevent people getting out of their responsibilities, bastardising children and defeating dependants of their support and inheritance. He declared at the Lambeth Council in 1200 that no marriages should be celebrated without the Church's 'Bann' being published thrice beforehand and the ceremony taking place publicly in the presence of a priest. (The Lateran Council in 1215 spread this all over Christendom and Pope Innocent III got the credit, but it was a British invention.)

Unfortunately, it did not work. The powerful theology of Peter Lombard declaring that *concensus non concubitus facit matrimonium* did not prevail against the evidence that a man promised to marry a woman and had intercourse with her. No parson was needed in England until the Council of Trent in 1563, and the old secret marriages were valid until 1753. Their spirit lives on in the euphemism delicately applied to informal unions nowadays of 'Common Law marriage'. This dignity is frequently applied to people who appear in courts for one reason or another, and the people who use the term should know better. It is no marriage at all. The only valid marriage celebrated in England is one which satisfies the requirements of Parliament. A Common Law marriage abroad could be recognised here as valid, but here in the home of Common Law, there is no longer any such thing. *Hardwicke's Act* of 1753 was designed to stop the clandestine marriages by the unfrocked, spurious and crooked parsons of the Fleet Prison district. Adventurers married comfortably-off youngsters and so prevented the arranged marriages for which their families yearned.

Something had to be done for passion, and thus began the Gretna Green trade. Clandestine marriages lasted in Scotland until 1939. Nowadays the age-limit is the attraction. No parson was needed, merely a witness and traditionally he was the blacksmith in the first village over the Border. Over his anvil they forged the bond of matrimony with the *verba de praesenti*. Even that formality was otiose. As some men discovered when they carried a girl over the Border and possessed her on the strength of a promise not kept, they were wedded nevertheless. They called it marriage *subsequente copula* up there, but it was no more than the old *verba de futuro*, and that was enough to make a man pay maintenance.

The formless marriage had disadvantages for a woman particularly. Lord Chancellor Hardwicke was no Women's Lib. supporter but his Act made the first real move for women's rights in marriage since the Middle Ages. A widow not married in church had no rights in her husband's property. The one-third interest for life in his estate went only to the woman who had been 'endowed' at the church door. Marriage in church was a kind of retirement insurance for which the astute woman had to be vigilant. The present day marriage service of the Church of England contains it. There are espousals in the body of the church with each party saying 'I will' and the contracting of the marriage with 'I do'. The modern view is that the marriage is then complete from the ceremonial aspect (*Quick* v. *Quick* [*1953*] *V.L.R. 224*). However, as we shall see, consummation is as necessary now as ever.

Before and at the actual ceremony, formalities are required. They can be of two kinds, civil and religious, and this dual approach to marriage is the result of religious discontent in Georgian days. Jews and Quakers could marry lawfully by their own rites in England, but Dissenters and Catholics could only lawfully marry according to the rite of the Established Church. Accordingly, in 1836 the marriage law was reformed to permit them to marry according to their own ritual, and at the same time was created the civil marriage by Superintendent Registrars.

Now a marriage licence is a dispensation from publishing banns in church. First permitted as an act of grace by the *Act Concerning Peter Pence and Dispensations 1533* (*28 Hen. VIII c. 21*) it can be the best way to go about getting married because an 'undue' publications of banns or a failure to publish can make a marriage void. A 'common licence' is granted by the Bishop of the diocese, through his Chancellor or one of his Surrogates, contacted through the parish Vicar or Rector. Marriages under the Church of England rite must be solemnised by a Clerk in Holy Orders (as they are called since the Reformation). Common licence or banns permit marriage in the parish church or authorised chapel which is the usual worshipping place of either the man or the woman, or in the parish or ecclesiastical district in which either has resided for 15 days.

Some clergymen will not marry people who have been divorced, and when they wish to remarry in church, they have to find a parson willing to do it.* Some years ago some of the 'no remarriage after divorce' faction complained of arranged 'residence' qualifications in the parishes of parsons willing to marry such people. But a person can have, in law, more than one residence. University students 'reside' there during term time as well as at home (*Fox* v. *Stirk* [*1970*] *3 W.L.R. 147*). A man working away from home during the week resides at his digs. Essentially it means not just being on a temporary visit. Someone who stays at a parish just to get married there might well not reside there, but a marriage is valid even though the residence condition is broken, or the church is not the usual worshipping place of either party.

---

* A Conscience Clause in the *Mat. Causes Act, 1965*, says a clergyman cannot be compelled to marry a divorced person whose spouse is alive.

172

However, *Section 25* of the *Marriage Act, 1949*, makes the marriage void if both parties knew that the building was not one in which banns were allowed to be published, or if there were no banns, or no properly issued Registrar's certificate. This could occur where the name in which the publication took place was a false one. And thereby hang some problems. Suppose Mrs Smith, when widowed, lives with Mr Brown, because he is not free to marry, and becomes known as Mrs Brown. Her daughter, Miss Smith, will very likely come to be known in the locality as Miss Brown. If her banns were given out in the name of 'Smith', no one would know whose impending marriage was being announced. If she is cited as Brown, the name is false. For this quite common dilemma, Parliament has provided no remedy. There is nothing unlawful about being known by a name which is not your own (so long as it is not to achieve some dishonest purpose).

The judges have protected the honest person with more than one name. The case is *Chipchase* v. *Chipchase (1941) 2 All E.R. 560; P. 37.* A deserted woman had banns published in the name by which she was known for two years. This concealed that she had been married before. That was an undue publication, but the basis of the decisions was that there must be intentional concealment to amount to undue publication.

If when the banns are called for a person aged between 16 and 18 someone publicly dissents the celebration of the marriage in spite of this will make the marriage void. But a marriage by licence or Registrar's certificate is not rendered invalid by lack of consent to the marriage of a minor. The hazards of marrying after banns are therefore considerable. Banns, common licence and notice to a Registrar are all effective for three months. If the couple 'knowingly and wilfully intermarry' after the three months has run out, the marriage could be void. It is uncertain whether they have to know merely that the time limit has passed, or whether they would have to know that the effect of that would be to make the marriage void. Lord Penzance left this point undecided in *Greaves* v. *Greaves (1872) L.R. 2 P. & D. 423.*

The powerful safety factor of a Special Licence is that it permits the marriage to be solemnised anywhere and at any time. Such a potent authority can be issued only by the Archbishop of Canterbury under the authority of the *Act Concerning Peter Pence and Dispensations 1533*—which is not affected by the 1949 Act (*see s. 79* [6]). Actually, you get them from the Master of the Faculties (who is also the Dean of the Arches). They cost £25.

By comparison, the certificate of a Superintendent Registrar 'With Licence', is extremely good value. (These are the ones printed in red.) Application is needed to only one Registrar in whose district either party has lived for 15 days. He does not have to display the notice of marriage in his office, and unless an impediment is raised or a 'forbidding' takes place, he *must* issue the certificate and licence after one day has elapsed since the giving of the notice. Thus all can be arranged in a couple of days for a cost of only 75 new pence.

It must be confessed that these licences are no good for weddings in churches or chapels where marriages may be solemnised under the Church of England rite.

The certificate of a Superintendent Registrar 'Without Licence' permits marriage in any church or chapel where banns may be published or in the registration district where either party resides, or where is the usual place of worship of one. At 37½ new pence it is the cheapest form of marriage permit. But notice has to be given by each party to the Superintendent Registrar of the registration district in which he or she lives (and has lived for a week). The form of the notice requires their addresses and occupations and marital status, and a statement of the church or other building in which their marriage is to take place.

Even if the notice is given in a false name, however, the marriage can be valid. Lord Penzance had considered (*Holmes* v. *Simmons L.R. 1 P. & D. 523*) that a notice in false names would be no notice at all. But in *Plummer* v. *Plummer* (*1917*) *P. 163* th eprinciple of using whatever name you like was upheld. 'Although the notice or declaration may be wilfully false, yet the marriage itself will be valid' said the judge.

This upset an ingenious argument in *R.* v. *Lamb* (*1934*) *50 T.L.R. 310*, where a prisoner contended that he could not be guilty of bigamy because he had married in a false name in 1914, and by his real name in 1933. The reasoning was that there was in the 1914 ceremony no 'due notice' to satisfy the 1836 Act, and therefore, the first ceremony being void, the allegedly bigamous marriage was valid. The Court of Criminal Appeal however held that the first marriage was valid, notwithstanding the false name, and confirmed the conviction for bigamy.

(When bigamy was first made a felony, in 1603, and for a long time thereafter, the penalty was death, which at least prevented arguments about the status of the innocent party thereafter.)

Section 49 of the *Marriage Act, 1949*, provides that if any persons knowingly and wilfully intermarry without having given due notice to the Registrar (unless by banns or ecclesiastical licence) the marriage is void.

The Registrars accordingly have to keep Marriage Notice Books. Just as anyone who wants to object to the grant of an ecclesiastical licence can enter a *caveat* with the diocesan Bishop, so there is a process for objecting to the Registrar. A *caveat* holds up the issue of the Bishop's licence until the diocesan chancellor (a professional lawyer) decides whether it should be granted. (By *s. 29* of the *Marriage Act*, anyone making a frivolous objection can be made to pay damages to the person seeking to marry.)

When an objector enters a *caveat* with a Superintendent Registrar, the official can satisfy himself whether to grant the certificate or refer the matter to the Registrar General. Only rarely are such questions referred to the court.

The most effective block is for a parent or guardian simply to write 'Forbidden' beside the entry in the Marriage Notice Book. The Certificate cannot then issue until the court has consented.

The time for forbidding or warning is short in the case of a Registrar's Certificate With Licence, but Without Licence, the Notice must be displayed in the Register Office for three weeks before issue of the certificate. Either kind of certificate enables a marriage to be solemnised in a Register Office, a church which is a Registered Building, or in the Jewish or Quaker form. Jewish marriages often take place in restaurants with elaborate ceremonial recorded for the law by synagogue officials. The Quaker records go back long before the records of English marriages were required by law. No religious ceremony is permitted in a Register Office. If some religious ritual is observed as well as a Register Office marriage, the legally binding one is the Registrar's. No marriage may be solemnised in a Registered Building without the consent of the Minister or one of the Trustees, Deacons or Managers. Roman Catholic Registered Buildings are subject to a similar restriction requiring the consent of the Officiating Minister. There must also be two witnesses and a Registrar of the registration district in which the building is situated or the Authorised Person for the Registered Building.

There is no record of any song along the lines:

As we stood before the Authorised Person
In that little old Registered Building on the hill
And solemnised our union in such form as we thought fit to adopt
Including 'I do' and 'I will'.

But why? A Register Office marriage With Licence is hardly less clandestine than one in the marriage shop alongside the Fleet Prison, or after a stirring pre-war drive to Gretna. It is certainly cheaper. The romance of avoiding publicity and thwarting the hierarchy is available at no risk at all to the status of matrimony. And yet there is always a possibility of some obscure technicality causing a legal lacuna. For a milennium, the lawyers have retained the romance in marriage. Small thanks they get for it.

One essential whether in church chapel or Register Office is open doors. This simple requirement goes some way to prevent the

175

worst excesses of irregular marriage. In *Cooper* v. *Crane (1891)* *P. 369*, for instance, the man set up the marriage without telling the girl, then called for her, walked her all unsuspecting to the church, and on the steps pulled out a pistol and threatened to blow out his brains if she did not go in and marry him. Had the doors been open already, this carry-on might have been observed by the celebrant, and the ceremony refused. The wife would then have been spared the necessity to apply to the court for an annulment, which was refused because she was apparently not sufficiently frightened out of her wits to vitiate her consent.

The earliest legal recognition of the actual words 'Fate worse than death' occur not in a case of forced marriage, but in the Petition to the House of Lords upon which *Field's Annulling Bill (1848)* *2 H.L.C. 48* was based—and which did not succeed. The aptly named *Lawless* v. *Chamberlain (1889) 18 O:R. 296* resulted in a valid marriage even though the father of the pregnant bride flourished a pistol at the husband.

Chancellor Boyd explained that the father was very feeble, and soon put down his gun. The Minister was sufficiently concerned to ask the bridegroom if he had any deep-rooted objection to being married, and the man shrugged and said 'Let it sliver'. This, ruled the Chancellor, amounted to consent whilst not under actual compulsion.

Mr Joseph Jackson QC has discovered the original shotgun wedding to be the case of *Cannon* v. *Cannon* in Tennessee in 1928 (*7 Tenn. App. 19*). The father's gun was indeed loaded and he said to the groom: 'You Goddamn son of a bitch, you have ruined my daughter and I'm going to kill you if you don't marry her'.

However consent is vitiated, the effect is to avoid the legal effect of the purported marriage. If one partner is insane to such extent that he or she does not comprehend the nature of the transaction, it is void. This defect is raised quite often by persons other than those immediately concerned, who would benefit materially from the marriage being void. But it is not necessary to go to the length of proving insanity. Non-comprehension is enough. In *Valier* v. *Valier* (*1925) 133 L.T. 830* an Italian who did not understand English was taken to a Register Office by a determined woman and taken through the ceremony without understanding what was going on. They never co-habited thereafter, nor consummated the union and he was granted a nullity decree. In *Mehta* v. *Mehta (1945) 2 All E.R.* the mistaken belief was that the 'marriage' was a ceremony for religious conversion.

Even where the effect of the ceremony is appreciated it might still not be valid because its form, or some essential condition was incomplete. In order to prove defects of ceremony the evidence of

176

experts in the laws of foreign countries is often necessary, because the persons seeking such decrees are often women who have been abroad to marry and wish to avoid the effect of the ceremony. These are different cases from marriages of convenience, which can be annulled on the basis of imperfect consent. A rich Hungarian woman, fearing that the Communists would imprison or kill her, married a Frenchman in order to escape with him from Hungary. They never lived together nor consummated the union and it was annulled (*H.* v. *H.* [*1953*] *2 All E.R. 1229*). However, in *Silver* v. *Silver* (*1955*) *2 All E.R. 164*, a German woman had married an Englishman in order to remain in England. They lived separately, but it was 29 years before she sued to obtain an annulment. Mr Justice Collingwood ruled that having freely chosen to be man and wife, they were validly married—even though it was a marriage of convenience. The difference between Mrs Silver and Mrs H. was that the latter was in fear and married to escape. She did not intend to be a wife. Mrs Silver intended to be a wife in order to stay here.

The basic defect in a void marriage is that the relationship of husband and wife, which was anciently created in the *sponsalia*, never existed. The rights of coverture consequently never arose. Intercourse between the parties could not mend the defect except in so far as it was evidence that the defect did not exist. The great pre-occupation of our civilisation with the distribution of wealth gave rise to the earliest inquiries whether marriages were true and lawful associations. Adulterous desires furthered and fostered the inclinations to terminate marriages and the device most usually employed was that the spouses were relations. A high degree of efficiency in the termination of marriages developed from this wantonness.

This doctrine developed from the same Christian dogma which demanded the sexual consummation of marriage. This was the '*carna una*' doctrine in Genesis, requiring husband and wife to become 'one flesh'. This duty to consummate was established as the post-Reformation law of England in *Manby's Case* (*1626*). Even though the ceremony of marriage be perfectly lawful, it was capable of being rendered ineffectual if there was no consummation. The defect is completely different from and ostensibly less logical than the impediments of want of ceremony or lack of capacity. However, since the sexual act united firmly those who were informally promised, what more logical than that the absence of it should disunite those formally espoused ?

The effect of the reasoning is to make of the ceremony of marriage, whether civil or religious, merely the method of fixing that instant in time after which sexual intercourse has legal force. The principle, whose determination was inevitable after Richard of Anesty's case,

177

did not actually fall to be decided until the case of *Dredge* v. *Dredge* (*1947*) *All E.R.* (*1947*) *P. 30*—a case of non-consummation, where a child conceived before the marriage ceremony was born after it. The question for Mr Justice Willmer was whether that prevented a finding of wilful refusal to consummate under *s. 7 (1)* of the *Matrimonial Causes Act, 1937*.

> '*Apparently, the possibility that a child might be conceived before the marriage and born afterwards had not occurred to the draftsman in the framing of this section of the Act . . . Curious and unhappy as the consequences are, I do not think that the fact that the child born after the ceremony of marriage would be bastardised is any ground for withholding the decree if I am otherwise satisfied.*'

In *Wing* v. *Taylor* (*1861*) *2 Sw. & Tr. 278* it was demonstrated that the ancient laws never suggested that carnal knowledge without matrimony could create affinity of relationship. The mediaeval Canon Law, however, did. Roger Donington's marriage was annulled because he had intercourse with his wife's third cousin before the marriage (*2 Coke's Institute's, 684*). *The Year Book 29 Edward III folio 31* records an even worse case where Thomas, before marriage, had stood godfather to his bride's cousin. This was affinity by spiritual relationship—the very danger which all the faithful are bound to declare if they know it, when they hear the banns published:

> '*If therefore ye know of any impediment of consanguinity, affinity or spiritual relationship you are bound to declare the same to us as soon as possible.*'

Mr Shelford (*Law of Marriage and Divorce, 1841, p. 15*) described the canonical ingenuity in nullity proceedings as 'rendering applications necessary and frequent to the Holy See, from every one of which they knew how to draw large fees and perquisites'. However justified that stricture, the most ambitious canonist could hardly have envisaged the ramifications of the intellectual disciplines he perpetuated.

Coitus before marriage might have legal implications, of course, such as imprisonment for a non-consensual indulgence, or liability for the support of a bastard. But after a ceremony capable of being valid in law, sex seals for all time that change of status which will affect the course of history, if only to the extent that it determines who will own a semi-detached house subject to a building society mortgage. And not only *inter partes* are these matters of moment.

Mr Dodsworth was one of His Majesty's Inspectors of Taxes to whom it occurred to raise against Benjamin James Dale an additional assessment to income tax for the years 1928 to 1933 inclusive. The incontrovertible evidence showed that this taxpayer and Miss

Kathleen Richards had and solemnised a ceremony of marriage at All Saints' Church, Marylebone, on the 22nd October, 1921. On the 23rd October, 1933 a final decree of nullity was made declaring that marriage 'absolutely null and void to all intents and purposes'.

No doubt that case was selected because of the happy coincidence of dates which would leave the requisite calculations uncomplicated by vulgar fractions. Aptly enough, it was on the 22nd October, 1934 that the Inspector claimed before the Commissioners £90 in respect of each of those five years against Mr Dale, as being the additional personal allowance to which a married man was entitled, and which Mr Dale had enjoyed. Wrongly, said the taxman, because he was not married. Even though his wife might be apparently married to him, he was not entitled to the personal allowance of a married man whose wife was living with him.

The Revenue lost, not, aptly enough on the marriage law, but on the tax law. That was one 'intent and purpose' to which they *were* married. The foundation of this law of unity of persons in marriage and all its consequences was regulated in a detailed and arbitrary way by *Chapter 18* of *Leviticus*.

> '*The prohibited degrees were those within which intercourse between the sexes was supposed to be forbidden as incestuous, and no distinction was made between relationship by blood or by affinity,*'

said Lord Chancellor Campbell (a great reformer in many branches of law, including divorce) in *Brook* v. *Brook* (*1861*) *9 H.L.C. 193*.

What Leviticus actually forbids is that you 'approach and uncover the nakedness of' a large variety of relations. Henry VIII maintained it in its full force by an act of 1541 forbidding marriages 'prohibited by God', though Archbishop Parker modified the degrees a bit in 1563. They were incorporated in a Canon in 1603 and codified in the Book of Common Prayer. However, these incestuous marriages were not void, but merely voidable.

The difference is so clear, according to Sir John Nicholl that 'no person who ever looked into any elementary book on the subject is ignorant of it', (*Elliott* v. *Gurr* [*1812*] *2 Phill. 16 and 18*). It is nevertheless a bold man who will be so sure that his marriage is void that he will just go ahead and marry someone else, without bothering to get a decree. The maximum sentence for bigamy is still seven years (*Offences against the Person Act, 1861 s. 57*). Courts can be quite soft on it nowadays, but a stretch inside is not beyond possibility.

A void marriage creates only a meretricious union in which the couple are not man and wife. A voidable marriage is one which is defective in such a way that a competent court can annul it, but until that decree is pronounced, it is a lawful union. It follows that if no such decree is pronounced, it remains lawful in spite of its imperfections. Since Common Law was prepared to uphold marriages which had never been celebrated, it is not surprising that it upheld marriages which had been celebrated—even wrongly. The improvements to the law of marriage in 1835 altered the law of incestuous marriages, and provided that marriage within the prohibited degrees was void, and not merely voidable.

Wholesale encroachment upon the principle began with an orgy of permissive legislation in this century. There was the *Deceased Wife's Sister's Marriage Act, 1907*, after which presumably a horde of impassioned widowers carried off their wives' sisters to the altar. Why the *Deceased Brother's Widow's Marriage Act* had to wait until 1921 is hard to understand. Eight of Archbishop Parker's decrees went with the *Marriage (Prohibited Degrees of Relationship) Act, 1931*. The *Marriage (Enabling) Act*, 1960, swept away much of the affinity doctrine by permitting marriages within those eight degrees if the former spouse is still alive after divorce or nullity. The prohibited degrees are now your parents, children and grandchildren, sisters and brothers. A man cannot marry his son's wife or his wife's daughter by another marriage even after the appropriate divorces. Nor can he marry his grandson's wife in similar case, nor his aunt nor his mother-in-law. It is to be hoped that the passion for reform which has characterised the recent past is now spent. It is well to know these things because in order to get a licence to marry the intending couple must, by *Section 16* of the *Marriage Act, 1949*, swear to the belief that there is no impediment to the marriage.

Whether a marriage be void or merely voidable the decree of the court is the same. It still follows the form the ecclesiastical courts employed in declaring that the marriage is and always has been void to all intents and purposes, and thus, said Lord Goddard, Chief Justice (in *R.* v. *Algar [1954] 1 A.B. 279*) 'it perpetuates a canonical fiction'.

'The fact that in both cases the decree is the same cannot alter the fact that the two cases are in this respect quite different,'
per Lord Green M.R. in *De Reneville* v. *De Reneville* (1948) P. 100.

The result is that if the validity of a marriage become important to other people—in for instance an inheritance dispute—the question whether it is void or voidable can be inquired into and if it is void it will be treated as never having existed, whilst if only voidable, it will not be ignored unless a decree of nullity has been pronounced. But even such matters can cause status problems. Mrs Ryan had £2,000 damages in the hands of the High Court for the death of her husband. She married again and applied for the money to be paid out to her since she was no longer his widow. But the court held that she was still the widow, even though remarried, and she could not have the capital but only the income. *Taylor (formerly Ryan)* v. *Cheltenham and Hereford Breweries Ltd.* (*1952*) *1 All E.R. 1135 C.A.*). In another case, Mr Justice Harman (as he was then) had to decide whether a woman was entitled to an inheritance as the widow of her husband. She had been married again, but that marriage had been annulled. The other interested parties naturally contended that she was not a widow any longer, but the judge said she was. Had she stayed married the result might have been different (but it would not if Mrs Ryan's case was correct).

It therefore appears that once a widow, always a widow. But it is comparatively easy to stop being a wife. It might be beyond a woman's powers ever to become one. For the obligation to consummate presupposes the ability to do so. 'It has always been held that the contract of marriage implies the ability to consummate it,' said Sir Samuel Evans, President of the Divorce Court, in *Dickinson* v. *Dickinson* (*1913*) *P. 198*. His actual decision in that case was overruled two years later in *Napier* v. *Napier* (*1915*) *P. 184*. He had held that wilful refusal to consummate was a ground for nullity, following the reasoning that consummation was necessary. But the true ground of annulment was declared in Napier's case to be inability. The great civil lawyer, Dr Lushington, had declared in 1845 that the only question on a nullity case was 'whether the spouse is or is not capable of sexual intercourse' (*D.* v. *A. 1 Rob. Ecc. 279*). The Victorian and earlier consistory judges disliked impotency cases. Lushington said that Sir John Nicholl had 'the strongest aversion' to them. Lushington nevertheless made our modern law of incapacity. What has to be achieved, he said, was *vera copula*. If a woman was capable of that but would never conceive, the marriage was valid because it could be consummated, even though no child would ever be born. The degree of satisfaction achieved is irrelevant (*Sy.* v. *Sy.* *[1963] P. 37*). In order to give time and opportunity to achieve matrimonial union nullity cases could not succeed on this ground before 1820 unless the parties had been together three years. This *triennalis cohabitatio* was to exclude demure or coy behaviour from the field of inquiry.* Lord Stowell did not think much of incapacity cases.

> '*A person need not be a profound psychologist to know how rarely the structure of the body is deficient for the purposes of our nature. Malformation is not common in our sex and perhaps is still more uncommon in the other.*

---

* It is still required for a divorce.

The wealthier class of woman who wanted to end a marriage in the late 18th Century could readily resort to inability. The case of the Countess of Essex in 1613 (*2 St. Tr. 786*) had led to rumours that she sent another woman to be examined in her place by the jury of matrons. When Mary of Modena gave birth to the Old Pretender in 1688 the King's enemies put it about that the baby was not really hers but smuggled into her apartments in a warming pan to maintain the Stuart succession. The birth was well attended by witnesses in fact.

Gynaecologists appointed by the court to inspect people alleged to be incapable have replaced the juries of matrons. But frequently the evidence of physical disorder is not conclusive or even persuasive of inability. As long ago as 1776 Attorney-General Thurlow was arguing in the Duchess of Kingston's case that a person need not be impotent to everyone of the opposite sex (*20 St. Tr.*). By 1853, Lushington was asking 'Who by possibility can say that such a man is necessarily impotent as to all women?' The psychological block was part of our law. Lord Hodson in *Wise* v. *Wise* (*1944*) *P. 56* said that cases where there was no physical incapacity 'far outnumber' those where malformation exists. Capability proves nothing, it was held in *L.* v. *L.* (*1949*) *1 All E.R.*, where the incapacity is psychological.

Between Napier's case in 1915 and Herbert's Act, in force from the 1st January, 1938, wilful refusal was not a ground for an annulment. But in *G.* v. *G.* (*1924*) *A.C.* (a Scottish case) there was a decree for wilful refusal caused by not obstinate or capricious behaviour but by 'invincible repugnance'. The refusal was treated as evidence of the incapacity, an inconsistency which involved blaming someone for failing to do something he or she could not do.

The basis of the ecclesiastical law of nullity being inability, the person who suffered from the inability was logically entitled to seek the decree. There was no blame. The court was concerned only with the effectiveness of consummation, and the possibility of conception is irrelevant. Conception can occur without full consummation (*Snowman* v. *Snowman* [*1934*] *P. 186*).

Mr Gerald Abrahams has written of the Common Law that 'notoriously, it does not define'. Nor did the ecclesiastical law, so far as what exactly amounted to *vera coupla*. If the judges had to do that, said one, they would be in an impossible position. Every case turns on its own facts. Parliament has declined to define it, too. This, together with the possibility of conception without full consummation—for instance by *fecundatio ab extra* can create difficult cases. I recall a case before Mr Commissioner William Latey QC some years ago, in which a man claimed to be impotent *quoad* his wife, who did not defend the suit.

He testified to her bearing a child, and the judge raised an eyebrow. 'Snowman's case, my lord,' began counsel. The judge nodded.

The petitioner told of the birth, some years later, of a second child. 'Snowman, no doubt?' queried the judge. Counsel nodded. The man told of a third child.

'What do you say about this?' asked the judge of the advocate. 'Very fertile woman, my lord.'

'Maybe, but I see you have also pleaded for divorce (he pronounced the "i" as in "high") on the ground of desertion. You had better proceed on that.'

'If your Lordship pleases. May he see his discretion statement? Now, tell my Lord, please. Is that all the adultery you have committed?'

Marriages are also voidable where either spouse is mentally disordered to such extent as to be unfit for marriage and the procreation of child, or had communicable VD at the time of the marriage.

Until the abolition of the action for damages for breach of promise of marriage on 1st January, 1971, the plaintiff's unfitness for marriage was a good defence, just like all the ordinary defences in contract cases such as for example that the contract was never made. In the last analysis this is all that a nullity suit comes down to. Unchastity, impotence or insanity all counted in this jurisdiction, and there were even cases where the unfitness for marriage was held to exist on proof of tuberculosis (*Jefferson* v. *Paskell* [*1916*] *1 K.B.*) or of an abscess on the breast of a man (*Atchinson* v. *Baker* [*1796*] *Peake. Add. Cas. 103*). It never was apparently held that a man's unchastity made him unfit for marriage, but often that a woman's did. Once it was so held where the woman had a baby out of wedlock 12 years before (*Bench* v. *Merrick* [*1844*] *1 Car. & K. 463*).

Merely to discover that a woman was less well off than had been hoped or expected was not a ground to permit a man to jilt her. But when it was a case of a man being induced to propose because of the false promise that her father would leave her property, though, in fact, he was on the brink of bankruptcy, the man was entitled to call off the marriage without risk of damages (*Wharton* v. *Lewis* [*1824*] *1 C. & P. 529*).

This digression merely illustrates that if a man found out what was wrong with the girl before the wedding, he ducked out at his peril in damages. If they went through with the marriage, and he tried to have it annulled, he might be met with a plea of 'insincerity' and his knowledge of the defect could prevent the nullity decree from being granted. The statutory grounds for annulling voidable marriages last mentioned depend on the petitioner being unaware of the fact when the marriage takes place, the case being begun within a year of the marriage and the absence of intercourse after discovery of the facts. They might better have been made grounds of divorce, as logically wilful refusal to consummate should be—since it occurs

183

after marriage and not before.

But the logic is gone from marriage now that there is no automatic inheritance of lands by an eldest son. A man is now bound to maintain other men's children who become 'children of the family' when he marries their mother. Henry VIII and Anne of Cleves married for political reasons when he was old. No doubt other people to this day see fit to emulate them and for devious reasons preserve the *locus poenitentiae* of non-consummation. But they are rare. And so the law prescribes no ritual of any particular description for the actual performance of this obligation. The parties are free to undertake it when, where and how they chose, subject only to the criminal law about indecent behaviour in public places. So powerful is the obligation that Sir Matthew Hale considered that a man could not be guilty of rape upon his lawful wife 'For she hath given herself up to that thing, which she cannot retract' (*Pleas of the Crown Vol. I 486*).

The Legal Incidents Of Coverture

'With all my wordly goods I thee endow . . .'

THERE IS, in the Chambers of Horrors at Madame Tussaud's exhibition of waxworks, a bath. This homely utensil is of a most convenient design, being suitable for comfortable ablutions upon the hearthrug before a cosy fire, and not at all suitable for plumbing into cold tiled bathrooms. Its place in English legal history is assured, if somewhat overlooked. It was purchased in 1912 by one George Joseph Smith, an expert in the law relating to husband and wife, whose learning was all the more remarkable since he spent his adolescent years in a reformatory and much of his young manhood in prison.

He had married in 1898 the lady who was to remain his only legal wife, and ten years later, he 'married' another, who stuck by him in all his later vicissitudes. In 1910, he happened to be passing under the name of Henry Williams when he found it convenient to 'marry' a Miss Bessie Munday, whose father, a bank manager, had left her £2,500 in a trust fund.

Now the *Married Women's Property Acts* began a century ago—indeed if Women's Lib. needed a suitable topic for a centenary celebration they could do worse than take up this one. However, since they remained largely unappreciated until the Second World War, the idea of women having money 'tied up in trust funds' was just one of those inconveniences with which the middle class put up. The actual tying up was often achieved by a legal device called a 'restraint upon anticipation' which some students think was an erotic practice. Until they were abolished in 1949, they could be troublesome, because a woman whose fortune was subject to one could only have the income, and never get her hands on the capital. They were devised, of course, in the days when 'husband and wife were one, and the husband was that one' and the idea was to prevent husbands getting control of their wives' capital, as the ordinary law entitled them to do. Now it did not take Mr Smith alias Williams long to get his new 'wife's' spare cash from her vigilant solicitors. He was, after all, much better entitled to it than she was, having been decent enough to marry her. But when he went back to his usual (if not real) 'wife', Bessie still had her main fortune.

Two years later he forgave her and took her back, and as an earnest of their undying devotion and intention to live happily ever after, they made mutual wills. For although she could not have the capital herself, she could dispose of it by will. It was then that Mr Smith alias Williams went out and bought the bath, and took it to their house at Herne Bay. He bated the ironmonger down by half a crown, and the bath turned out to be worth the money.

For Mr Smith in spite of his absence of formal legal education, had evolved a means of circumventing the restrictive effects of the trust deed which governed his 'wife's' fortune. The will she had made in his favour was the first step. But that, of course, was of no effect until she died, which she did on 13th July, 1912, by 'misadventure from drowning from some fit' in that bath. That was the verdict at the inquest. When the will was proved, he inherited the £2,500 with which he and his steady 'wife' enjoyed a short vacation. It is only fair to concede that this way round trust restrictions was not immediately appreciated in the world of the law.

The following year a woman who was Alice Burnham until her 'marriage' died in a bath at Southsea (one fitted into a bathroom). The former Miss Margaret Lofty died in yet another bath at Highgate, the day after her 'marriage' to Mr Smith, to whom she had left all her property under his then alias of 'John Lloyd'. These events had received publicity, which had come to the notice of Alice Burnham's family who went to the police. In March, 1915, Mr Smith was arrested and charged with having made a false entry in a marriage register. But one thing led to another and after 120 witnesses had given evidence he was convicted of murdering Bessie Munday. With that grasp of the details for which he was famous, Sir Richard Muir, the senior Treasury Counsel, persuaded the jury that the actual machinery by which the restrictive trusts were evaded was by seizing the legs of the lady bather and up-ending her so that she drowned in the bath.

It is for this rather than his other innovation that Mr Smith is remembered. Nobody knows how many others he practised upon.

It is, of course, trite to remark that many couples do not dwell upon the sordid commerce of whose actual name shall be recorded as the owner of their first dwelling. The decision is frequently based upon some expedient to facilitate the procuration of a mortgage or to take advantage of a residence qualification on a housing list. Before the War, it was taken for granted that the breadwinner was the sole provider of the residence as well. But the social upheaval which caused women MPs to shake their wise heads and complain about the 'latch-key' kids awoke in the hearts of women who worked for wages an alien attitude apparent when the exigencies of the times precipitated matrimonial conflict. The housing shortage which Winston Churchill said would have to be solved by something like a military operation had something to do with it, no doubt.

During the Second World War the Services all operated divorce assistance legal services as welfare operation. Afterwards the Law Society continued the service from which developed the Legal Aid System. The cost of divorce is thus reduced and can be paid for by instalments. Solicitors can now offer this useful service at very competitive prices. Never far from their minds is the 17th Section of the *Married Women's Property Act, 1882*, which provides (as amended by the demands of recent reformers):

> '*In any question between husband and wife as to the title to or possession of property, either party may apply by summons or otherwise in a summary way to any judge of the High Court of Justice in England or in Ireland according as such property is in England or in Ireland, or (at the option of the applicant irrespective of the value of the property in dispute) in England to the judge of the County Court of the district . . . and the judge . . .* may make such order *with respect to the property in dispute and as to the costs of and consequent upon the application* as he thinks fit . . .'

And so on. Was there ever such a section in all jurisprudence? No limits on jurisdiction; no definition of principles. It was of a different statute that Lord Justice Goddard (as he was then) said:

> '*The Court . . . is really put very much in the position of a Cadi under the palm tree. There are no principles on which he is directed to act. He has to do the best he can in the circumstances, having no rule of law to guide him.*'

> **Metropolitan Properties v. Purdy (1940) 1 All E.R. 188.**

But many judges have applied it to Section 17, and thoroughly enjoyed doing it. Because of the system of binding precedent, however, that happy condition no longer obtains. Diligent law reporters have printed so many of the judgments from under the different palm trees that the practitioner in the arid desert of the High Street is not always sure what advice to give to his client. Some points are simple, of course. For instance, notwithstanding that it is a Married Women's Property Act, a married man can make an application under it. Though Lord Sumner did point out, 'Generally speaking, the Act of 1882 was a Married Women's Property Act, not a Married Man's Relief Act.'

It is not simply a question of who paid for the house and the furniture. That question is a dominant one, but seldom simple. It is bedevilled by the names which appear on the documents of title. One spouse, when the marriage breaks up, will frequently assert the maxim of 'Equity is equality' in support of the contention that joint names means equal shares. There is a school of judges, mainly the senior judges of County Courts, which follows this doctrine pretty consistently. The reasoning which found a great deal of support in the 'Forties and 'Fifties was based upon a principle of Equity called 'The Presumption of Advancement'. This means that if a man pays for something which requires to be registered to complete the acquisition of ownership, such as shares, or a house, and has it put into his wife's name, the law presumes that he intended her to have it. This is less naïve than at first appears. There is a legal presumption when a person makes such a disposition to a comparative stranger, that he intends him (or her) only to be a mere nominee.

But with a member of the family—at least the closest ones—the inference was of a complete gift, both of legal and beneficial interest. Now the Law Lords (*Pettitt* v. *Pettitt* [*1969*] *2 All E.R. 385*) all said that this presumption of 'advancement' is less strong nowadays than it used to be. The reason is that wives work nowadays and so do not need presumptions of advancement.

The Law Lords were equally emphatic that English law knows nothing of 'Community property', the common murder motive in Perry Mason cases. Many American states have developed laws which pool the property of husband and wife during marriage. The problem, according to the highest court in our land, is simply one of deciding what intention the parties had when the property was bought, when there is no evidence about it because the husband and the wife never considered it.

Lord Evershed, Master of the Rolls, had suggested a way of performing this feat of knowing better than the spouses themselves, as long ago as 1948 (*Re Rogers' Question* [*1948*] *1 All E.R. 328*).

> '*What the judge must try to do is to conclude what at the time was in the parties' minds and then to make an order which in the changed conditions, now fairly gives effect in law to what the parties, in the judge's finding, must be taken to have intended at the time of the transaction itself.*'

In a later case he remarked that that sentence had inspired a registrar and a judge, in the same case (one on appeal from the other), to reach diametrically opposite conclusions.

Once you discard equality and advancement presumptions and accept the wife as putting in value by working and saving from the housekeeping and being a good manager you embark upon an exercise in logistics and cost effectiveness which was hazily conceived in the post-war years in the 'common purse' doctrine. Lord Justice Romer (*Rimmer* v. *Rimmer* [*1952*] *2 All E.R. 863*) saw that case as one where equity was equality. The wife paid the deposit for the house in 1935—£29. The husband became responsible for the mortgage payments. But the wife paid some of these whilst he was on war service. When they parted in 1951, the house which had cost £460 was sold for £2,117. Their shares were held to be equal even though the wife had actually paid more than the husband.

Equality prevailed in *Fribance* v. *Fribance* (*1957*) *1 All E.R. 357* where 'the wife went out to work and used her earnings to help run the household and buy the children's clothes, whilst the husband saved'. And so the cases went on, stories of money put in tins for this and that expense; or regular savings from extra work and deductions from housekeeping. Wives got fractional shares—often half—in the proceeds of houses which were held in their husbands' sole names. This seems to be the doctrine sealed with the approval of the Law Lords in *Gissing* v. *Gissing* (*1969*). But the claimant must prove that the legal owner holds the house at least partly in trust for her.

But whereas Pettitt's case made it clear at least that where the title deeds show the intended shares, the court will not look beyond that, the valuation of contributions under the 'common purse' is subject to exceptions which place men at disadvantage. The Court of Appeal had held that Mr Appleton, a skilled woodworker, who had enhanced the value of his wife's house, should take the value of his work and materials out of the increase. But the House of Lords reversed that and held that one spouse cannot by doing work on the other spouse's property, acquire an interest in it. Lord Diplock thought that if a husband gave up full time work to improve the wife's property, he could acquire an interest (*Jansen* v. *Jansen* [*1965*] *3 All E.R.*). But a Do-it-Yourself enthusiast can expect no proprietary reward for his exertions.

Nevertheless where the claimant has supplied some of the money, as well as doing some of the work the law will recognise a substantial share. The Court of Appeal increased the share of a mistress to one-third of a bungalow she helped to build (*The Times*, 20th January, 1972). The trial judge had allowed only a twelfth. This immediately alerted the legal profession. When, just after the War, Lord Denning invented the 'deserted wife's equity' to stay in the matrimonial home, it enjoyed an uneasy acceptance in our law until the Law Lords decided in *National Provincial Bank Ltd.* v. *Ainsworth* (*1965*) *A.C. 1175* that no such thing existed. Parliament, however, provided by the *Matrimonial Homes Act, 1967*, that a wife should have rights of occupation, and if she claimed an interest in the place she could protect it from defeat by sale by registering a Land Charge Class F. It has long been possible to give notice of claims in this way by registering them as equitable charges. Whether that decision foreshadows a specific protection for deserted mistresses, time alone will tell. Lord Denning did say that the principles between man and mistress were the same as between husband and wife.

Uttered in the year in which wives can for the first time claim to be separately assessed to Income Tax, that might be more accurate than hitherto.

Whether the wife has the foresight to insist upon the matrimonial home being put into joint names, or whether she has to rely, in the event of a break-up, on her wifely qualities, her chances of getting a share without actually putting any capital in are now extremely fair. Since the enactment of Section 4 of the *Matrimonial Proceedings and Property Act, 1970,* a court in a divorce suit can order either party (i.e. a husband) to transfer property to the other (i.e. a wife) or for the benefit of any child. This is done by reference to the relative means and assets of the parties, the history of the marriage and the standard of living. This decision is taken entirely irrespective of intentions as to ownership or the other considerations. Of course, you have to have a divorce, a nullity or a judicial separation to do it, whilst it is theoretically perfectly possible to have Married Women's Property proceedings whilst still the best of friends. (Smart people can have divorces in that comforting condition.)

One can quite see that the Law Lords would have been wrong to recognise 'community of property'. The husband has, of course, a perfectly good claim upon his wife's property. Unhappily there is seldom any property upon which the claim can operate. As Blackstone put it:

> '*By marriage, the husband and wife are one person in law; that is, the very being or legal existence of the woman is suspended during the marriage,*'
>
> Commentaries i. 442.

She was, he said, 'consolidated into the husband under whose wing, protection and cover she performed everything and is therefore called in our law-French a *feme covert* femina viro co-opetera'. There is no trace of any merging of the husband in the wife. This may account for the failure of non-contributing husbands to secure shares in the matrimonial property. No judge has had the courage to say so. The nearest was, of course, Mr Justice McCardie in *Gotliffe* v. *Edelston (1930) 2 K.B. 378. Inter alia* he pointed out that a husband was still liable for his wife's necessaries even though her income was much larger than his, and she refused to pay a penny towards the expenses of their home.

> '*So great a favourite is the female sex of the laws of England,*'

he said (quoting Blackstone).

In 1962, eighty years after the main Married Women's Property Act consolidated the wife's advantages, Parliament decreed that husband and wife should be able to sue each other just as if they were strangers. By that time they virtually were. In the old days when a man acquired his wife's property on marriage, he also became liable for her debts and wrongs. To save himself from bankruptcy, he needed to command obedience. The degree of discipline permitted to him was the subject of disagreement for three centuries. Chief Justice Hale, in *Lord Leigh's Case* (*1674*) *3 Keble 433* defined the husband's power of *castigatio*—an ecclesiastical remnant of the Roman *dominium*—as permitting him only to admonish or confine the woman to make her subject to his will.

But Sir William Blackstone (*Commentaries i. 445*) found Common Law support for corporal punishment. Although wife beating was obsolete then (1765) in polite society, 'the lower rank of people, who were always fond of the old Common Law, still claim and exert their ancient privilege'. A foreigner might be forgiven for believing, on a Monday morning at a magistrates' court in a poor neighbourhood, that the principle remains unshaken. But it has gone, and it meant the end of marriage proper, said the *Nineteenth Century Magazine*, in 1891. The change was remarked upon by that great authority on marital rights, Mr Nicholas Forsyte ('In Chancery', John Galsworthy), who was very upset about 'that Jackson case'.

Mr Jackson had secured a decree that his wife return to him and render him conjugal rights. But this daughter of the Lancashire bourgeoisie decided to defy the court, as was already not uncommon. The expected result was, of course, that she would be in desertion and that her husband would put her aside. But he was not that easily put off. As she walked out of church one Sunday he and two stalwart companions (one of them a solicitor's articled clerk, who doubtless instigated the plot) seized and 'with no more force than was necessary' bundled her into a cab and took her to the matrimonial home.

There she was confined. A nurse was engaged to look after her. She was highly nervous and indignant but the only physical injury she suffered was a bruised arm. Her family declared that the nurse was a gaoler, and one judge so found. But she was free to go where she would in the house. The only display of anger manifested by Mr Jackson was that he threw her bonnet in the fire when she did not surrender into his arms on arrival at the house.

Her family issued out a writ of *habeas corpus* alleging that she was illegally imprisoned, and Mr Jackson admitted that he had confined her, and declared that he was entitled to. Bacon's Abridgement did say that a husband might keep his wife 'by force within the bounds of duty and may beat her, but not in a violent and cruel manner'.

191

But that was only *castigia*, when you looked into it; the power to tick your wife off, which no doubt fell into desuetude for ineffectiveness or impossibility of performance. Fifty years before, Mr Justice Coleridge had said (*in Re Cochrane [1840] 8 Dowl. 633*) that for the happiness and honour of both parties the law placed the wife 'under the guardianship of her husband, and entitled him, for the sake of both, to protect her from the danger of unrestrained intercourse with the world by enforcing cohabitation and a common residence'.

However, the court was much impressed by the fact that in 1884, Parliament did away with imprisonment for refusing to obey a decree of restitution of conjugal rights.* If the court could not lock her up, said the judges, Mr Jackson certainly could not.

Lord Esher did not entirely destroy a husband's power over his wife. The great Master of the Rolls said that: 'If she was on the staircase about to elope, or in some other way setting off to go to her paramour, the husband might seize her and pull her back'. But otherwise, according to the bachelor Mr Justice McCardie, 'From the date of their decision, the shackles of servitude fell from the limbs of married women and they were free to come and go at their own will' (*Place v. Searle (1932) 2 K.B. 497 @ 500*).

Thenceforward a decree of restitution of conjugal rights was a hollow mockery of a judgment. Failure to comply with it was not only inevitable, it was what was intended when it was made. Technically it turned the disobedient spouse into a deserter—which he or she had to be before it was granted. It was abolished on 1st January, 1971. The law had never been able to make anyone carry out the duties of matrimony. After Jackson's Case, it would not even make one spouse live with the other. Marriage was practically as fragile as living in sin. Raging equality was stemmed for a generation or so whilst dependent wives occupied their husband's homes, impelled by the sheer necessity for bread and shelter. No one thought about the women's right to decide where the family home should be. The proletariat lived near their work and the middle class kept up with the Joneses. It was rather taken for granted that the huband chose, in the sense that he was the person on whom the economic pressures bore most directly. But in *Dunn v. Dunn (1948) 2 All E.R. 822* Lord Justice Denning (as he was then) commenced that saga of judicial innovation which he is carrying on no less energetically today.

The wife, he declared, has a right to be heard. This is no more than

---

* Imprisonment had been established as the punishment only by the progressive administration of 1813. Previously, the penalty was excommunication by the Ecclesiastical Court.

recognising *de jure* the ordinary state of affairs *de facto*, but it is dignified now as a principle of law.

> '*The decision where the home should be is a decision which affects both the spouses and their children. It is their duty to decide it by agreement—by give and take—and not by the imposition of the will of one over that of the other. Each is entitled to an equal voice in the ordering of the affairs which are their common concern.*'

Anything more calculated to undermine harmonious marriage is impossible to conceive. Inevitably, each having right on his or her side, the impasse is soluble only in the Divorce Court, and the *Legal Aid and Advice Act, 1949* became necessary. Its timely provisions enabled the legal profession to expand to cater for if not to contain the rising tide of matrimonial unhappiness.

From the purely legal standpoint, the doctrine of 'constructive desertion' burgeoned. 'Constructive' is a term of great utility to legal theorists. It does not mean that the spouse who has decided to bring matters to a head by clearing out is doing something constructive. It means that even though the act which gives a right to a legal remedy has not been done, the law presumes that it has. Desertion connotes that the deserter has left the deserted spouse. But where the wrongdoer drives the innocent party away, he or she has not left the matrimonial home. Lord Merriman put it much more accurately when he said

> '*Desertion is not the withdrawal from a place but from a state of things.*'
>
> **Pulford v. Pulford (1923) P. 18.**

Lord Denning said this follows when 'such an arrangement is frustrated by the unreasonableness of one or the other'.

It is not timely to digress to the definition of the degree of unreasonableness which will found a decree in this jurisdiction. A conventional view of the cases suggests that the husband is entitled to the last word because he is the breadwinner and has to live near to his work. On the other hand, a man cannot insist on his wife living under the same roof as his mother (*Munro* v. *Munro* [1950] 1 All E.R. 832). By a curious oversight there is no reported decision on the impossibility of living with his wife's mother.

Once cohabitation is achieved the failure to render the expected rights after consummation is no ground for annulment. Nor was it a ground for divorce on the ground of cruelty until 1965. Then in *Sheldon* v. *Sheldon* (1966) 2 All E.R. 257 a decree was granted on that ground where the spouses had slept together for six years without marital relations. There was no evidence of inability, merely refusal. In *Evans* v. *Evans* (1965) 2 All E.R. 789 the wife was held to be cruel

193

though her reason for refusing was fear of childbirth, but in other cases long abstinence based on disinclination for sex was held not to be cruel.

For what married couples are bound to give to each other is consortium, not just sex. And the law demonstrates this in cases where outsiders, not the spouses, prevent it for them. In *Best* v. *Samuel Fox & Co. Ltd.*, the husband was rendered impotent by the injuries inflicted by the defendant's negligence. But the wife was not entitled to damages for the loss thus occasioned to her of normal marital relations. The husband, the direct victim, could have substantial damages to compensate him for the disability. The wife's loss is not recognised by the law of compensation for injuries though it is the very foundation of the law of marriage.

Consortium is companionship and sharing the home and recreation and sometimes the business of each other and bringing up a family —or indeed, enjoying life together without children.

> '*Sexual relations are doubtless a most important part of the marriage relation, but if age or illness or even disinclination impair the potency of either of the spouses who continue to live together as husband and wife, I do not think the consortium is affected. It would be only if on this account one of them withdrew and decided to live apart. In truth I think that the only loss that the law can recognise is the loss of that part of the consortium that is called* servitum, *the loss of service,*'

said Lord Goddard in Best's Case. Therefore, a man's damages for his injuries are increased if his wife leaves him after he is stricken. Mr Justice Hilbery (in *Lampert* v. *Eastern National Omnibus Co. Ltd.* [*1954*] *2 All E.R. 719*) was prepared to allow damages for the loss of consortium to a woman so disfigured in an accident that her husband left her. But she failed to prove that the defendants were at fault. Thus a wife can get nothing for her loss, but her husband will get more damages if she leaves him because of it.

The loss of consortium and service was the damage for which the homebreaker had to pay damages in seduction cases. The Permissive Parliament by legislation which took effect on 1st January, 1971, abolished seduction together with breach of promise of marriage and damages against adulterers. For there allegedly is something sordid about putting a price on a woman because she has been seduced. There is apparently no such obloquy attaching to a woman who suffers food poisoning after eating tinned salmon. Another Mr Jackson recovered damages in 1909 for the loss of his wife's services from the sellers of the defective food (*Jackson* v. *Watson* [*1909*] *2 K.B. 193*).

By losing the menial services of a wife a man suffers a legally recognised wrong. By losing her love and capacity to make love he does not. The basis, according to Best's Case, is that:

> '*companionship, love, affection, comfort, mutual services, sexual intercourse—all belong to the marital state. Taken together, they make up the consortium; but I cannot think that the loss of any one element, however grievous it may be as it undoubtedly is in the present case, can be regarded as the loss of the consortium within the meaning of the decided cases. Still less could any impairment of one of the elements be so regarded. Consortium, I think, is one and indivisible. The law gives a remedy for its loss and for nothing short of that,*'

said Lord Justice Birkett.

Even should an awakened public opinion resent the absence of compensation for deprived spouses, there is no means by which a change can be ensured. Parliament changes these things if it likes and when it likes. There was no general clamour for the abolition of enticement. As Lord Porter pointed out in Best's Case:

> '*I do not think it possible to say that a change in the outlook of the public, however great, must inevitably be followed by a change in the law of this country. The Common Law is a historical development rather than a logical whole, and the fact that a particular doctrine does not logically accord with another or others is no ground for its rejection.*'

Which is naught for your wife's comfort.

However, back again to Mr Justice McCardie for her advantages:

> '*At every point of research, on every aspect of the case, I find nothing but confusion, obscurity and inconsistency. I find privileges given to a wife which are wholly denied to a husband and I find that upon the husband there has fallen one injustice after another.*'

> **Gotliffe v. Edelston (1930) 2 K.B. 378.**

That case arose simply because a couple got married after a car accident. (They would probably have married had they not had the crash.) And the insurance company wanted to find out if they had to pay damages to the wife who had become one with the driver. Before they were united in wedlock, they were free to sue each other. If one drove negligently and injured the other, he (or she) could be cast in damages. By reason of the fortuitous enactment demanding compulsory motor insurance in the *Road Traffic Act, 1930*, the injured party would not only get judgment, but his or her insurers would actually pay the money. But husbands and wives could not sue each other—except for divorce and maintenance. A thoughtless marriage before the insurance cheque was actually cashed could ruin everything. It was altered in 1935, no doubt because the un-limited lethal potentialities of women drivers precipitated a change which seven centuries of the Common Law had not found necessary.

A married man had, until the *Married Women's Property Acts* and the *Law Reform Act* of 1935, the dismal prospect of being sued by his wife's victims. He was pretty helpless even to defend the action.

> '*Till judgment, he was nothing but a party to the action, joined for conformity. After judgment, he was bound. Before judgment, he could escape this inexorable doom only by parting with his spouse, his money or his life,*'

said Lord Sumner.

Mr Justice Rigby Swift pointed out that a husband being liable for his wife's civil wrongs could be liable to pay damages to the wife of the man whom she enticed away (*Newton v. Hardy [1934] 149 L.T.R. 165 and 168*). As Sir Percy Winfield put it (*Law of Tort Edition 1954*):

> '*It might be less expensive for a man to keep a dog with a savage temper than to marry a wife with a venomous tongue. He could kill the animal, he could not even lock up the woman. And while he was not liable for the dog's bites unless he knew of its evil disposition, ignorance of his wife's vices was no excuse.*'

One of the great feminist legislative advances, the *Law Reform (Married Women and Tortfeasors) Act, 1935* provided that a man should not be responsible for his wife's torts, such as negligence and slander. A price had to be paid for this great economic emancipation of Englishmen. By a master stroke, the Act also enabled a married woman to own and deal with property just as if she was *feme sole*. Women were thus duped not only into accepting financial responsibility for their own affairs, but deprived of the economic foundation of their husbands' fortunes.

However, the pernicious undertones of the old subjection of women still affect some situations. A husband might be liable for his wife's negligent driving, for instance, because he owns the car and his wife is his agent to use it. Those who can afford the initial outlay give their wives motor cars of their own. You can buy nice little cars for less than a thousand pounds, and considering how much damage your wife can do, they are well worth it. But they must be absolutely given so as to belong to the wife completely.

The 1935 Act was not pure unadulterated relief for married men, however. It provided a lesson in lawmaking of the kind to which many a reformer could fall foul. The fiction of legal unity which we inherited from God's law had another consequence besides making a man liable for his wife's damaging actions. Since they were one, neither could sue the other for debts and damage to property, however maliciously caused. The *Matrimonial Causes Act, 1857* (as well as 'inventing' judicial divorce) had provided that when they

196

were judicially separated, husband and wife could sue each other. But by an accident in the 1935 Act, which repealed a bit of a later Act, which had replaced the relevant part of the 1857 Act—if you follow me—the old Common Law rule revived.

Husband and wife were therefore precluded from suing each other in many cases. A wife might want to sue her husband for negligence, whilst they were yet on the best of terms. The husband might be delighted to admit liability. Suppose they were in a car crash. The wife was badly hurt. His insurance company could pay a large sum in damages. His wife, a passenger, was in no way to blame. Perhaps another driver was, but perhaps the husband was genuinely at fault.

It was odd that a man might be covered by a policy of insurance which indemnified him against the claims of passengers (and although not until very recently demanded by law, many motor policies did cover passengers) and be unable to compensate his wife, but bound to compensate his mother-in-law sitting in another passenger seat.

This limitation was well illustrated by a libel action heard at the Chester Assizes by Mr Justice Macnaghten in 1930—*Ralston* v. *Ralston*. The husband and wife had parted in 1899, and the wife later started in business in Ludlow as a garage owner. In 1929 she happened to be on holiday and visited a churchyard in Anglesey where she saw a gravestone inscribed: 'In loving memory of Jennie, the dearly beloved wife of W. R. Crawshay Ralston . . .'

The wife's name was Edith. She sued her husband for libel, contending that the meaning of the epitaph was that she was not married to him. The judge accepted that this was a libel. But husband and wife were one—even when they had been apart for 30 years. Her counsel sought to get round that by relying on one of the sections of the *Married Women's Property Act, 1882*, which enabled a limited right of action by a wife against a husband 'for the protection of her separate property'. The 'separate property', he argued, was her trading reputation. The judge rejected the contention, saying, 'It cannot be said that chastity is a necessary qualification for the management or ownership of a garage'.

The case would be differently decided today. The *Law Reform (Husband and Wife) Act, 1962*, gives husbands and wives the same rights of action against each other for torts, which are civil wrongs independent of contracts, and contracts, as if they were not married. But the Act reserves to the trial judge the right to stay the action if it seems that no substantial benefit would accrue to either from the case going on. Or he can stay the case if it would be better brought under the 17th Section of the *Married Women's Property Act, 1882*, which, as we have seen, has only recently come into its own.

The old doctrine of unity now has one sole survivor. When husband and wife swop gossip in speech or writing, no action for slander or libel can be taken because of the publication thus made. For not only could there be no publication because husband and wife are one (*Wennhak* v. *Morgan* [*1888*] *20 Q.B.D. 635*), but the relationship makes the communication privileged, and it would be against public policy to permit an action on it. On the other hand, if a slanderer defames the husband to the wife or the wife to the husband, in speech or writing, the slanderer can be sued by the victim. And probably would be, if he was worth a writ.

The Common Law demanded of a husband that he maintain his wife and child in a manner suitable to their rank and station. Parliament has never said so in so many words. In the Summary Jurisdiction Acts which founded the powers of magistrates to order maintenance for wives, and the statute law relating to divorce and separation, the standard of living was not specified. The *Matrimonial Proceedings and Property Act, 1970*, belatedly lays down a host of matters to be taken into account, which the courts have been considering for ages. To this day, the practice books mention that maintenance for a wife pending divorce proceedings was commonly an eighth of the family income, on the authority of a Consistory case which pointed out that she could not have much because she had likely committed adultery. In practice the courts work on a third of joint incomes, and several cases can be cited to show that that is not a rule with the force of law. Maybe not; the judges do it.

But the Common Law could not expect a woman to take matrimonial proceedings for financial support. It did not entrust the provision of bread and covering to the vagaries of its ritual-ridden courts. It simply constituted the wife her husband's 'agent of necessity'. He could not revoke this implied authority to pledge his credit for necessaries unless he expressly instructed a tradesman not to supply her. Even if he had forbidden his wife to pledge his credit, the shopkeeper or landlord could recover against him when the wife disobeyed. This rests upon the same principle expressed by Lord Kenyon in *Philp* v. *Squire* (*1791*) *Peake 114* when excusing people who harboured a married woman because she falsely told them that her husband ill-treated her. If the law were otherwise, no one would dare to protect a married woman. Where circumstances forced a wife to live apart from her husband, without desertion, he was bound still to maintain her (*Lilley* v. *Lilley* [*1959*] *3 All E.R. 283*).

The wife was not entitled to impoverish the husband by extravagance (*Land* v. *Ironmonger* [*1844*] *13 M. & W. 368*). She could pledge his credit only for 'necessaries', clothing for herself and the children, household equipment, food, medicine, the attention of doctors, and where appropriate, the wages of servants. On 1st January, 1971, the wife's agency of necessity was abolished. Section 41 of the *Matrimonial Proceedings and Property Act, 1970*, did it. Such is progress.

Of course, you do not nowadays see in the newspapers the advertisements by which men gave notice that they would no longer answer for the debts of their estranged wives. The importunities of the door-to-door salesmen of encyclopaedias could not saddle a husband with necessaries—though the vacuum cleaner men might have done better. And the right had always, like all forms of maintenance, been defeasible if the wife committed adultery. Grocers and butchers no doubt found it tiresome having to ask all their women customers who wanted tick whether they had committed adultery. It may very well be that they will go on letting women have credit after they part from their husbands. Should they do so, they might with advantage observe whether they wear wedding rings. They might, of course, have pawned them to buy necessaries. The foundation of the agency of necessity was that

> '*women if they could take nothing without permission from their husbands will be left to perish, Tantalus-like, from thirst and hunger, amid the overflowing exuberance of their husband's plenty.*'
>
> *Manby* v. *Scott (1660) 1 Lev. 4*.

But not only husbands and wives co-habit. Mistresses live with men, and they, too, are entitled to pledge their men's credit for necessaries, whilst they co-habit (*Ryan* v. *Sams [1848] 12 Q.B.D. 460*). This right has not been abolished. Mistresses are thus better off than wives.

Now whilst it was perfectly lawful to beat, castigate and lock up your wife—particularly if you belonged to the lower orders, there were some judges who rather disapproved of it, and one of them was Lord Stowell. He was the younger brother of Lord Eldon, who did so well in law and politics that he wrote to him, 'Come south, Jack,' and his brother would help him prosper. He became the chief ecclesiastical judge and thus came to decide the case of *Evans* v. *Evans* in 1792. He decided that a wife did not have to go back to her husband and render him conjugal rights if the husband had treated her cruelly. His attitude might have been because they were Scotsmen, and it had been possible to get a divorce in Scotland since the Reformation. However, the best that Stowell could manage was to hold that a wife was entitled to stay away from her husband if his conduct was so 'grave and weighty' as to justify it.

Day in and day out, lawyers who probably do not appreciate the antiquity of that proposition and magistrates who certainly do not, consider what exactly amounts to 'grave and weighty'.

'I await with some philological excitement an example of conduct which is "grave" and without being "weighty".

Lord Justice Diplock *(as he was)* **in** *Hall* **v.** *Hall (1962) 1 W.L.R. 1246.*

Since *Evans* v. *Evans*, wife beating and similar tactics in the battle of the sexes have occupied the attention of Parliament as well as the courts. The particular kinds of behaviour which would qualify a spouse for relief became the subjects of technical limitations of stupefying complexity. The whole topic was overlaid by class prejudice. The lower orders, knowing full well that they had Coke on their side, believed in wife beating and their social superiors saw no reason to deprive them of that comfort, which did nothing to raise wages. The Upper Classes, of course, appreciated that wife beating was not gentlemanly, but they had to regard matrimony from the viewpoints of Property and Sin, in that order.

The 1857 revolution did not do away with judical separation, and many a wise woman took that in preference to divorce, for why should a woman 'Give' a man his freedom when he had taken from her the best years of her life? Judicial separation was still an expensive business, and in 1892 the bright notion of protecting women whose husbands could not afford to run two homes, or even to run one and to drink as well, occurred to Parliament. It enacted that when a man had been convicted of an aggravated assault on his wife, the court which convicted him could order that she be no longer bound to co-habit with him if it considered her future safety was in peril.

The advantages to a wife who had had the living daylights knocked out of her was obvious. She was free to go off and live alone, or with their children under 10. The husband could be ordered to maintain them. Exactly how he did so whilst in prison for the assault is not clear. By 1879 a woman could get an order because her husband was an habitual drunkard. In 1886 'courts of summary jurisdiction', which was the compendious title of JPs in Petty Sessions and the Police Courts of the big towns, were empowered to order deserting husbands to maintain their wives, and similar orders against those who 'wilfully neglected to maintain' them.

By various enactments the powers of those courts—since 1952 all called 'Magistrates' Courts'—have been altered in details. The important thing is that unlike the divorce jurisdiction, their power to adjudicate depends upon the person applying to the courts residence, not upon domicile. It is often difficult to find people against whom summonses have been issued, but if they happen to be in Scotland or Ulster or Commonwealth citizens, or only living here while it suits them, the court has power to make orders. The greatest indirect customers of these courts are the Departments of Social Security. They can insist upon deserted wives claiming maintenance from their husbands, and so that the expense to the taxpayer of maintaining the family is mitigated as far as possible. Contraception still being virtually unknown among the indigent, this is more of a gesture than an economic success. The magisterial jurisdiction is apparently efficient from the productivity viewpoint. It makes large numbers of orders quickly. This is possibly because magistrates become so used to believing all they are told by police-men about motorists, pilferers and layabouts that they are quite prepared to believe the worst of anyone. It is also attributable to a tendency among summoned husbands not to turn up.

It would be quite wrong, however, to believe that magistrates always make orders in favour of complaining wives. The British tradition of uncertainty in litigation is probably as strong in the Magistrates' Courts as in the House of Lords, though in the former the supporting casuistry is not nearly so well done.

The great virtue of the Magistrates' Courts until recently has been their speed. A woman with a strong case on cruelty, desertion, adultery or neglect to maintain can get an order in most cases within a few weeks of the bust-up. Such people are often unable to sue for divorce because they have not been married three years, nor deserted for two years. Sometimes they do not want to be divorced. However unpopular it might be with progressive committees and MPs, there is an attitude among many people that a woman who has given the best years of her life to a man is entitled to withhold his 'freedom'. The law of the Magistrates' Courts is quite well designed for them.

The complaining spouse must prove his, or more usually her, case. The degree of proof required is dealt with elsewhere in this work. The degree achieved depends in fact upon the prejudices of the tribunal. By no means all the bad decisions come from lay magistrates. A charming Stipendiary was greatly impressed by the forthright admissions of a coloured man. Yes, he had burst open the lavatory door when his wife was sheltering therein from him after he had thrown the clock at her. Yes, he did hit her with the chamber pot. But this was because she had aggravated him with her extrava-gance. To her counsel, the Learned Magistrate said:

'This is the East End, you know. And he said he was sorry.'

He was, however, persuaded that that was 'cruel', though it took some doing. Since it was not the only time that the husband had been so vexed, and the wife had issued her summons within six months of the assault, he was able to 'adjudge' that he had treated her with 'persistent' cruelty. (Why cruelty had to be persistent to entitle the victim to an order from the Justices while one cruel act by itself permits a judge to dissolve the marriage has never really been explained. The reason is clearly that the lower orders are entitled to beat their wives to some extent at least.)

Once satisfied that the man had been cruel, however, the Stipendiary was able to order him to pay maintenance of £4. 10s. a week for the wife and £2 a week for each of the five children. He also ordered that the wife be no longer bound to cohabit with him. His pay, according to him, was £16. 10s. a week, so he had £2 for his board and keeping. Such orders are explicable on several grounds, and quite often the magistrates are not as daft as they look. Many of them, whose origins are working class, or who are still in that *stratum* of society, know perfectly well that many people of that and every other class see nothing wrong in perjury about means. It is explicable on grounds of hatred of spouse or quite often by conspiracy with spouse, who knows perfectly well that certain overtime and bonuses are paid to the husband, or that he has sidelines of varying decrees of honesty and income tax sensitivity. If the case has only been brought at the insistence of a Social Security officer, honour is satisfied if the husband can get out cheaply, leaving the main burden of expense to the taxpayer. Magistrates, professional and lay (most of them), know this perfectly well. They therefore multiply the income to which a man admits by a variable quotient.

The best course for a man who has two wives (or more) to keep, is to be absolutely excoriatingly honest. It is hard work, but worth it. You will only be believed when accused before magistrates if you prove your innocence with utmost certainty, and probably not then. But to turn up without even a wage slip is inviting disaster. The multiplier will be at least two.

I proffer with some diffidence the theory that in the majority of courts of summary jurisdiction, and quite a few divorce courts, the multiplier increases—perhaps only fractionally—for a husband who complains of his wife's extravagance. The extravagance of a woman who was supported and had to provide for five children on the wages of a £16. 10s. a week immigrant is a little difficult to condemn. But those more fortunate might properly complain of it. In *Callot* v. *Nash*, the wife was an American girl. In the early Twenties that of itself was practically enough for a verdict against her. Captain Nash pleaded that he was not liable for the goods she had from the plaintiffs because they were not necessaries. Socialistic reforms have done away with the agency of necessity of a wife, but it will take more than legislation to do away with the reasoning of Mr Justice McCardie. 'Even the most expensive dress she would wear but three times only.' One evening dress cost 2,400 francs and was called 'Pecheresse' (or female sinner).

> 'Her catholicity of profusion was remarkable. She threw herself beneath the fatal curse of luxury. She forgot that those who possess substantial means are trustees to use them with prudence, charity and propriety. She forgot that ostentation is the worst form of vulgarity. She ignored the sharp menace of future penury. Dress, and dress alone seems to have been her end in life.'

The husband won. Her dress bills were so enormous that he was bound to do it. She did not go into the witness box. She was the customer, in her own name and in the names bestowed upon her by her two previous husbands. McCardie's brilliance fixed liability on that ground. But it will not avail every husband for the mere fact that the wife was rich in her own right did not mean that the husband had no duty to maintain her. Consequently, suppliers of women's clothing are worse off now that the agency of necessity is abolished, but husbands are no better off. The mere fact that they can defend actions by couturiers and jewellers does not mean that they can get out cheaply in maintenance claims by their wives. And should they allege extravagance against their wives, they will discover that it is a poor excuse for their own delinquency.

Before the maintenance order is made, however, the 'matrimonial offence' must be proved. This concept has theoretically been abolished in divorce. It has not actually been abolished; if anything it is a bit more rigidly circumscribed than it was. But to get a separation order and maintenance in the Magistrates' Court, the old law of the matrimonial offence still has to be satisfied. Parliament was given no answer when this inconsistency was pointed out during the reform of the divorce law. Change was foreshadowed, but it appears to have been overshadowed. Parliament apparently can do anything but it can't do everything.

The actual grounds available for Separation Orders in Magistrates Courts are still adultery, persistent cruelty to the spouse or children, desertion, conviction on indictment of any offence involving an assault on the complainant, conviction summarily of wounding, grievous bodily harm or actual bodily harm or a common assault for which the sentence was more than a month in prison; knowingly infecting the spouse with VD, habitual drunkenness or drug addiction, and wilful neglect to maintain. A wife forced into prostitution by her husband can also get an order. The complaint should be made within six months of the behaviour complained of. Many of these classes are 'continuing offences' and so there is no effective limit. But a complainant must issue the summons within six months of the last bashing or adultery on which he or she relies.

Magistrates quite often dismiss applications for separation or maintenance orders, where the case seems to be to them six of one and half a dozen of the other. By this means they ensure that the Department of Social Security will continue to support the wife whilst the husband spends his wages on drink or other women or a motor-car. There is a class of person whose standard of living depends on the sympathy of the magistracy for 'inadequate' people and they do quite well out of it.

There are plenty of Justices of the Old School who do actually try to make maintenance defaulters pay up. Of the 'absconder' a correspondent of *The Magistrate* for November, 1970, declared that six weeks' imprisonment was the only way to deal with those who had disappeared for three months or more. He pleaded with his brethren that after a time or two inside, they learn the lesson. He then pointed out that most of the excuses:

'I never got a copy of the order',
'I never got a receipt',
'She won't let me see the children',
'Her mother said she does not want my filthy money',
'She has committed adultery',
'I've someone else to keep and cannot afford it',

are irrelevant.

In every such case the defaulter can take some proceedings himself if he wishes so as to get the order varied if he is right in law and is believed on the facts. But they seldom put the excuse forward until they are well in the taxpayer's debt.

The same gentleman considers that Attachment of Earnings Orders are a waste of time for the Magistrates and their staff unless the employer of the person bound to pay maintenance is a concern of reasonable size and reputation. Even employees of such firms often feel it worthwhile to change jobs to dodge a deduction for unwanted wife and children.

This class of our society is subsidised to the extent of £50 million. Large arrears caused by genuine poverty which can usually be proved quite easily by doctor's certificate or proof of real inability to get work are often remitted in part or whole. Spouses get quite good at telling the tale to take advantage of remissions. This magistrate cited the often canvassed case of the defaulter who did win the Pools, and, of course, his wife could not recover the several hundred pounds he had been forgiven. Nor was he so conscience-stricken that he paid up anyway.

Had that been a County Court judgment unpaid for some un-roadworthy motor-car or ghastly veneered furniture the pool promoters bounty would have benefited the creditor. Magistrates might well decide not to remit large arrears 'to give him a chance'. Chances are what these fellows are looking for, like Mr Smith. Other men of all classes can put themselves in his class now. *The Housing Act, 1969*, has made extravagant provisions for Government grants for home improvements. No man need be denied access to a bath nowadays.

Putting Asunder

DIVORCE is necessary in order to make adultery legal. It has always had for its purpose the enabling of people already married to contract more marriages without incurring the penalties of bigamy. Until 1823 this was punishable by death. Other attractions were the disinherison of an unwanted wife; the capacity to marry a more desirable wife; and the legitimation of issue who would otherwise have laboured under the disabilities of bastardy.

The law of adulterine bastardy developed to protect the social and economic power of the aristocratic order. It did it with great efficiency and now that we are all capitalists some find it convenient to get divorced now and again. This great social advance has resulted in the past generation in the law of divorce becoming confused because of a lot of somewhat 'pi' considerations creeping in. When A. P. Herbert's Act in 1937 enabled women to get divorces merely because their husbands were cruel it was hailed as a great social advance.

All that Herbert's Act did was to free more cruel spouses and their victims to make further marriages even though they had no inclination therefor. The divorce lobby, ever since John Milton started it after marrying a girl whose father's politics were different from his, has always insisted with typical Reforming cant, that by enabling further marriages to be lawfully contracted, divorce *prevented* adultery and was therefore desirable from the public policy viewpoint. All it actually did was to legalise it.

The first essential for a divorce is a valid marriage. By divorce we mean nowadays the dissolution of the status of a married person. It developed, of course, from the power of *patria potestas* which the Roman paterfamilias possessed over all his family and household. Originally the power of life and death, their rights were curtailed. But they could still put aside their own wives and the wives or husbands of those subject to them. There is nothing unusual now about a mother telling her daughter or her son that she or he must divorce. Every day, a large number of mothers go into witness boxes all over the country to play their part in the dissolution process. The commonest rubric until 1st January, 1971, was a few words to the effect that the petitioner lost weight to a noticeable extent whilst yoked to the respondent, but has recovered proper dimensions since the parting. This was evidence of injury to health, now no longer necessary for divorce, but still essential for Maintenance and Separation Orders in a Magistrates' Court.

The function of the judiciary is to prevent the alteration of matrimonial status developing into a sort of planned obsolescence consumer industry dominated by mothers-in-law. They are a bunch of Canutes overwhelmed by what Mr William Latey QC, a vastly experienced Commissioner in the Divorce Court, has designated in a learned work, *The Tide of Divorce (1970)*. But to this day, some give the dissolution of marriage anxious consideration and insist on the strict proof of things which others are more easily persuaded about. 'I will not be a rubber stamp,' declared His Honour Judge Leon in 1958. He spoke for many of his brethren, but it was not recorded in any learned work—only the centre page of the *Daily Mirror*.

The turning out of Roman women was done, no doubt, for all sorts of reasons, good and bad, but the common cause, scholars believe, was adultery. God has been credited with a deep concern over adultery. The Archbishop of Canterbury, however, was on record during the campaign for divorce reform supporting the view that a single isolated act of adultery should not break a marriage. This mental attitude is impossible to reflect in a law. Laws are simply situations. When certain things have happened, certain results follow if, *and only if, the legal process is invoked.* Spouses begin divorce proceedings by filing at any Divorce County Court petitions more or less in *Form 2* in the *Appendix to the Matrimonial Causes (Amendment No. 3) Rules, 1970*. These are obtainable for a few pence from law stationers, ready made out for desertion, adultery, and so on, and only need filling up with the name and details.

Behind the Iron Curtain, they have tried rubber stamp divorce at post offices and other state departments. But this approach is falling into disfavour. Civilisation proceeds apace, and the importance of status changes in personal law is appreciated. The growing numbers of rights and restrictions compel a bureaucratic approach. The object of the study of divorce in the future will be to acquire expertise in the manipulation of the status-change for economic advantage. Careful study of the history of divorce reveals that that has always been the object of taking proceedings.

A ritual more complex than the mating dance of the capercailzie is essential. By providing the courts with a wide variety of information the parties disarm themselves and enable the courts to control them. This the courts have to do in order to be just not only to the parties but to all the other people affected by their status and behaviour.

Until 1923, a woman wishing to divorce her husband in England had to prove against him not only adultery, but some other matrimonial offence as well. A husband, however, could always get rid of his wife (by separation before judicial divorce was invented) for adultery alone. The reason was not simply that women were inferior. The law gave the man the right to repudiate not merely his wife's morality but the legitimacy of the issue born to her after the adultery. 'God makes the heir' was the cornerstone of economic power for centuries. The eldest son living after the death of the father was heir-at-law to whom passed the father's freeholds. For a long time this inheritance could not be sidestepped by the father's will. It was intolerable in the eyes of the English men of property that a suppositious child might inherit that which belonged by God-given right to the heir begotten by a man upon the body of his lawful wife. Modified somewhat, this doctrine endured until 1925.

Other matrimonial offences came to be recognised because of their tendency to lead to adultery. In the Dark Ages before the Normans came divorce was permitted, for example, as the result of the capture of the other spouse by the Vikings, who came here to pillage and rape. The Penitentials of Archbishop Theodore recognised the wisdom and validity of this. It was, after all, merely forced separation, like desertion. After the ecclesiastical power wrung from the Conqueror the principle that the control of marriage by the church courts was the temporal law of the land as well as the spiritual law of the Church, the spiritual bases for divorce were added to the physical. An instance is the Pauline Privilege, where one of two unbelieving spouses became converted to Christianity, and was allowed to contract a further valid marriage with another Christian.

Here we observe the beginnings of the great religious controversy over remarriage after divorce. The Roman Christians had excommunicated those who remarried after putting aside a spouse. But the law of the Empire permitted it. To this day, no clergyman of the Anglican Church is bound to re-marry a divorced person. *Section 65* of the *Matrimonial Causes Act, 1965*, is a conscience clause which leaves it up to the priest to choose whether to give this legal right. The Bishops were deeply divided when the *Divorce Bill* of 1857 was debated in the House of Lords. Nowadays they are divorce reformers of enthusiasm and originality. But still they cannot compel the remarriage of divorcees in church. The Bishop of Southwark quoted the speech made in 1857 by the Bishop of London in *The Times*, 15th January, 1971, to compare theory and practice. Between 1715 and 1857 there were 317 private Acts of Parliament for divorce. Not one bishop voted against any of them. Three of the petitioners were Anglican priests.

The bishop set out his own Pastoral Regulation to clergy, 'Although clergy have the legal right to marry a divorced person, all four Houses of Convocation have urged the clergy not to avail themselves of this right'.

The people denied marriage in church have, of course, the right to go elsewhere to get married, after complying with all the qualifying conditions as to residence and so on.

When the Ecclesiastical Courts dominated the law of marriage, 'divorce' did not mean what it means today. Didactic practitioners in the Divorce Courts nowadays open suits by telling judges that the petition is for 'dissolution' and that is right. When the consistory courts granted those 'judicial separations' which were known as '*divorce a mensa et thoro*' the decree stated that:

> '*We do pronounce decree and declare that the said . . . ought by law to be divorced and separated from bed and board and the mutual cohabitation with the said . . . her husband until they shall be reconciled to each other; and we do by these presents divorce and separate them accordingly . . .*'

This was merely a dispensation from the duties of marriage which did not destroy the relationship of husband and wife. It can now be done quite simply and cheaply by an order of a Magistrates' Court containing a 'non-cohabitation clause'. It can still be done by the Divorce Court, of course, but since Quintin Hogg's Act (*Maintenance Orders Act, 1968*) abolished financial limits on the powers of magistrates to order maintenance, Legal Aid committees often refuse to assist people to proceed in the Divorce Court, because they can get the same result more cheaply in the Magistrates' Court. But if the case is brought in a Divorce Court the respondent can pray for dissolution instead of separation.

The Magistrates' Courts' matrimonial jurisdiction is still based on the old law, and differs from the law of divorce in important ways, separation is on the same basis as ever. The supervision of all the courts handling the breakdown of marriage, and divorce maintenance of spouses and children, and separation; division and succession to property because of marriage changes is now handled by the newly created Family Division of the High Court. The practitioners there accordingly have to deal in the old and the new law allegedly founded upon different theories and principles. But there need be no confusion because, of course, the new law is not very much different from the old. It only looks as if divorce has been reformed. All that has actually happened is that a couple of extra grounds have been given—divorce by consent and by the initiative of the 'guilty party'.

The infinite variety of means and motives for getting one's own way and spiting someone else are nowhere better observed than in a matrimonial cause. The judges and lawyers can become very wise and sophisticated because of their constant exposure to the ingenuity of litigants. Matrimonial cases are nowadays seldom tried by jury.

Jury trial has never been so much used in matrimonial cases as in others. One man justice is preferable to popular prejudice. This is no doubt one of the great benefits inherited from the Ecclesiastical Courts. For Jesus Christ himself was never so arbitrary as the Evangelists. When the woman taken in adultery was brought before him the mob leaders pointed out that the Law of Moses required her to be stoned to death. It was clearly a trap for him. If he said 'Stone her' he would be exposed as an enemy of the people. If he said 'Don't' he would be opposing the law.

He wrote something in the sand, we are told, but we are not told what. He then invited 'him who is without sin among you to cast the first stone'. No one did, and this was perhaps because what he wrote revealed that he knew a thing or two of the sins of the demagogues. For this theory, I am indebted to a sermon by Father Clifford Howell of the Society of Jesus. The principle underlying it no doubt inspired the great judges who have tried matrimonial causes in England in the past two centuries. Founded in religious casuistry though the law was, they were able by the creation of judical rules without the aid of Parliament, to protect the weak. Parliament in reforming the law of divorce abolished many wise rules in the name of progress.

There is nothing to prevent it passing an Act which defies the laws of nature. By the *Act 37 Hen. VIII*, it enacted that the children born of Elena by Sir Ralph Sadler were legitimate. She was the wife of Matthew Barr, who had disappeared. Believing herself a widow, Elena 'married' Sir Ralph, in 1534, but some years later, Matthew turned up again. To regularise the position, Parliament declared that the second marriage would be made valid by virtue of the Act, and of Barr securing a *divorce a mensa et thoro* (on the ground of Elena's adultery with Sadler). This, the first of the 'Parliamentary divorces', was therefore really nothing of the kind, but a declaration of legitimacy and validation *ex post facto* of a bigamous marriage. The one thing which it did not do was to destroy the original marriage to Matthew Barr, and nor did the decree.

A century later, Lord Rees got a similar Bill through the House of Lords by only two votes. The Bishops opposed it because the Whigs intended it to be an up-to-date precedent for a divorce for Charles II from Catherine of Braganza. But even in the 16th Century some theologians were claiming that the Church Courts could actually dissolve marriages, by God's authority. The Puritan clergyman Henry Smith wrote that:

> '*Divorcement is the end of marriage, and divideth them that were one flesh, as if the bodie and soul were parted assunder.*'

> '*The disease of marriage is adultery, and the medicine thereof is divorcement.*'

Luther and others had rejected the indissolubility of marriage. The Reformation here overthrew the temporal authority of Rome but refused to depart from those mediaeval doctrines which Henry chose to believe. You were as likely to burn for being too Protestant as to be disembowelled for being a Papist. English theology has never favoured extremes. Accordingly, it was no surprise when Henry Smith's theory was rejected by the Star Chamber in 1601. This was the case where the Widow Peaze had married Hercules Fuliambe, by right of which marriage he claimed the Aston Estate in Yorkshire. Archbishop Whitgift, giving the judgment of the Council, declared that the remedy for adultery was only divorce from bed and board and not dissolution, which was described as *a vinculo matrimonii*—'from the bond of matrimony'.

What had happened was that Hercules had a sentence of divorce from a Consistory Court before he married the widow, which he contended left him free to remarry. The verdict against him set the course of the English marriage law for 256 years. Divorce *a vinculo* was actually a decree of nullity, on the grounds of the 'diriment impediments' known to the Canon Law, such as consanguinity, bigamy, duress and impotence. Judicial divorce existed in Scotland from 1536, and no one thought that was not a Christian country. It is sometimes claimed that one of the foundations of the campaign for judicial divorce in England was a speech to a prisoner by Mr Justice Maule in 1844, to a man who was convicted of bigamy at the instance of his wife's seducer. The judge told him that he should have gone through the Parliamentary divorce procedure at a cost of over £1,000.

> '*You will tell me that you have never had a thousand farthings of your own in the world, but that makes no difference. Sitting here as an English judge, it is my duty to tell you that this is not a country in which there is one law for the rich and another for the poor. You will be imprisoned for one day, which period has already been exceeded as you have been in custody since the commencement of the Assizes.*'

Like so many legal fables that is subject to some qualification, Robert Walton, who was counsel on the Midland Circuit at the time, says the prisoner was gaoled for four months, which rather knocks the bottom out of its reforming spirit. At any rate there was support for Divorce Reform. The Bishops were in favour by a two-thirds majority. The Court for Divorce and Matrimonial Causes was set up with power to decree dissolution in favour of a husband for adultery by itself, or to a wife for adultery coupled with incest, bigamy, cruelty, two years' desertion, rape, sodomy or bestiality. At first the decrees were absolute, and the marriage was dissolved by the judgment in the suit, but three years later the decree *nisi* was introduced. It means 'unless' and creates a delay after which the final decree will issue from the court unless some ground is shown why it should not. This is a protection against defrauding the court by a false case. The period of delay has varied, and is now six weeks.

The official who has to consider the independent objection to the final decree is the Queen's Proctor, who has no means of investigating all the divorces granted each year and can only effectively do so when someone gives the game away. The effective preventive of divorces being granted against the justice of the case was really the rules about trial of these actions.

For the creation of the new court and the new law did not prevent the old law of the Ecclesiastical Courts continuing to be the law, so far as it was not changed. The Act expressly provided that it should. Thus there came in the document which has caused so much trouble to so many petitioners, but which was never ordained by Parliament —the discretion statement.

In an Ecclesiastical suit the person accused was entitled to undertake a process aptly called 'recrimination'. He or she could allege that the petitioner had by his or her own behaviour become disentitled to the relief prayed for. The adulterous wife could say she was driven to another man by her husband's behaviour. That was 'conduct conducing to adultery'. Or she could contend that his cruelty disentitled him, or his own adultery. The adultery of the petitioner became the commonest of these 'discretionary bars to relief'. The judge had to decide whether in all the circumstances he would grant a decree or withhold it.

The practice grew up of requiring a petitioner who had committed adultery to make a candid revelation of it on a signed paper which was kept in a sealed envelope until the judge opened it at the trial. Anyone who did not do so, and yet was detected in anything which pointed to an adulterous association was thereby branded a liar and liable to fail in his claim for a divorce. Since 1st January, 1971, this valuable document and the prayer for 'discretion to be exercised' in the petition, have no place.

Since the *Divorce Reform Act*, 1969, theoretically, divorce no longer depends upon a matrimonial offence having been committed. In fact, of course, it does, because the facts necessary to be proved before a divorce can be granted are the old offences. But a general dilution of the law has been achieved in order to make consent divorce and easy divorce available in the name of progress. Baroness Summerskill called it a Casanova's Charter, and well it might be. Few men can afford to support two families. The Family Allowances indirectly encourage the begetting of children. (Lady Summerskill favoured them.) The real loser by the reform of the divorce law is the taxpayer.

For though divorce is inspired by adultery, it is often, like most litigation, a financial dispute. And the simplification of the dissolution of the bond has done nothing to simplify the financial disputes. However, the new basis of divorce must be examined. According to the Law Commission a good divorce law should have two objects:

'(i)   *to buttress, rather than to undermine, the stability of marriage: and*

(ii) *when, regrettably, a marriage has irretrievably broken down, to enable the empty legal shell to be destroyed with the maximum fairness and the minimum bitterness, distress and humiliation.'*

Curiously enough, no one has thought to get rid of the old rule that a husband is bound to give security for the costs incurred by his wife in seeking advice and taking proceedings against him for divorce. Its origin is, of course, the omnipresent principle that a solicitor must be paid, disguised as the husband's responsibility for his wife's debts. Which solicitor would start work without funds? A woman without means could never get legal representation unless her husband was compelled to answer for her charges. The odd result is therefore that a man will be liable to pay the bill for his wife's unfounded suit for divorce against him.

This has been mitigated somewhat by the *Legal Aid and Advice Act, 1949,* which has caused more divorces than anything else. When a person applies to the Law Society for Legal Aid, two sifting processes take place, as a matter of course, which need not occur when a person instructs a solicitor privately. One is that the applicant's statement of the case has to go to a Certifying Committee which decides whether—assuming the story to be true—there is a case fit to be put before the court. This is decided on the assumption that the evidence will prove the facts, and in the light of the law. The other process is the assessment by the Social Security Department of the applicant's means and ability to contribute to the expense of his or her own case. Married women often have not sufficient means to make a contribution. A middle-class woman, instructing a solicitor, might find her means disqualify her for Legal Aid. It is her husband who might be ordered to give security for her costs.

Whether this is maximum fairness might be a straightforward question. But it can cause bitterness. Supposing the solicitor is either in funds or to be paid by the Legal Aid fund. There remains the completion of the law stationer's form setting out all the details of the marriage and family. Divorce petitions used most often to be drafted by counsel. They used until 1965 to have to have an affidavit at the bottom in which the Petitioner swore that the statements therein were true. This is no longer required, perhaps out of deference to the sanctity of the oath.

A divorce petition is the product of 2,000 years of tradition. Under the *Lex Julia de Adulteriis* of 17 B.C. a Roman husband who put his wife aside had to deliver to her a tablet formally setting out the repudiation, in the presence of seven witnesses, as the Jews did with their divorce procedure of *Ghet*. No more than that was required. But a petition for dissolution presented to a Divorce County Court is only the beginning nowadays. Divorce County Courts are the originating courts in all cases since the 1967 Act created them. Of course, divorces had been heard in County Courts, by County Court judges, for 30 years before that, but the law would never admit it. The judge was always acting as a High Court Commissioner then and had to be called My Lord, instead of Your Honour. Even when Mrs Justice Lane was appointed to the Bench at first she had to be called 'My Lord'.

The petition states the maiden name of the wife and that at a certain date and place the petitioner was lawfully married to the respondent. It then states that they have cohabited in England or Wales or not as the case may be, and that they were domiciled in England and Wales. If they are not, there can be no divorce unless the wife is petitioning and has lived here three years.

It then lists all the Children of the Family. A Child of the Family might be a child of neither spouse. It could be adopted. It could be a child of a party to a former marriage of one of the parties, which has been brought up in the family the subject of the case. It could be a child of one spouse but not the other. The petition also states whether there is any dispute over whether any child is a Child of the Family. It lists children taken into care by local authorities. It states whether there is any maintenance required for children of whom the respondent is not a parent.

Petitions used to set out the arrangements for custody and up-bringing of the children. But now there is a separate form on which that has all to be dealt with in detail, including the arrangements for education and upbringing. There is much more about children in the primary divorce papers than about divorce. There has to be stated therein whether any earlier proceedings have taken place about marriage or the children, and whether co-habitation has been resumed after any orders of courts.

There has then to be a revelation of any financial agreement or arrangement for support of the respondent or the children. Where the divorce is claimed because the spouses have lived apart for five years, and on no other fact, any financial provision proposed by the petitioner for the respondent has to be set out. This is because under this provision 'guilty parties' can get a divorce against the will of their spouse, subject to the court's power to refuse in hard cases.

Only then does the petition state that the marriage has broken down irretrievably. This, by *Section 1* of the 1969 Act, is the sole ground on which a petition may be presented to the court. The section does not say in so many words that it is the sole ground for divorce. Why not is difficult to imagine. The next section says that the court 'hearing a petition for divorce' shall not hold that the marriage has broken down irretrievably unless the petitioner satisfies the court of one or more 'facts'. It then lists the facts. It therefore becomes clear that the Act is about Divorce.

The first fact is that 'the respondent has committed adultery and the petitioner finds it intolerable to live with the respondent'. Many people, after their marriages break up, continue to live in the same house or flat. Sometimes they do not speak to each other and keep to separate parts of their establishment. Others 'go their own way' in a 'civilised' manner. Quite often, the wife still does a bit of cooking or washing, the benefit of which is taken by the husband. Such people have to tell the judge in all seriousness that they find it intolerable to live with the respondent.

Exactly how this has simplified the old ground of divorce for adultery is not immediately apparent. The idea occurs that it was inserted 'to buttress, rather than to undermine the stability of marriage'. There is a clue in *Section 3*, '*Provisions designed to encourage reconciliation*'. *Subsection (3)* of that provides that where after the petitioner has discovered that the respondent has committed adultery,

(a) *if they live together for up to six months, it is ignored in deciding whether the petitioner finds it intolerable to live with the respondent,* but

(b) *if they live together over six months the petitioner cannot get a divorce on the proof of that particular adultery.*

The 'intolerable to live with' requirement is therefore apparently a smoke screen for a limitation on the right to get a divorce for adultery. Its ineffectiveness has been buttressed (if such a thing can happen to ineffectiveness) by a decision of the court (*Goodrich* v. *Goodrich* [*1971*] *115, Sol Jo, 303*) to the effect that finding it intolerable to live with a spouse need not be because of the adultery sued upon to end the marriage. It can be intolerable to live with someone who is unhygienic or totally absorbed in his stamp collection. If he has committed adultery, the combination, unlikely as it is, between the circumstances is good proof of breakdown.

The *fons et origo* of this curious complication of the law concerning adultery, which is fairly old established, is no doubt that celebrated utterance of the Archbishop of Canterbury that divorce ought not to break up a marriage after an isolated act of adultery. The Reform lobby needed something more to convince Parliament. Anything, it seems, will do.

There was a doctrine of the Ecclesiastical Courts which continued into the Divorce Court that a person who 'condoned' adultery by his or her spouse could not get a divorce on that adultery. Lord Justice Lopes defined condonation as:

> '*complete forgiveness and blotting out of a conjugal offence, followed by cohabitation, the whole being done with full knowledge of the circumstances of the past offence forgiven*'.
>
> **Bernstein v. Bernstein (1893) P. 292.**

It was an absolute bar to divorce. The court had to decide, first whether the petitioner knew all about the offence and then whether he or she truly forgave and reinstated the guilty one. The condonable offences were adultery and cruelty.

Now, in *Worsley* v. *Worsley (1730) 2 Lee 572*, it was recognised that condonation is given on the implied condition that the guilty spouse commits no further offence. It followed quite naturally therefore that if the forgiven spouse behaved badly the condoned offence 'revived'. The kind of conduct needed to revive was described by Lord Justice Bucknill as that which 'makes decent married life impossible'.

The judges had to contend with a wide variety of behaviour advanced as reviving past wrongs. That is relatively unimportant in trying issues between husband and wife. The whole story of the marriage has to be told anyway. The law requires it. Even if it did not, it is physically difficult to stop people telling all the details of the matters giving rise to their differences. The judges decided all these questions as matters of fact, applying the criteria of reasonable people. In *Cundy* v. *Cundy (1956) 1 All E.R. 245*, for instance, it was contended that when a woman, whilst gardening, permitted herself to be kissed on the neck by a man, she did not thereby revive the adultery she had committed with a different man 19 years before.

Individual cases of condonation and revival led to difficulties in decision and different views of the same facts by different judges. This is inevitable in every field of law. But what is extracted as law from a decision of a superior court is the principle of legal reasoning and not the artificial assimilation of the facts. *Henderson* v. *Henderson (1944) A.C. 49* set the authority of the House of Lords

217

upon the proposition that if a husband had sexual intercourse with his wife in the full knowledge that she had been cruel or committed adultery, he was conclusively presumed to have condoned her wrong. In that case the wife promised to break off with her lover as a condition of her husband taking her back. After forgiveness and intercourse, she said the following morning that she did not see why she should not go on seeing the lover. The Law Lords held that the condonation was complete and he could not rely on her adultery before then. The reasoning was that to permit the husband to have intercourse and then get a divorce was immoral, and that the wife risked conceiving a child in the act of intercourse.

But the Lord Chancellor, Lord Simon, said that a wife would not necessarily be barred from suing on earlier adultery by the husband, after intercourse. A wife may not be her own mistress and may not be able to support herself or find anywhere else to live. The circumstances might conspire to make her agree to intercourse with a guilty husband. Nevertheless, the law was criticised because, it was claimed, it deterred estranged couples from trying to reconcile, for fear of losing the chance of divorce by condonation. Of course, if the alleged condonation was procured by lies it would not be a bar to divorce at all. An example of that was *Roberts* v. *Roberts (1917) 117 L.T. 157*, where the wife said she was not pregnant, but she was.

The way round this suggested by the Royal Commission on Marriage and Divorce in its 1956 Report was to relax the severity of the rule affecting the husband, so that intercourse after forgiveness need not bar divorce if things went wrong again. This would have put men in the same position as women. What was actually done, in the *Matrimonial Causes Act, 1963*, was to put women into the same position as men. Instead of making the sexes equally well off, they were confirmed in their equality by being made equally badly off. In this way, no doubt, Parliament impressed on the Royal Commission that just because they took five years to make a report, they need not think they could tell Parliament what to do.

One of the other suggestions of the Royal Commission was, however, that a month's trial reconciliation should not constitute condonation. The 1963 Act extended that to three months. The 1969 Act extends it to six months. But *s. 9* and *Schedule 2* of the 1969 Act abolish, among other things, condonation. Instead there is the Draconian rule that on the first moment after the expiration of six calendar months from finding out that the husband or wife has committed adultery, the innocent one cannot divorce for that adultery.

This condonation still affects Magistrates' Court Separation Cases, but in the Divorce Court it is now irrelevant whether the resumption of cohabitation was caused by the deception of a guilty spouse. A man who cons his wife into taking him back can dodge being divorced if he fools her for six months. A woman who claims forgiveness and continues to cuckold her husband can avoid being put asunder and retain her meal ticket. The stability is buttressed by fraud, and the judges are powerless to prevent it. And bishops as well as free-thinkers voted for it.

What exactly 'living together' entails, is not explained in the Act. 'Living apart' is. There is no reference to why they lived together. It is presumably therefore irrelevant whether they lived together because they were reconciled or because they hoped to be reconciled. Whether sharing the table but not the bed is 'living together' will have to be found out.

But it means, of course, that any spouse who can persuade his wronged partner to try to work it out and patch it up has a good chance of staving off divorce. Unless the innocent one is sufficiently resolute to run off to the solicitor, he or she can spin out the qualifying period. No promises can affect the matter. No further bad behaviour such as cutting short money or staying out late on his own can affect it. Playing for time is the only essential.

Unquestionably, the stability of marriage, in the sense of keeping it going, is buttressed by preventing innocent, wronged husbands and wives from getting divorces. The 1969 Act in its preamble declares itself to be an Act 'to facilitate reconciliation in matrimonial causes'. If a woman cannot get divorced, she might well decide to put up with the fact that her husband is an adulterer and stay where he pays the rent and puts the food on the table. It is certainly arguable that if a person has sexual intercourse with a number of different people he or she is contributing to the happiness of the populace more than the selfish and conventional person who keeps himself or herself to his or her spouse.

No doubt the proponents of divorce reform considered that any injustice occasioned by the tidying up of the adultery provisions might be compensated for by the next 'fact' by which irretrievable breakdown of the marriage can be established. This is 'that the respondent has behaved in such a way that the petitioner cannot reasonably be expected to live with the respondent'. Applying normal rules of syntax to this somewhat vague proposition one might suppose that 'cannot reasonably be expected' involves some objective analysis of the behaviour. One knows, of course, some splendid men with irritating habits. Nail biting, sniffing, smoking cheap tobacco, and keeping rabbits are all to some extent unacceptable. Whether they would be grounds for divorce depends upon the weight to be given to the word 'reasonably'. This is perhaps the hardest worked and least understood word in the language of the law. The old 'ground' which this 'fact' replaces was cruelty. Many liberties were taken with the meaning of that perfectly straight-forward English word. The conduct, said Lord Justice Harman, characteristically, had to be 'cruel' (*Le Brocq* v. *Le Brocq* [*1964*] *1 W.L.R. 1085*). But there was laid on to the cruelty the further requirement that

> '*there must be danger to life, limb or health, bodily or mental, or a reasonable apprehension of it, to constitute legal cruelty*'.
>
> per Lopes L. J. in *Russell* v. *Russell (1895) P. 322.*

This requirement of injury to health was endorsed by the House of Lords in that case, and endured until the 1st January, 1971, in divorce, and exists still in the cruelty which has to be proved before magistrates in Separation and Maintenance proceedings. It is therefore more difficult to get an order from the magistrates which keeps two people married than it is to get a divorce. Precisely how this buttresses the stability of marriage is a little obscure, particularly since a person can only start magistrates' court proceedings in the district of residence, but a divorce petition can be filed in any Divorce County Court. There is no reason at all why a resident of Newcastle should not sue for divorce in the Bournemouth County Court. Without such a geographical discrepancy being necessary, solicitors cannot be blamed for starting their cases in courts not inconveniently distant, where the judges are more easily satisfied. They are not yet rubber stamps.

Equiparated with cruelty must be 'constructive desertion' a fiendishly complicated phenomenon which is capable of being reduced to the simple proposition of one spouse saying to the other, 'I shall not put up with this a moment longer'. The technical description of the conduct which will justify a spouse in feeling driven away was Lord Stowell's celebrated 'Grave and weighty'.

What constitutes the conduct has expanded since then. It meant physical brutality at first. Drunkenness alone was never held to suffice in a reported divorce case until 1947.

It is to be observed that the idea that mental cruelty has no place in the English divorce jurisdiction is entirely misconceived. Nagging was established as behaviour which could be cruelty by *Atkins* v. *Atkins (1942) 2 All E.R. 637*. Constant dripping wears away stone, said Mr Justice Henn Collins.

Various doctrines have altered these fields of law slightly from time to time. From 1951 'expulsive conduct' such as would found 'constructive desertion' was considered to be possibly different from cruelty. The instance was, of course, that a spouse might tell the other to get out but not offer violence or even impoliteness. However, 'grave and weighty' conduct had to amount to cruelty it was held in *Ogden* v. *Ogden* (*1969*) *3 All E.R.* Thus for 18 years a spouse driven out could get a divorce more easily than now.

Under the old law the desertion period needed to found a suit was three years before the presentation of the petition. A cruelty petition could be presented without delay, so long, in most cases, as the marriage had lasted three years. The difficulty arose when no injury to health could be proved to satisfy the rule in *Russell* v. *Russell*, or the conduct of the guilty spouse was not 'aimed at' the other spouse, as required by *Kaslefsky* v. *Kaslefsky* (*1950*) *2 All E.R. 398.*

This was held not to be necessary by the House of Lords in *Gollins* v. *Gollins* (*1964*) *A.C. 644* where the husband, according to Lord Justice Harman merely 'hung up his hat in the hall'. He did not go to work but simply dissipated his means, and those which his wife provided for years by working hard to run a guest house, in making some unproductive experiments with agricultural machinery. The work and worry of bringing up a family under those conditions made his wife ill, and he was adjudged to be cruel. In the case which immediately followed it, the Law Lords held that intention and state of mind were irrelevant in considering whether a spouse was in fact cruel, and so mental illness affecting the guilty spouse was not a defence to a cruelty suit. Although the *Divorce Reform Act* avoids the word 'cruelty' it is plainly what is meant by the provision about conduct up with which no one should put. It is designed to make it easier to confess to, no doubt. Many cruel people defended suits simply because they could not face the fact that they were cruel. The neighbours would read that word in the papers and their good name was gone. The limited vocabulary of the draftsman could find nothing to put in its place except 'Behaved in such a way that the Petitioner could not *reasonably* be expected to live with the Respondent'. The old law is still available to assist in putting a meaning to that turgid phrase. The standard by which conduct should be judged is subjective. O. Henry wrote a short story about a woman who loved her man for the black eyes he gave her. The law would be quite objective about those:

> '*Whereas a blow speaks for itself, insults, humiliations, meannesses, impositions, deprivations and the like may need the interpretation of underlying intention for an assessment of their fullest significance*',

said Lord Pearce in the Gollins case.

Lord Justice Singleton had put it several years before. The conduct had to be a wrong, 'By *this* husband to *this* wife'.

Consequently any spouse can find practically anything cruel, and, more important any judge can agree or disagree, as he chooses. One man can be divorced for an excessive devotion to football causing him to neglect his wife socially. Another wife might put up with physical assaults and then much later seek a divorce with success. A couple who just ignore each other or sulk would be well advised to seek a consent divorce after two years' separation, but there are still judges about who would not grant what is still after all a discretionary remedy.

> '*Cruel, is not used in any esoteric or "Divorce Court" sense of that word, but the conduct must be something which an ordinary man would describe as cruel if the story was fully told*',

said Lord Justice Harman in *Le Brocq* v. *Le Brocq* (*1964*) *1 W.L.R.*

All that the Gollins case really did was to get rid of the necessity for the cruelty to be intentional. Many lawyers thought that it would lead to decrees for long toenails or smoking in the bath. The 1969 Act has encouraged that approach. But even in undefended suits decrees are still refused by some judges.

Many people think that a judge has a damned cheek to refuse a divorce. It is none of his business, they feel. But our rulers in Parliament have baulked at letting people be put asunder just because they want to be sundered. After the Royal Commission in 1956 the climate of reform was all for consent divorce yet when a Bill was initiated in 1959 it could not get through. The 1969 Act places a two-year limit on it before which the parties have to 'live apart'.

Presumably the rulers know that they cannot effectively prevent matrimonial unhappiness but hope to teach people not to be too keen to repeat the experiment.

The conduct complained of must be judged 'in the light of the whole history of the marriage' said Lord Reid in *King* v. *King* (*1953*) *A.C. 124*. The marriage service might contain an undertaking to cherish the spouse in sickness and in health. Therefore although not a defence to a cruelty suit, the fact that the spouse accused was a sick person is something for which the complaining spouse should make allowance. Refusal of intercourse for six years was held to be cruelty in *Sheldon* v. *Sheldon* (*1966*) *P. 62*. But if there is a reason for refusal—for example the fear of injury to health or of conception for a good reason—it is not.

It has yet to be held that the failure to afford physical love is 'behaving in such a way that the Petitioner cannot reasonably be expected to live with the Respondent'.

One judge had to confess that he did not understand why a lady should be angry when a toilet roll was put on its holder in such a way that the end dropped from the back and not the front. It was only one incident of many but it demonstrates how obtuse the judiciary can be. The public thinks from what they have read and heard in reports from Parliament that getting a divorce is now a certainty once it is 'put in for'. By and large this is true but some judges still perversely prevent it. There is so far very little guidance in the law reports over what situations give rise to the inability reasonably to expect a man to live with a woman. Lord Goddard, with untypical helplessness observed once that the court could not order a husband and wife to live happily together.

What is happening therefore, as it always does when Parliament cannot say what it wants, is that the profession is making up slowly and vaguely, a body of law for itself. Already the requirement has become corrupted by being described as 'intolerable behaviour'. This is a gross distortion of 'cannot reasonably be expected'. The subsection says nothing at all about the behaviour being 'intolerable'. A petitioner who relies on a spouse's adultery has to say that he or she finds it intolerable to live with the adulterer. But the 'behaviour' which warrants a parting does not have to be intolerable. Naturally, the whole reasoning is overlaid by the long experience of 'cruelty'. 'Long periods of silence' and 'depriving her of his society' were frequently pleaded as cruelty, but on their own were not enough. They could perfectly feasibly amount to conduct such that one person could not 'reasonably' be expected to live with another. Many people tolerated gross cruelty for years. When they finally advanced it as a ground for divorce they were often met with the retort that they had condoned it, or that it could not be cruelty because they put up with it. The commonest instance of this was meanness in family finance. This has two sides: a husband keeping a wife short of money or a wife being extravagant and a bad manager. It is in truth the commonest cause of breakdown of marriage and incapable of investigation with any accuracy. Being impossible to prove or disprove, it is ideal as a basis of complaint against a spouse.

As an element of cruelty it has long been a means of divorce. Now, presumably, it is a means of divorce on its own. Since a woman can no longer pledge her husband's credit for necessaries she has to sue him for adequate maintenance either with or without divorce. While she is about it she might as well get rid of him. How this buttresses the institution is not clear.

People who really cannot put up with their spouses often leave them. The one who goes can then be accused of desertion by the one who stays, and has to show 'just cause for leaving' to establish 'constructive desertion', which amounts to the same thing as proving cruelty or 'behaviour'. It therefore seems pointless to wait two years before alleging desertion. If the marriage was more than three years ago, the party leaving can allege that the other behaved so that he or she could not live with them, and that tactically spoils a cross-petition on desertion. Being first into court always helps. Thus both parties can be expected to rely on 'not reasonable to live with' in most cases. If both are saying that, why should the waiting period of 'consent divorce' be two years?

The only reason that there can be is that consent divorce was unacceptable to the pressure groups for the 1969 Act. It has been easy enough to get a consent divorce for a generation, simply by one party not bothering to defend. Spouses defended Divorce suits either to get maintenance ('alimony' is what it is called in separation cases) or to stop the wife getting maintenance. There was a rule that no complaint could be made in maintenance proceedings which had not been raised in the suit for divorce. But there was in 1970 an important decision of the Court of Appeal (*Tumath* v. *Tumath* [*1970*] *1 All E.R. 111*) to the effect that in maintenance proceedings, the complaints of the parties are not limited to those raised in the suit for dissolution. This means that a man who objects to paying maintenance because of his wife's behaviour need not bother to defend the suit for divorce. So popular has this policy been that anyone who defends a divorce action now is regarded as an obstructionist kink. Defended divorce suits are still possible, but it was in effect abolished by the Law Society in 1966, when it decided to be much more sparing in permitting legally-aided litigants the services of Queen's Counsel for long cross-examinations about who was to blame for throwing the Sunday dinner at the dining-room wall, and even longer legal arguments about whether four letter words were 'expulsive conduct'. These actions were caused simply by the filing of complaints designed to reduce or obliterate the claims for maintenance. Once the spouse saw all his or her own complaints set out in numbered paragraphs, a wealth of self-pity overwhelmed him or her and 'British Justice' had to be done. This means no more than insistence upon the day in court.

To some people the idea of standing up in public and talking about their intimate affairs is paralytic. To others it invokes a sense of embarrassment, adventure or repressed wickedness. When they do it, they find they like it, and do not want to stop. Both spouses want divorces. Each wants the satisfaction of being in the right, or to do the other down financially, or both. Quite often, before Gollins case, after a long trial the judge would award a decree to neither. Cruelty could founder on the absence of injury or the lack of intention. Whether comparative effects of the behaviour of each is such as to lead to one or either not being 'reasonably expected to live with' the other is a refinement yet to be defined. For the court cannot just say it is satisfied that the marriage has broken down irretrievably. It must find one at least of the five 'facts'. Those practitioners who have seen couples reconcile four or five times in as many years will have reservations about the irretrievability of any breakdown. But if a petitioner proves a 'fact' he need not worry about whether the marriage has broken down. Practically any judge will take it from him. What else can he do?

Section 2(1) of the 1969 Act says that:

> '*the court hearing a petition for divorce shall not hold the marriage to have broken down irretrievably unless the petitioner satisfies the court of one or more of the following facts*'

A mnemonic for the 'facts' could be:

A is for Adultery and cohabitation intolerable
B is for Behaviour with which you can't put up
C is for Continuous desertion for a couple of years
D is for consent Divorce two years from breaking up
E is for the Erring Spouse putting aside the innocent

Mr William Wilson, who piloted the Bill through the House of Commons was very proud of it notwithstanding that it permits a blameless spouse who does not want a divorce to have one forced upon him or her at the instance of a guilty party. He stressed that the court would have power to require from such a person financial provision of half joint capital plus maintenance payments. It was not enacted in that form. The court has to be satisfied that the financial provision is the best that can be made in the circumstances.

No doubt it was realised that a half-interest in a slum tenancy and a Social Security dole is not wealth beyond the dreams of avarice. Parliament often has to recognise that the capacity for procreation of the idle and indigent is in inverse proportion to their ability to support their wives and children. Even those capable of earning a reasonable competence for one family are usually incapable of supplying motor cars and television sets for two. That eminent East Anglian farmer who hailed originally from the hard land of Hungary spoke not only of the British agricultural community when he opined that it would never be right until 'they close all the Corn Exchanges and castrate all the farmers'.

The real potency of financial want as a cause of marriage breakdown is that it drives women out to work, where they meet men with whom to commit adultery. Their husbands can then divorce them on that ground.

A Roof Over Your Head

'There is no law against letting a tumbledown house . . .'
Chief Justice Erle.

HAVING, perhaps, got married, you need somewhere to live. The contract of marriage having created a status, others crowd in upon you. Another contract makes you a householder. Contracts for the disposition of real estate are the staple of the legal industry. Seldom made without the benefit of a solicitor they are no different in principle when not so blessed.

Everyone understands the law of real estate in its essentials. What everyone does not understand are the theories about it expounded in the law books. Everyone knows you can rent or buy, or live with your in-laws.

Buying involves down-payments and legal costs. The roof over your head becomes a millstone round your neck. Buying covers buying leasehold and freehold property. That is where the complexity begins. A home owner is radically different from a mere renter. But to the lawyer, a weekly tenant is as much a lessee as the holder of a thousand year lease.

The similarity is not merely technical. Parliament has made the slum tenant practically a Grace and Favour resident, but the price of protection is great in other than money terms. A protected tenant may of course, have much better value for his money than a house owner, and much greater security of occupation. But the owner can make a capital profit when he sells and the tenant says good-bye to his rent money for ever. The owner-occupier knows that he must mend everything himself for his own advantage. The tenant spends as little as possible on his landlord's investment.

Very rich people do live in rented places. But most tenants are poor. Poverty is at the root of the law of landlords and tenants so far as it concerns housing, and maybe where it touches shops and factories, too. The Law Commission's first report in 1965 suggested a simplification, modernisation and codification of this branch of the law.

It has a very simple foundation. A lease and a freehold are

different only because with a lease the length can be ascertained with certainty. The duration of a freehold cannot. It does not matter how long either lasts until it has to be paid for. The duration then controls the price. A never-ending freehold is therefore expensive. So is a lease for a thousand years. Large sums of money are often borrowed. Many of our sophisticated legal structures are founded on debt. The lease is a development of usury. Money is a store of wealth as well as a means of exchange.

For its hire, a price must be paid. Henry II's Treasurer wrote a description of his department's work called the *Dialogus de Scaccario*. This tells us that Jews could lend money up to a maximum interest rate of 43⅓ per cent—two pence in the £ per week. Christians could take no usury under pain of mortal sin. Edward the Confessor had declared that the rule he learned at the Frankish Court would run in his land. The usurer was an outlaw whose substance was forfeit to the King. Madox (*History of the Exchequer*) tells us, 'Under the Norman and early Angevin kings the Jews were employed as a sponge to suck up the wealth of their subjects and be periodically squeezed to supply the wants of the Crown'. The Royal way of putting it was that the moneylenders were 'under the King's protection'.

The fiscal morality was no better during those cheap money days than in our own inflated age. Our Chancellors depend upon us smoking ourselves into early graves. The later Angevins 'spread the load' by winking at Christian usury. By the times of Glanvill—1187— a living usurer would not be prosecuted. But when he died, whether or not he left a will, the King took all his estate. It is not, technically, the origin of the Death Duties, but it will do.

Some mediaeval lawyer worked out the way round usury by which you could save your soul as well as your money. It has rarely worked since. But if you allowed someone by contract to occupy a piece of your land for a definite time, you could make money. A small sum each week or month was a rent. A lump sum such as we call a premium or merely the price of a lease, was called a fine. Had you lent your money, you could have lost it. Usury was illegal; the King's judges would not make the borrower return it.

But the rent was more than the interest, with no risk of crop failures. Landowning became the best racket in the Middle Ages. The landowners and lawyers kept it that way. Indeed, many of the lawyers became landowners. The status of landowner did not extend to a tenant. He had a contract, and if he could not pay the rent, he was ejected. Of course, leases are now legal interests in land. But their birthmarks are still the certainty of the time for which the tenant is entitled to possession. The natural, logical consequence of that certainty enables the period of another phenomenon to be fixed with equal certainty—the notice to quit. The price of the right of possession must be a precisely ascertainable sum in cash or kind, paid at regular intervals, even if it is only 'one peppercorn, if demanded'.

Some monastery scribe, spreading the inky contents of a cow's horn on long-lasting sheepskin with a broad-bladed quill, drew up the first lease. The phraseology was that used in charters given by Kings to towns and guilds 'know all men by these presents . . .' When all those present had crumbled to dust, those skins would prove the rights. Their authenticity was proved by the designs imprinted in the seals of scarlet wax. The *Law of Property Act, 1925* says that grants of legal estates are void unless made by deed. A deed is a 'sealed writing'. We use posh paper and plastic seals.

Most tenants have only a rent book. Landlords can be fined for not providing them (*Housing Act, 1962*). The absence does not, as Citizens' Advice Bureaux ladies so passionately believe, make the letting illegal. But it is good County Court ammunition in eviction cases, a smear implying that the landlord is a bit of a Rachman.

Woolworths' rent books are lawful because there is no need for a deed where the letting is for less than three years. You might live all your life on a weekly tenancy in one house. But your actual contract is from week to week. Since the wicked Tory *Rent Act of 1957, Section 16*, any tenancy needs at least four weeks' notice to determine it. People who pay rent weekly usually hope to stay months or years in their houses. But the law imputes to them and their landlords an agreement to occupy from week to week. It is a lease. A 'Periodic lease', as the lawyers say, desperately trying to fit modern protection from eviction into the logical lawful reasoning of centuries gone by.

Practical lawyers are much more pragmatic, and they speak firmly of weekly tenancies. Thus came to be named the 'tenancy agreements' so beloved of the landlords of West Kensington, Notting Hill, and some local authorities. Why these are not named 'leases' is perhaps because they are for less than three years. So be it, they are still leases, but seldom so-called. But that doctrine deserves one important reservation. Sometimes they are not leases. Sometimes very cunningly, they are referred to merely as agreements. They contain words which it is hoped will be construed by County Court judges as proof that no relationship of landlord and tenant was created between the landlord and the tenant. If that ruse succeeds, then the dreaded *Rent Act, 1968* has been circumvented.

This statute, latest of an ignoble line, suffers markedly from that vice which afflicted its forebears. As the rain falls upon the just as well as the unjust, the Rent Acts ruined the reasonable landlord much more easily than they reached the Rachmans. The judges therefore developed a doctrine. The particular judge whose name is coupled with this, as with others, is Lord Denning. He is now Master of the Rolls, an important judicial office which only a century and a half ago enabled the holder to dispose of sinecures for profit.

The doctrine is the simple one that whatever label the parties— or either of them—put upon a relationship in their agreement documents, the court will decide for itself what is its 'essential nature'. This is a juridical expression of an intention to take no notice of the plain words on the paper when it suits. For a tenancy to exist, said Lord Justice Denning, as he was, in *Facchini* v. *Bryson (1952) 1 T.L.R. 1386*, there must be 'occupation of right'—such as the law recognises as creating an interest in land. Exclusive possession is a consideration of the first importance in this decision, said Lord Justice Jenkins in *Addiscombe Garden Estates* v. *Crabbe (1958) 1 Q.B. 513 @ 528.*

Important, but not conclusive. Always there must be sought that chink in the great castle of the law where a skilful practitioner can gain a foothold and climb the rampart. Was there, the Court of Appeal asked in these cases, an intention to create that rather businesslike relationship of landlord and tenant? Such intention can be lacking in a family arrangement, such as a house owner's son paying the mortgage instalments whilst he lived in his father's house (*Errington* v. *Errington [1952] 1 K.B. 290*). He was not a tenant, said the judges. Nor was a tenancy created where the arrangement was an act of generosity or friendship—*Foster* v. *Robinson (1951) 1 K.B. 149.* 'Did the circumstances and the conduct of the parties show that all that was intended was that the occupier should have a personal privilege with no interest in the land?' asked Lord Justice Denning in *Cobb* v. *Lane (1952) 1 All E.R. 1199.*

If a landlord can show that there was no contractual tenancy the Rent Act does not protect the occupier, and an order for possession of the property is much easier to get. The rent protection system was introduced as a temporary measure in 1915, when munitions workers in Glasgow rioted over evictions and rent increases. Control of the amount of rent has to go with security of occupation, because if tenants can be evicted arbitrarily the pegging of rents is impossible. What we call law wages a perpetual struggle with the natural law of supply and demand. Thus the tenancy became virtually a life freehold conditional on paying the rent.

Anyone who could get into a house as a tenant was practically unmovable. But the judges reached back into the common law for the 'licence'. One of these occupations ineffectually protected is nowadays so called. Chief Justice Vaughan who decided *Thomas* v. *Sorrel in 1673* (and reported it as well) ruled that:

> '*A dispensation or licence properly passeth no interest nor alters*

or transfers property in anything but only makes that lawful which without it had been unlawful.'

This was approved as the modern law by the House of Lords, in *National Provincial Bank Ltd.* v. *Ainsworth* (*1965*) *A.C.*

A landlord might be quite willing for people to occupy his premises for payment, but not so as to be legal tenants. This jam-on-both-sides attitude usually commands little judicial sympathy. But when Mr Torbett let an employee of his company, Mr Faulkner, occupy a house which he owned and deducted 'rent' from his salary, it was held not to be a service tenancy but a mere licence. There was no need to fall back on 'intention' because the company, a separate legal person, had no legal interest in Mr Torbett's house, from which to grant a legal right to Mr Faulkner. There is nothing slavish about the adhesion to doctrines once established.

Of course, those payments were not 'rent' in the strict legal sense. They were payment for 'use and occupation' otherwise called 'mesne profits' (pronounced 'mean'). A feudal lord's estate was called his demesne in Law French. Mesne profits are nothing more than damages for trespass. If the amount demanded for use and occupation is excessive, a court can reduce it to a true compensation for the use of the land. (Houses and all real estate are 'land'—*Law of Property Act, 1925 s. 205.*)

'Rent' is fixed, certain, a service rendered in return for exclusive possession. There are still in Lincolnshire strips of land farmed by the mediaeval system, but no one works on the lord's land in return for his own land holding. When the lease ends, or is broken, and the tenant stays in possession he becomes a trespasser, and has to pay damages for his trespass, usually at the rate of the rent, but maybe less—perhaps even more.

Rent-free occupation by employees like farm workers gives rise to licences not tenancies, when they are required to occupy a house in order to do the job, like a stockman, they are licencees. If the house goes with the job and a rent is paid, they are tenants so long as the occupation of the house is not an essential requirement for doing the job. Fringe benefits secure rent protection, but genuine tied cottage occupation does not. But the Acts were not made to benefit farm workers.

The Rent Act covers all lettings of premises with rateable values in Greater London (defined in the *London Government Act, 1963*) under £400 a year. Elsewhere the limit is £200 a year. This covers most leased properties. Sections 85 and 86 make it a crime to require a premium for the transfer of tenancy. A lot of people were afraid to sell their leases at a profit in case they were prosecuted.

There was in fact no need for fear. The matter was decided as long ago as 1921. Mr Julius Harris took an assignment of a flat in

Abercorn Place for the modest premium of £70, but stopped it when he discovered certain defects. When sued on the cheque he pleaded that it would be paying an illegal premium; contrary to *Section 8 (1)* of the *Increase of Rent & Mortgage Interest (Restriction) Act, 1920.* Mr Justice Shearman said that a 'grant' was the creation of a tenancy by landlord and tenant.

> *'An assignment of a tenancy does not come within the operation of S. 8 (1) of the Act.'*

> *(1921) 1 K.B. 653.*

There was nothing to worry about after all.

It was unusual to see the well housed Hampstead socialists withering under the lash of social justice, but Rent Restriction is essentially a phenomenon affecting the lower orders. A dwelling let at less than two-thirds of the rateable value is not protected. Rateable values of parts of houses can be fixed by the County Court.

The weekly, fortnightly or other periodic tenancy created by no more formal act than paying the rent collector every Monday creates a 'term of years' because of *Section 205 (1) xxvii* of the *Law of Property Act, 1925,* and even when the tenant is behind with the rent, he will not be thrown out unless the County Court judge thinks it reasonable to do so (*Section 10, Rent Act, 1968*). The grounds for possession to be ordered by the court go right back to the start of the Acts, and they have not changed really since 1933. Over all of them has hung the necessity for 'reasonableness' in making the order. In 1924, a Mr Shrimpton asked a judge to evict a tenant called Rabbits. He wanted the place for his daughter and son-in-law and the judge said that that was reasonable. But on appeal to the Divisional Court, Mr Justice Acton said, 'Because a wish is reasonable, it does not follow that it is reasonable for a court to gratify it.' The case was sent back to be re-tried, to see if something more reasonable could not be done.

Reasonableness, therefore, is not enough. A special kind of justifiable reasonableness is requisite. Nor is that all. There are specific grounds for possession as well as reasonableness, and one is no good without the other. Arrears of rent will get a protected tenant evicted. Just how much arrears is not certain. It depends largely on whether your judge is a landlord man or a tenant man. It depends on whether it is a hard case or genuine hardship. Judges give poor people more than one chance. Landlords wishing to sell with vacant possession find this tiresome. Landlords wishing to relet to tenants who will pay more—even perhaps illegal premiums—find it downright scandalous. There are a great many landlords who cannot get enough out of their houses to make them pay, and cannot get anything like their true worth on sale because they are occupied by protected tenants. So long as they pay the rent, the landlord is thrown back on the other grounds for possession.

Case Two, Part One of *Schedule Three* of the 1968 Act is descended from the common forms of lease and permits a possession order 'where the tenant or any person residing at lodging with him or any subtenant of his has been guilty of conduct which is a nuisance or annoyance to adjoining occupiers, or has been convicted of using the premises or allowing the premises to be used for immoral or illegal purposes'.

Noisy wireless has been held a nuisance or annoyance.

There are many 'goings on' which would not found a charge of brothel keeping, but they can perfectly easily be a nuisance or annoyance. However, in *Platts* v. *Grigor* (*1950*) the County Court judge held that although the tenant brought men in for immoral purposes, there was no nuisance or annoyance to the adjoining occupiers.

Evidence of such user is often difficult to get. An illuminated bell-push with the name tablet endorsed 'Yvette' is pretty conclusive in the Westminster County Court, the district of which covers Soho. But it might have less telling effect in a provincial court. In cases such as that, for divers reasons, it sometimes transpires that the tenant whose name is on the rent book or tenancy agreement is totally unaware of the activities of the person who is in actual occupation of the premises. Indeed, it is not unknown for such tenants to have no personal acquaintance with the occupier, and even to be unaware of his (or her) identity. Now a tenant who sublets at a higher rent than the controlled rent, or without the consent of the landlord, where this is needed by the tenancy agreement, is liable to be evicted.

Which is only fair, for the profits of prostitution should not be rent-controlled as well as tax-free.

We have seen that the combined effect of the Common Law and the activities of Parliament made the casually created contract of letting most residential property into a virtual freehold. 'Landlord's right to recover possession is now a right to go to the County Court for an order for possession,' said Sir Raymond Evershed (later Lord Evershed), Master of the Rolls, in *Marcroft Wagons* v. *Smith* (*1951*) *2 K.B. 496*. An owner-occupier behind with the mortgage money has more chance of being evicted than a tenant behind with his rent.

But the licence was not the only subtle doctrine developed to escape from the clutches of the Acts. They apply only to 'separate dwellings'. A single room can be a separate dwelling but it is often the case that two families, or a family and some single person share to a greater or lesser degree. Here was a fertile field for the cultivation of a doctrine. Lawyers love 'degree'. That is why Lord Justice Harman was able to say of the Rents Acts that they were 'the best 20th Century example of judge-made law—the chief architect of the new system was Lord Justice Scrutton' (*Parkin* v. *Scott* (*1965*) *196 E.G. 989*).

Landlords massed their forces for escape through the sharing loophole. Sharing a kitchen for cooking was sharing which took the premises out of control. Sharing for just washing or getting water from a tap in the kitchen was not. The 1968 Act limits unprotected shared accommodation to those cases where 'living accommodation' is shared. What, the judges are now asked, is 'living accommodation'. Suppose the wash basin is in the lavatory. Suppose the access to lavatory and coal cupboard is through the kitchen. Injunctions to restrain unauthorised use of a bathroom assume important tactical significance.

Landlords who wish to live in their own houses can get possession if it is reasonable, and if they provide suitable alternative accommodation for the tenant. If they want it for themselves or their immediate family the same applies. But an order for possession can only be made where the landlord owned the property before the 23rd of March, 1965, and 'greater hardship' would be caused to the landlord than the tenant. Availability of other accommodation is a consideration here.

But why only those who owned before the appointed day? Greater hardship is now an old established principle. It is really the recognition that Rent Acts are with us, like the poor whom they protect, for ever. If before Harold Wilson you bought a house and were so unwise as to get posted to Bahrein for a year, and let it, you could be pardoned for not taking your tenant's statutory immovability into account. But now the Rent Acts are no longer a temporary expedient for the relief of social misfortune in the First World War, everyone must take them into account.

How you carry on paying your mortgage whilst you are working away is your affair. You could permit someone to occupy it under licence—which some judge might say was a tenancy. You could let it at a rent less than two-thirds the rateable value. You could let it furnished and hope that the tenants do not ruin your treasured possessions and that the law is not changed while you are away. If you find that none of these courses can be achieved without expense and uncertainty for you, you must remember that Mr Wilson's pledge of social justice for all applies to you as much as to anyone else.

A good way of getting rid of an unwanted tenant is to provide another, better house for him close to his work and his children's schools, at a lower rent, and in a neighbourhood he finds acceptable.

If you pay his removal expenses and buy him new curtains and find him a garage so that he does not have to leave his new car in the street, he might very well accept the alternative. Technically, of course, the alternative only has to be similar as regards rent and the needs of the tenant and his family. It can, in fact, be a different, even a smaller part of the original premises. Many long-established tenants do not mind giving up unnecessary rooms in return for security.

But the well-advised protected tenant has to be fussy about his needs because his protected tenancy passes to his widow on death and after her death to some member of the family living with them —even if the successor was illegitimate. The bastard child of a protected tenant is therefore stronger in expectation than that of a rich man who has made a settlement of a million pounds. The weekly tenancy of the poor has in half a century become a veritable estate of inheritance, requiring no more formal muniment than more or less regular endorsement of a sixpenny rent book.

Solicitors get nothing out of this level of conveyancing, but they become experienced in the litigation of possession cases. Even a successful landlord is normally out of pocket on the costs. One County Court judge calls costs 'an incident of the relationship of landlord and tenant'. Accident might be a better word.

The commonest question, perhaps, in such cases was germinated by the absence of protection—comparatively speaking—for 'furnished' accommodation. When the immediate post-war housing shortage was at its height, bamboo tables and art pots had not achieved the dignity of antiques in the estimation of the cognoscenti. Islington was not then fashionable; junk shops in Camden Town were just that. Victoriana were neglected and brass-knobbed bedsteads and their saggy springs were so plentiful that every Static Water Tank in the East End of London contained at least three.

The provision of such bric-a-brac and a few strips of lino emboldened landlords wishing to evict occupiers of rooms to claim that they were 'substantially' furnished. Two cases in the House of Lords (*Palser* v. *Grinling* and *Property Holding Co.* v. *Mischeff* (1948) A.C.) laid it down that this state of furnishedness was a question of fact for the County Court judge to decide. There was already evolved a mathematical formula by which the 'value to the tenant' was calculated. What was and is done is to ask the landlord and the tenant what the furniture was worth. The actual cost of furniture on hire purchase or credit sale terms in furniture chain stores, is a curious phenomenon. It depends mainly on taste or the absence of taste and can be very high or very low. There is no such difficulty with the valuation of second-hand furniture. It is practically valueless.

Most landlords value the furniture in an apartment according to the first criterion, and tenants habitually adopt the latter. The judge, who is totally unprejudiced by having seen the goods, is therefore free to arrive at any value he chooses within the upper and lower limits. He then has to decide how long a 'purchase' this value should be in order to arrive at an annual value for it. He might say three years or five, or he might have actuarial theories of his own. He then calculates what was the percentage of the annual rent represented by the annual value of the furniture and decides whether this is in fact 'substantial'. The Court of Appeal at different times has refused to disturb proportions between 8 per cent and 20 per cent, all of which have been found 'substantial' by different judges. The word 'substantial' itself was once construed by a judge as meaning 'not insubstantial'.

The great advantage of this scientific analysis is that it enables judges to evict people who ought to be evicted and to protect people who ought to be protected. The Law Lords refused to bless it expressly in case it became too rigid and inflexible, and perhaps the best course is for a judge to say 'in all the circumstances I do not (or I do) think that this furniture is substantial'. That is a finding of fact which cannot be appealed if the rateable value is under £200. It is a very bold lawyer who will say for sure whether a given quantity of furniture in a particular house or flat actually makes it substantially furnished. Quite apart from anything else, the elementary mathematics of judges are prone to error, except in the case of Lord Denning who was a Wrangler, and his maths are too good for anyone else to understand.

There was an Act in 1949 which enabled tenants of furnished accommodation to have their rent reduced by order of a Rent Tribunal, if it considered it too high. While proceedings were pending before this Tribunal, any notice to quit was of no effect, and the Tribunal could in addition suspend its operation up to six months. They could therefore get security of occupation up to a maximum of six months plus the time it took for the case to be heard, plus any unexpired portion of the notice period. These provisions are continued by the *Rent Act, 1968*, but the Francis Committee on the Rent Acts has refused to recommend that the whole protection of the Act be spread over furnished as well as unfurnished dwellings. This is a source of great disappointment to the organisations which work to help the homeless, and of no great comfort to those who insist that the real poor are the landlords.

Immigrant landlords in the converted-flat zones of big cities and their immigrant tenants are no very good reason to impose the rigours of the endless tenancy upon people who for all sorts of individual reasons part with possession of their houses or flats. Nor is Mrs Elsie Raum a village Hampden sticking up for their rights. Parliament is perpetuating injustice because if people who want their houses to live in themselves could get them easily, thousands of little Rachmans (or should it be Rachmen?) would be able to tell County Court Judges that they want houses to live in themselves (or for their daughters), and once they have them they can sell them with vacant possession for their market prices.

Of all the acres of print expended upon the social problem of bad housing, two characteristics have received little recognition. The first is that lawbreakers do not seem to mind whether they break old laws or new ones. The second is that a very large number of the populace will never be able to raise the capital sum required for a deposit on a decent house, nor pay the instalments required to discharge a sufficiently large mortgage loan. The only ways they can own houses are by advances of practically the whole price. This facility, like subsidised rent, is available only through local government agencies.

Local authorities are too virtuous to need any such control as the Rent Act. A council tenant who does not look after his window box, or who parks his car outside the proper space can be evicted by notice without any right of appeal. (It happened at West London County Court to a Hammersmith tenant on the 6th of April, 1971.) In the main, local authorities are benevolent despots. When they evict for arrears or nuisance, overcrowding or painting the front door the wrong colour, it is only after agonised appraisal in the housing management committee. Arrears of rent can be quite readily forgiven, or allowed to accumulate out of charity for the weaker brethren. After all, even council tenants have votes at local elections, even if they do not have any security of tenure under the law.

Since Lord Chief Justice Goddard confessed that he did not understand the Rent Acts during the 1940s, they have endured an unfortunate reputation. The old control system lasted from 1919 to 1939 and there are still some tenancies within it, but that matters little. There was 'new control' from 1939 to 1957, and this technically still exists. But the Tory Act of 1957 decontrolled 800,000 houses in one blow, and prevented thousands of others from becoming controlled. Labour did not abolish that decontrol, for all that Harold Wilson said they had done. From the 8th of November, 1965, it 'regulated' tenancies which were not 'controlled' within the rateable value limits I have given. Both classes are under the 1968 Act, 'protected'. The houses that were controlled before 1957 and stayed controlled are still controlled, and the rents can only be increased in the highly technical ways provided. The 'Fair Rent' scheme applies to regulated tenancies if and when they are brought into it. But the restrictions on recovery of possession apply to both rented and controlled, i.e. 'protected' tenancies alike. It is really very simple.

Difficulties have been experienced with some of the phrases in the Acts, because 'The Acts were passed in a hurry and the language used was often extremely vague,' said the 'architect' himself, Lord Justice Scrutton (*Skinner* v. *Geary* *[1931]* 2 *K.B.* 546 @ 561). 'Houses or parts of houses', 'let as a separate dwelling', 'board attendance or use of furniture', 'greater hardship' and many more exercised the etymological capacities of judicial philologists.

The doctrines emerged from the exigencies of life for, as Lord Goddard said, 'The court cannot specifically enforce an agreement for two people to live peaceably under the same roof' (*Thompson* v. *Park* *[1944]* *K.B.* 408). And so they developed such conceptions as sharing living accommodation even though 'it is not the function of any judge to fill in what he conceives to be the gaps in an Act of Parliament'. Lord Morton in *Major & St Mellons R.D.C.* v. *Newport Corporation* (*1952*) *A.C.* 189. Sharing a lavatory does not take the dwelling out of protection. Several people can share lavatories and still have 'separate dwellings'. They've been doing it for generations in the Gorbals. Farm cottages did not have lavatories. But a kitchen is an essential room when you cook there, but not when you just wash there (*Cole* v. *Harris* *[1945]* 1 *K.B.* 474). If you rent a room but do not sleep there it is not a dwelling, and so not protected.

But do not lean too heavily on old cases. 'I doubt whether that court in the early days of the Rent Restriction Acts appreciated fully what it was doing,' said Lord Justice Scrutton himself in *Gee* v. *Hazelton* (*1932*) 1 *K.B.* 179.

Right up to 1968 there was the celebrated enigma of *Section 12 (6)* of the 1920 Act which said:

> '*Where this Act has become applicable to any dwelling house or any mortgage thereon, it shall continue to apply thereto whether or not the dwelling house continues to be one to which this Act applies.*'

That provision was many times cited, often argued, but never once acted upon in 47 years. But the other conundrums were solved. As was said in *Brown* v. *Brash* (*1948*) 2 *K.B.* 247 @ 254, 'The clear policy of the Acts is to keep a roof over the tenant's—or someone's —head'.

But the landlord and tenant law was forged long before England became a property-owning democracy—even before Sir William Harcourt QC, the Liberal Cabinet Minister said, in 1894, 'We are all Socialists now'. The lease was a collection of well settled conditions and covenants, all authoritatively pronounced upon or elaborately constructed by conveyancers out of words which had been authoritatively pronounced upon. There are common forms of provision for agricultural leases and leases of factories and warehouses; of mines and quarries, and fisheries and shooting. There are short leases and long leases, particularly where land is leased in an undeveloped state for the purpose of building thereon.

Infinitely variable though the details be, they are designed to one end and adherence to that principle is the first essential for comprehension of leases. They are to give the freeholder control over the tenant's occupation of the land. Judges and Parliament have whittled away the rights of freeholders, but their lawyers have returned to the task, patiently sapping and mining away in the libraries and the courts. Obligations in sealed deeds are enforceable by law whether or not value was given therefor. For breaches of these obligations there can be litigation over whether the tenant should pay money or be enjoined by orders which, if broken, will see him imprisoned for contempt of court. But the great sanction is the proviso in so many important covenants that if the tenant breaks it, the landlord can put an end to the interest in land created by the lease. The tenant thus loses that for which he paid dearly. No matter how much the premium, if the rent is not paid, the lease is forfeit, unless a sympathetic court will 'relieve against the forfeiture' which is only done on payment in full of all the arrears and the costs.

Victorian landlords found in this the way to make the wayward tenant toe the line and to control development. Thus was born the 'restrictive covenant', the earliest form of town planning. Its ambit is wide. It might forbid putting out washing on a clothes line, or burning garden refuse, or building a house below a certain rateable value.

It need not be in a lease. Conveyances of freehold also contain them. I knew a wealthy builder who built a glass-fronted mansion in a posh suburb. His wife started getting phone calls from the neighbours about his site van being parked outside. This, they considered, was 'carrying on a trade or business' and they had all covenanted not to do that in that desirable residential area. He bought a Land Rover and a flat cap and the complaints stopped, which was curious, because some people thought the underlying reason was that his wife wore her curlers in the garden.

No doubt you have wondered why there are no buildings in the middle of Leicester Square. Well, a Mr Tulk sold it to a Mr Elms, and took from him a covenant not to build on the middle. Leicester Square was afterwards sold to Mr Moxhay, who knew of the covenant, but nevertheless started building. But Mr Tulk sued him on the covenant (*Tulk* v. *Moxhay* [*1848*] *2 Ph. 774*) and Mr Moxhay was prevented from building there in breach of the covenant. The reason was that Mr Elms paid a low price for it because of the restriction, and it would be inequitable to let Mr Elms make a great profit out of it by selling it free of the ban. Moxhay would have been bound by the covenant even if he did not know its actual terms, because a purchaser of land, even though he does not make proper inquiries, is deemed to know everything he would have found out if he had. You can apply to the Lands Tribunal to have restrictive covenants removed from land.

The heyday of the restrictive covenant was during the creation of the desirable places, like Hampstead Garden Suburb and other 'best parts', as well as the Garden Cities. But they are still common, particularly in shop leases, where a parade of shops is intended to supply all the different wants of the neighbourhood. Unfortunately, grocers disapprove of greengrocers selling tinned fruit and vegetables. Chemists disapprove of grocers selling aspirin. Newsagents selling stocking tights upset the haberdashers. Landlords preside over these little differences but they are not the main bone of contention in the world of landlord and tenant.

5, Brunswick Place, Sept. 19, 1842.

'*Lady Marrable informs Mrs Smith that it is her determination to leave the house in Brunswick Place as soon as she can take another, paying a week's rent, as all the bedrooms occupied but one are so infested with bugs that it is impossible to remain.*'

This is a faithful reproduction of the letter which commenced that celebrated action which shook Victorian landladies to the middle of their stays, and filled with immense foreboding those gentlemen who sought security for their old age in rents.

Lady Marrable was dragged through the courts by Mrs Smith (*1843*) *11 M. & W. 5; 12 L.J. Ex. 223.* Lady Marrable had taken the house for five weeks, and Mrs Smith wanted five weeks' rent, bugs or no bugs.

The somewhat novel proposition for which Lady Marrable contended was that in the letting of a *furnished* house, there is always to be implied a condition that it is reasonably fit for human habitation. Edwin Chadwick's *Public Health Act* was only six years old at the time. He and his like, although powerful in the counsels of Prime Minister Peel, were regarded by the landed interest and the lesser property people as all of a piece with the violent Frenchmen who only half a century before had consigned so many of their betters to the guillotine.

Not for another five and thirty years was the Bug Case confirmed in *Wilson* v. *Finch Hatton (1877) 2 Ex Div. 336,* where the drains were very bad.

But even when it became a doctrine, it was one which was satisfactory to the late 19th Century conscience. Fitness for habitation was a requirement only for *furnished* accommodation. Well, the right sort of people did take furnished houses: for The Season, or for a holiday, or for a couple of years home from India; or during the shooting, hunting or similar periods of socially essential diversion. Progress rather demanded that when they took a furnished house it should be above reproach—not that it would be, but that it should be.

Furnished houses would, it was true, be let by other gentlefolk, but they were rather descending into trade by doing it. If you were any class at all, you could afford to shut up your establishment and go away without trying to profit by your absence. That really was rather reducing land owning to the level of Trade. Now Trade had a simple, inflexible rule. The seller must deliver. However lousy the goods he had to deliver. The carriage trade sent back what it did not want and the tradesman could wait for his money and he would not be paid for what was rejected (this is the basis of the Sale of Goods Act). The tradesman could and did insure against this kind of loss by overcharging. All that was done in *Smith* v. *Marrable* was to vindicate the God-given rights of Class over Trade. Once properly understood, it raises no difficulties of principle and it is easy to understand why it is still the law, and not much extended.

Altogether and totally different was the lasting principle which affected *unfurnished* lettings. These must be viewed from an entirely different standpoint. A gentleman would by judicious marriage and crafty mortgage acquire more than one estate. Each might have a mansion house, several farms, dower houses, and other residential properties. That was his due, being born in the right bed had made of him a gentleman, and the basic right of a gentleman was to live in style upon rents. The tenants might vary in class, but Great Heavens they were still tenants. Was a man to have to guarantee to every tenant whom he was good enough to grant the privilege of occupying one of his bits of Britain that the roof would not leak or that the walls would not crumble?

The Common Law had endured upwards of six centuries without finding it necessary to require a house let say, on a seven-year lease, to remain standing for even a week. *Caveat emptor*. If you bought a horse and it went lame, hard luck. If you bought a house and it fell down, you built it up. Having been permitted by rent service or fine or both to achieve at least the outward appearance of land holding by the benison of an English freeholder the tenant had the same right as a freeholder—to mend what broke.

So jealously was this right protected by the law that if the tenant did not build up again what fell down, the freeholder could recover from him the loss in value to the reversion. This principle supports in large part the honourable profession of building surveyor, whose detailed 'schedules of dilapidations' still strike terror into tenants whose leases are running out in spite of the mitigating influences of Parliament.

'Fraud apart, there is no law against letting a tumbledown house,' declared Chief Justice Erle in *Robbins* v. *Jones* (*1863*) *15 C.B. 221*. This salutary principle, like all good things, has endured and remains the law practically unsullied to the present day. Some Governments have tried to interfere with the doctrine, by imposing minimum standards of hygiene and soundness upon houses intended for and occupied by the lower orders. But the powerful rationale underpinning the philosophy has protected it from any serious in-roads. Landlords, as well as tenants, have Members of Parliament. Some landlords are Members of Parliament. You can restrict rent, you can give security of tenure. And when the tenant is living securely in the dump he will find out just what a dump it is.

Not that there were not attempts to extend the Bugs Case. Mr Carr put so much flour into the warehouse he leased from the Manchester Bonded Warehouse Company that the floor gave way, and brought down the building. The tenant seemed to think that he should not pay rent whilst the warehouse lay in flour-covered ruins. The Court of Commons Pleas very reasonably explained that to agree with him would be the same as saying that there was an implied condition that a rented warehouse would remain standing for the whole period of the lease, and they could not do that ([*1880*] *5 C.P.D. 507*). He was entitled to exclusive possession of the ruins, and he would need it, to build the new warehouse. Whilst he was doing that, he had, of course, to pay the rent, he being in occupation.

In the same year, another tenant, Mr Anderson, complained in the Queen's Bench that his landlord, Mr Oppenheimer, ought to pay for all the tenant's goods which were ruined by water from a burst pipe. Mr Anderson was cute enough to sue under that 'usual' covenant which assured him of 'quiet enjoyment' of the premises. There is one in every well-drawn lease, and most badly drawn ones, too. With every appearance of reason he contended that you are not quietly and peaceably holding the premises when all your stock is floating sodden down the stairs on a raging torrent. He was reminded rather sharply that *Smith* v. *Marrable* was a furnished letting, and that its implications did not extend to ordinary leases of houses, lands, shops or warehouses. Vice-Chancellor Bacon, in *Powell* v. *Chester* (*1885*) *52 L.T. 722*, would not even allow that there was in a lease an implied covenant for a sufficient water supply. At least the tenant could not complain that his floods were bad ones.

Tenants were not only well advised to get the strength of the insurance companies round them. They were bound to insure to the extent which the landlord required, and pay the premium to him, as additional rent, and they could be turned out if they did not. No Act of Parliament has ever sanctioned this practice. But it is hallowed by time, it is done in every well-prepared lease nowadays, and has been going on much too long to stop without legislation.

It might have been taken for granted since a furnished letting carried with it an implication that the house or flat should be habitable, that there would be a similar implication that mere lodgings should be habitable, if furnished. Though, as generations of landladies have made plain to their lodgers, they are entirely free to go elsewhere if the rooms do not suit.

Of course, people who let lodgings were not of the same degree as those who let more capacious establishments. Of course, a quite good class of person did sometimes take lodgings of a superior kind. A doctrine developed, but closely circumscribed so that the rights of landowners should not be encroached upon more than was absolutely necessary. The Court of Appeal held that although there is one that lodgings are habitable when let, there is no warranty that they will stay habitable all the time they are let. (*Sarson* v. *Roberts* [*1895*] *2 Q.B. 395.*)

The natural consequence is that if a tenant lets bed bugs get into the premises once he is in occupation—or even if he does not let them but just cannot prevent them—it is not the landlord's fault. Furthermore, if he has the lease drawn up by someone with any idea at all, he will have at least a sporting chance of being able to evict the tenant for letting it happen. This will entail serving on the tenant a notice under *Section 146* of the *Law of Property Act, 1925*, specifying the breach of covenant committed (other than non-payment of rent) and requiring it to be remedied within a reasonable time and payment of money compensation.

Letting the bugs in could be nuisance, or letting the premises fall out of repair. If the notice is not complied with the lease could be forfeit. A quick fumigation, a tidy-up. A new tenant at a higher rent, and inflation is catered for.

Parliament, eternally vigilant and conscious particularly that by far the majority of voters live in houses, appreciated that something had to be done to make rented accommodation fit to live in. As early as 1957, the *Housing Act* by *Section 6*, gave a protection to both furnished and unfurnished houses. It imposes upon the letting the implied condition that the house shall be fit for human habitation not only at the beginning, but throughout the period of the lease. The defects which make a house unfit, it says, are instability and damp, absence of light, water, air, sanitation, cooking facilities, and disrepair which could cause damage to life, limb or health.

It is true that it only covers houses let at rents up to £80 in London and £52 elsewhere. Its ramifications, therefore, are less than total. Oddly enough, it does not say whether the rent is for a year, month or a week. Lawyers, steeped for centuries in the Common Law climate of becoming a tenant at your peril, and implications that leases are by the year unless otherwise expressly designated, construe it to mean that the rent period is a year.

There is no constitutional means of asking Parliament what it meant. That is left to the judges for the good reason that if you asked Parliament, it might very well not be able to tell you. However, if some bold spirit likes to sport the costs on the chance of being right, a court might say otherwise. If it was held that the rent period was a week or even a month, there would overnight be a revolution in English property circles such as never happened before. There would be so many bankruptcies of landlords that a relief operation on the Asian Earthquake scale would be required to succour them.

As things are understood at the present—and there is no court decision on it—if your rent is a pound a week or less, you are entitled by law to a house that is fit to live in. If you can afford something better, you have no grouse if it is a dump.

There is an exception, however, for those who occupy under leases for less than seven years. Under such contracts, the landlord has to keep the structure and exterior (including drains, gutters, and exterior pipes) in repair. He must also keep the sanitation and means of supplying (but not of using) water, gas and electricity in repair. For instance, he has to keep the electricity main and the fuse box in repair, but not the electric fire. And he must also thus maintain the space and water heating. But there may be none. This privilege applies whether the dwelling house is furnished or not.

No doubt these matters were raised by the tenants of Mr Peter Rachman with him when the *Housing Act, 1961*, enacted these provisions by *Sections 32 and 33*. There is no reported authority on the matter but it may have been over this provision that his tenants were visited by his agents who bit their ears off. Ear cropping was considered to have fallen into desuetude with the dissolution of Star Chamber in 1660. But this is perhaps an instance of how foreign-born property magnates quickly pick up old English ways.

The cardinal principle of our law is of course that everyone is equal under it. It might therefore be considered that those who enjoy the benefit of expensive if unexciting buildings, and up-to-date sanitation in council houses, would be the best-off householders in the land. They have to put up with the neighbours, of course, but don't we all? Subsidy and security (real if not apparent) should satisfy. But the council tenant has no implied warranty of fitness for habitation attaching to his house.

When Mr Sleafer took hold of his front door knocker to slam the door shut at the flat which he rented from the Lambeth Borough Council, it came away in his hand. This caused him to stagger back and hurt himself against some railings. He claimed damages from the council for his injuries. He argued that the door was defective because it jammed and would not shut properly unless it was slammed. He could, perhaps have put his hand in the letter box, to get a better hold, but the most convenient way was to pull it by the knocker.

His counsel did not contend that a defective door knocker made a house unfit for human habitation. But a defective door did, he argued. But the judge refused to imply a condition to keep the premises in repair or fit for habitation (*1960*) *Q.B.* Oddly enough a landlord, a decade earlier, was held liable to compensate a passer-by, who was injured because the premises by which he was perambulating were defective. The house was occupied by a weekly tenant. There was no explicit agreement between him and the landlord about who was to keep the property in repair. In the absence of the responsibility being cast upon the tenant by the landlord, the landlord must be responsible to the third party, said the court. (*Mint* v. *Good* (*1951*).)

Can you wonder, therefore, that landlords put conditions in leases and in the small print on rent books making tenants liable for repairs? Think how many people walk along streets past houses. Anyone could be walking past a property of mine and be hit on the head by a falling slate. (It has happened to me, which might explain a lot.) When the liability is expressly cast upon the tenant, it does not matter whether he is negligent or not in failing to repair. His duty is absolute. He has contracted to repair, and repair he must. This was clearly laid down in *Paradine* v. *Jane, in 1647*. They had no nonsense then about landlords being responsible under the Housing Act for the limited structural liability in leases of under seven years in any event. So strong is our sense of justice that when a tenant was unable to repair because he would be acting illegally by doing so (having been refused a building licence for the work) he was excused the repairs, and allowed to pay money damages instead. (*Eyre* v. *Johnson* (*1946*).)

It often seems to students of English law that our courts are more ready to imply responsibilities upon private individuals than upon public organisations or officials. Similarly, they are more likely to imply duties under Acts of Parliament than under private contracts. In our grandfathers' days this was less apparent. Indeed, some Victorian judges fertilised the seeds of anarchy in their intolerance of Government interference. But that reprehensible tendency has been arrested. So have many people who agree with it.

A landlord who is obliged to keep premises in repair under a lease (and there are some such) does not have to take any action unless and until he is informed of disrepair. This does not at all conflict with *Paradine* v. *Jane*. That is a law for the tenant. There is a different law for the landlord. He, after all, does not live in the demised premises, does he? The process of informing is called by lawyers 'giving notice'. You can have 'notice' of anything. You can have 'constructive notice' of something which means that although you do not know it, the law presumes that you do.

But the law is not so harsh as to leave landlords at the mercy of perils of which they are not aware. Nevertheless, the tribulations of property owning are such that landlords often entrust their affairs to solicitors even before anything goes wrong. In return for fees acknowledged by everyone except *Which?* and the Prices and Incomes Board to be extremely reasonable, the solicitors draft leases for them. Drafting a lease demands a thorough understanding of the law of real property, leases, Town and Country Planning, Local Authority By-Laws, drainage, nuisance, trespass, Occupiers' Liability and contract. Law libraries are lined with books containing precedents, which are model clauses drafted by eminent conveyancers since time immemorial and brought up to date each year by the underpaid and overworked qualified staff of law publishers. You will seldom find one covering the precise case with which you are dealing but diligent search will yield something pretty close. The demise of a Mayfair flat is not all that different from that of a less salubrious apartment. ('Demise' in this context is a technical word for 'lease'; not 'death' or 'destruction'.)

There is another way, but only if you are on the Roll, i.e. happen to be a solicitor. You can then go to a Law Stationer and for $17\frac{1}{2}$ pence buy a printed form of lease with a lot of blank spaces in. By filling them up with the details of who is the landlord and what is the rent, you have a do-it-yourself Lease. It is a great help to know what to put in, by way of 'special conditions' or 'unusual covenants'. But it is even better to know what to cross out. The wise solicitor, even if he drafts his lease in this way, has it typed on thick 'judicature' paper afterwards to make it look as if he worked it all out himself. There is nothing to stop him using the filled-in printed form except sheer common sense. If the client sees that all that was done was to fill in a form, he will think he can do it himself next time.

Granted, that might lead to costly litigation which might prove profitable if the client is rich. But it is likelier by far to lead to the loss of a right, and some blameless person might suffer. If the person liable—the home draftsman—cannot pay the costs, the opponent will have to pay them himself.

Unless therefore, there is one of the statutory provisions over-

246

riding it, a provision making a tenant liable for repairs is effective. The basis of this law is the old law of 'waste', a beautiful old English word expressing the concept with dignity. In Latin it is 'vastum' and the meaning of the verb 'devastate' is well known. Anything which a tenant did which reduced the value of his lord's land had to be paid for. Just so that it should be clearly understood, the *Statute of Marlborough, 1267*, put it into writing and the *Statutes of Marlebridge* and of *Gloucester* applied it to estates held under settlements. These are just as much the law as the *Rent Act, 1968*.

There are two kinds of waste: 'voluntary' where the tenant does something to cause the waste, and 'permissive' when he does nothing to cause it. It is not waste to use premises for the purpose for which you rent them. Though the unfortunate Mr Carr, whose flour brought down the Manchester Bonded Warehouse, had to pay the rent, he was let off the damages for wrecking the warehouse because it was reasonable to store the flour there.

But the law of waste is behind the rule that even where there is no express covenant by the tenant to repair, there is one implied that the tenant will use them in 'a proper and tenantlike manner', which means to keep them in repair and at the end of the term deliver them up in the same state and condition as when the tenancy began, except for 'reasonable wear and tear'. *Marsden* v. *Edward Heyes, Ltd. (1927) 2 K.B. 1.* No doubt a landlord could recover from his tenant if he was liable to a passer-by for something the tenant should have repaired by these criteria.

A couple of hundred years ago Lord Kenyon said that a tenant from year to year is bound to commit no waste, and to make reasonable and fair repairs, such as putting in windows or doors that have been broken by him, so as to prevent waste and decay of the premises. If it is a short lease, e.g. seven years, and the foundation crumbles he does not have to rebuild the whole house, but just repair it as well as he can (*Lister* v. *Lane (1893) 2 Q.B. 212*). But he cannot get away with letting the place fall down to dodge liability and in *Haskell* v. *Marlow (1928)* a deceased tenant's estate was held liable for permitting waste and decay.

The tenant's liability extends not only beyond the grave. It begins with the signing of the lease and continues even when he assigns the whole term of the lease on sale to someone else. (*Shaw* v. *Kay [1847] 1 Exch. 412.*) He therefore has to make the assignee liable to indemnify him. Both he and the assignee are liable for the covenant 'runs with the land' like the Leicester Square covenant. (*Spencer's Case [1583] 5 Coke's Reports 16a.*)

Interpretation of a repairing clause must take account of 'each word used' said Lord Justice Fletcher Moulton in *Lurcott* v. *Wakely & Wheeler [1911] 1 K.B. 905* and of 'the age, class, locality and

247

general condition of the premises at the time of the demise.'

'Tenantable repair' is a 'very slight liability' not requiring premises to be put back in original condition, it was said in *Crawford* v. *Newton* [1886] 36 W.R. 54. But you got a lot more decorating for a ten pound note then. There is no liability to re-paper walls unless expressly reserved, but painting must be done as necessary to preserve woodwork.

Lord Esher, Master of the Rolls, said in *Proudfoot* v. *Hart* (1890) 25 Q.B.D. 42 that although a covenant to 'keep and deliver up the premises in tenantable repair' did not say that the tenant had to *put* them into that state when they were not so at the beginning of the term, he had to do that. Only thus could he discharge the obligation to deliver up in repair.

That is the law today. All turns on the standard of repair upon which the landlord can insist. Said Lord Esher: 'The state of repair necessary for a house in Grosvenor Square would be wholly different from the state of repair necessary for a house in Spitalfields.

'. . . If the tenant leaves a house in Grosvenor Square with painting only good enough for a house in Spitalfields, he has not discharged his obligation.'

But . . . 'Take again the case of a house in Grosvenor Square having an ornamental ceiling which is a beautiful work of art. In course of time the gilding becomes in such bad condition or so much worn off, that the ceiling is no longer ornamental. I should think that a reasonable tenant taking a house in Grosvenor Square would not require a gilded ceiling at all. If that be so, on the mere covenant to leave the premises in tenantable repair, I should think the tenant . . . was not bound to regild the ceiling at all.'

What could landlords do in the face of such rabid republicanism? Specific covenants for regilding ceilings had to come.

'Repair' and 'renew' are not words which express a clear contrast, said Lord Justice Buckley in *Lurcott* v. *Wakely & Wheeler*: 'Repair always involves renewal; renewal of a part; of a subordinate part; a skylight leaks; repair is effected by hacking out the putties, putting in new ones and renewing the paint. Repair is restoration by renewal or replacement of subsidiary parts of a whole. Renewal as distinguished from repair, is reconstruction of the entirety, meaning by the entirety not necessarily the whole, but substantially the whole subject matter under discussion.'

Since the Second World War, the value of real property has gone up even quicker than the cost of living. Reversions therefore do not suffer by waste, for they are worth more anyway. But they would be worth even more if they were in better order. But this argument will not avail against a bill for dilapidations under a repairing covenant because it is totally independent of waste. If the tenant has bound himself to 'paint, varnish, colour, paper, and cleanse all those parts usually and habitually painted, coloured, varnished, papered and cleansed' at some intervals like 'every three years and at the end of the term' he must do it even if the decor is still quite nice. He might get his own back by doing it in bad taste. That might not fulfil the contract for a well-drawn lease would make it dependent on 'the reasonable satisfaction of the landlord'. I once came across a chap who got away with stairs with matt black treads and orange rises, but that was in Chelsea.

The great case of waste was not a landlord and tenant case but one where Lord Barnard had settled Raby Castle upon himself for life with remainder to his son, the Hon. Mr Vane. Lord Barnard's settlement deed provided that he held 'without impeachment of waste', which meant that he was not liable for depreciation of the castle's value by the time his son inherited. According to the report of 1716, 'Lord Barnard, having taken some displeasure against his son, got 200 workmen together, and of a sudden, in a few days, stript the castle of the lead, iron, glass, doors and boards to a value of £3,000'. The Court of Chancery made him make it good anyway. He makes the modern fixture-pincher look pathetic.

'*Quicquid plantatur solo, solo cedit*', is the maxim which expressed the principle that whatever was attached to the land became part of it. Still powerful law, it would logically prevent the tenant from taking away his curtains when he moved. But things are only legally 'annexed' when the fixing is so strong that work would be needed or damage caused to remove it. A factory lessee, whose machinery has to be fixed firmly to work properly, had better set only bolts in concrete and screw his machines to them. If he sets the legs of the machines in the concrete floor, he might loose them (*Jordan* v. *May*, *1947*).

Tenants can take ornamental or trade fixtures. In *Spyer* v. *Phillipson* (*1931*) a wise tenant put up antique panelling in a leased house, by a fastening which made it fairly easily removable. The court held it was a 'tenant's fixture' which he could remove before leaving. Once he leaves, unless he gets permission to go back for a fixture from the landlord, the tenant has lost it. Even if you wanted to sell your curtain rails, curtains and carpets, but the new tenant moved in before you were able to make a deal with him, you will not be able to charge him for them.

But you may have to pay for your waste or want of repair, nevertheless. Unless they were caused by Act of God the tenant is not liable for those. Nor, in the High Court of Justice at least, is God. The landlord is without a remedy, because his insurance might not help either. (No case against Him has ever been established in what we know as 'the Supreme Court', though it is apprehended that a conflict of jurisdiction might arise.)

Just what a tenant should do after one of God's acts depends more on personal inclination than any rigid law. Sir Edward Coke said that if one of God's storms takes off the roof, the tenant ought to cover the rafters to stop them from rotting. But he also said that if a house has no roof at the beginning of the lease the tenant can let it fall down without being liable for waste. The product of the two doctrines appears to be that you should not sign a lease before a storm. If you do, you will be liable for all the damage, with the prospect of compensation in Heaven.

A Place Of One's Own

'No doubt the maxim "quicquid plantatur solo, solo cedit" is well established. The only question is what is meant by it?'

Mr Justice Williams in *Lancaster* v. *Eve (1859)* 5. C.B.N.S.

HARDINGE GIFFARD, Earl of Halsbury, who gave his name as general editor to a 45-volume encyclopaedia of all the Laws of England said that the 'equity of redemption' of a mortgage was something he had never understood. And with the sublime indifference which so often characterises the ignorant, he said he could not see the sense of it anyway. Actually he was a brilliant lawyer who kept his faculties to the age of 96.

If any was required, that is a superb example of the wisdom of the statement that if Conveyancing is to be reformed, the land law has to be put right first. The equity of redemption is one of the finest ornaments of the diadem of that peculiarly English goddess, Justice. Like so many of her qualities, it need not be understood in order to be appreciated.

It is what enables you to buy your own house; although the house is not paid for, it is yours while you buy. That is freedom. Any rise in its value is yours. You do not even have to pay Capital Gains Tax on an owner-occupied house. If you make a loss, that is yours, too. You do not have to pay tax on that, either.

Money may or may not be the root of evil, but moneylending is the root of most of English private law. A mortgage is technically a lease, nowadays. The classical English mortgage actually transferred the ownership of the property to the lender, and he promised to convey it back when all the debt, interest and costs were paid. But even if the day of redemption had gone by, the Chancellor in his court of Equity, would compel Sir Jasper the lender to transfer back a valuable property on repayment of debt and costs and interest. That is the equity or right of redemption. It means that the owner gets the profit, even though he owes a vast sum on mortgage. For the maxim of Equity is 'once a mortgage, always a mortgage'.

251

The three-thousand-year lease which the modern building society gets as security, like any other lease, carries with it the right to possession. So, naturally, did the old mortgage by transfer of ownership. Building societies and other benevolent usurers are entitled to possession of the premises secured by their loans, 'before the ink is dry on the mortgage' in the words of Lord Justice Harman (*Four Maids Ltd. & Dudley Marshall (Properties) Ltd. [1957] Ch. 317*).

The building societies do not want to live in your house. But they are thereby entitled to take possession if you do not pay the instalments. You cannot deny them that right. You granted them a lease for three thousand years in return for the loan they made to you.

Of course, it is rather a long time, and though the freehold is for ever, the actual value of the freehold reversion, discounted until the end of that three thousand years is not great. But the retention of that freehold reversion is what makes a suburban bungalow owner a fee tenant in chief under the Queen. The owner of his own little bit of England.

The theory works very well for leaseholds as well. A mortgage is made of leasehold land by creating a term a day or two shorter than the actual interest of the purchaser of the house or flat. (It is perfectly possible to have a 'flying freehold' of an upstairs flat, but these can have auxiliary problems.)

The great complexity of the land law of England would be greatly simplified if teachers of law thought of it in terms of ordinary people buying houses to live in, instead of as a remarkable legacy from feudalism. It certainly is that. But most things have histories. People have been drinking water and washing in it for a long time, but many of them do not know that it is compounded of two parts of hydrogen to one of oxygen. They are content to know that it is necessary.

A man who is buying a house has two problems; raising the money and making sure it is not going to be a troublesome purchase. The first is covered by the law of mortgages, the second by the laws of contract and of ownership of land.

The law of mortgages, so far as the ordinary man is concerned, is that he and his family can be thrown into the street if he does not pay the monthly instalment. But even if things get that bad, the equity of redemption will assist him. Because of it, if the building society sells the house to pay its loan, any profit must be paid to the owner. And right up to the sale he can redeem the property if he can find the money—perhaps by a loan from some other source.

It may very well be that Lord Halsbury realised all this perfectly well but could not understand why this salutary law should have a funny name like 'equity of redemption'.

Since 1st February, 1971, this ancient right—which owed nothing to Parliament in its inception—has been supplemented for the first time in history by a power for the courts to postpone the operation of a possession order against a mortgagor by *s. 36 of the Administration of Justice Act, 1970.* Judges and lawyers have been bending the rules for years to achieve something of the kind.

For whilst a tenant of a rent-controlled house could owe as much in rent as the place was worth without any real risk of being chucked out—unless his County Court judge was tougher than most—an Englishman who was the legal owner of his house could not, theoretically, stop the mortgagee taking possession of it— before the ink was dry.

The difference between law and life is nothing to wonder about. For all the apparent disadvantage of being an owner, in fact by paying 8½ per cent in mortgage interest and making yourself owner, you can increase your investment by about 10 per cent a year. If you have profit, who needs rights? Consequently, you decide to buy instead of paying rent so that your landlord can buy more houses to let to mugs.

You have seen the house. You like it. It is for sale. You are prepared to pay a price the owner is willing to accept. There is nothing in the world to stop you giving him the money, and he moving out and you moving in. It would not make you able to prove that you owned the house, but so long as no trouble arose you could live out your life there.

If you had no written note of your agreement to buy, you could go ahead with your arrangements to move in and he could sell it to someone else—even if the other chap did not offer more money. Your deal would not be enforceable. It would be perfectly legal. But the courts would not enforce it.

But you would not want to commit yourself to buying until you had arranged a mortgage, or had it surveyed, or had a solicitor assure you, after the vague and mysterious things they do that the deal was 'all right'.

You have therefore been told by your friends or picked it up in the rapid speech of the estate agent's negotiator, that you have to say you will buy 'subject to contract'. If you are ignorant of this the solicitor's first letter on your behalf will say that you have agreed to buy 'subject to contract'.

If you have a sticky vendor, he could come back at them with the charge that it is not subject to contract at all, that you are legally bound to go through with the deal at the price. And he could produce the receipt for the holding deposit signed by him over the sixpenny stamp. If it does not say 'subject to contract' you could be bound. The court might allow you to give evidence that it was only provisional on all the details being sorted out.

You will have appreciated that 'subject to contract' means that although you have agreed to buy you have not bound yourself.

There is a great deal of nonsense written about putting an end to 'gazumping', which means selling to a higher bidder whilst 'subject to contract' or, in the cases of developers, raising the price before contract. With deference to Mr Kevin Macnamara MP, if his Bill to fine people who sell for more after a 'firm offer' and to make them compensate the would-be purchaser is to have any bite, it would virtually force people to contract before they had arranged their finance or arranged to sell their present home—which are usually interdependent because the 'bridging loan' depends upon the sale of the old home. Delays in real property sales are usually caused by purchasers who have to get rid of their existing houses—often delayed because of the profiteering prices they ask of their purchasers. For many owner-occupiers, a sale going off is a financial disaster when they own the house but not when they do not.

The natural development of his Bill would be to force people to stipulate that an offer is not to be treated as 'firm' or in any sense binding, which is the existing law, and the reason for stipulating 'subject to contract'.

'Gazumping' hurts only those who are not selling a house to buy one. Anyone who has wrung the last penny out of his purchaser cannot complain of someone doing likewise to him.

It follows that 'subject to contract' means 'no contract'. Can he sell it over your head to someone else? Yes. If he does, what happens about the money you have to pay your solicitors and surveyors? You lose it. You have had an expensive lesson in property buying. The law gives you no sanction. However, economic force does. He is probably desperately anxious to sell to you because he can see that you will get a mortgage without much trouble whereas the other desperately interested viewers are all too poor. They have young children and their wives cannot work. Or they cannot get big enough loans.

You must be very careful to stick to the rubric. Do not embroider. 'Subject to a formal contract being prepared by my solicitors', wrote one man. He was bound to complete the purchase. What that meant, said the Chancery judge, was that the vendor and purchaser had made a legally binding agreement, which should be enforced, and simply added a rider to it that the *formal* technical contracts would be drawn up later. If they were bound, why bother? In ordinary sense, why indeed. But contracts for the purchase of real property and other valuable things often contain a large number of terms besides the main bargain. They might be important, but not affect the main purpose.

If you get stuck with the house from the word 'go' you can either go ahead and look cheerful and try to get some compensation for defects afterwards, or refuse to proceed and perhaps be sued. If it turns into contentious business, the solicitor will be your solicitor only if he is specifically instructed for the purpose of carrying out that business. It is not included in the conveyancing charges. It would be a great deal extra.

The secret of modern soliciting success is to have a good photo-copying machine. With one of those, a Solicitors' Diary and Kelly's Draftsman a man can put up his brass plate with confidence. If the diary is current he will be assured of success—for the staple of this profession is Conveyancing. It has been described as the 'dynamic' aspect of the law of real property. Its spirit is about as combustible as camel dung, but the implication is to suggest the process of transferring property from one owner to another.

There is a widespread fallacy that this has to be done by a solicitor. This is untrue. Every Englishman has an undeniable right to make his own catastrophes of his own affairs. This applies to property transactions as well as to do-it-yourself interior decorating and car repair.

There are available little books to tell you how to do your own Conveyancing, and the kind called Registered Conveyancing is supposed to be within the competence of an intelligent person. Registration of title to land in some official system was called 'the necessary process' by Mr Justice Wilberforce (as he was then) in *Re Hewitt's Contract (1963) 1 W.L.R. 1298 @ 1305*. Like other necessities it is unconscionably long in spreading, having been the subject of an unsuccessful Bill in Parliament in 1652 the words of which were similar to those of the *Land Registration Act, 1925*.

Although Lord Birkenhead—'Galloper' Smith to the Irish—did away with the feudal system by his 1925 property legislation it is with us still in the regime of unregistered dealing in real property which applies over most of the country. (As a matter of fact, Smith did not work out those 600 pages of property law. It was done by Sir Benjamin Cherry.)

A noisy minority claiming to represent public opinion consider unregistered conveyancing a reproach to the legal profession. No one complains about barbers who do not use electric clippers, but lawyers on the make have been victims of public jealousy for centuries. But it took them a long time, with Parliament's help, to turn the law into the treacherous morass it is, and they deserve their fees for guiding the ignorant travellers across it. Not for nothing are some of the conveyancing processes called 'searches'.

At this point one has to consider the theory of the English land law, if one is to have any idea at all why people go to solicitors for guidance.

Law students are told in their first classes and the little books from which they cram that the monuments to English legal thought in the jurisprudential world are the doctrine of estates in land and the law of trusts.

Land, because it stands out in all weathers but still lasts longer than any human being, cannot be 'owned' according to this theory. However, people can own 'interests' in it which come to their ends at different times and in different ways. All the interests which are less than the infinite, inheritable ownership free from all rents and obligations can exist at the same time as it. Each of these has to be capable of proof by evidence in a lawsuit if necessary. The evidence is usually a document. If you have not got your document you cannot prove your rights.

That Eminent Victorian, Augustine Birrel, QC, was speaking about a similar abstraction called Copyright when he described it as 'a bundle of rights'. That is what ownership of land is, and exactly what those rights are is set out in highly technical language on the deeds of title. All you have to do to prove you are the freehold owner of your bijou suburban residence is to produce your title deeds, which you cannot do because the building society will not let you have them.

That is the English Law of Real Property in a nutshell. But as Lord Macnaghten said it is one thing to put a case in a nutshell and entirely another to keep it there. The intelligent reader will have wondered why photocopies are not made of all these so-called deeds—overprinted *Copy* in red like insurance policies—and these copies handed to the proud houseowner in an attractive plastic wallet embossed in gold with the name and telephone number of the building society, insurance company, estate agent and developer. I wonder too. Maybe no one else has thought of it yet.

Before photocopiers were invented 'abstracts' of all the deeds showing title had to be typed, and new deeds still have to be. Before that they had to be handwritten, and the monumental labours of the old quill drivers were the foundations of many lawyers' fortunes because deed draftsmen and 'law writers' charged by length.

In A.D. 673 Archbishop Theodore produced to the Council of Hertford a book based upon the *Corpus Juris Canonici*. It said that the Pope had power to declare laws for the universal church. Already Aethelbert of Kent, convert of the saintly Augustine, had written out the 'dooms' or law of Kent in the Roman fashion, but in the language of the country—the first Germanic laws in a Germanic language.

When the glory that was Rome departed the indigenous law remained. But the foundation of conveyancing, the Anglo-Saxon 'landbook' is Italian in origin. These 'deeds' as they came to be called became gradually more common and as Maitland said the Land Law of the 13th Century became the Land Law of 20th.

Now Glanvill and Bracton, the law book writers of the Middle Ages, wrote about people owning land. But in those days only the magnates bothered about deeds and charters to prove their ownership. You can see some in castles and museums now. Possession may never have nine points of the law, but a man's right to land was common knowledge. When he was put into occupation, the lads of the village walked round with him to get to know the boundaries with him and he was given a twig or lump of earth by the former owner as a token of his 'holding' the land.

When John de Warenne, Earl of Surrey, was asked by the Quo Warranto Commissioners in 1278 'by what warrant' he held lands once owned by the Crown, he took down his sword from the castle wall declaring:

'This is my title deed. My ancestors came over with King William and won their lands by the sword. And with this same sword I will maintain them against anyone who tries to take them from me.'

Nowadays you sometimes read of an old lady barricading herself in her home and defying the men from the Ministry and their Compulsory Purchase Order with her husband's ancient shotgun. The difference between her and Earl John is that he got away with it.

The law is the same for castles and bungalows. Freehold is the heritable estate (only a corruption of the latin 'status'). A person put in possession of land was said to be enfeoffed, that is given the 'fee'.

When you buy a freehold house, the conveyance says that you hold it 'in fee simple, absolute in possession'. It uses those archaic words because they express the particular technical meaning of the interest you own. In later times a lot of land came to be owned by people who were the peasants on the lands ruled by the likes of Earl John and his successors. They paid him a 'quit rent' which meant they were not bound to work in his fields as feudal service for their holding of land. As evidence of their right they had a copy of the roll kept by the Steward of the Manor who ran the Manorial Court. Thus they were called 'copyholders' and the documents allowing them to enter into possession after buying such land were called 'admissions'. When they had a mortgage they made a 'conditional surrender' of the land to the Lord of the Manor. They got a 'warrant to vacate' signed by the Lord when it was paid off.

The *Law of Property Act, 1922*, turned all these copyholds into freeholds on 1st January, 1926, and the quit rents and services were all compounded for by 1935 in payment of compensation for the 'manorial incidents'. The deed showing this was done was called either an 'extinguishment agreement' or a 'deed of enfranchisement'.

Since property which was last dealt with forty or more years ago is commonly sold today, all these kinds of document as well as wills and mortgages and conveyances are to be found in 'title deeds'. And it is perfectly possible for it to turn out after all that time that the owner of land is not the owner of it—or at least of bits of it.

Said Mr Justice Romer in an 1898 case:

> *'When I consider the state of the laws of this country concerning land, and the difficulties under which even a perfectly honest and careful vendor labours, it does not appear to me to be reasonable to impute to him knowledge of all possible defects of title for the purpose of such a clause as this'.*
>
> *(Re Woods and Lewis' Contract—about delay in completion of a sale caused by 'wilful default'.)*

Since then, of course, the law has been simplified by the reformers and expanded by them too, so that it is now, if anything, more complicated than ever. Various slightly scatty systems have been propounded, notably one that title should be evidenced by something like a car log book. 'Bookland' indeed. Forgery of logbooks—which do not prove title anyway—is a cottage industry at the bent end of the motor trade and the opportunities for fraud in loose-leaf systems of accounting have not yet been exhausted by even the most assiduous criminals. The reason that all titles are not registered is that property owners were too mean to do it voluntarily when it was introduced in 1872. Landowners see no profit in paying for a registration from which someone else will profit—the purchaser. Compulsory registration was legislated for in 1925, but only brought into operation for the land rush in a few places in the Dodge City days before the war. It is now compulsory in Greater London, Middlesex, Surrey, Kent, Berkshire, Eastbourne, Hastings, Croydon, Oxford, Oldham, Leicester, Canterbury, Manchester, Salford, Huddersfield, Blackburn, Reading, Rochdale, Coventry, Bedworth, Nuneaton, Rugby and Sutton Coldfield.

If you do not register a title on the first transfer after the compulsion order, any transfer of the land is void until you do. And you have to pay the fees for registering. Apart from running his offices at Lincoln's Inn Fields, Durham, Gloucester, Harrow, Lytham St Annes, Nottingham, Stevenage and Tunbridge Wells, the Chief Land Registrar guarantees all the titles on his Register. Anyone who suffers loss from a flaw in one will be compensated from public funds. Before being registered, therefore, a title has to be good enough to satisfy him, just as it has to be good enough to satisfy a purchaser.

When someone buys property, he wants to own it, and there is a fair chance that he will do that as things are today, although Lord

Justice Harman pointed out (in *Sheggia* v. *Gradwell* [*1963*] *1 W.L.R. 1049* @ *1062*) that contracts for the sale of real property are not like other contracts because of the difficulties of title, and the doctrine of specific performance. This is the law by which someone who does not want to go through with a deal can be forced to. And if he will not sign the necessary documents, then the Registrar of the Court will and the judgment and order of the court will become a title document.

A real property purchase contract is not like other contractual documents which merely prove that a deal has been done. It is itself a document of title. Lord Greene said so in *Eccles* v. *Bryant*. The reason for this is the doctrine called Specific Performance by which the court will force an unwilling party to go through with the deal and not let him back out from a binding obligation.

Equity, that all pervading mystique which distinguishes English law from less sophisticated systems has made of a purchaser with a binding contract the owner of an interest in the land.

If you are able to call for the land to be conveyed to you, you can sell it before it is yours perhaps at a good profit. This is one of the property developer's arts.

You do not exchange contracts unless you are sure you can and want to go through with the deal.

If there is written evidence of a binding contract and one side tries to break the contract that might happen. Or at least there might be some damages or compensation to pay. But nobody picks up his solicitor in his car and takes him house-hunting to vet any incautious move. Most people fancy themselves as bargain drivers. (The old form of property transfer up to the middle of the last century was called a 'bargain and sale'.)

There are still some people who do not know about 'subject to contract', though most people pick it up from friends or fast-talking estate agents and their 'negotiators'. As long ago as 1877, in the case of *Winn* v. *Bull* (*7 Ch. D. 29*), 'subject to contract' was recognised by the law to mean that the matter remains in negotiation until a formal contract is executed. 'That is, if the contract is recorded in two parts until the formal contracts are exchanged,' said Lord Justice Maugham (brother of 'Willie' Somerset Maugham) in *Trollope* v. *Martyn* (*1934*) *2 K.B. 436*. And there we have the beginnings of the modern ritual between solicitors in a conveyancing transaction, a process like the mating dance of the Blackcock.

If you sign a note saying 'I agree to buy No. 14 Paradise Gardens from Mr Smith for £5,000. £50 initial deposit paid', and sign it, you will find yourself stuck with it in all probability. If it is riddled with rot and the flank walls are tottering, or if there is a new road to be built right through it in two years time so that you cannot unload it on some other mug, the judge will only remind you of the maxim *caveat emptor.*

Now, as Lord Justice Fitzgerald said, 'That does not mean in law nor Latin "take chance"; it means "take care".' A seller cannot foist upon you a bad title in such a case. But there are a host of things more likely to make you want to back out than a bad title. Rotten drains or bad foundations or a bad roof or dry rot could put you off well and truly. But if you are bound you have got to lump them. And even if you want the house desperately a credit squeeze on mortgage loans, or difficulty in selling your own house may prevent you from going through with the deal and thus lay you open to an action for breach of contract.

For protection of their own estates, estate agents are not above suggesting acceptance of lower than asking price. They may, after all, be selling the purchaser's present house, and a whole chain of purchases may depend on the purchase by a vendor of his next home. At any given time half the population might be linked in an enormous chain of conveyancing. Bank managers used to spend Saturday mornings ticking off people who had contracted to buy new homes before getting contracts to sell their old ones. Now, customers have to take time off from work to go to the banks for their supplications.

It is vital, therefore, not to be bound to go through with your purchase by reason of having signed an unequivocally binding contract note. But you must beware not to embellish with unwise caution the hallowed rubric. In *Winn* v. *Bull* the words were 'subject to the preparation and approval of a formal contract' and in *Riley* v. *Troll (1953) 1 All E.R.* the words were 'This agreement is subject to formal contract to be prepared by the vendor's solicitors if the vendors shall so require'. Both these were ruled to be the same as 'subject to contract', and so the purchaser could escape. But in *Branca* v. *Cobarro (1947) K.B. 854* the words were 'This is a provisional agreement until a fully legalised agreement drawn up by a solicitor and embodying all the conditions herewith is signed'.

The layman might think that was a pretty business-like expression much to be preferred to 'subject to contract'. Mr Justice Denning, who is now Lord Denning, Master of the Rolls, thought it was not binding. But the Court of Appeal held that it meant that what was to be done afterwards was the formality of the usual contracts between solicitors. That is the test. Do the words mean that the deal is done and only mere formality is to follow? Or do they mean that there is no intention to be bound until 'the stately saraband' between solicitors (as Lord Justice Buckley has called it) is brought to fulfilment?

Since 'subject to contract' means that the seller can back out, too, if he gets a better offer the temptation is great. Mr Justice Sachs in *Pimms* v. *The Tallow Chandlers in the City of London (1964) 2 Q.B. 547* said that this situation is

> '. . . *so often referred to as a gentleman's agreement, but which experience shows is only too often a transaction in which each side hopes the other will act like a gentleman and neither intends so to act if it is against his material interests*'.

A very common kind of introduction to a solicitor is achieved when you go to inquire if a building society will lend you money for a house. You learn that they will and that Messrs Snodgrass are very good on property. Solicitors must not advertise. At the law office you will find a retired policeman minding the door and the switchboard. He will tell someone that there is 'another conveyance from the Mutual . . .' to see him and you will be on the lawyers' gravy train.

The first letter that your new-found solicitor will send the seller's solicitor will state that he is instructed to act for you and that you have agreed to purchase the property for a certain price 'subject to contract'. If the seller does not then come back and claim that the deal is binding already, you have scored a point. It will become difficult (though nothing is impossible in litigation) to claim that later on, when something goes wrong.

They play by the rules, these fellows, and knowing the rules is the important thing in what follows. For oddly enough there is not often litigation over a pure conveyancing question these days. The main cases have been 'contract or no contract'. But we are not yet out of that limbo and nowhere is that more amply demonstrated than in the first movement of the symphony which is Inquiries before Contract or 'Prelims'.

There is no duty imposed by the law on the seller or his solicitor to answer a lot of the questions which are addressed to them by purchasers or their solicitors. Indeed the idea of drawing up and publishing model sets of Conditions of Sale was to avoid making inquiries before concluding a binding contract. But the conditions provided that where matters came to light which affected the value or utility of the property, the purchaser could rescind the contract unless the seller put them right.

This was the hope of the brave new property world after 1925, but it was not realised then that great changes would soon follow. After 1st July, 1948,

> '*Ownership of land, generally speaking, carries with it nothing more than the bare right to go on using it for its existing purposes.*'

That is what Sir Desmond Heap, the Comptroller and Solicitor of the City of London says, and he is a foremost expert on planning. He might have added that if the Government or one of its adjuncts likes to force you to sell your land to them, you cannot do anything about it in most cases.

The form used by Mr Gomm's solicitor when he was buying from Gilchester Properties (see [1948] 1 All E.R. 493) was couched in the courteous terms of pre-war business.

> '*Perusal of the contract for sale and purchase of the above property will be much facilitated if the vendor's solicitor will be good enough to reply to the following questions:*
>
> *(1) Please supply copies of four tenancy agreements stating which are or have been statutory tenancies either under the Rent & Mortgage Interest Restrictions Acts 1920 to 1933 or under the Rent and Mortgage Interest Restrictions Act, 1939, and give the standard rent of each flat.*'

That might just as easily have been a planning or title query. As it was, it called for a possibly difficult decision of law in the case of any tenancy because they are notoriously technical. But the trouble arose over none of those troublesome things. The reply simply stated the rents inaccurately. Mr Justice Romer, as he was then, found that this wrong information induced the purchaser to enter into the contract.

However, he also found that it was given innocently. Therefore, although if he had applied to the court in time he could have rescinded the contract, he could not claim damages or compensation for the misrepresentation. The Common Law allowed a loss caused without fault to lie where it fell. In *Heilbut, Symons & Co.* v. *Buckleton* (1913) A.C. Lord Moulton, in characteristic language, declared:

> '*It is, my Lords, of the greatest importance in my opinion, that this House should maintain in its full integrity the principle that a person is not liable in damages for an innocent misrepresentation no matter in what way or in what form the attack is made.*'

Important or not, the *Misrepresentation Act, 1967*, totally reversed that law and made it not only possible but highly probable that a person could be made to pay damages for an innocent misrepresentation. We have not yet begun to see the ramifications of this change.

Fraudulent misrepresentation, of course, always has entitled the victim to damages and to get out of the contract if he wants to. But proving fraud has never been easy. Just why Parliament should put the innocently mistaken seller in the same position as the fraudsman in many cases is not easy to comprehend. The Act does not make damages payable in every case—it depends on the discretion of the judge. But it would be a good idea to insure against mistakes if you could, or to disclaim liability expressly. And just how much that will simplify and improve the law of real property sales is anyone's guess.

Mr Gomm's case established that an answer to a Preliminary Inquiry was not a Warranty for which, if it was wrong, the seller would have to pay damages. It could still possibly amount to a misrepresentation, but that could not land him in trouble if it was innocent, in those days.

Consequently, although they were not bound to answer all these questions, sellers' solicitors got into the spirit of doing it and co-operation nourished the property boom. Sir Raymond Evershed (as he then was) when Master of the Rolls, in 1952 confessed (in *Mahin* v. *Ainscough 1 All E.R. 337 C.A.*) that he did not know how universal this practice of asking questions before contract was.

Of course it was going on between all solicitors and it had to because of the Town and Country Planning laws, if nothing else. No one wants to buy a property and find he cannot use it for some purpose. Since the *Misrepresentation Act*, Inquiries before Contract assume a sinister role. For a generation they have been evolving and growing in range and number. It is a middle-aged solicitor or clerk nowadays who remembers that they started as a professional courtesy. Everyone is now a dragon's tooth, pregnant with a High Court action based on the *Misrepresentation Act*.

There has just been a new form put out by the Solicitors' Law Stationery Society, *Conveyancing 29 (Long)*. Although there are short forms for ordinary dwelling houses the long form is often used.

Courtesy demanded that the purchaser's solicitor strike out the 'non-applicable' questions. But the new form makes no concessions to traditional courtesy and comes in to battle like Mick McManus. About Registered Land, it wants to know whether all the documents leading to first registration will be handed over on completion of the sale. Once title is registered you do not need the previous deeds, and though they are nice for making lampshades no one could call them essential.

The previous edition of the form asked separately about the drains, water, electricity and gas supplies. Did they connect to the public services? Did they have to pass over other people's land to do so, and what Easements or Wayleaves were there over these lands?

Now, all the questions about 'services' are lumped together and the seller is asked to specify which 'main services' are NOT available. What is a 'main service'? Dare the seller forget the telephone? How much damages for misrepresentation would there be for that?

Is having the dustbin emptied a 'main service' or a shared central heating oil supply or a communal TV. aerial?

Another inquiry wants to know if the vendor is aware of any 'informal arrangements' affecting the property not in the contract and 'not immediately apparent on inspection'. When we go on holiday the woman next door feeds our cat. She comes in by the side gate and sets out the contents of the food tins in the shed. Is this an informal arrangement which if not observed could result in some curious complaint? It has its *quid pro quo*. We lend her husband our rotary mower.

The form does say 'please' when asking for details of 'the following matters which *may* have affected the property *at any time*: flooding, structural, building or drainage defects, subsidence, woodworm, rising damp or dry rot and electric wiring failing to meet the requirements of the appropriate Board'.

Who dares to commit himself to the past history of a house long before he owned or even saw it? The courts might, of course, soften the blows rained on the seller by the combined furies of the *Misrepresentation Act* and the Inquiries, but who wants to be first into the murky waters of litigation? The solicitor has a choice. He can be evasive or refuse to answer. If he does the first he will receive 'Further Inquiries'. If he refuses to answer, the purchaser might be advised not to buy. And then you could well have a desperate seller (who has bought another house in anticipation of selling this one) suing him on the initial agreement, claiming that it was a concluded and not a tentative contract. A whole succession of sellers and buyers could be in similar quandaries.

'Perhaps you will kindly instruct your solicitor to write to my solicitors with the necessary agreement,' wrote Mr High to E. R. Ives Investment (*1967 2 Q.B. 379*) and it was held to be a binding contract. What a tangled web of ruinous litigation could be spun from little things just because one decides to move house.

While the seller's solicitor is struggling with the Prelims he comforts himself with having sent the Draft Contract to the purchaser's solicitor. The purchaser's chap probably asked for it in his first letter. A contract which just names the parties and the property and the price is called an 'open' contract. All the odds and ends about when completion of the sale will take place and the giving of possession, and the deposits to be paid and the conditions about late completion, and the title that will be proved are all then implied from the general law. The idea of Conditions of Sale is to 'close' the contract and pin down the other side. It is more honest to follow the words of *Gibson's Conveyancing* and confess that the object is to throw upon the buyer the expense of investigations which would otherwise fall on the seller, without putting the buyer

264

off. But the usual thing is for a printed form of conditions to be used.

The Law Society's Conditions of Sale are favoured by some conveyancers, the National Conditions by others. Why, if there are standard forms of contract, does not everyone follow the same rule and make one legal code to cover the whole system of property transfer? Why use a solicitor, if he will not apply special expertise, but merely use a printed form? Well, these two printed forms are copyright and should only be used by a solicitor. And they are just a beginning. Some of the printed conditions are excluded and other 'special conditions' are added in most cases. For the Home Conveyancer there is a set of standard conditions which are called the *Lord Chancellor's Statutory Form of Conditions of Sale, 1925.* They were made under the property legislation of that time and they only apply to contracts made by correspondence. They are very seldom used.

They are subject to any stipulation excluding or modifying them in the correspondence, although they can be expressly included in any other contract. This, of course, suggests that other contracts which would be enforceable to deal in land are contemplated and would perhaps restrict the meaning of the word 'correspondence'. Obviously it means letters, but does it only mean letters sent through the post? The courts have never in their forty-five years' existence had to interpret these conditions to decide so. Suppose an offer be made orally, but accepted by letter. Is that 'by correspondence'? What if a note of acceptance is put through the letterbox of an estate agent or solicitor by the purchaser personally, and not sent by prepaid post? Is that 'by correspondence'? Suppose the deal be made by telegram?

This posting business is very important in the law of contract apart from real property deals. In 1818, twenty years before Rowland Hill brought in the Penny Post, it was settled that if the parties have expressly or impliedly agreed to use the post as the medium of communication an offer is accepted—and a binding contract made— the instant the letter containing the acceptance is put into the post. (*Adams* v. *Lindsell* [1818] *B & Ald. 681.*)

In *Byrne* v. *Van Tienhoven* (1880) 5 *C.P.D. 344* frailty in the postal system was recognised by Mr Justice Lindley:

> '*It may be taken as now settled that, where an offer is made and accepted by letters sent through the post, the contract is completed the moment the letter accepting the offer is posted, even though it never reaches its destination.*'

Go to any County Court and you will see why people are, in the eye of the law, bound by letters they do not—so they say—get. One debtor after another will have failed to receive his bills, the summons, and any other missive unwisely consigned to the mails.

In *Eccles* v. *Bryant & Pollock* (*1948*) *1 Ch. 93*—of which we shall hear more—Lord Greene came within an ace of deciding whether the Undelivered Acceptance rule governs real property contracts. The earliest time that a postal contract would bind, he said, was the time at which the last of two counterparts was posted. Or, it could be that there was no contract until each party got the part signed by the other. And then he said: 'It is not necessary here to choose between these two views.'

Judges do not often feel entitled to express statements of general application. They confine themselves to the cases before them and leave legislation to Parliament. The answer to the question, when does a correspondence contract involving real property bind? is: Don't know.

Now that we have got to the Conditions of Sale, you will remember the 1930s idea was to design conditions to make Preliminary Inquiries unnecessary. The idea was brought to fruition by *Condition 13* of the National Conditions and *No. 20* of the Law Society's. These provided for rescission if immediately before the contract became binding a land charge or a planning matter which had not been disclosed came to light. The purchaser could serve a 'Condition 13 Notice' requiring the seller to get rid of the problem as a term of the contract. These conditions, in both forms of contract, can be excluded by leaving in or striking out a word 'not' in the Special Conditions. And of course, most solicitors exclude them. Having got as far as exchanging contracts, who is going to let the buyer off the hook? He's had all his silly questions answered, hasn't he?

But even then there is the actual clinching of the contract. The usual way is for two copies of the draft to be exchanged. If the contract is typed the standard forms might be included by express reference or the forms themselves might be used. Until recently they had to be signed over a sixpenny stamp (to pay the stamp duty on the contract to make it valid for production in evidence. This has been done away with.)

The purchaser will amend the draft contract in red ink if he does not agree with the original form, but this is not common on the standard forms. Special Conditions are used to insert or exclude other provisions. When the two proper copy contracts are all signed they will bind when exchanged. It is probably best if a solicitors' clerk walks round to the other solicitor's office and hands over his client's part in exchange for the other side's. But that cannot be done when they are miles apart. Curiously enough most solicitors use the post.

In *King* v. *O'Shee* (*1951*) *158 E.G.* the defendant's solicitors did not post his part. They rang up the other side and said he was pulling out. Mr Justice Harman said they were entitled to do so. There was no binding contract. Suppose a contract part is posted and fails to arrive? This was the question which Eccles's case did not decide. But if all the solicitors in the country make contracts through the post does that not count?

It used to. Lord Hardwicke said as long ago as 1744, 'The uniform opinion and practice of eminent conveyancers has always had great regard paid to it in all courts of Justice' (*3 Atk. 203*). Lord Denning, now Master of the Rolls, said in 1953 that the practice of the profession 'makes law'. (*Re Devonshire Settled Estates. 1 Ch. 218.*) But Lord Justice James in 1879 said that though practice might be part of the law, 'a modern practice in which some solicitors differ from others' was not. (*Re Ford & Hill. 10 Ch. D. 365 @ 370.*) Mr Justice Danckwerts was urged in 1956 to accept the evidence of solicitors as to what is usual. But he did not accept that he had to let that overcome his own experience and the decided cases. (*Goody* v. *Baring 1 W.L.R. 448.*) Can it be that these solicitors are not 'eminent' conveyancers?

The Law Society Conditions require the parts despatched by post to have been actually delivered before a binding contract is made. But in the general law there is nothing. If a letter goes astray, and the sensible sender rings up to check its arrival, and confirms his acceptance, has the contract been made by correspondence so as to bring it within the Lord Chancellor's conditions of sale? All this fascinating uncertainty has yet to be resolved by costly litigation.

Quite often both buyer and seller use the same solicitor. One may recommend the other. They may think that if he does two sides, he will do it for the price of one. In the absence of specific agreement they will probably be disappointed there.

What happens on exchange of contracts then? Does he stand at the end of his desk with one part in his right hand and one in his left?

We know what happens according to law when there is only one solicitor, and one document. This happened in *Smith* v. *Mansi* (*1963*) *1 W.L.R. 26*, where seller and buyer signed the same copy of the contract. When one claimed he was not bound because there was no exchange, the court said that the deal was binding the moment they had both signed. But we do not know what happens if there are two copies of the contract and one solicitor or two solicitors and one document.

In some ways the mortgage is the least troublesome part of the business. Actually persuading the building society manager to let you have the loan may be extremely difficult but it presents no legal problems. You do not have to have the precise terms of the mortgage worked out laboriously as you do when the advance is made by a private lender. If you do not like any of the provisions of the building society's printed form of mortgage you are entirely at liberty to do without their money.

A modern building society mortgage is a much more comprehensible document on the face of it than the so-called 'classical English mortgage'. It rarely begins with the forbidding Gothic tocsin 'This indenture of mortgage'. It can be headed 'Mortgage Deed' and have a space for the Land Registry Title Number at the top. It calls the borrower 'The Borrower' and not 'the mortgagor'. It calls the lender 'the Lender' and not 'the mortgagee'. The two latter terms confuse nearly everybody, including estate agents and surveyors and bankers, and they are confused in some of the little guide books about property transactions. Then, in very clear language it recites that the Borrower acknowledges that he has had the money specified in some Schedule or other. The actual price, property, and other variables on these printed forms are all inserted in numbered Schedules. The main, printed part states in clear and up-to-date language that in consideration of the sum of money advanced the Borrower as Beneficial Owner charges the property described in another schedule with repayment of the sum advanced together with interest and other 'moneys covenanted to be paid' or 'otherwise secured by this deed' and it says that those payments are 'charged' on that property 'by way of Legal Mortgage'.

It will then set out umpteen covenants full of terms and conditions against parting with possession without the building society's approval and Material Change of Use being forbidden, and binding the unfortunate freeholder to insure in such a sum as would build another Buckingham Palace on the site if it burns down 'in some office to be approved by the Lender'. What it does not say is what a 'Charge by Way of Legal Mortgage' is. Nor does it set out the most important characteristic of the transaction. Why not, is incomprehensible. As long ago as 1904, Lord Macnaghten in his speech in the House of Lords in *Samuel* v. *Jarrah Timber and Wood Flooring Co. Ltd. (1904) A.C. 323* said:

> '*No one, I am sure, by the light of Nature, ever understood an English mortgage of real estate.*'

He can be forgiven because he was Irish. Maitland had been telling Oxford undergraduates for years that a mortgage deed suppressed the truth and misled the parties. 'It does not explain the rights of the parties; it suggests that they are other than really they are'. (*Lectures on Equity, 1913 reprint, p. 269.*)

That, of course, referred to the 'classical' mortgage which was a conveyance on condition to convey back on repayment of the loan.

But the modern ones are no better. The simple truth is that however it is expressed or inferred—and it is quite possible for a mortgage to exist without a scrap of paper—it is only ever security for a loan, and not an outright parting with ownership of the property. Said Lord Eldon, 'Once a mortgage, always a mortgage.'

The borrower might have his land taken from him by the lender, for failure to pay the moneys as they fall due, or for some other breach of covenant. If the lender is in possession and some interest is in arrear for two months, the *Law of Property Act, 1925, s. 103 (ii)* enables him to sell the property and give a good title to the purchaser, even though he is not the owner. This might look like a contradiction of once a mortgage, etc. but it is one of the great improvements in the law for which lenders have so much to be grateful. If they make a profit on the loan—and lenders are under strict obligation to get the best price they can, which is easier nowadays than ever— the profit, after the mortgage debt, with interest to date and costs, must be paid to the borrower.

This must be carefully distinguished from 'foreclosure' as practised by Sir Jasper. Even now a Chancery decree can be obtained 'closing' the right of redemption of a mortgage. If the property has not realised the amount of the loan and accrued interest, on sale, the borrower might just as well be foreclosed. If the property is not disposed of, and yet the court still sees fit to foreclose, it will 're-open' the transaction if in fact there is any chance of a payout coming to the borrower.

But the essence of the transaction is for the borrower to get the profit, or get his property back before sale on paying up what he owes. The lender cannot keep the profit. Before 1926 the principal debt was most often payable in a lump sum and the interest was to be paid at specified intervals. The arithmetic was easy: £1,000 at 5 per cent meant that £25 was paid every six months. The borrowers were often landowners who had inherited property and were raising money on it. When the clerks and artisans started raising sums of money far beyond anything they had ever possessed in order to buy their little corners of England, different considerations began to appear. The capital was often paid back bit by bit, and so the interest diminished. The idea became more and more usual of borrowing for a determinate period, not an indefinite one, but long enough for the repayment to be made in small sums from small incomes. Only in case of sale would there be a repayment of the whole amount outstanding.

Those monuments of thrift, the building societies, fostered this social advance. Their common way of charging interest now is to nominate a day in each year of the term, say 1st January. The interest for each year is the amount represented by the rate specified in the mortgage from that day until the same date in the next year. During the year, twelve repayments will be made, and part of each will be capital. The borrower will therefore over those months be paying interest on money he has already repaid. But even at this slightly hidden rate the building societies charge less for their loans than finance houses which lend on second mortgages or old properties which building societies do not like to advance on. The usual limit for an advance from a building society is 80 per cent of the value, or 90 per cent with premium interest on the odd 10 per cent, and they do not like houses more than forty years old. But after a satisfactory survey they will lend on very old ones.

There is often nowadays a provision in a building society mortgage for interest to be raised or lowered. Before the war quite a few of them put their charges up when they were not entitled to. They were still good value and the borrowers were members of the societies, and so they got away with that illegality.

The way the deed provides for the usual rights under a mortgage without actually saying so is by using the ancient form which provides for the whole sum loaned to be repaid on a certain day one month or six months from the date it was lent. This is called the 'legal' date for redemption. The mortgage cannot be redeemed before then. It is a loan for a definite time. The only effect is that interest for that length of time is payable in any event. If redemption does not then take place, the lender can enforce all his rights, but because of equity of redemption, all he does is accept interest and repayment of capital if that is agreed for until redemption. Thus this particular contract expressed by the insertion of that 'legal' date for redemption is bound to be broken and lender, borrower and surety and anyone else concerned all know it perfectly well.

The object could be achieved much more simply by stating,

'This agreement shall always be a security only, and shall not vest in the Lender any rights of ownership, without prejudice to his rights of possession and sale on default by the Borrower.'

But it is too late now for such a revolution. When the property is registered at the Land Registry, of course, the copies of entries on the Register are tied into a folder which is called a Charge Certificate, made after the filling up of a simple buff form. The word 'mortgage' meant 'dead pledge' and was different from the ancient live pledge (*vivum vadium*) under which the lender of money entered on the land charged and helped himself to the profits and rents until the debt was paid. Under the dead pledge, the borrower was left in possession to use the property as best he could to pay back his debt.

The advantage of rights against the land is that they endure with it. The rights of a lender are similar to rights created by different

270

kinds of obligation. A legal mortgagee can take possession of the land, but the other rightholders might not be entitled to do that. The legal owner of land might be under a duty to use it for the benefit of somebody else. As O. Henry put it, 'a trust is its weakest point'. The Court of Chancery enforced trusts by having trustees who did not do as they were ordered put into prison. That is the basis of the maxim, 'Equity acts in person'. Not so much in as on.

When the Franciscans came here in the 13th Century their vows of absolute poverty bound them to own nothing, but they needed shelter for themselves and the poor for whom they cared. Sympathisers used their own money or that given as alms to the monks to buy property and whilst they were the legal owners, the monks used them. The attractions of this device were manifest at the time because wills of land were not allowed, it had to descend to the eldest son, and according to the feudal tenure on which it was held, the Crown would take a hefty slice on succession. By giving one's property to trustees, this could be avoided. When one trustee died, the survivors merely made another in his place.

But trusts arise without extravagant schemes. If a woman gives her husband some money towards buying their house, she can thereafter claim that he is a trustee of it for them jointly in particular shares. This kind of thing is more common now than the great disputes over the inheritance of earldoms like the Sussex Peerage Case and the Titchborne Claim. One of the commonest disputes is where a woman who has not contributed anything is described in a conveyance as a joint owner with her husband of property which they hold as trustees for themselves in equal shares. Some husbands regret having had that clause inserted because it makes Married Women's Property Act proceedings a foregone conclusion. It is estimated that half the houses in the country are held on trust in this way—often without the owners realising it because their solicitors put the clause into the conveyance from force of habit. However, it is possible for the court to vary such a 'post nuptial settlement' after hearing evidence of the creation of it and the behaviour of the parties. It then becomes very material to consider what shares are proved. Joint bank accounts, cheques and other records of payments made for the mortgage, the rates, and other expenses connected with the property are the stuff of these disputes, and there are of course always stories of money handed over in the presence of this or that in-law, and loans procured from better off relatives. If all this kind of thing happens before marriage, and the marriage is either called off or breaks down, the *Married Women's Property Act* may not be available, and a full-blown action in the High Court for a declaration of the trusts will be required. This may well entail the public recollection of conversations between the parties whilst 'in that

glamour which precedes the romatic severity of a formal engagement'
(Mr Justice McCardie again, in *Gotliffe* v. *Edelston*.) Recollections of
intention in such circumstances tend to differ.

There are three certainties required to create a valid trust—the
certainty that a trust was intended so as to bind the legal owner;
the certainty about what he was to do with the trust property and
the profits from it; and the certainty what the trust property actually
was. It is surprisingly common for people to be uncertain of the
extent of real property until they get into a dispute about it. Then
they become remarkably certain. A strip of land a foot or so wide
can cause a very bitter boundary dispute. There is frequently a
blackmailing aspect to these actions, where for instance, someone
can sell off part of a big garden for building at several thousand
pounds per plot. If, as is common, the planning permission depends
on there being access, or certain minimum width of frontage the
land available for development might be a bit tight. A neighbour
who can set up some claim to a foot or two on the boundary could
command a handsome price for it if he is right—an application of
the Neighbour Principle* not encouraged but quite definitely
enforced by the law. The actual description and definition of the
land sold in a conveyance is the part called 'the Parcels'.

> '*When describing the parcels in a conveyance or a lease convey-
> ancers have to do the best they can with the facts supplied to them
> and it is only now and again that confusion arises,*'
> **Lord Sumner in *Eastwood* v. *Ashton (1915) A.C. 900*.**

Since 1949, Legal Aid has permitted poor people to bring their
cases of confusion before the courts, and resist the importunities of
their wealthier neighbours. The County Court judges are sick of
such actions. Even though they are concerned not with law at all,
but with questions of fact, the facts are so often obscure that presumptions of fact and law are the only way of resolving them.

> '*Certain it is that the whole of the costs of this litigation could have
> been saved if one or other party had used a few staples and a roll
> of wire.*'
> **Lord Justice Diplock *(as he was)* in *Jones* v. *Price (1965)
> 2 All E.R. 625*.**

Lord Kinnear did say that:

> '*It is the duty of the conveyancer framing a disposition upon sale
> not to take for granted that he is to follow the exact terms of the
> description of the existing title, but to make full inquiry into the
> facts in order that he may be able to describe correctly the subject
> to be disposed.*'
> ***(1910) A.C. 537.***

---

* See page 322.

Solicitors, however, seldom go down to the land with hammer, staples and wire. Few of them possess gum boots. Few ever go to look at the land. I recall a disconcerting affair where a solicitor bid successfully for a large piece of land on which a consortium of estate developers—of all of whose companies he was of course a director—proposed to build a couple of hundred semi-dets. A gentleman who asserted the right to a new business tenancy under *Part II* of the *Landlord and Tenant Act, 1954*, then wrote to him saying that he assumed that compensation for the loss of that tenancy would be generous, because the development would be extremely profitable.

Close examination of the tumbledown shed in one corner of the fields would have revealed that there were a couple of practically derelict lorries there, which were driven by his ragged-trousered sons about that business which is now described as 'salvage merchant'. The area covered by their operation was enough for twenty houses. There was of course a special condition of the contract precluding compensation for any misdescription. It cost quite a bit to get rid of that merchant, which could no doubt have been saved at the expense of a drive round to look at the land, and requiring the vendor to get rid of the occupier before completion. But that was in the days before the *Misrepresentation Act*, and now no doubt a vendor who does not disclose an occupier is in dire trouble—and will rely heavily on his exemption clause.

Ideally, the parcels give measurements from a positively identifiable landmark, and state from which part of it they proceed. Often, though, they are inserted merely as measurements from the frontage on the street. Often there are no measurements at all, and the property in identified merely by name or number and address, and the boundaries are then what they appear to be, by looking at the property. The degree of encroachment which can quite innocently occur in course of five years, by the growth of hedges and replacement of fences is remarkable. Most often, however, there is annexed to the conveyance a plan. These plans disprove the Confucian dogma that a picture is worth a thousand words.

The rule of construction is that the written parcels and measurements dominate the plan. The plan is often declared to be there 'by way of identification only'. That is fine when there are descriptions and measurements in the parcels. But when the plan is for identification only and there are no dimensions or bearings in the parcels, the person holding under the deed is in a weaker position than his neighbour with whom he is in dispute, if the neighbour has a deed of title which describes his land better. The ancient and modern rule is simply that a person who claims land must succeed on the strength of his own title, and not the weakness of someone else's. But where a big estate has been broken down, those parts of it which are best described in the deeds will be much more easily proved than those which are held on vague deeds.

If the parcels clause says the property is 'more particularly described in' the plan, then it dominates the words. In some conveyances you see

'more particularly described in the plan attached to these presents for the purposes of identification only.'

This is obvious rubbish and contradicts itself and is used surprisingly often. If it is used in connection with a parcels clause which has no measurements, bearings or features in it, a judge may feel driven to rely on the plan anyway to resolve conflicting evidence about what the position on the ground used to be. He can of course go and have a look himself, and when he does he often comes to a conclusion which suits neither party. But if the opposing party has a clearer deed, he will usually win.

Mr Justice Swinfen Eady said *in Re Sansom and Narbeth's Contract (1910) 1 Ch. 741* that whilst he would not say every purchaser was entitled to have a plan in the conveyance, in all cases where it would assist the description a purchaser could insist on one. Solicitors in suburbs often say that their clients will not pay for professionally prepared plans. A few guineas for a surveyor is money well spent, however. Conveyance plans are often taken from the Ordnance Survey. But since it was done in 1922 and revised in 1956, the boundaries have to be checked and the map brought up to date by adding buildings.

A try-on nearly came off when a neighbour asserted a boundary which would have stultified a profitable sale for development at the back of a big garden, by reference to a building shown on the Ordnance. Since there were no Nissen huts in that district in 1922, the blackmail failed, but only because the lawyer went and looked at the site.

The Director-General of the Ordnance Survey grants licences to reproduce his copyright maps for a small fee. A skilled draftsman can get down to an accuracy of one foot on the 1/1250 scale. However, Ordnance Survey maps are not themselves evidence of private boundaries (*O.S. Act 1841, s. 12*) and a deed ought to declare that the Ordnance Survey is agreed and accepted as correctly delineating the boundaries when they are used.

If all that is conscientiously carried out, and then some office boy runs a nice thick HB pencil roughly over a tracing paper you ought to finish up with a conveyance plan right to within six or eight feet. If it is a new house being built on the plot, you might find that it looks as if it is in a different position from that shown on the plan. This can happen if the most diligent of conveyancers and draftsmen prepare the parcels and the plans for the purposes of getting the planning permissions and building by law consents. For they are not to blame if some navvy in the footings gang knocks the pegs into the mud in the wrong places. You can, of course, resist a boundary dispute with your splendid plan. The Local Planning Authority might make you pull your new house down because it is in front of the building line, and so you had better make sure that the builder does not try to exempt himself in the contract.

Easements are not well named. They seldom ease relations when they are disputed, and their enjoyment—which is legal parlance for use—often causes difficulties between neighbours. They involve rights of people who own land to do things, or prevent things being done on the lands of their neighbours. Simple, ordinary things, like

'to pass and re-pass thereover for the purpose of access to and egress from the said messuage with or without vehicles plant and animals',

which is a right or easement of way. It is not uncommon for them to give rise to these 'interminable lawsuits' on which Mr Pickwick's counsel, Serjeant Snubbin was engaged—'about the stopping up of a pathway leading from some place which nobody ever came from to some other place which nobody ever went to'.

This need have nothing to do with a public right of way. It might exist for dustmen to cross a backyard to get the bins, or for coalmen to deliver. There was one which was never actually litigated about access to outside lavatories after the sales of a row of cottage to their sitting tenants. The lawyers settled it because they felt sure the court would say that it was an Easement of Necessity.

On speculatively built modern estates it is common for the estate developer to save a bit of frontage on each plot and so make room for another pair of semi-dets. in the street. This is achieved by means of the 'shared drive-in' between two unconnected houses. It is wide enough to permit a car to be driven to the garage at the rear of each house. Usually the neighbours are owners of the soil to the mid-line and owners of rights of way over their neighbour's halves of the drive-in. Obstructing the drive is therefore an interference with the neighbour's easement and a trespass to his half. Not a few County Court actions—and even some more expensive High Court actions, have arisen from this thoughtless discourtesy. It is perfectly simple to phrase an injunction restraining obstruction of the drive, and breach of it would be a contempt of court punishable by imprisonment.

In principle this is the remedy in all easement disputes, though of course damages can be awarded for interference and trespass as well as injunction.

An easement has to be required for the enjoyment of the property. You may put up a notice board in your garden to advertise goods. Your neighbours might successfully complain about it to the Town Planning authority. But whether you can keep it or not, or whether it advertises soap powder or chapel services, it is not an easement. The property can be enjoyed without it. On the other hand, if you live in a block of flats, easements to pass over the hall and stairs and passages to get to your flat are essential. They can be interfered with by leaving a pram in such a position that you cannot get past. The pram owner might have an easement to leave prams in the passage, though she probably has not. Easements for the use of bathrooms and lavatories, and to cross gardens to get coal from coalsheds probably cause as much trouble as easements to hang out washing to dry, because the use of their property by others irritates many people. But easements are not merely domestic rights. A seventeen-day case in the High Court over rights of sheepwalk in the West Country showed that they can be of great commercial value. One expects rights of sheepwalk to have feudal origins. It is tiresome to discover that urban back entries have them too.

Existence of an easement necessarily predicates that one property shall be 'the dominant tenement' and have the benefit of the right and the other 'the servient tenement' be subject to the right. In *Suffield* v. *Brown* (*1864*) *4 De G. J. & S. 185* the easement was for bowsprits of ships to poke over the land on a dockside. The law books say that the classes of easement are not closed. Some ingenuity is, however, required to invent new ones, because of the necessity angle. There are all sorts of other rules. An easement cannot be created to permit branches of trees to hang over someone else's land, for example (*Lennon* v. *Webb* (*1895*) *A.C.1*). However, an easement to go on to your neighbour's land to trim your own tree or hedge is quite common. They cause nearly as many quarrels as rights of way.

The person whose land is overhung has the right to abate the nuisance thereby created by lopping the trees himself. He can also dig up and cut off those roots of the tree which trespass over his boundary (subject of course to the Council's Tree Preservation Order if any). That must await the discussion of the law of tort. There is no point in complicating matters.

The most apt purpose of an easement, perhaps, is the right to use a neighbour's lavatory (*Miller* v. *Emcer Products* (*1956*) *Ch. 304 72. L.Q.R. 172*). But as long ago as *1610* (*William Aldred's Case 9 Co. Rep. 57b*) Chief Justice Wray held that no right to a nice view from your windows or your lawn was known to the law. 'The Law does not give an action for such things of delight'.

Such things can be protected by restrictive covenants or other contracts. Indeed, they are the reason for the development of such

276

socially advantageous covenants as not to hang out washing; not to build property below a certain rateable value; not to erect corrugated iron or asbestos garages and the other entrenched laws of bijou development. Easements were a necessary invention of the lawyers. Parliament never had the wit to invent them. They arose from necessity. There is, for example no natural right of support for a building

'The owner of the adjacent soil may with perfect legality dig that soil away, and allow his neighbour's house, if supported by it, to fall in ruins to the ground,'

said Lord Penzance in *Dalton* v. *Angus (1881) 6. App. Cas. 740 @ 804.*

No doubt when that happens one is quick to allege an easement of support and claim damages for its infringement. That will raise the fascinating question of how the easement was acquired. It can of course be gained by being expressly granted in deeds or in Acts of Parliament. The only quarrel then is about the precise extent of the easement, and whether the proper conditions are satisfied. Any conveyance of land grants all the rights necessary for its enjoyment unless a contrary intention appears therein—*s. 62, Law of Property Act, 1925.*

That is a grant. The opposite of a grant is a reservation. If a seller of land gives something he has power to give, that is fine. If he wishes to keep back something out of what he is selling, he has to do it in plain terms. Suppose a landlord owns a row of houses and sells them all. There might be an alley alongside one, by which the dustmen go and turn along the backs of all to empty the dustbins. If the houses farther away from the alley are sold first, or at the same time, as the one nearest, the conveyances will automatically confer on them the rights of way for the dustmen to go across the back garden nearest the alley. It having been retained, for the time being, by the landlord, and being a right reasonably necessary (and in existence at the time of the sale) for enjoying the houses, it will pass under the section. But if the house nearest to the alley is sold first, there will be no easement unless it is expressly reserved in the conveyance. For a seller of land is not allowed to 'derogate from his grant'. This 'legal maxim embodying a rule of common honesty', as Lord Justice Younger called it (*Harmer* v. *Jumbil [Nigeria] Tin Areas Ltd. (1921) 1 Ch. 200* gives way only to the very strictest necessity. The reasoning is the 'earliest in time, strongest in law' rule and it is just the sort of thing people employ solicitors for. It is also just the sort of thing solicitors forget.

The necessity for a reservation also stems from the original common ownership. Whilst one person owns several adjoining properties, each property cannot acquire binding rights over the

277

others. A man cannot have rights against himself. All the learning on the subject is set out in *Wheeldon* v. *Burrows* (*1879*) *12 Ch. D. 31* @ *49* which is the leading case even though it just repeats a lot of others, leaves some out, is *obiter dictum*, and is not exhaustive. But it is much easier for a judge to look there than at 30 or 40 other books, many of them old and hard to get. The rule is two rules, anyway, of which the first has been overridden practically by *S. 62*, and the other one is fascinatingly uncertain. It clearly provides that if you are crazy enough to buy a house with no way of getting to the road without walking across someone else's land, he is bound to let you. But so stringent is the necessity rule that no right will be implied unless there really is no other, permitted way, of getting out of the place. If you could get to a bus stop by nipping across a yard of land, instead of going round by a mile-long path or drive, no way of necessity would be implied.

Lord Justice Thesiger, laying down the rule in *Wheeldon* v. *Burrows*, said that this rule about implied reservation of easements is 'subject to certain exceptions'. Ways of necessity are one. Lawyers have ever since been trying to find out what the others are. Lord Justice Greer in *Aldridge* v. *Wright* [*1929*] *2 K.B. 117* said that the exceptions extended only to contemporaneous sales. But all is not lost. The law has long permitted the creation of rights by proof of long use. The Common Law followed the Roman Law in imagining that if a man enjoyed a right without force, openly and without acknowledging that he was being permitted to do so, he owned the right. Lord Penzance said in *Dalton* v. *Angus* that this business called prescription depended upon the owner of the servient tenement acquiescing, and thereby acknowledging the dominant owner's right.

And so the Common Law presumes a valid right if it has been used 'from time whereof the memory of man runneth not to the contrary' (*Littleton's Tenures* [*1481*] *170*). The memory of man, according to the Common Law of England, goes back to 1189, the year when Richard the Lionheart came to the throne, and no further. It is called Time Immemorial. This memory was fixed by the first Statute of Westminster in 1275, which is still the law. It is often tiresome to prove that you and your predecessors enjoyed a right in 1189. It is impossible when the building for which you claim it was not built then.

By 1864 (*Darling* v. *Clue 4 F & F. 329*) the courts had evolved a doctrine, analogous to time-bars on lawsuits, and accepted proof of continuous use of the right for 20 years as proof of use since 1189, unless the servient owner proved it was impossible, because the houses were not built or for some other reason. That did not meet every case and so the judges invented another fiction, as they often have done over the centuries, usually to make Parliament's laws work. This one, however, was called by Mr Justice Lush a 'revolting fiction'. It had begun in 1761 and soon achieved respectability. It simply involves the judge saying, when long use has been proved, that there must have been a deed granting the easement, but he supposes it has been lost. The use is evidence of what the deed granted, and the court will uphold it. It is the Doctrine of the Lost Modern Grant, though as Chief Justice Cockburn pointed out

'. . . *neither judge nor jury nor anyone else had the shadow of belief that any such instrument had ever really existed.*'

Unlike use since 1189, it cannot be rebutted by impossibility, because it has never existed anyway. But the logic gives way when it is proved that during the whole time in which the fictitious grant could have been made, the land was occupied by someone who had no power to grant it, such as a life tenant under a trust or a company whose memorandum of association contained no power for it to grant easements.

It has to be confessed that this body of law had flaws in it. Accordingly, Parliament in 1832 enacted a *Prescription Act* to do away with uncertainty in this field of jurisprudence. It provided that an easement enjoyed 'without interruption' for 20 years could not be defeated by proof that it began after 1189. And one which was enjoyed for 40 years became 'absolute and indefeasible'. However, the periods have to be enjoyed immediately before any action about the claim of right begins. Consequently, if you enjoy a right of way for 20-odd years, and then someone new moves in next door and starts to object to you using it, you cannot always rely on your long enjoyment. Because if you spend a long time haggling before going to law, you will not be able to claim that the 20 years immediately before the action started was the period when you used the way, without force openly and without specific permission. You have to be quick with your writ.

You get a little grace, however, because of the peculiar construction given to 'without interruption'. An interruption does not count unless it has lasted a year. The effect therefore is that you can establish your rights by proof of use for 19 years and a day and 39 years and a day respectively. Because the servient owner could then not prove a year's interruption. Of course, you cannot issue the writ until the 20 years have passed, because you need to prove 20 years' use. But you need have no fear of a plea of interruption succeeding. Equally clearly, if you issue the writ a day late, the interruption period will count, because it will have lasted a full year.

Having secured the great advantage conferred by the *Prescription Act*, the only subject to argue about is whether the servient owner consented. He will of course describe in detail all the many occasions when he specifically pointed out what a good chap he was to permit you to go on his land. The absolute rights obtained by 40 years' use will only be defeated by written consent. Only the fee simple owner can prescribe, but the *occupier* of the servient tenement can permit a neighbour to acquire rights with which the owner will be burdened, when the occupier leaves. In the same way, a tenant of the dominant tenement might acknowledge to the servient owner that the right is permissive and so destroy his landlord's easement. One way to cut out a qualifying period is by proving that the occupier of the servient property was mad, or under age. It does not count if the servient landlord just thinks his tenant was mad.

Rights of light are much easier to get now than they were. The 20 years—19 and a day actually—is the only period applicable to them. But since the period has to be next-before any action, the only way to get an unchallengable right is to have a lawsuit (*Hyman* v. *van den Bergh* [*1907*] *2 Ch. 516*). Disputes over obstruction of light are splendid affairs with long statements from surveyors about the readings on their light-meters at various dates and times, from all sorts of positions in the rooms of the dominant property. The trigonometrical calculation of the diminution of a shaft of light by reference to the height of a wall a specified distance from a window is even less comprehensible than the calculation of interest in money-lending actions. Local councils get automatic statutory authority for much of their development works under the Town Planning laws. But any other person building a new place might find his neighbour claiming rights of light. Fortunately, the mere existence of windows in the existing building does not count as a claim of an easement of light. You still have to do something further to establish your claim, such as putting up a board bearing the legend 'ancient lights'.

The air raids of the Second World War started up prescription periods for rights of light for a great many people and so just before the 20 years from 1939 expired, Parliament stepped in to see fair play. *The Rights of Light Act, 1959* enacts that where an action for a right of light was begun after 13th July, 1958, and before 1st January, 1963, or if any later action sets up a period beginning before 1963, the prescription period must be 27 years instead of 20— or, of course, 26 years and a day in fact. But for this timely step, all the existing owners could have got injunctions preventing bombed sites from being built upon, except perhaps by single-storey buildings.

Rights similar to easements are those such as shooting, fishing, and cultivation rights, which are known as *profits a prendre*. They can be acquired by prescription. As well as by action at law, easements and profits can be enforced by that curious kind of lawful self-help known as abatement. If a servient owner bars your right of way, and you are sure from what has gone before that your right is sound, you can break open a locked gate or barrier in order to enforce your right. You must use no more force than is absolutely necessary to vindicate your rights, and cause no injury to people not concerned, and do nothing which could cause a breach of the peace. Magistrates' courts have no jurisdiction in claims of right or title to property. But they quite often have to deal with abortive abatements.

The Best Of A Bargain

'*A person named Hampden got it into his head that it was a popular error to suppose that the world was round, and advertised a challenge in the newspapers to any scientific man to prove it, each side to deposit £500 to abide the issue . . . eventually the referee decided in favour of rotundity . . . Hampden objected and demanded back his money. . . . In an action, it was held that Hampden was entitled to recover his deposit, the affair being a mere wager.*'

Shirley's Leading Cases, 1903

'LEY EST RESOUN' insisted the early Common Lawyers. Their logic marched through the Reformation and the Renaissance and the Age of Revolution to the present. A promise without a price is a gift. One made for *quid pro quo* is a bargain. And English law enforces bargains, not mere promises or gifts. Gifts are not enforced by the law unless by will after the donor is dead. The legal name for the price is 'a consideration'.

Lord Mansfield, Chief Justice of the King's Bench from 1756 to 1784 tried to do away with the necessity of 'consideration' to make an intentional contract binding under English law. But the other lawyers and the House of Lords were against him (*Rann* v. *Hughes* [*1778*] *7 Term Reports, 350*). The great legal historian William Holdsworth wrote in 1925 that it was useless to try to rationalise the Common Law by 'pure reason and foreign analogies' because it was too well established even when Mansfield tried to overturn it. Perhaps the European Economic Community will achieve what the founder of our commercial law system failed to do. But the two centuries have seen 'consideration' virtually reduced to a legal fiction, whilst the anomalies and anachronisms survive.

If I owe a man £10 and he agrees to take £5 in full discharge of the debt, the law does not approve the deal. He can sue me for the fiver he forgave and get judgment. There was no 'consideration' for the forgiveness. However, had the £5 been paid before the £10 fell due expressly for the advantage to the creditor of early payment, there would have been enough 'consideration' for the lesser sum to be a full lawful satisfaction of the greater. This is the kind of doctrine condemned as

'hairsplitting distinctions of exactly that kind which bring the law into hatred, ridicule and contempt'.

Yeoman Credit Ltd. v. Latter (1961) 1 W.L.R. 828 and 835.

The real evil is that the English law of contract as expounded sounds at first so straightforward and logical. One person makes an offer. The other accepts. 'A promise against a promise is good consideration.' But that is not all: the promise which amounts to consideration must be some detriment to the person giving the promise. And, of course, in order to give 'business efficacy' as Lord Justice Bowen called it, to commercial bargains, the courts are prepared to spell out consideration whether it was intended or not. On the other hand, where the relationship of the parties confers only apparently social or moral obligations the legal remedy of enforcement of contract is often denied. Ostensibly, what people intended by their transactions ought to be enforced by the courts, and what they say and do should lead the judges to decide what they intended. But it does not always work out like that.

The celebrated Mrs Carlill informed the Carbolic Smoke Ball Company that in spite of diligently inhaling the pungent fumes of the Carbolic Smoke Ball as instructed on the packet, she had been stricken by influenza. The company, notwithstanding their advertisement that they would pay £100 to anyone catching 'flu after taking the treatment, took refuge from her claim in a multitude of technical defences which somewhat undermined their statement that they had deposited £1,000 with their bankers to cover claims as an act of good faith.

Unconscious, perhaps, of the pun, they asserted *inter-alia* that the advertisement for the Smoke Ball was a mere puff, and not an offer. It was, said the judge, an offer to all the world.

'If I advertise that my dog is lost and that anybody who brings the dog to a particular place will be paid some money, are all the police or other people whose business it is to find lost dogs to sit down and write me a postcard saying that they have accepted my proposal?'

The finding of the dog—the performance of the contract—was the acceptance. The case is the great Awful Warning to Advertisers. Even though it is difficult to take you seriously, it might be profitable to take you at your face value. In a proper law book, the basic principles of the subjects are taught first, which is why the law is difficult to learn. Fundamental conceptions are not for tyros to trifle with. The essential underlying philosophy of the law should never be attempted lower than the Court of Appeal or some learned periodical. At the lower levels of judicial decision, the 'common sense approach' has many adherents, but is more honoured in the breach than the observance. Few people acknowledge my old physics master's dictum that it should not be called common sense at all because it is very uncommon.

Mrs Carlill's case was really an action for damages for breach of a collateral condition or warrantry. Having paid the price she got the smoke ball. That was a perfectly lawfully enforceable sale of goods. In order to succeed in her claim she had to prove that she relied on the cure claim and was induced by it. There was no separate consideration for the assurance that it would cure influenza. Mrs Carlill paid her money for the smoke ball. In their eagerness to attract custom the sellers put in the extra statement. She caught the influenza from the malign machinations of the streptococci. The 'bargain' theory is distorted somewhat, by including something besides the goods sold in the contract. Strictly speaking there was no lawful bargain for the guarantee of a cure.

Of course, the company had only itself or its advertising agents to blame. Comparatively few people regard the everyday transactions we all make as proper contracts, comparable with the awfully solemn ritual involved in acquiring a place to live. But buying an evening paper or a ride on a bus are all contracts too. The contract of marriage and the resultant economic stringency awakens in many people a sensitivity to contractual rights. Girls who threw away clothes they found unsuitable, take them back to the shop when they are married women. Men who never considered the existence of the electric light company behind the switch have check meters installed in their homes to see if they are being overcharged. Generations of people dissatisfied with what they have bought have really created the English law of contract, by implying all kinds of conditions. The law provided compensation for individual instances of failure of contractual terms.

So many people bought broken-winded, or spavined horses that the Common Law judges soon got used to awarding damages against horse-copers. Judges had bought wrong 'uns themselves and readily believed that the seller said the horse was sound. The rule is, of course, still *caveat emptor*. But that, said Lord Justice Fitzgerald does not mean in Law or Latin, 'take chance', it means 'take care'. If the man takes care in the choice of an article, but relies on something the seller said he might establish as a ground for compensation. An 'innocent' misrepresentation enabled the victim to rescind the contract so long as the other party or anyone else had not altered his portion for the worse. Once the purchaser has used the goods, it was practically impossible for this to be done. But no

damages could be recovered for 'innocent' misrepresentation—
only for 'breach of a warranty'—and a representation need not be
a warranty. Mrs Carlill's cold-cure was a warranty.

Progressive lawyers considered this state of affairs a reproach to
justice. The *Misrepresentation Act, 1967*, was enacted to make
damages recoverable by people who enter into contracts after misrepresentations have been made to them—innocent or not. Just why
someone totally innocent should have to pay damages is not easy
to understand from the standpoint of justice. Parliament has therefore left it up to the judge to decide whether the victims of the
innocent should get damages or not. The representer can escape
liability by showing that he did not make the representation negligently. If there is an exemption clause restricting liability for misrepresentation it is void—unless it is considered fair and reasonable
in the circumstances.

This improvement in the law has achieved the best of all worlds.
Ostensibly a death blow to *caveat emptor*, it affords good defences
to sellers. Because they seem more vulnerable they have to carry
bigger insurance, and they can justify larger profit margins. This
naturally inflates prices, but not to such an extent where it is worth
suing over most consumer goods. It is much better that Parliament
should make sweeping changes than that the law should develop
haphazardly.

The curious rule that payment of a lesser sum at the time due
cannot satisfy a debt is called *The Rule in Pinnel's Case (1602)
5 Coke's Reports 117a*. That was a case of debt due on a bond and
so no consideration was needed anyway. But the ancient principle
was expressly upheld in *Foakes* v. *Beer (1884) 9 App. Cas. 605*, a
decision of the House of Lords much criticised by the law to this
day. The plaintiff had promised to take no further legal proceedings
on a judgment if the defendant paid agreed instalments. The
defendant paid as agreed, but the plaintiff went back on her word
and sued for interest on the principal debt, and won. Sir George
Jessel, Master of the Rolls in the later Victorian years, described the
doctrine as one of the mysteries of the Common Law, and if he
would not justify it, it is useless for anyone else to try. But, of course,
the lawyers have worked out several doctrines to mitigate its effect.
Payment of a smaller sum at a different place or before the date—
at the creditor's request—is a satisfaction, because the creditor gets
paid earlier. There is a new separate contract which is legally binding
because it has its own consideration. And there is of course, consideration if the creditor agrees to accept some different thing to
that to which the contract entitles him. These differences were
expounded in Pinnel's Case itself:

'The gift of a hawk, a horse or a robe is good. It might be more beneficial than the money.'

For even then, as now, the courts did not concern themselves with the adequacy of consideration. If you pay too much or charge too little, you will—unless you are a victim of fraud, misrepresentation or some definite breach of a contractual term—get no remedy from the law of England. Judges cannot sit in court all day sorting out what things are worth. (Though when they assess damages, that is exactly what they do.)

This is the Cloud Cuckoo Land of contract. The law requires for enforceability of a simple contract, a consideration which is real, not illusory. And yet you can discharge a debt by a smaller sum if the creditor request that it be paid by negotiable instrument, for instance an open cheque (but not, of course, a crossed one). And, of course, cheques bounce. They are frequently not worth the paper upon which they are written. But if a cheque bounces and there is no payment, the old full amount is payable still. That sanction for collection of the cheque seems to be a pretty poor reason for allowing it to do what hard cash could not do on the due day. This, like the *Rule in Pinnel's Case*, is another mystery of the Common Law.

Of course, the thing given by way of substituted consideration has to have value. There is, for instance, no consideration to be found in promising not to sue someone on a claim which has no foundation in law—*Poteliakoff* v. *Teakle* (*1938*) *2 K.B. 816*. On the other hand, a compromise of doubtful legal proceedings is a perfectly valid contract. Even a claim which is actually bad in law is believed to be valid—*Callischer* v. *Bischoffsheim* (*1870*) *L.R. 5 Q.B. 449*. Otherwise compromises of actions would be impossible, and 'the Law favours an end of actions'—though it is very difficult to get the public to believe this.

The real foundation for the rule is of course that even perfectly sound claims are the subject of Dutch Auction bargaining because of the 'hazards of litigation'. These include *inter alia*, the lies and innocent inaccuracies of witnesses; the difficulty of locating the building where the court sits by the time one's presence is required; the gullibility or prejudice of the judge; his judgment of the importance and value of facts; and a very poor last, his quality as a lawyer. The diligence of the professional advisers of the parties in the initial preparation of a case is of the highest importance. Luckily for the professional advocates, their performance on the day usually has little effect on the outcome of the dispute. Not that they are not essential. Only they can explain the controversy to the judge in the available time and get him on the right wavelength.

This is because the people who get involved in actions—particularly in the County Courts—are always coming up with curious bits of accountancy like letting the other party have a postal order to pay off a different debt because the person's brother-in-law could procure some desirable article. (Much merchandise which falls off lorries is trafficked through the inner suburbs of London and other great cities in this fashion.)

Third parties related by marriage play important parts in many disputes. They turn into incredibly complicated affairs. In simple cases the rules are clear enough. If someone else pays off part of your debt for you, and that is accepted in full satisfaction, the creditor cannot go back on it. The absence of consideration between debtor and creditor does not matter because the new arrangement is between creditor and third party. In consideration of the creditor forgiving the debt, the third party will pay him something. That is a good consideration and the court will not inquire into its adequacy. If, however, the true condition of affairs was that the third party was the debtor's agent, all is just as if the debtor himself was dealing with the creditor. The authority for payment of a smaller sum by a third party being good satisfaction is *Hirachand Punamchand* v. *Temple* (*1911*) *2 K.B. 330*. It is worth remembering. If you have neither cheque book, horse, hawk nor robe about you, you should not let a good offer go by, but get someone else to settle up for you.

Should such an opportunity present itself in respect of a bet, the loser can prevent himself from suffering whatever consequences attach to a welsher. The law recognises none. If a friend asks you to stand him the stake for a bet, be prepared to be a loser. The English law of the illegality of wagering transactions is less moral than muddled. If a person lends money to another to make payment of a betting loss it is a payment 'in respect of' a wagering contract within *S.1.* of the *Gaming Act, 1892.* However, if you lend someone his stake money for his pools coupon you can sue him to get it back because pools are not wagers.

The importance of gambling in English social history has led to some rather curious laws, the logical foundation of which is no doubt some broad general intention to encourage thrift. In the result it has made of gamblers, *qua* their failing, second-class citizens who, in a scientific analysis of Status might find a niche. That this should have been done by Parliament only half a century after Charles James Fox was wont to stake a fortune on the turn of a card indicates its shortcomings as a barometer of public opinion. Before the *Gaming Act, 1845*, the Common Law was able to hold wagers perfectly lawful in cases where the judge thought they should be honoured, and illegal when they did not. That is real judging, not simply adding up a lot of bits of statute and coming out with a mechanical answer. Immoral activities like lotteries and cock-fighting were unlawful, and so was everything else which a judge considered to be 'against sound policy'. In *Gilbert* v. *Sykes (1812) 16 East 150* a bet on the life span of Napoleon was ruled against sound policy because it might lead someone to assassinate him in peace time, or not to in war time.

But the importance of the game of chance in our law is not confined to sporting and similar uncertain transactions. From it developed the splendid principle of the 'unenforceable' contract. This is not unlawful. It is not against the law to make an 'unlicensed moneylending' transaction or to give a guarantee not in writing. The courts simply will not assist in enforcing such contracts.

However, that is to anticipate somewhat, for *s. 18* of the 1845 Act declared gaming and wagering contracts not merely unenforceable but null and void. That was a vast improvement in morality, no doubt, and a bit of a blessing for some people. No judgment will be given on an unenforceable contract for that would be enforcing it. But if the contract is null and void and of no effect; any money paid under it must be given back. The person who has been paying under a void contract might have had considerable benefit—perhaps occupied a house or had possession of a motor car for months or years. But he can get back what he has paid for these benefits if a court declares the contract void. He cannot do so if it is unenforceable. The immediate consequence for gamblers was that a losing bettor could get back his stake money. Exactly how that might discourage gambling is a little difficult to follow.

However, the remarkable expansion of the bookmaking industry is tribute to the great sense of honourable obligation which characterises the sporting fraternity. It could be merely ignorance of the law, but it is in fact based upon the eagerness of the punters to have the opportunities to lose more money in the future. Many gambling cases have turned on the question whether a consideration could exist which was not tainted by the Gaming Acts. The undesirability of being declared a defaulter in a sporting club is more clearly appreciated by a man who feels sure that he must make the big tickle sometime. In *Hyams* v. *Stuart King (1908) 2 K.B.* the Court of Appeal actually held lawful a losing punter's promise to pay his debts in consideration of the winner not declaring him a defaulter. But in 1949 this decision was reversed by the House of Lords (*Hill* v. *William Hill (Park Lane) Ltd. A.C. 530*).

The technical ground of the decision was that the promise was not void but merely unenforceable—and so the stake money could not be returned, either. It has been apparent in other fields of contract as well that the natural consequences of avoiding transactions might not be so conducive to honest endeavour as was formerly envisaged. Unhappily, upright behaviour has not always characterised sporting transactions. Bookmakers often had—and have—other interests of a business nature and there were many actions—and still may be—for 'goods sold', loans, 'accounts stated' which were in truth gambling debts. However, in *R. v. Weisz (1951) 2 K.B. 611* it was held that a solicitor who issued a claim by writ for an 'account stated' which was really founded on a bet was guilty of contempt of court for the attempted deception. Very few solicitors have been imprisoned under the stringent power the Supreme Court wields over its officers. That case was *verbum sapientum.*

But not all chancy propositions are wagers. The essence thereof is that one party has to win, and the other to lose. There is therefore no wager in a football pool. When the investor loses, the pool promoter does not win. The money merely forms part of the fund distributed to the more fortunate after subtraction of the expenses and remuneration of the organiser. If the investor is among the winners, it is not the promoter's bounty that enriches him. But, it may be objected, do not the losers lose and the winners win? Quite so, but there is no contractual nexus between the investors. Each sends his stake to the promoter, upon terms that in certain events he shall share in the pool and in return for being so included, he pays the *pro rata* price for inclusion. The same principles exactly apply to the Tote. Such institutions are merely selfless servants of the public, paid for their services out of the corpus of the finances of the enterprise. Premium Bonds are more than halfway to constitutional acceptance of this legal casuistry, and no doubt a National Lottery will emerge as the antidote for some future financial crisis. It is overdue.

A further important element of a wager is the uncertainty of the event which determines the destination of the money. This is not so straightforward as it might appear. An insurance of my life is not invalid although it is uncertain when I shall die. It is lamentably beyond doubt that I shall do so. On the other hand, when, say, Phil Bull says that a particular horse will win a particular race, or when Lester Piggott mounts a horse, there is very good ground for believing that the result is not in doubt. It is a much more certain forecast than when I might die. But the degree of uncertainty is not considered by the law to be relevant. It is created by the parties merely choosing to disagree about what will happen. The converse of this is that it does not prevent a contract from being a wager— and therefore unenforceable or void—that either or both parties have no real doubt about the outcome.

What makes an insurance different from a mere wager is that the insured person or policyholder—who may be different people— have 'an interest' in the result. Insurance is an extremely ancient business—some say 3,000 years old—and has been practised here

290

for at least six centuries, and no better description of this vital element has been found than that. One would have thought that having staked a bet on a race, the punter had an interest in the result, but that is only common sense, not Common Law. The fact that he stands to win or lose a large sum of money confers no interest of itself.

However, if a farmer is prudent he will write insurance on his next year's crop. It might be a good year, and so the prices will be depressed. It might be a bad year, and yet he will have a better produce than other farmers and so reap the best the market can yield in the way of profits. In a good or bad year, some blight or a cigarette end might destroy his crop, and he will receive in insurance the valuer's assessment of the loss he has suffered. Any events less certain are hard to imagine, but that is a perfectly good insurance, and a great deal of such business is written every year because the farmer has an insurable interest in his trading profits. However, wagering contracts of insurance (a contradiction in terms) are void. In *Re London Commercial Reinsurance Office Ltd.* (*1922*) *2 Ch. 67* marine insurers had to pay back the premiums in respect of some policies so avoided. This was all in line with *s. 18* of the 1845 Act which enables a loser to get his stake money back from a stakeholder so long as he claims it back before the stakeholder pays it to the winner. The winner, gets his money back too. It is only rarely that the law says loser takes all.

The winner can actually manage to enforce his claim in some cases. A negotiable instrument such as an open cheque is void if given for a bet, there being no consideration. But a holder of the cheque in due course from the bookie can enforce it unless the punter proves that the holder did not give value for it, in good faith, i.e. without knowing it was for a bet in the first place. The same restrictions on action at law apply to money 'lent for gaming'. But the *Gaming Acts of 1710* and *1835* which make this provision only apply to such loans and to winnings. If a losing punter, in return for not being declared a defaulter, gives a cheque for the debt, the bookie can sue him on it. However, if the bookie, thinking that the loser's cheque might bounce, prefers to take a cheque from someone else in settlement, that friend in need may well remain one indeed. For his Samaritan gesture will be a payment 'in respect of' a wagering contract and so because of *s. 1* of the 1892 Act he will not be able to enforce the loan against the loser.

Having got the tiresome money part out of the way, it is appropriate now to consider for the first time the basic essentials of a contract. Anyone can tell you that there has first to be an offer capable of acceptance, unequivocally accepted by the opposite party, with consideration moving from the person getting the benefit.

Anyone can similarly tell you that the contract must be for a lawful purpose; that the parties must have the capacity to contract; and that they must be intending at the time to make a contract having legally enforceable consequences, and be of one mind about what it is and under no mistaken apprehension. Those are commonplace. Very few people, however, can tell you in every case just what is an offer.

Even a pragmatist might be persuaded that to put goods on display with price tickets on them is an offer by their owner, the shopkeeper say, to sell them at the price to such people as wish to purchase. To do so in a self-service supermarket with placards in the window declaring in letters two feet high, 'Special Offer' might be considered pretty convincing evidence that the traders were making offers. Well, they are not. What they are doing is inviting shoppers to 'treat'. Not to *a* treat, but to treat or bargain with them over the price.

How many people say to the counter assistant (the servant or agent of the shopkeeper) when they are buying a packet of soap powder labelled 'special offer', 'I will give you two bob for that', instead of tendering the marked price of eleven new pence? It is, of course quite unheard of, and if you did it you would soon achieve a local reputation of being some kind of nut. But the theory of the English law at the present day is that the purchaser in a shop makes an offer to buy and that conversely the shopkeeper does not offer to sell anything. (*Pharmaceutical Society of Great Britain* v. *Boots Cash Chemists Ltd. [1952] 2 Q.B. 795; [1953] 1 Q.B. 401.*) The reasoning behind this ostrich-like attitude is that if the other, more obvious policy was adopted, then as soon as the shopper picked up the article he (or more likely she) would be bound to pay for it because she had accepted the shopkeeper's offer. This is manifest nonsense because it overlooks the basic necessity in every law of contract— British and foreign—that the party must have the intention to make a legally binding transaction. Anyone picking up something to inspect it is doing no more than trying to find out if it is something he or she might in the fullness of time care to buy—other things such as price, size, type being evaluated, and acceptable to them.

The reasoning of the Boots case means that by making, across the counter, a general inquiry about availability or even merely pointing, the shopper is in danger of having made an offer that has not in common sense been made accepted by the acutely commercial shop-keeper or the commission-hungry assistant. The shopper is logically denied the opportunity to inspect and a bullying assistant can force goods upon him. The case itself dealt with a self-service emporium, and the purchaser's offer was constituted by taking the goods to the checkout point. But the *reductio ad absurdum* of that is that the purchaser is thereby denied any opportunity to offer a different price —the very thing he is supposed to do in the first place. Thousands of people change their minds about purchases every day, and mercifully, the subject matter of their cogitations is usually of too little value to make it worthwhile troubling a court with this question of intention to accept or contract. Customers owe it to themselves to be right, whether or not the law is on their side.

The paradox was something of a problem for the draftsmen of that monument to Consumer Protection, the *Trade Descriptions Act, 1968*. This replaced the old *Merchandise Marks Acts* which made it a crime to apply a false trade description to goods sold or 'exposed for sale' or in the accused's possession 'for sale'. The criminal law is the only effective means of protecting shoppers.

Since, however, the Common Law would not have it that the goods in a shop are being offered for sale, either that had to be changed or some formula devised to enable consumers to be protected as the Women's Institutes wanted them to be. Consequently, the offences of applying false trade descriptions under the 1968 Act affect people who 'supply or offer to supply' goods for false descriptions. *Section 6* provides:

'*A person exposing goods for supply or having goods in his possession for supply shall be deemed to offer to supply them.*'

The greatest difficulty was in avoiding any reference to 'Sale' goods or prices in *Section 11* which deals with them. It is an offence to indicate falsely that the 'price at which the goods are offered is equal to, or less than, a recommended price or the price at which the goods . . . were previously offered'.

And the Section implies a condition that the goods were offered at the non-sale price for one month in the previous six.

But the words 'offered at a price' refer in each case to the offer to 'supply' goods. Not, of course, to sell them. The offers to buy come from all the eager people who queue up outside the windows bearing the enormous 'Sale' notices.

No purer logic is to be expected on the question of acceptance of an offer when made. But logic is deceptive. Hydrogen and oxygen are both inflammable, and one would expect a combination of them to be highly so. So incombustible is the best known one that it is used for putting fires out. Analogously, you can take advantage of some contractual offers without actually accepting them. I do not mean in the Smoke Ball Case sense, for the sniffing of the medical smoke is acceptance. But when the Household Insurance Company made an offer of shares, a Mr Grant wrote a letter accepting the offer. He posted it, but it never reached the company. Nevertheless, he was made a shareholder by the Court.

After Rowland Hill instigated the reliable Penny Post it became so necessary to daily business that it was more convenient if someone was bound by some acceptance he never received than that the business could be disrupted by people changing their minds while letters were in the post. Had Mr Grant's shares fallen in value while his letter was in the post, he might not have wanted them, but he would have been bound. His case was actually decided the year before *Byrne's (1879) 4 Ex. D. 216 C.A.* But he was held to have acquired the shares even though his acceptance was not in fact communicated to the company. Company-issuing houses, conscious of that great freedom of contract which we all enjoy, and wishing to know where they stand, invariably insert a condition in their offer documents which makes it a condition of the contract of purchase that the acceptance shall be received by them.

However, a person making an offer cannot impose liability under a contract upon someone by stipulating that silence shall be deemed consent. Mr Paul Felthouse wrote to his nephew offering to buy his horse for £30. 15s. 'If I hear no more about him, I consider the horse mine at that price.' The young man did not reply, but he did tell the auctioneer who was selling up his stock that the particular horse was not to be included in the sale. The sales people made a mistake and the uncle sued the auctioneer for conversion of 'his' horse. He lost.

> '*It is clear that the uncle had no right to impose on the nephew a sale of his horse for £30. 15s. unless he chose to comply with the condition of writing to repudiate the offer,*'

said the judge.

There are enterprising merchants who if they are aware of *Felthouse* v. *Bindley* [1862] *11 C.B. N.S. 869*) do not observe its spirit. They are a bit more sophisticated than those tally men of the Thirties who used to insist to the poor and elderly that goods had been ordered, and leave them in the front passage from which physical disposition they could pretend an acceptance.

The judges of the County Courts have little sympathy for 'inertia sellers' whether they operate by post or with their feet in the door.

Litigation over unsolicited goods has not been very considerable. Much of it was default procedure for comparatively small sums in the County Courts. Some of these proceedings were brought by debt collectors who had taken assignments of the debts from the sellers which were unenforceable unless written notice was given to the debtor (*Law of Property Act, 1925, s. 136*). The expense of defending such claims was such that many people did not bother, but allowed themselves to be fleeced. I recall a County Court claim for about £3 for a magazine subscription defended by a taciturn business man who thought it worthwhile sporting three times that sum on a solicitor to teach the magazine distributors a lesson. They thought it worth sending a solicitor from London to deepest Hertfordshire—no doubt 'on principle'. The principle may have been the legitimacy of employing a spurious 'student' to solicit subscriptions for a variety of not very desirable foreign magazines, or merely '*pour encourager les autres*'.

The weakness of the case for the distributors was not merely one of trading morality, but that they could not trace and make to testify the 'student' who had made the contract on their behalf. Few commercial people understand the law of evidence. They blithely assume that an invoice is analogous to Holy Writ.

The judge pointed this deficiency out to the ill-tempered solicitor whom they employed, and recalled that an adjournment had already been had—at their expense—to trace the selling agent. This advocate appeared to labour under the Carson complex of believing utterly in the rightness of his client's case. Unfortunately for him, the defendant stolidly insisted that the absent 'student' told him that he was under no obligation to take a year's subscription if he was dissatisfied—a proposition only to be extracted from the printed order form with some philological difficulty. He added for good measure that he had never received the additional special offer material promised, and was accordingly entitled to regard himself as not bound by the contract.

This solicitor could not understand that the goods for which he sought to hold the defendant liable were unsolicited. The 'student' may very well have tried to sell a subscription, but unless he extracted an order and performed the precedent conditions he had not made the goods into solicited goods. Unsolicited does not merely mean goods delivered out of the blue. It is equally applicable to goods which are foisted upon one. The judge made a special order for costs in favour of the successful defendant even though the claim was for less than half the amount limiting the lowest scale of costs.

The distributors had therefore to pay him about £30 costs and did not get their £3. The figures were vastly different in another case involving unsolicited goods. But this was no County Court squabble over a few pounds.

Stephen Wragg was eleven years old in 1962 when he read in the *Buster* an advertisement inviting him and anyone else with a shilling to bless himself to forward it to the advertiser and receive 5s. 9d. worth of stamps. 'World's Biggest £s. Fill your album—have swopping material for months.' When Stephen's packet of stamps arrived there was with it another packet 'on approval', stated to be worth 28s. 6d. He had not requested them and was surprised to get them. His mother disapproved of this selling technique. The 28s. 6d. worth of stamps was not sent back and neither was the price.

The law applicable to such a situation was theoretically clear, but practically problematical. The delivery amounted to an offer, and no sale could be forced on the recipient. *Section 35* of the *Sale of Goods Act* provides that a purchaser accepts goods if he intimates that he accepts to the seller; or does something inconsistent with the seller's ownership; or retains them after a reasonable time.

Throwing them into the dustbin could be considered inconsistent with the seller's ownership, and retention would also amount to acceptance. To put them in the post back to the seller would seem the clear course. Easy enough with stamps, but some importunate sellers deal in fairly bulky goods, and many people do not see fit to pay postal charges for something they do not want. This is something some of the sellers rely upon.

Broadway Approvals Ltd. sent two 'friendly reminders', the second of which stated that the 28s. 6d. packet had been sent 'at your request'. These notices Stephen's parents deliberately ignored. The solicitors for Broadway Approvals Ltd. then sent a standard form of letter demanding a remittance. His parents told the story to the 'Frank, Fearless and Free' newspaper *The People*. A reporter interviewed the director of Broadway Approvals Ltd. and as a result an article appeared headed 'What a Way to Run a Business'. 'Scaring Kids with Solicitors' Letters,' which Broadway Approvals Ltd. and its director considered one-sided, and so they sued *The People* for libel. The jury found that the article defamed them, but that the opinions in it were fair comment on a matter of public interest. However, the paper was in their eyes guilty of malice, and so they lost the protection of fair comment, and they awarded the company £5,000 damages and it's director £10,000. Naturally the newspaper appealed.

> '*It was difficult to resist the feeling that the result of the trial was wrong and unjust,*'

said Lord Justice Davies ([*1965*] *1 W.L.R.* @ *p.* 820).

The Court of Appeal held that the jury had been misdirected and that the damages were disproportionate, and so there should be a new trial on the issues of fair comment and damages. The jury trial had taken four days in 1964 and the appeal six in 1965. The costs might therefore have been as much as the total damages. It is clear that up to then the only person (other than lawyers) who got anything out of the case was Stephen, who got the solicited 5s. 9d. worth of stamps for his shilling. History does not relate whether Broadway Approvals Ltd. got back the 28s. 6d. packet. For the case, though a technical authority on libel, hardly dealt with the law of unsolicited goods. *Paragraph 6 (viii)* of the Defence pleaded that Broadway Approvals Ltd. were well aware that they had no legal right to require Stephen to return the 28s. 6d. worth of stamps or to sue for the price. Apart from anything else, of course, he was an infant, and bound to pay only for necessaries.

Due mainly to the efforts of Arthur Davidson MP there has now passed into law with effect from the 12th August, 1971, the *Unsolicited Goods and Services Act, 1971.* A recipient of unsolicited goods can send notice that he does not want them. The sender then has 30 days in which to collect them. If he does not do so, the goods are deemed to be an unconditional gift. If such a notice is not sent, the property passes to the recipient in six months and he has to pay for the goods. The due time for sending the notice is therefore six months less 30 days plus such time as it takes for the notice to be delivered to the sender.

The second section makes it an offence for a person not having a reasonable belief that there is a right to payment in the course of a trade or business to demand payment for unsolicited goods or to threaten legal proceedings or any other collection procedure. The maximum fine on a summary conviction is £200. There are similar sanctions over directory entries: *Section 4* makes it an offence to send unsolicited publications describing or illustrating human sexual techniques. A first offence attracts a fine of up to £100; subsequent offences £400. But the permission of the Director of Public Prosecutions is required for a prosecution. Presumably a certain legal expertise is necessary to define 'unsolicited soliciting'.

Never Never Land

*'Hire purchase is: somebody acquiring goods which
they do not want, from someone they do not know,
with money they have not got.'*

H.H. Judge Lawson Campbell.

IT STARTED with the distribution of sewing machines by the Singer
Company but the earliest litigation about it filled the financiers
with doubt because the financing of a heating system for a nursery
market garden's glasshouses raised the ancient doctrine of things
becoming 'annexed to the freehold' and so unrecoverable.

This is why the financing of central heating systems is by 'personal
loans' rather than hire purchase. Hire purchase is not, by our law,
money-lending. One can obtain tax-relief on the interest elements
of advances thus made for the purposes of a trade, profession or
business, and one could be forgiven for believing otherwise.

What really dictates whether things are paid for in cash or upon
credit is whether the price is a large sum or a small one. The great
property legislation of 1925 was designed to make the disposal of
real estate more simple, like that of personal property. In theory,
there is no difference between selling a car or anything else. The sale
of land, however, creates an 'estate'. The conception of an estate
is employed in trafficking in such things as shares and even other
abstractions like copyrights, or dignities, like earldoms. No doubt
it is permissible to call them 'things'. It is an insult to apply that
term to a human being, and it is no bad working rule to limit it to
those things which the law calls chattels. This word derives from
catella, meaning cattle. Wives were once thought of in the same
category, and indeed the 19th Century Mormons called their wives
'heifers'. Do so in England today and the woman could divorce you.

When Sir Mackenzie Chalmers, the Judge of the Birmingham
County Court, reduced into beautiful English the principles of the
law of sale produced in the course of three thousand years of
Western civilisation, he made a much better job of codifying the law
than a good many draftsmen since. Modern professors can pick
holes in it, but it should never be forgotten, as Bacon said in 1601:

*'All men of the law know that a Bill which is only expository to
expound the Common Law doth enact nothing.'*

It merely sets out in unarguable form the existing law, and in it the chattels with which people deal in the ordinary course of trade every day are described as 'goods'. It has no application to mere private transactions. The difference between a good and a chattel is probably that between live and dead stock, from the historical viewpoint, but the act says in *s. 62* that goods are:

> '*all chattels personal other than things in action and money, and in Scotland all corporeal movables.*'

'A thing in action' is a legally enforceable right, like a claim under an insurance. By *S. 1 (1):*

> '*A contract of sale of goods is a contract whereby the seller transfers or agrees to transfer the property in goods to the buyer for a money consideration, called the price.*'

The third subsection is informative:

> '*Where under a contract of sale the property in the goods is transferred from the seller to the buyer the contract is called a sale; but where the transfer of the property in the goods is to take place at a future time or subject to some condition thereafter to be fulfilled, the contract is called an agreement to sell.*'

and the fourth, conclusive:

> '*An agreement to sell becomes a sale when the time elapses or the conditions are fulfilled subject to which the property in the goods is to be transferred.*'

Anyone reading that might be led into believing that if he bought anything on hire purchase, it would become his when he had paid for it. The elapsing of the time and the fulfilment of the conditions might be equated with the paying of the instalments. But they are not and the notion is completely wrong. Hire purchase is not sale. Credit sale is sale. Conditional sale is sale. They are both covered by the *Hire Purchase Acts* to greater or lesser extent. But they are not hire purchase. And hire purchase is not sale.

Whether a sale has occurred depends entirely upon whether the property has passed. Whether a sale is intended depends totally on whether it has been agreed that it is to pass. All depends on whether there was the same thought in the minds of seller and buyer at the same time. Since the seller is usually a limited company acting through its very fed-up servant who is thinking of his commission or her boyfriend, and the buyer thinks of the goods as 'mine' anyway, this *concensus ad idem* is highly unlikely. Nevertheless, it is the basis of the law of contract.

It is, however, possible to judge the mind of man. Judges judge it all day every day. That is why there are so many disappointed litigants. But Parliament has in the past few years determined to cause a bit of justice to invade the harsh commercial world of the sale of consumer durables.

They have faced up to the fact that not only is the motor industry the biggest export earner we have, but that it is not only the citizens of the district covered by the Old Street Magistrates' Court whose proclivities are as described by the Stipendiary Magistrate, Mr Neil McElligott:

> *'People round here think a motor car more necessary than a spare pair of socks.'*

We are all equal under the law, but no class of person is more equal than those who sell motor-cars. Whether they sell limousines from palm-fringed showrooms or bangers from bombed sites, they are all regarded in the same light by the judges before whom the disputes over the transactions are tried. There are disputes about hi-fi record players and washing machines, central heating systems and furniture. But the splendid variety of our laws of sale and bailment owe most to the motor car. In the *Seven Stars* in Carey Street one can sometimes find a gathering of half a dozen 'outside clerks' all agreeing to persuade their clients to chip in £50 to pay out the true owner of a few cubic feet of scrap steel on its way from the crushing machine to the foundry to start life again as a marvel of modern engineering. No doubt there are two logbooks for it, the first issued when it was originally registered to roll out of a show-room, pristine and desirable.

By that time, the car was actually second-hand. Mr Justice Wynn-Parry decided in 1960 that a car stopped being 'new' when it had number plates put on it and was driven from the showroom. The car in question had been offered as 'new' when it had been resold immediately on delivery and having run only 'delivery mileage'. And of course, 'as new' can mean something very different from 'new' when the subject is a motor-car.

When a car has been registered and licensed it has acquired an identity and its existence is in many cases recorded in the archives of Hire Purchase Information Limited. The transaction which rewards the manufacturer, the Customs and Excise and the main agent in roughly equal proportions is usually financed by one of those 'industrial bankers' who write most of the credit business in these islands. (They must not describe themselves in their corporate names as 'bankers' without leave of the Department of Trade.) These are the institutions which the Chancellor of the Exchequer utilises to control consumption of goods and money. With a wave of his Regulator he creates a boom by reducing minimum deposits to one-fifth of the price, and allowing three years or so to pay the balance (with interest at rates somewhat difficult to ascertain). When the Gnomes of Zurich are on the warpath he waves it in the other direction, and the minimum deposit becomes one-third, and the balance must be paid in a few months.

As a matter of law, very few of these concerns are banks. Nor are they moneylenders. They call themselves 'finance houses'. They used to be known as 'hire purchase companies' but hire purchase, believe it or not, is on the decline. Credit is not. Just that kind called hire purchase. From the two cases of *Lee* v. *Butler* (*1893*) *2 Q.B. 318* and *Helby* v. *Matthews* (*1895*) *A.C. 471*, it appeared that there were at least two kinds of 'hire and purchase agreement' basically. In the first, the hirer became owner of the goods automatically on payment of the last instalment. But that, said the Court of Appeal, was an 'agreement to buy' within the *Factors Act, 1889*. In the latter case, the hirer was entitled under the agreement to return the goods to the owner at any time. Even though he automatically became owner on paying the last payment, he had the option until then of returning the goods. Consequently that was not a sale or agreement to buy.

These cases, and most of the other hire purchase and kindred cases, have come before the courts because the original hirers parted with the goods for love or money to other people. If the goods were theirs to dispose of they were perfectly entitled to. If they were not paid for, the debt remained in existence but the property in the goods belonged to the debtor. If there was a mere hiring and the hirer parted with possession, there were all the fearful remedies which the English Common Law had developed from the ancient writ of *trover*. There was the tort of conversion, and the crimes of fraudulent conversion and larceny by a bailee. Conversion was what was alleged against Mr Matthews in buying the goods from the hirer. Said Lord Herschell:

> '*If Brewster agreed to buy the piano the parties cannot by calling it a hiring or by mere juggling with words, escape from the consequences of the contract into which they entered.*'

This 'option to purchase' became therefore the characteristic which prevented a transaction from being a sale or agreement to sell. In sale, the ownership passed with delivery, whether the price was paid or not. In an agreement to sell, it passed whenever the conditions upon which it depended had been performed. But where the transaction could be aborted before the property passed, it was not an agreement to sell but a mere offer. Since the hirer had no ownership or legal right to deal with it, he could not validly dispose of it to someone else.

Nemo dat quod non habet, said the ancient maxim. You cannot give what you have not got. At the turn of the century the finance houses liked to be able to get the goods back. Consumer durables in those days were durable, like Mr Brewster's piano. The earliest 'hire-and-purchase' was one by the Singer Sewing Machine Company. Carson used to tell of an old, deaf Irish County Court judge, who thought a case was about a musical instrument, 'probably a harmonium', when it was in fact about a Singer machine. The importance of being able to re-possess made the finance companies very keen on the option to purchase. They started putting provisions for options to purchase in all their written agreements. The law did not then require the agreements to be written, but the practice soon became widespread. Since the option to purchase was such a great benefit, many of the companies thought the hirers should pay for it. There is a legal reason for charging as well, namely that the consideration for the hire is past, and that a new consideration for the actual passing of property is necessary to make the contract enforceable. Whether it was selfless desire to protect the interests of hirers or enlightened self-interest is probably irrelevant now.

The 'automatic ownership' kind of agreement came in the fulness of time to be known as a 'conditional sale agreement', perhaps because of the case of *Scammell* v. *Ouston* (*1941*) *A.C. 251*, where a man agreed to buy a lorry on 'hire purchase terms'. The House of Lords held that this contract could not be enforced because it was so vague that the necessary elements of the contract could not be defined.

There were so many different kinds of hire purchase terms that the court could not decide what the parties meant. At that time, it is true, Parliament had defined it as a 'bailment of goods under which the bailee may buy the goods or under which the property in the goods will or may pass to the bailee'. But it covered only sales of livestock up to £1,000 in value and other goods up to £300 value. Many cars were therefore excluded before the war and all new cars after the war.

In the 1964 Act, which was replaced by that of 1965 a remarkable Parliamentary metamorphosis took place. A conditional sale agreement was defined as any sale agreement for goods under which the price or part of it was made payable by instalments until the conditions were fulfilled. Credit sale agreements, where the purchaser becomes owner straightaway and pays the price by instalments are not within the *Hire Purchase Acts* unless the price is payable by five or more instalments and the seller remains owner until the conditions are performed. This would be the natural meaning of a conditional sale agreement. But the distinction is only important to purchasers who sell the goods before they are paid for. In the grand design of the national economy they are all the same under the Regulator. The

Hire Purchase and Credit Sale Agreements (*Control*) *Order, 1964,* as amended every financial crisis by Amendment Orders, provided for the deposits and buying periods. The 1965 Act extended the application of the statutory control of agreements to goods worth £2,000 bought by human beings, not companies. Credit sale agreements for prices under £30 are excluded.

As well as the coverage being widened, the detailed provisions and consumer protection of the latest Acts is considerable. Consequently, the wiser finance houses are giving up hire purchase, and going in for pure hire, personal loans and credit sales. Until the *Finance Act, 1968,* the purchaser got more income tax advantage from those. People in business on their own account still do. They are the discerning purchasers. But most people scarcely bother to read the form. They might find that what they thought was a hire purchase transaction was in fact a straight sale and that they have merely borrowed the money from the finance house.

An extremely common kind is headed 'Loan Agreement', describes the finance company as lender, provides for payment of instalments —the whole outstanding balance to become due in certain events— an agreement to insure the goods and an authorisation to pay the money to the seller, and provisions for rebates for early settlement. The schedule sets out the property bought and the price, but it says nothing about taking the goods back, or the financiers needing a court order to get them back after a certain proportion has been paid.

This is moneylending, but without the grave limitations imposed by the *Moneylenders Acts.* Hire purchase is not moneylending. Lord Denning has said so in *obiter dicta,* but then he always did call a spade a shovel. There are several judicial statements to the effect that the transaction in suit in the case before them were not moneylending. Such contracts attract the power of the court to re-open and re-make 'harsh and unconscionable' bargains, and calculations of interest which would daunt a Senior Wrangler, and the precise formalities of signing detailed contracts before the money is handed over. There used to be a struck-off solicitor who roamed the corridors of the Law Courts looking at the Masters' Lists. He would wait outside the Master's room and when some debtor appeared for a case which looked a bit moneylenderish he would offer his expertise at finding technical defences by which the debt could be avoided. But they would not avail a hirer wishing to go in for legal welshing.

Hire purchase business is:

> '*their real function is the lending of money . . . Although that may be the object and the intention for which they exist the question is not with what object they employ their money, but the*

Mr Justice Porter, in *Olds Discount Co.* v. *Cohen (1938)*
3 All E.R. 281.

Legally, the owner does not lend money. He buys the goods from a dealer and hires them to the person who wants to use them for a rent. The real death knell of hire purchase as a financing system in the car trade was the decision of *Financings Ltd.* v. *Baldock (1963) 2 Q.B. 104* where the Court of Appeal said that default in payment of two instalments was not such a breach of the contract as to amount to repudiation of it. If a contract is broken, the innocent party can often treat the breach as putting an end to the contract, and be free to sue for damages for the breach and yet not be bound to perform his obligations under the original contract. Consequently, the common practise among what Professor Guest has called The Black Sheep of Hire Purchase, was to send 'recovery agents' to 'snatch back' a car when the hirer was one or two payments behind. The transaction was usually outside the Acts in those days, because most second-handed cars cost more than £300.

The recovery agents would sell the car, because the hire purchase company would have nowhere to keep it. The agents would have outlets in the motor trade, because usually they were the dealers who had sold the car in the first place to the hirer. It would not realise much, of course. It would be so difficult to sell that a very low price would have to be accepted. The purchaser was usually the dealer's own firm. If the 'cash price' was £500 the hire charge would have made the hire purchase price £700. But it would fetch only 'trade price'. The trade price is fixed in the second-hand car trade by reference to the Bible, otherwise *Glass's Guide*, the contents of which are a closely guarded secret among the car traders and their acolytes.

Under the economic law which makes every season of the year the wrong time for selling to the trade; and black cars, coloured cars, two-tone, and one-colour cars unsaleable, the lowest 'book' price (dependent on 'condition') would make such a car worth about £250. The finance company which had paid the dealer £400 of the £500 'cash' price would therefore have 'lost' £150. It might also have had to pay for repairs to put it into sufficiently good order for the 'recovery agent' to buy it. The hirer would see this situation as having paid £100 down, and all the monthly instalments save one or two, lost the car, and been dunned for about £250 in the County Court, for breach of contract.

The right to determine the contract has to exist under the general law, and not merely under the special terms of the contract, said the court in *Yeoman Credit* v. *Waragowski (1961) 1 W.L.R. 1124.* If the breach of contract is bad, and the breaker shows thereby that he is disregarding the contract, he can be sued for breaches before and after the innocent party elected to end the contract. (*Overstone Ltd.* v. *Shipway* (*1962*) *1 W.L.R. 117; Bridge* v. *Campbell Discount Co. Ltd.* [*1962*] *A.C. 600.*) But the mere failure to pay a couple of instalments entitled the financier to sue only for the arrears.

Followed swiftly by the Acts of 1964 and 1965, these cases practically ended true hire purchase in cars. The *Moneylenders Act, 1900* was passed to control the ravages of back street moneylenders, and the smarter ones 'up West' who got the younger sons of the Edwardian smart set 'in their clutches'. The law against usury was finally abolished in 1854. Later Victorian morality thought that Parliament ought again to forbid what God no longer did. However, it excluded pawnbrokers from the wages of sin because they were already legislated against; Friendly Societies and Building Societies because they encourage Thrift; bodies entitled under special Acts to lend money and

> '*any person bona fide carrying on the business of banking or insurance or bona fide carrying on any business not having for its primary object the lending of money, in the course of which and for the purposes whereof he lends money; or any body corporate for the time being exempted from registration under this Act by order of the Board of Trade . . .*'

These bodies are subject to legislative control over the form of their contracts or conditions of their loans and the interest they charge. They do not need to have moneylenders' licences.

The essence of the exceptions from the obloquy of usury appears to be this: Any concern which lends other people's money can do it as it likes and charge what interest it likes. Anyone who systematically lends his own money is treated like a criminal and is virtually unprotected unless he charges little and follows a complicated ritual. It is much better to be a Bank if you wish to trade in usury. But it is not easy to be a Bank. United Dominion's Trust is one because the other Banks treat it as one of them. Such acceptance is much more cogent than even the *imprimatur* of the Inland Revenue or the Department of Trade.

In *U.D.T.* v. *Kirkwood* (*1966*) *2 Q.B. 431*, Lord Justice Harman said:

> '*The only point on this appeal . . . can be shortly stated in the form of question and answer: Q. When is a moneylender not a moneylender? A: When he is a banker.*
>
> '*. . . as Farwell, L. J., observed many years ago* (Litchfield v. Dreyfus [1906] 1 K.B. 584) *it is a perfectly respectable trade, but the Legislature has thought fit to enact that he who carries it on must be registered as such.*

> '*It is notoriously difficult to define the business of banking and no statute has attempted it.*
>
> '*. . . It was said in a dissenting judgment in* Davies *v.* Kennedy (1868) 17 W.R. 305 *that a banker is one who is considered in commercial circles to be one, but on the whole I have come to the conclusion that reputation alone is not enough. There must be some performance behind it.*
>
> '*I regret to find myself unable to subscribe to the views expressed by the Master of the Rolls on this topic. His judgment seems to me to prove that U.D.T. is not a banker.*'

Be that as it may, that opinion triumphed. All of these weighty matters seldom trouble the prospective customer when he begins to chaffer with a car dealer. He is more concerned how much he will get for his existing car in 'part exchange'. Now this oddly enough is a sale. He sells his old car to the dealer. The dealer may sell the new car to him or he may sell it to the finance house—depending on what kind of transaction is currently being employed. It may very well be that the dealer is kind enough to advertise 'existing h.p. accounts settled'. The idea is to provide that lump sum of money which the Regulator decrees must be paid as a deposit, without actually finding any money.

It has from time to time occurred to the motor merchants that the idea is to sell those motor cars gracing their forecourts for profit to themselves. Hungry for motor cars the public unquestionably is and the only really common difficulty is a shortage of money in the customer. Quite frequently his existing car is not one which would command a great price and might even prove an encumbrance to the dealer. It therefore occurred to some of them that since the finance house is going to pay the balance of the price of the purchased car anyway, no great harm will be done by relying upon a legal fiction, namely that the deposit has been paid. In order to ensure that the whole cash price is then paid by the finance house, the price inserted on the form has to be inflated by the amount of the deposit which like the Wise Steward in the Bible, the dealer has forgiven. This is known colloquially as 'booking', but under its other name of obtaining money by deception is highly criminal, and several motor dealers have served prison sentences to prove it. If the purchaser knowingly takes part, he of course becomes a conspirator, and if he sees it through, he 'obtains a pecuniary advantage by deception'.

If the customer actually does trade-in his old car but the deal falls through—perhaps because the finance house does not accept the customer—then he can serve a notice of cancellation on the dealer and if his old car is not returned to him in practically as good condition as it was, he can recover from the dealer a sum equivalent to the part exchange allowance. Since the oldest adage in the motor

307

trade is 'Any fool can sell a car but it takes an expert to buy one' the part exchange allowance is unlikely to be anywhere near enough money to pay for a similar replacement. In the result the dealer can sell the traded-in car with impunity.

Exactly how this protects the consumer—which is the avowed object of Parliament in passing Hire Purchase Acts—is a little obscure. But for the provision, the customer would be able to allege in an action against the dealer that the sale of his old car was conditional upon the purchase or taking on hire of the 'new' one and that since that has not occurred the dealer is in breach of contract.

The ordinary measure of damages for breach of contract is the value of the damage actually flowing from the breach—in the case of loss of a car, its replacement value in the open market. In these circumstances, one could not get back the car from the person who bought it from the dealer. For the dealer is that splendid creation of the Law Merchant, now immortalised in the Factors Acts, a 'mercantile agent'. The existence of these middlemen necessitated by the vast expansion of commerce since the Middle Ages, gives the lie to the proposition that you cannot give what you have not got.

For the purposes of the *Factors Act, 1889*

> *'the expression "mercantile agent" shall mean a mercantile agent having in the customary course of his business as such agent authority either to sell goods or to consign goods for the purpose of sale, or to buy goods, or to raise money on the security of goods.'*

A purchaser from a genuine mercantile agent in the course of his business in selling such things gets a good title to the goods even though the true owner did not want them sold to him. But only such transactions have that effect. Pictures given to a man to sell on commission if he could were not validly transferred because he was an insurance agent, not a picture dealer (*Hayman* v. *Flewker* [*1863*] *32 L.J.C.P.*).

If the customer is in possession of his old car under a hire purchase or conditional sale agreement he has no title to pass to the dealer. The agreement probably provides that even if he 'parts with possession' of it he has broken the contract. On the other hand, if he has it on 'credit sale', the property has passed to him, and he merely owes the money for it—unless there is a provision for it to be recovered in which case it is not true credit sale. He can then perfectly lawfully sell it to the dealer or anyone else, but he still owes the price to the financiers.

Since the *Sale of Goods Act s. 12 (1)* makes it an implied condition of a sale that the seller has title to the goods, even if the seller believes in good faith that *he* has, the full price can be recovered against him by a purchaser on proof that he had no title—even though the purchaser has had the benefit of the use of the car for months—*Rowland* v. *Divall* (*1923*) *2 K.B. 500.*

However, when a car that is on HP is offered for trade-in and the dealer requests and receives from the finance house a 'settlement figure', this will probably be treated by the courts as the finance house waiving its rights to treat the disposition as a breach of contract (*Wickham Holdings, Ltd.* v. *Brooke House Motors Ltd.* *[1967] 1 W.L.R. 295*). When the finance house has been settled up, the ownership of the car does not go straight to the dealer, but theoretically passes through the customer. The effect is that the customer is selling to the dealer, not the financier (*Bennett* v. *Griffin Finance [1967] 2 Q.B. 46 C.A.*). In this way, contract is performed and the benefit of any early settlement relief of interest is secured.

The wise dealer, when offered a car in part exchange, makes an inquiry with Hire Purchase Information Ltd. to discover whether it is owned by any finance house. Unhappily for the customer, it sometimes turns out to be. The simplest way in which this can arise is by buying from a 'private owner'. Sharks there may be in the deep waters of the motor car trade. But they sport in the shallower seas of individual enterprise as well. The advertisers in the classified columns include some folk whose consciences do not extend their beneficence to finance houses.

Attempts to consult them about such matters a couple of years later often result in the discovery that they have disappeared without trace from their former haunts. A not inconsiderable number of people have to remain mobile simply because of the unwelcome solicitations of the Inland Revenue and other creditors. Being the purchaser from the untraceable rogue is an unhappy fate. There is no defence to a conversion action by the true owner. Nor is there any to the claim for the price from the purchaser from you. If you can find the rogue, he will have no defence against you. But since he is hardly likely to be able to pay anything if you bankrupt him, and you can no longer imprison him for non-payment of a judgment debt, the law gives you little but sympathy. In the unlikely event of his having a job you could get an Attachment of Earnings order. If you do he will probably change his job and disappear again.

Not all dealers are wise enough to check whether the vehicle they are taking in is already on hire. It must be confessed that those who do not might be motivated by the sad situation in which the customer will find himself in the event immediately herein before described. This solicitude is perhaps in some cases tempered with the realisation that if the customer turns out to have no title, he will not buy the 'new' car. There are times when the Regulator has created a climate when trade could not be regarded as brisk. At such times, silence appears to be golden.

However, the acquisition of the 'new' car will involve, in a large number of cases, a finance house. The financiers as a rule conduct an independent check with the information service, but that is of course confined to the car being acquired from the dealer. Any query on the trade-in will not arise until the dealer tries to finance its disposition to someone else. Which he may not do. He may dispose of it through the trade, by cash sale or barter. This is how the 'string' conversion actions arise, sometimes with half a dozen parties all claiming that their vendor had no title. The sensible course is to make up an *ad hoc* co-operative and share the loss of the original true owner. There are earnest people who write to the papers demanding to know why buying and selling a house is not as simple and straightforward as buying a car.

The trade-in came of age with the 1965 Act, being immortalised by Parliament therein. It is of course the soul and inspiration of car sales and a few other consumer durable trades. But whereas cooking stoves, televisions and vacuum cleaners command only a few pounds part exchange value to sweeten the housewife's pride in her domestic machinery, part exchange has a Freudian significance in car trading. Nothing makes an insignificant wage-slave feel more virile than forcing a hard faced motor salesman to give him more money for his old car. The flowering of his self-esteem is perfected when between them they hatch up a mighty plot to do it by reducing the price of the new car to compensate for the reduced trade-in price of the old one. The customer knows that secondhand cars are virtually impossible to sell. Several of his friends have had no end of trouble. The national freemasonry of motor traders has all of us locked in an economic straightjacket and the key is *Glass's Guide to Used Car Values*.

When Judge Bassett ruled at the Ilford County Court, he would not accept Glass's Guide as Holy Writ, when tendered as proof of value—or lack of it—of a motor car. One astute advocate rather imposed it upon him by calling as an expert witness no less an authority than the compiler himself, who described, in great detail, his researches into used car values for the month concerned. Automobile anthropology of this order is the exception rather than the rule. The values given in the guide are of three main classes, each circumscribed with reservations, but the main purpose is open to every car dealer. He can use the book to justify offering what he wants to pay for any car and no more. This is not a conspiracy or a restrictive practice. All he is doing is to offer a price for an article the customer wishes to sell. Unless that is done, the new car cannot be acquired whether it is required, subconsciously, to satisfy the customer's image or, practically, to enable him to perform some necessary motoring. Whilst 'booking' is illegal and criminal, artificial adjustment of the trade-in value of the 'old' car is no such thing. Is it not a principle of the law of contract that the adequacy of consideration will not be inquired into by the courts? Freedom of contract reigns in the used car trade just like anywhere else. True, this requires escalation of the price of the 'new' car. By taking an optimistic view of the value of the trade-in, a large advance sometimes can be obtained from the finance house. Enough to give the dealer a profit on the sale of the 'new' one by itself. The trade-in can then be 'sold in the trade', which might be a euphemism for the breaker's yard. But no crime has been committed. The customer is paying back more in instalments than he otherwise would have done, and everyone is happy, including himself.

Should it happen that the finance company will not accept the transaction because of the age and type of car, the whole deal will fall to the ground. If that should happen, the customer will perhaps want his old car back from the dealer. *Section 15* of the 1965 Act provides that if the trade-in is not returned in as good condition as when sold, within ten days of a Notice of Cancellation being served on the dealer, the hirer can recover from him money up to the part-exchange value as compensation.

It must not be forgotten, however, that when the trade-in was delivered to the dealer, a simple sale took place. The dealer therefore acquired the property in it the moment it was delivered. In any case, the dealer is a mercantile agent, and if he sells it to some eager purchaser within hours of taking it in, the Factors Acts will give a good title to that purchaser and the trader-in will be left to his remedy against the dealer. My own inclination would be to make the purchase by the dealer conditional expressly on the contract for the 'new' vehicle being performed by the finance company. Then if the dealer disposed of the trade-in car, one could sue him for its market value, which might very well be more than the 'part-exchange' price which is the maximum recoverable under the cancellation provisions of the statute. This Act is one result of the great campaign for and on behalf of the Select Committee on Consumer Protection.

The traded-in car will often itself be subject to a hire purchase agreement which means of course that the hirer has no title to sell it. The 1964 Act protects the title of a purchaser from a private person of a vehicle 'sold' in this way. But since it is usually left to the dealer to settle the hire purchase on a traded-in car it has been said by Lord Justice Harman that if the finance company informs him of the 'settlement figure' it is waiving the provisions of the agreement against assignment and parting with possession. (*Wickham Holdings* v. *Brooke House Motors* [1967] 1 W.L.R. 295 C.A.)

There are two parts to most finance company documentation

systems. On one part of a form the customer proposes that the financiers should buy the car from the dealer and rent it to him. Then there is the hire purchase agreement itself. If and when executed by the company, this will govern the transaction. When the customer signs the forms and 'drives away in ten minutes' he probably regards all as settled except the transfer of his insurance cover to the 'new' car. There is, of course, no concluded contract between him and the dealer, nor with the finance house. If he crashes the car and is covered by insurance he will have to pay the money to the dealer. If he is not insured he will have to pay money to the dealer out of his own pocket. He will also have to compensate anyone he injures or the dependants of anyone he kills. With the delivery condition of some secondhand cars, neither of these possibilities is remote.

If the transaction should be refused by a finance house the dealer will no doubt offer it elsewhere. He wants to sell the 'new' car. The standing of the customer and the condition, age and value of the vehicle determine whether a finance company will accept a proposal which is only an offer by the customer. Of the condition, they rarely if ever know anything. Of the price, they probably make a pragmatic assessment of the probable value if snatched back by an ordinary-reasonable car dealer. In the ordinary cases where this process results in the finance company thinking the transaction acceptable, the acceptance is notified to the dealer and the customer, and the dealer will get the balance of the price of the car. The finance house relies upon the lawyers who draft its standard forms of contract to protect it against exigencies of fate. But for its further protection it often has a 'recourse agreement' with the dealer. This provides that, in consideration of the commission paid to the dealer for introducing business, the dealer will, when required by the finance company, pay up the customer's liability to it and have the debt assigned to him (or *it* if it is a company) so that he can sue the customer for breaches of his obligations.

Since the dealer might well be acting as 'repossession agent', and thereafter buying repossessed cars from the finance company he is impaled on the horns of a dilemma. If he bids a small sum for a snatched-back car, he is increasing the amount he will himself have to pay to the finance company under the recourse agreement. That will of course increase the amount of the debt assigned to him. But motor dealers know better than most that it is one thing to get a judgment for a sum of money, and entirely another to get the money. The finance company by this means, of course, dispense with having to store and re-sell (after putting into saleable condition as required by law) a variety of goods. They really deal only in one commodity: money. It has great virtues of convenience of handling.

312

The dealer, however, by offering a sufficiently small amount to purchase the repossessed car can protect himself against the burden of his recourse agreement by making a decent profit on its sale. The person who underwrites all this, the insatiable consumer, is the one for whose benefit the whole system exists.

Analogy is a dangerous form of argument in any field and doubly so in the law. The circumstances which reveal that a dealer keeps a stock of the contract and proposal forms and physically transmits the completed forms to the finance house, might lead one to suppose that he is an agent of the company. The fact that he gets commission on business introduced would reinforce the conviction. The fact that he was enabled to buy the lease of his bombed site, and stock of motor cars for sale with a loan from the finance company might be regarded as conclusive. But the dealer is not at common law the agent of the finance company. He is an independent entrepreneur who sells things to the company for it to rent to the consumer. He was not the general agent of the company even when it employed him to collect instalments, or seize the car if the customer defaulted.

The purpose for which no finance company wishes to recognise the dealer as its agent is the actual selling or taking on hire. There is always a chance that during what the *Hire Purchase Act, 1965* calls 'antecedent negotiations' the dealer or his salesman might say or do something to indicate that acquisition of the car would be advantageous or desirable. It is possible that such a statement might turn out to be less than 100 per cent accurate. Even without such unwise representation, the responsibilities of a hire purchase finance company are extremely onerous. In the ordinary way, the law requires one who lets a thing on hire to provide something which will enable the hirer to enjoy the use of it. Sewing machines are for sewing, washing machines for washing; televisions ought to work. The owner is, after all, getting rent. In the absence of any express provision providing that he shall not, the owner would ordinarily be liable to provide another article which would work, or pay damages, or lose rent, for such time as it did not work.

The device employed for the protection of finance houses from the imperfections of modern mechanical apparatus is called an 'acknowledgement clause'. By signing an agreement containing such clauses, the customer 'acknowledges' such unlikely facts as that the machine is in perfect working order and condition. But they seldom stop there. He also acknowledges that the finance house does not know what condition it is in. He also acknowledges that he has not made known expressly or by implication the purpose for which he required the machine. This provision sometimes strains one's credulity.

For what purpose does one ordinarily require a mechanical

excavator? Or a washing-up machine? No doubt motor cars are capable of a wide variety of uses. I saw one once which was labelled perfectly truthfully '2,000 miles only. One owner from new'. The fact that it had crashed on the Col du Lecques during a Monte Carlo Rally could not detract from the perfect veracity of those two statements. But that is the nature of motor cars. They are capable of a wide variety of uses, within the limitation of being driven round the face of the Earth. Ingenuity could no doubt devise some employment for a knitting machine which did not constitute fair wear and tear, such as using wire instead of wool. The finance company likes to provide against such contingencies.

There has for ages been implied into a contract of sale a condition that the goods should be of merchantable quality when the seller's business is supplying such goods and the buyer expressly or impliedly makes known to him what he wants them for and thereby indicates that he is relying on the seller's skill and judgment. Now it is, of course, by no means inevitable that a person who sells cars possesses skill and judgment as to whether the cars are of merchantable quality. But the law imposes another condition and that is that they shall be reasonably fit for the purpose for which they are required. It is even more unlikely that many of the people who sell cars will know such things for the breaking down of parts of motor cars is frequently a secret, unobservable and sudden occurrence. Nevertheless, *s. 14(1)* of the *Sale of Goods Act, 1893*, imposes that responsibility on sellers. Not just motor dealers; everyone who sells anything as a business, whether or not he is a manufacturer.

Fiat Motors Ltd. were held liable to the Bristol Tramways Company in a celebrated action in 1910 because the motor omnibuses they supplied were not suitable for use in hilly districts, and broke down. The essence of buying and selling has always been *caveat emptor*, and sociologically inclined writers have seen such provisions as a limitation upon the rule. But it was the common law long before the Act was passed to codify the law of sale. And *caveat emptor* does not mean 'take chance', it means that the buyer must take care. Be that as it may thirty years later the Court of Appeal held in *Drury* v. *Buckland* (*1941*) *1 All E.R. 269* that the conditions of fitness implied by the *Sale of Goods Act* did not apply to hire purchase transactions, because they were not sales. By then the *Hire Purchase Act, 1938* had provided that when the hirer made known the use for which the goods were required there was to be implied a condition that they were reasonably fit for such use. Of course, that covered only goods up to £300 in value.

The agreement Lombank Ltd. had with Mrs Lowe, a 65-year-old widow—and a 'careless optimist' according to one judge—acknowledged that she had not made known to them the particular purpose for which she required the car—a small Morris of a type of which many thousands have run about our roads. Mr Justice Diplock, as he was then, said that that clause was an attempt to evade the Act

> '*Which only the size of the print in which it is set out prevents one from calling blatant.*'

Among the other things Mrs Lowe had signed was an acknow-ledgement that she had read and understood fully the agreement containing all the acknowledgement, exclusion and other clauses. She had not. So ignorant was she, that when the car proved 'utterly unroadworthy' she spent her own money on having it repaired, but it kept on breaking down. She was a little put out by this because the dealer had told her it was in near-perfect condition. This availed her not, against the finance company in 1960 (*1 W.L.R. 196*). But although they contended that she was bound by her signature to the confession that she had not made the purpose for which she required the car known to the finance company, she won her case. The judge thought Lombank 'bold' to argue against the inference that a widow of 65 who buys a rather ordinary car wants it to drive about in from place to place. I do know of a case where an elderly lady part-exchanged an E-type Jaguar for a 'batwing' Mercedes, but pre-sumably even Lord Diplock, as he now is, would concede that that is an unusual case.

But the enthusiasm of the dealer in that case did not bind the finance house. In *Andrews* v. *Hopkinson* (*1957*) *1 Q.B. 229*, Mr Justice MacNair had ruled that a hirer had a remedy against the dealer himself for representations made warranting the condition of a car taken on hire purchase. The dealer had told the customer:

> '*It's a good little bus. I would stake my life on it.*'

It is as well that he did not, for the steering broke and it crashed and injured the customer. The legal logic of the decision has been doubted, but in the 1964 Act, and again in that of 1965, Parliament made finance houses liable for the sales talk of the dealers. They are made agents of the companies by sections *12*, *16* and *31* of the 1965 Act. It also covers credit sale transactions up to £30. There is no corresponding protection for the dealer, and so if he is worth suing he can be. The agency makes the finance house responsible for 'representations' which includes any undertaking or statement whether or not it is a condition or warranty. A condition is an essential element of the contract, and a warranty is a collateral statement for breach of which damages can be recovered. Breach of a condition brings the contract to an end if the innocent party so desires. Furthermore, the *Misrepresentation Act, 1967* now gives a right to damages even for innocent misrepresentations as a result of which someone is induced to make a contract. The inflationary effect of all this consumer protection must be considerable. The finance houses and dealers probably just charge more in order to buffer their losses from successful complaints.

Dealers are also made agents for the purposes of receiving notices of cancellation and return of the goods where agreements are signed at any place other than 'appropriate trade premises'. This is the celebrated 'cooling off period' enacted in 1964 to protect the public from itself.

For four days after the receipt of the second statutory copy of the agreement, the customer can repent the bargain and cancel the transaction. The theory is that the wife signs the form to get the salesman off the doorstep and that the husband comes home and says he does not want the encyclopaedia. Few motor cars are sold in this fashion. It may be a nice question whether, from the aesthetic viewpoint, a motor dealer's premises are 'appropriate', but this provision is unlikely to bother them a great deal.

Of course, by *s. 27* of the 1965 Act, the hirer can always, right up to the last instalment, terminate a hire purchase agreement. In the Depression, I believe, finance companies in America were besieged by wives begging them to repossess the families' cars to buy bread. Without the statute, a finance company could hold a hirer to the contract. He has to give notice to anyone entitled to receive payments, and then by *s. 28* must pay up the balance of half the hire purchase price. If the agreement specifies a smaller amount, he must pay that. But I know no instance of a smaller amount being payable. If the customer has not taken reasonable care of the goods, the finance company can get damages against him for their loss thereby caused.

All of this difficulty is avoided when the transaction is by credit sale over £30 or personal loan (usually by promissory note). The property in the goods having passed to the customer on completion of the sale, the finance company can get money judgment for defaults and enforce it with bankruptcy or distress proceedings. The law regards these transactions as *ejusdem generis* those transactions—nowadays increasingly rare—where a purchaser with money in his hand buys and pays for and takes delivery of an article available for sale.

Where a seller agrees to deliver goods pursuant to such a contract, he can be made to pay damages for late delivery. A tradesman might need his new van for work on Monday morning, and if he has to lose trade or hire a replacement, he can recover his loss from the motor agent who has broken the contract of sale. Conversely, then, the purchaser does not take delivery when the ordered vehicles is tendered, he breaks the contract. With highly desirable cars in short supply after the War, dealers were grateful for the breach of such contracts for there were plenty of *nouveau riche* willing to pay over the odds, and freedom of contract, as we all know, is a sacred principle. Nowadays very few cars are so desirable that the demands of the export market make them worth paying too much for. Motor dealers, therefore, incline to legal action against people who order cars and then do not want them. In the ordinary theory of the law, damages for breach of contract are such as flow naturally from the breach (*Hadley* v. *Baxendale* [*1854*] *9 Exch. 341*). If the dealer sells the car elsewhere, the damages would therefore be his actual loss, i.e. the amount by which he lost on the sale compared to the contract sale, and some damages for the extra time he had the machine on his hands including storage, or interest on capital. But in *W. L. Thompson* v. *Robinson* (*Gunmakers*) *Ltd.* (*1955*) *Ch. 177*, Mr Justice Upjohn, as he then was, held that the dealer could recover the profit he lost on the contract sale even though he eventually sold the vehicle to someone else, or returned it to the main agent without being charged any damages in turn for breach of contract. *Section 50* of the *Sale of Goods Act* provides that the damages are the loss 'directly and naturally resulting' in the ordinary course of events from the breach of contract by the buyer.

Whether or not they understand the nature of the liability for failure to complete the contract, or wish to return the goods after taking delivery, purchasers often put forward some justification for doing so. These are often described by lawyers who should know better as 'fundamental breaches of the contract'.

Now a contract comprises various conditions either expressly provided for or implicit. If I order a white Triumph car with black seats, and the dealer tenders a white Rover with black seats it is obvious that he has not fulfilled the contract. However excellent the Rover, it is not a Triumph. The non-fulfilment is exactly the same if the Triumph tendered is green with red seats. It may be difficult to get the required colours, and many dealers wisely take several choices in order of preference from the customer. The tender of goods not according to the provision of the contract is not performance, and they cannot legally be foisted upon the purchaser. For the sake of getting something he was promised months ago he might accept them, but that is a variation.

Nor is the mere fact that a car will not go necessarily a breach of contract if the right car is tendered. It might need only petrol or some minor adjustment. Nevertheless the public are so fickle that even in straightforward sales, motor dealers often put on the back of their invoices conditions of sale. Other business people do likewise. Quite often the conditions are recorded on the back of a receipt. I have never understood, but will listen to an explanation, how it can be that conditions are imported into a contract which does not come to the notice of the purchaser except on the back of a piece of paper which he only received when the contract was concluded and the price paid. No doubt the doctrine of fundamental breach of contract has developed in the cause of side-stepping such hair-splitting. But it arises most often in conflict with exclusion clauses. These are perfectly lawful. It is not only possible but highly desirable that people should be free to agree to buy things as they stand, and without any warranty or condition attaching to the sale. Many a bargain has been picked up under such an arrangement.

The philosophy of fundamental breach, however, can override a perfectly proper exclusion clause. The reasoning is: granted that it is possible to exclude liability for a particular defect or defects; the defect here is so serious that the article is unusable and so the contract is completely nullified. The question therefore becomes: how bad is that bad? But it becomes confused when lawyers ask: 'Is this a fundamental breach?' before finding out if it is a breach at all. A car might be in an awful, unsafe, useless condition. But so long as no condition can be implied that it is roadworthy and usable, no action will lie. The price is an important indication of the usefulness of a car, or any other article.

In *Karsales (Harrow)* v. *Wallis (1956) 1 W.L.R. 936*, there were many old parts on the car where there had been new when it was taken on hire. As an emphatic indication that the hirer was supposed to put up with what he had agreed to hire, it was delivered at night to his house. The engine would not run at all; in all the condition was held to be such that the contract was fundamentally broken. Notwithstanding this precedent, in *Yeoman Credit Ltd.* v. *Apps (1961) 3 W.L.R.* a car was again returned to a dissatisfied customer during the hours of darkness. The dealer had promised certain repairs because the clutch, steering and brakes were so bad that the customer had taken an hour and a half to cover three miles. When the finance company sent a man to repossess it, he could not get it going. Again, fundamental breach was found proved.

A Little Knowledge Is
A Dangerous Thing

'The Common Law ought never to produce a wholly unreasonable result.'
Lord Reid in *Cartledge* **v.** *Topling (1963) A.C. p. 772.*

WHEN MRS SAYERS spent a penny in Harlow she did not appreciate that a chain reaction was set in motion which raised fundamental questions of the theory of the English law. Like the three old ladies, she was locked in, and might very well have stayed there from Saturday to Monday. Certainly, nobody knew she was there, even though she shouted out for about a quarter of an hour. An active woman, she deemed that the moment for self help had arrived.

The door was seven feet high but there was a space more than two feet deep over it, through which she might escape. She stood on the lavatory seat, and held on to the cistern pipe. Then she grasped the top of the door and put her right foot on the lavatory paper roll fastened to the wall. She was not up to the traverse from there to the top of the door, and had decided to descend when the roll of paper revolved, and she fell to the floor, injuring herself.

She sued the Harlow Urban District Council for damages for the injury. The judge of the County Court held that the Council were in breach of their duty as occupiers of the public lavatory, in having a defective lock on the cubicle. But the cause of her injury, he said, was her own dangerous action.

She appealed, and she won.

> '. . . *what she did was to explore the possibility of climbing over the door. That I cannot think was unwise or imprudent, or rash or stupid,*'

said Lord Justice Morris (*[1958] 1 W.L.R. 623*).

She was, however, one quarter to blame. The processes by which such judgments are arrived at mystify a great many people. Many of those people are lawyers. A person with a good memory can learn the principles of the law of torts. But he can never be very sure which principles will turn out to be the decisive ones in any particular case. It probably would not help much to have a code. The American Restatement of the Law of Torts occupies four main volumes and several supplements. The word itself is French, and means 'wrong'. The French do not have a law of tort.

In the *Code Napoleon* of 1804, Article 1382 provides:

> *'Every act whatever of man which causes damage to another binds the person whose fault it was to repair it.'*

The four succeeding Articles wrap up the whole subject. But they do not tell anyone how to divine what is the 'cause' which gives rise to the 'fault'. It may be utterly reprehensible in the Harlow Urban District Council to have dud locks on its lavatories, but it is not immediately apparent that that circumstance drives ladies to fall off toilet rolls. And it is by no means unusual for there to be more than one 'cause' of something happening. If I am run over at an accident 'black spot' the immediate cause is either that I did wrong, or the driver did wrong, or that it was a pure accident. A cause is that I had occasion to go to that place and cross the road.

One of the causes might therefore be that they sell the kind of bacon I like at Sainsbury's. But Sainsbury's would be very annoyed if I sued them because I was run over crossing to their shop. The courts do have to contend with this kind of reasoning. In *Stapley* v. *Gypsum Mines Ltd.* (*1953*) *A.C. 633*) the plaintiff's husband was killed by a fall of roof in a tunnel. He and his mate had seen the dangerous rock and tried to bring it down to make the roof safe. They could not manage it and so presumably thought it was safe. A little later it fell and killed Mr Stapley. The company's argument really seemed to be that it was not an unsafe system of working which led to the tragedy, but that the cause was that he was underneath the rock when it fell. Newton's law rather than Common Law.

The classification of causes is usually into 'proximate' causes and others, or *causa causans* as opposed to *causa sine qua non* in spite of Lord Shaw of Dunfermline's dictum that 'the day for canonising Latin phrases has gone past'. But even when you have isolated the *causa causans* you have to establish that it was 'wrong' in order to get damages. And it is in this sphere that the modern cases involving negligence and nuisance and the breaches of legal duties become confused by comparison with the old Common Law wrongs. They have a simplicity and directness lacking in modern wrongs. The man who called Robese Bindebeau a whore had to pay threepence damages in the church court, seven centuries before the *Slander of Women Act, 1892*, made an imputation of immorality in a woman actionable without proof of actual damage.

One Shepherd, 'a man not destitute of humour', was celebrating 'the happy deliverance of King James I', i.e. Guy Fawkes' Night, though he may have been affected not only by 'pious and patriotic spirit' when he threw the firework on the gingerbread man's booth in 1773 (*2 W. Bl. 892*).

The gingerbread vendor 'caught it dexterously and threw it away from him. It then fell on the shed of another gingerbread seller who passed it on in precisely the same way; till at last it burst in the plaintiff's face and put his eye out.'

Shepherd argued that he was not responsible when the squib had been through so many hands, 'but though he persuaded the learned Mr Justice Blackstone to agree with him, the majority of the court decided that he must be 'presumed to have contemplated all the consequences of his wrongful act, and was answerable for them', according to the 1903 edition of *Shirley's Leading Cases*.

Lord Radcliffe took a typically sanguine line about responsibility for negligence.

> '*There is certainly no turpitude involved in a failure to observe that standard of care, which after full inquiry, a court of law may find to have been the appropriate measure . . . Nor are the rules that determine them exactly graven on tables of stone.*'
> **Workington Dock and Harbour Board v. S.S. Towerfield (Owners) 1951 A.C. 112 @ 160.**

We know then that boorish behaviour is 'wrong'. But what about all the unintentionally inflicted discomforts? Lord Atkin was forced to admit:

> '*It is remarkable how difficult it is to find in the English authorities statements of general application defining the relations between parties that give rise to the duty of care.*'
> **Donoghue v. Stevenson (1932) A.C.**

Actually, it is relatively easy to find general statements, and equally easy to find contradictions. For negligence is a very modern legal wrong. Assaults and trespasses and slanders were remedied in the primitive tribunals of olden days but the idea that mere carelessness should be compensated grew only slowly. Few people sued the Regency Bucks for running them down during those drunken coach races along the Brighton Road. It could be done, but most judges would have thrown a case out, as was done in *Holmes* v. *Mather* (see p. 31).

> '*A party is not to cast himself upon an obstruction which has been made by the fault of another and avail himself of it, if he did not himself use common and ordinary caution to be in the right. One*

person being in fault will not dispense with another's using ordinary care for himself.'

Lord Ellenborough in *Forrester* **v.** *Butterfield (11 East 60).*

'Where there is a right there is a remedy' does not mean, 'Where there is a wrong there is a remedy'. You get no damages for a wrong unless you can show that the law gives you a right to them, because you were not entirely to blame and someone else was to some extent to blame. Miss M'Allister knew nothing of this when her boy friend Mr Donoghue bought her a bottle of ginger beer at Minchella's Café at Paisley. She drank a glass of it and when the rest was poured out there—hitherto concealed by the dark glass of the bottle—were the decomposed remains of a snail. She was nauseated, and suffered from shock and gastro-enteritis, according to her Statement of Claim.

Now it was clear that an action would lie at the suit of a purchaser of the polluted mineral water from a person whose business it was to sell it. The *Sale of Goods Act, 1893,* took care of that. But she was not the purchaser, merely his girl friend. She could not sue in contract but had to call in aid the law of tort, which as we have seen is a mispronunciation of the French for 'wrong', meaning 'right'. A preliminary question of law was taken up to the House of Lords before the case was tried, just to see whether such a claim could be entertained at law. Everyone knew that Baron Alderson in the Case of the Defective Stop Cock had defined negligence in law as:

'The omission to do something which a reasonable man, guided upon those considerations which ordinarily regulate the conduct of human affairs would do, or doing something which a prudent and reasonable man would not do.'

Blyth v. Birmingham Waterworks Co. (1856) 11 Ex. 781.

But does the reasonable man have to consider other people besides those he is actually dealing with? Is he to pause before he does anything and work out all the possible ramifications of his action?

'The rule that you are to love your neighbour becomes, in law, you must not injure your neighbour; and the lawyer's question, Who is my neighbour? receives a restricted reply. You must take reasonable care to avoid acts or omissions which you can reasonably foresee would be likely to injure your neighbour. Who, then, in law is my neighbour? The answer seems to be—persons who are so closely and directly affected by my act that I ought reasonably to have them in contemplation as being so affected when I am directing my mind to the acts or omissions which are called in question.'

Lord Atkin, *Donoghue* v. *Stevenson* (1932) A.C. 562.

She was therefore entitled to bring her action, and she did. Ten years later, in his Presidential Address to the Holdsworth Club, Lord Justice Mackinnon revealed something not generally realised south of the Border:

> *'To be quite candid, I detest that snail. At the trial, it was found that there never was a snail in the bottle at all.'*

Before getting down to the Neighbour Principle, Lord Atkin had let drop a sentence which might give a better clue to the real nature of the secret of legal liability.

> *'The liability for negligence, whether you style it such or treat it as in other systems as a species of culpa, is no doubt based on a general public sentiment of moral wrongdoing for which the offender must pay.'*

He hastened to add that objects of moral censure could not all be compensated in a practical world. Had he not, the celebrated case of Mr Pickles would not be still the law. He purposely and maliciously excavated his land in order to prevent the underground flow of water into the reservoir operated by the Mayor, Aldermen and Burgesses of Bradford. His reason was simple. It was to force them to buy him out at his price. It was blackmail. But Lord Watson said in the House of Lords in the Corporation's action (*[1895] A.C. 598*).

> *'No use of property which would be legal if due to a proper motive can become illegal because it is prompted by a motive which is improper or even malicious.'*

This has been described as 'the consecration of the spirit of unrestricted egoism'. Apart from that, it is a little odd that if a man like Mr Pickles damages a lot of people intentionally, he should escape liability; whilst many people who have no intention of injuring anyone in any way are daily held liable for damage. Lord Macnaghten appeared a little restricted in his view of Mr Pickles.

> *'He may be churlish, selfish and grasping. His conduct may seem shocking to a moral philosopher. But where is the malice?'*

That is not eclecticism. The rise of a litigious bourgeiosie had introduced such pace and variety into the law that almost for the first time the philosophical principles underlying the law were being considered by the judges. Briefless barristers wrote books about the law of civil wrongs and avaricious publishers sold them at prices as high as a guinea. By the turn of the century there were two power-fully opposed camps. Professor Salmond wrote of the law of Torts (plural) as separate kinds of wrong recognised by the law. Sir Percy Winfield wrote of the law of Tort (singular) a system united by

323

principle. The controversy rages still in the University Common Rooms. Just as with a crime, does there have to be a mental element, some knowledge of what one is doing, to make something 'wrong'. By its very nature, negligence is unintentional, but the law presumes that you should have known what you were doing. This is quite common in the older torts like conversion. If you used someone else's things as if they were your own, you could not deny liability. If you merely used them, but did not treat them as yours you could. Whether you did one or the other is a question of inferences at which judges are superb performers. The ability to infer better than anyone else is the genius of the eminent judge.

Unfortunately the Snail Case does not tell you exactly how to work out whether something will do a wrong to someone. That is a matter for inference, and the difficulty of measuring a reasonable degree of foresight, or care, or likelihood, is great.

> '*A greater risk of injury is not the same thing as a risk of greater injury.*'
>
> **Lord Justice Asquith,** *Paris* v. *Stepney Borough Council (1950) 1 K.B. 320.*

The matter is further complicated by the infinite variety of circumstances and personal knowledge which arise in negligence cases. The art of presenting and resisting them lies in working out arguments to make the obvious seem obscure and vice versa. After all, Lemuel Gulliver was made by Swift to inform the Houyhnhnms that a class of men existed in his land who devoted their lives to proving that black is white.

Academic lawyers write articles in the reviews about The Concept of Risk, and it is no mere intellectual exercise. Always there are binding precedents to distort the most promising theory. Consider those affecting the liability for the owners and keepers of animals. Mr and Mrs Behrens were midgets appearing in a booth at Bertram Mills' Circus. The booth operator's little dog ran out and barked and snapped at some passing elephants, one of which knocked down the booth and sat on Mrs Behrens.

> '*The elephant Bullu is in fact no more dangerous than a cow . . . But I am compelled to assess the Defendants' liability in this case in just the same way as I would assess it if they had loosed a wild elephant into the fun fair.*'
>
> **Mr Justice Devlin** *(1957) 2 Q.B. 1.*

The reason was that elephants were declared to be wild animals by the Court of Appeal in *Filburn* v. *People's Palace and Aquarium Co. Ltd. (1890) 25 Q.B.D. 258.* In 1953 a committee recommended that such presumptions should be abolished and the doctrine of 'reasonable care' applied to liability for animals. The *Animals Act, 1971*, has altered the Common Law rules 'imposing a strict liability for damage done by an animal on the ground that it is regarded as *ferae naturae* or that its vicious or mischievous propensities are known or presumed to be known' by its keeper.

The new rules are a kind of Albert Ramsbottom arrangement by which the keeper of a 'dangerous animal' is automatically liable for the damage it causes unless the damage is wholly due to the victim's fault. No liability is created for damage caused by an animal not of a dangerous species unless the damage is such as it is likely to cause or likely to be severe and the beast has characteristics different from other animals of the species, which were known to the keeper or the people for whom he is responsible. All of which should make very little difference to dog-biting cases. And it was the little dog that caused the trouble in the Behrens' case.

Objectivity is not logical in considering likely causes.

> '*If a person wakes up in the middle of the night and finds an escaping tiger on top of his bed and suffers a heart attack, it would be nothing to the point that the intentions of the tiger were quite amiable,*'

said Mr Justice Devlin in Behrens' Case.

Such a person's widow might well recover under the Animals Act. He can hardly be said to be at fault for having a weak heart. But what if he has a strong one and leaps out of bed either to trap the beast and return it to its owner or merely to escape in case it is not amiable? No doubt some counsel will be found for the menagerie's insurers to argue that his being rent limb from limb was entirely his own fault.

It will cast upon him the duty of exercising reasonable foreseeability as to the likely reaction of the tiger. Now reasonable foreseeability is probably the great underlying principle of the law which all the academics are seeking. It has caused a great deal of trouble. Some Arab stevedores at Casablanca were unloading the *Polemis* in 1917, and one dropped a wooden plank into a hold. It must have caught a piece of cargo and toppled it over so that a friction spark was struck. The hold happened to be heavy with petrol fumes, and the resultant explosion and fire damaged the ship. The owners were awarded £196,165 for the loss of nearly two years' charter, and so it is easy to understand why so many important lawsuits involve ships. They are well worth risking the costs about. The argument against liability was the sound enough one that sparks do not fly from wooden planks. But it failed. The charterers were made liable for the negligence of the stevedore even though the result was not foreseeable, because it was a direct consequence of the negligence.

Whilst the law about establishing liability for a negligent act or omission remained like that for forty years, the second important question, whether the damage claimed for was to be compensated, or was 'too remote', was governed by the foreseeability test. Millions of pounds have been expended in litigation over these two conflicting principles. Now they are technically reconciled, and foreseeability has prevailed, but at the expense of saddling the country with several thousand confused lawyers.

The vessel of reform was the dredger *Liesbosh* which was engaged on a contract for dredging the harbour at Patras when the defendants' ship rammed and sunk her. She had cost £4,000. The owners hired a replacement for a while for £6,839, which they then bought for £9,177 having in the meantime incurred sundry overheads of about £3,000, all of which they claimed, with interest. The defendants argued plausibly enough that having sunk a £4,000 dredger that was all they should pay. This kind of argument takes place daily in County Courts over the values of highly cherished motor cars maintained in 'showroom condition' by ardent and sometimes professional engineer owners. The dredger owners protested that they had been unable to replace it immediately, being 'financially beggared' by the loss of the *Liesbosch*.

> *'If I may venture to summarise and paraphrase the defendants' argument, it was that damages in law are awarded by way of restitution and not in relief of destitution,'*

said Mr Justice Langton.

He declined to strain his imagination after 'a notional phantom which will when intellectually captured be recognisable as the Normal Dredger Owner'.

> *'I can imagine few things more maddeningly provoking than to be called upon as a consequence of sinking a somewhat elderly dredger to pay a sum amounting to more than twice her value when generously computed.'*

He therefore followed the *Polemis* principle and gave damages for the direct consequences of the sinking. That, said the House of Lords, was wrong. But the reason they gave was that the cause of the damage was wrongly assessed. The owners of the *Liesbosch* had been involved in all that expense not just by the sinking but because they were too poor to buy another dredger straightaway. They rather implied that it is contributory negligence not to be able to replace your dredger immediately someone sinks it.

In 1961, the Judicial Committee of the Privy Council had another ship fire case, from Australia. The *Wagon Mound* was bunkering in Sydney Harbour. A thin film of oil spread on the water. Some welders on the plaintiffs' dock with great care inquired whether the oil would take fire from the welding sparks and in accordance with the finest scientific advice they were informed that the oil would not ignite. But some of the molten metal set on fire some cotton waste which burned on the oily water long enough to ignite the film of oil, and the plaintiffs' dock was burnt down.

Said Lord Simons:

> '. . . the authority of Polemis has been severely shaken though lip-service has from time to time been paid to it.
>
> 'After the event, even a fool is wise. But it is not the hindsight of a fool; it is the foresight of the Reasonable Man which alone can determine responsibility.'

How would one recognise a Reasonable Man as one's Neighbour?

It is curious, if not downright paradoxical, that judges—and rarely nowadays juries—should have to observe the law that they decide a case on the evidence produced, but that their assessment of the effect of that evidence should be pure conjecture. For very often they have to say to themselves: 'We know what these particular people did do. How do we guess what a reasonable man would do?' What kind of fellow is the Reasonable Man?'

Dr Richard Thorold Grant was one, even though he did not wash his vest and pants before he put them on. On 3rd June, 1931, just before we all became Neighbours, he went into the store of John Martin & Co. and bought two pairs of pants and two singlets in 'Golden Fleece' woollen material. This store was in Adelaide, South Australia, where of all places you would think you could not do better for woolly vests and pants. When he wore them he began to itch and his skin became inflamed.

In Australia they had a *Sale of Goods Act*, very much like ours and the good doctor claimed damages under *s. 14* for the injury. He had, remember, bought the goods himself. The investigations showed that his irritation was caused by free bisulphate of soda in the garments, and *Donoghue* v. *Stevenson* having been decided by the time his case was tried, the court ruled that not only were the goods defective so that he could get damages from the store, but the makers, Australian Knitting Mills Ltd. were also liable to him for negligence in not removing the sulphites in manufacture. Even though the sale contract was with the store and not with them.

This is a useful doctrine, because shopkeepers might not have insurance and might also be too poor to pay heavy damages. Large manufacturers might well be a sounder bet. The makers appealed to the Privy Council, insisting that their factory was thoroughly modern and that they had sold a million pairs of pants without complaint. Furthermore, those pants the doctor bought came out of a packet of six and the others were all right. They were completely ignorant of the excess sulphites. Overlooking the fact that Dr Grant was, too, they said he should have washed them before wearing.

'It was not contemplated that they should be first washed,'

retorted Lord Wright *(1936) A.C. p. 105.*

'If excess sulphites were left in the garment that could only be because someone was at fault,'

said Lord Macmillan.

But they held that a purchaser—or anyone else—injured by goods in a similar fashion, could recover damages only where the defect was hidden and unknown to the customer or consumer. But they made the manufacturer liable even though he, too, was ignorant. You can blame a ginger beer maker for snails in his bottles. You can blame a vest maker for something mysteriously in his vests. Dr Grant kept his £2,000 damages. The Reasonable Man, according to Lord Macmillan, must be presumed to be free from over-apprehension and from over-confidence. Farmer Menlove had a hayrick on his place in Shropshire which began smoking and gave every sign of spontaneous combustion. When his neighbour, Mr Vaughan pointed out the danger, he said 'Nonsense, I'll chance it'. The chance to which he referred, said Chief Justice Tindal in the Common Pleas Court in 1837, was the fact that he was insured in case the rick took fire, which it did even though—or perhaps because too late—he made a chimney through the rick. Mr Vaughan's cottages were burnt, because, said Tindal C.J. Menlove had not observed 'common prudence and foresight'.

An error of judgment, 'of itself', is not negligence. Lord Oaksey said so in *Latimer* v. *A.E.C. Ltd. (1953) A.C. 643.* Day in and day out this is argued as a defence in cases involving criticism of car drivers. But even when done with sufficient clarity to make it intelligible to lay magistrates it seldom succeeds, for an error of judgment can be negligence if it is an error a reasonable driver would not make *(Simpson* v. *Peat [1952] 2 Q.B. 24).*

'The standard of foresight of the reasonable man eliminates the personal equation and is independent of the idiosyncrasies of the particular person whose conduct is in question. Some persons are by nature unduly timorous and imagine every path beset by lions; others of a more robust temperament fail to foresee or nonchalantly disregard even the most obvious dangers.'

Lord Macmillan in Glasgow Corporation v. Muir (1943) A.C. 448.

This paragon has been variously described. 'The man who takes the magazines at home, and in the evenings pushes the lawn mower in his shirt sleeves' was an American variant on Lord Bowen's 'Man on the Clapham omnibus' which was also used to describe the person whose judgment would be the criterion of the fairness of a theatrical criticism in *McQuire* v. *Western Morning News* (*1903*) *2 K.B.* 100.

Another Scottish opinion required that he is cool, calm and collected and takes safety measures even in emergencies (*Ghannan* v. *Glasgow Corporation* [*1950*] *S.C. 23*). This conflicts with Lord Justice James's notion

> '*You have no right to expect men to be something more than ordinary men.*'
>
> *(1879) 4 P.D. 219.*

Mr Justice Maugham said that the law demands the standards 'of men, not angels' (*Jupiter & General Insurance Co.* v. *Shroff* [*1938*] *3 All E.R. 67*).

The *Interpretation Act, 1939* provides that in general the masculine shall include the feminine, but to the Common Law, apparently, there is no such thing as a Reasonable Woman. There was no debate about her capacity for seeing into the future in *Stone* v. *Bolton* (*1950*) *1 K.B. 201*. It was apparently taken for granted that she was perfectly entitled to stand on her own doorstep, outside a cricket ground, 100 yards from the wicket and protected by a 17 feet high fence round the ground. She was hit by a cricket ball. Cricket is much better catalogued and annotated than the Law Reports. There is even a book which records the cricketing performances of Lawyer–Cricketers in their clubs and universities! From the score books it appeared that only six times in the previous 30 years had such mighty sixes been struck. This was no doubt present to the mind of Lord Radcliffe during his speech in the House of Lords (1951) *A.C. 850*. He said that a Reasonable Man would neither have stopped using the ground for cricket nor would he put up higher fences.

> '*He would have done what the Appellants did; in other words, he would have done nothing.*'

Thus by the dominant juridical philosophy of the twentith century, we are all neighbours, if not friends and must behave reasonably. Which often means it is best to do nothing at all. Indeed, officious interference is pointedly discouraged. Neighbourliness gives rise to duty—recognised in the Ten Commandments. But forseeability demands that the duty be father to the relationship. Logicians might demonstrate the falsity of *post hoc, ergo propter hoc* but for the lawyer seeking an explanation of social responsibility, it replaces the privity of contract as the foundation of a duty. Actual geographical neighbours have always had duties *quoad* each other. Exactly what they are has always been a problem to divine, and it is always a nuisance to have to decide whether one's discomfort is something to be alleviated by good nature or by standing on one's rights. The use of the ordinary word 'nuisance' to describe a phenomenon actionable at law is confusing. The lawyer's definition of a private nuisance is even more so. 'An interference with the enjoyment of land' is only true if you qualify 'interference', 'land' and especially 'enjoyment'.

'Land' is of course, houses and buildings of all kinds as well as the territory on which they stand. But there are grave diminutions of its enjoyment which afford no remedy at law. There is, for instance, no remedy for a spoilt view. 'Such things of delight' are not protected by the Common Law (*Aldred's Case* [*1611*] *9 Coke's Reports, 58a*). The great legislative code of Town and Country Planning Control, and the National Parks, and Civic Amenities legislation seek to provide an overall benefit without leaving any rights of action between neighbours. It is cogently argued that such laws ensure the ruination of many a view. Regrettable though that may be, since there never has been a right to a view, who is thereby prejudiced?

You cannot make a nasty neighbour take down a fence or wall which shuts out a pleasant aspect from your windows. In *Potts* v. *Smith* (*1868*) *L.R. Eq. 311*, the fence was 23 feet high. Nowadays you need planning permission for a fence over ten feet high. If a man builds a high fence, with permission, the local planning authority probably will not ask the neighbours whether they mind it being built. On the other hand, if the neighbours complain to the officials about his fence, and the builder has not got planning permission for it, the officials will be able to prevent him keeping it there. Public inquiries for such things as fences are so rare as to be virtually unknown.

A footnote in Salmond postulates that the biggest 'spite fence' in the western world is a handsome terrace of six-storey houses on Dublin Bay, built expressly for the purpose of ruining the view from a nobleman's country house. But such things are often, from a majority viewpoint, desirable. The complainer is a lone voice. Tall buildings invade privacy by overlooking. You will look vainly for textbook references to a law against overlooking. Nevertheless there is a vociferous minority determined to legislate for a law of Privacy of indeterminate extent. There was once a law against overlooking, or at any rate, there might have been. Eighteenth-century cases seemed to support the proposition that a householder could be prevented from making new windows in a blank wall which would overlook his neighbour's domestic regions. But the court decided emphatically in *Turner* v. *Spooner* (*1861*) *30 L.J. Ch. 801* that no such right exists at Common Law or in Equity.

Suppose, however, that such windows be constructed in a wall which forms the boundary. If they are of the casement type, the encroachment into the air space of the neighbouring tenement when they are opened is a trespass. No injunction could be obtained to prevent the making of the windows, but one could be secured to prevent them being opened. Sash windows, or sliding windows, could of course be opened with impunity. And those very windows could acquire for the property which they lit and ventilated, the long-recognised rights of 'light and air'. The diminution thereof is a wrong which can be restrained and for which compensation can be awarded. Should such a right be acquired by the requisite length of usage the question whether a legally remediable infringement of it has occurred might lead to protracted and complex litigation. For the infringement will be found an action only when it is substantial. In a light case, the evidence might well be of photographers' light-meter readings at different hours of the day and different seasons and different conditions of weather and cloud cover. These will be tabulated for the various apartments affected, and readings will be made at several different spots in each room on each occasion. From these statistics it will be possible to compute some mean value of the amount of light which exists at particular hours of the day in each room. Then by a daunting trigonometrical calculation, the effect in diminution of light caused by the structure complained about can be made. This has to be done for each room.

If the structure's shadow is such as to reduce by a third the light which would otherwise come to the windows a remedy might be given. Injunctions are discretionary and depend on the 'balance of convenience'. The offending building might not have to be pulled down—damages could be given instead for the loss of the amenity of light. Putting a board on your wall saying 'Ancient Lights' does not create the right. It merely gives notice to all and sundry that you claim such a right. It certainly does not turn anything built in front of your window into an infringement of your rights.

Insult adds to injury if what is built enables you to be overlooked by highly-placed occupiers. Binocular sales in the high-block districts of our cities are booming. That of course is not eaves-dropping. The 1361 statute making that a crime affects only Peeping Toms under the eaves, not in the next-door tower block. But it could be a private nuisance whilst yet again it might not be. It is not always possible to state with absolute certainty what a judge might call a nuisance. Kenny's *Cases on Tort, 4th ed. (1926)* mentions a case in which a Balham dentist sued his neighbours in 1904 over the 'annoyance and indignity' they caused him by rigging up an arrangement of large mirrors in their garden to look into his premises. But he lost, there being no right of action. Only five years earlier, some trade unionists were successfully sued for a private nuisance by 'watching and besetting' premises.

The flexibility of the Common Law is the hall-mark of its superiority.

The Duke of Buccleuch failed to establish against the Metropolitan Board of Works any remedy for the loss of his privacy caused by the construction of a new road [*1870*] *L.R. 5 Ex. 221*). Ministries and municipalities enjoy that protection for all their invasions. If a Duke cannot establish a right in tort, lesser folk have little chance. The Duke of Rutland succeeded against Mr Harrison who stayed on the road to frighten the Duke's grouse ([*1893*] *1 Q.R. 142*). But that was because the Duke owned the moor over which the road was made. Harrison became a trespasser to the soil by abusing the road. Had the Duke owned only half the width of the road (as so many freeholds of subsoil extend) Harrison could have gone on to the other side of the road, and escaped liability. In *Hickman* v. *Maisey* (*1900*) *1 Q.B.*, a racehorse trainer successfully sued a man who moved up and down the road taking notes and timing horses in training. But again, the trainer owned the soil of the road.

You do not have to own the land to sue in nuisance. Being entitled to occupation is enough. But it is definitely a right of action dependent on property. English law is rooted in landholding. So powerful is the protection for the landed person that he is protected—when he *is* protected—against nuisances which existed before he had the property. This is, after all, only logical. If the fumes from my smelting works have wafted for years across the plot of land you buy, they have harmed no one. But when you build your new house, they are a nuisance to you. If I say you should not have come there, I am not minding my own business. If you chose to buy from your vendor, that was between you and him, and none of my business. I cannot plead Pickles' Case. He was doing as he was entitled to on his own land. My fumes are coming off my land on to yours. I am therefore a tortfeasor, and the law will not listen to me when I say you knew about my fumes when you came. Said Mr Justice Byles in *Hole* v. *Barlow* (*1858*) *27 L.J.C.P. 208*, it is no answer to an action for nuisance that the plaintiff knew there was a nuisance* and yet went voluntarily and pitched his tent near it.

Similarly, the defendant cannot say that the source of the nuisance is a reasonable use of his property.

---

* But tents are public nuisances and their occupants can be dealt with under the *Vagrancy Act, 1824*.

'If a man creates a nuisance, he cannot say that he is acting reasonably. The two things are self-contradictory.'

Mr Justice Kekewitch, *Attorney-General* **v.** *Cole (1901)* **2 Ch. 205.**

If it is no defence that the plaintiff came to the nuisance; nor that he was using his land reasonably, e.g. for burning bricks, which caused noxious vapours, how can a man ever defend an action of nuisance? It is arguing circularly, but the answer is that he can show it is not a nuisance. And the test is reasonableness. Once make a thing a nuisance, and the fact that it is reasonable use is no defence. But you must be reasonable in the criteria by which you decide whether something is a nuisance.

'That may be a nuisance in Grosvenor Square which would be none in Smithfield Market, that may be a nuisance at mid-day which would not be so at mid-night, that may be a nuisance which is permanent and continual and which would be no nuisance if temporary or occasional only.'

Chief Baron Pollock (dissenting) in *Bamford* **v.** *Turnley* **(1862) 3 B. & S. 66.**

But just as the reasonableness of the use to which the defendant puts his land is of itself irrelevant if a nuisance is created, so, equally logically,

'The law still is that any person who actually creates a nuisance is liable for it and for the consequences which flow from it, whether he be negligent or not.'

Mr Justice Devlin in *Farrell* **v.** *John Mowlem & Co. Ltd.* **1 Lloyd's Rep. 437.**

Can it be that I am defenceless against my neighbour's complaints? It can, but it does not necessarily follow. Important distinctions of detail enable apparently conflicting decisions to be made. When counsel in a nuisance action adopted a man of the world attitude to the tiresomeness of car doors banging and engines starting up, he put in the other side of the balance, a few years back, the great convenience of having a garage and service station in the basement of the particular block of luxury flats in West London. 'Those of us who live in flats in London . . .' began the judge. Nuisance is a subjective test.

Mr Soltau complained that when the Redemptorist Fathers moved into the house next door to his in Clapham, they 'rang a harsh and discordant bell at the most unnecessary times'. He spoke for the neighbours when he said that it

'is offensive alike to our ears and feelings; disturbs the quiet and comfort of our houses; molests us in our engagements, whether of

333

amusement, business or devotion; and is peculiarly injurious and distressing when members of our households happen to be invalids; it tends also to depreciate the value of our dwelling houses.'

Soltau v. De Held (1851) 21 L.J. Ch. 153.

Modern Clapham would be closer to the Smithfield end of the scale of values than to the Grosvenor Square end. How much the Redemptorists' bell had to do with it is inestimable. But Mr Soltau won. A similar decision today would be highly unlikely. A precedent is authority only for the principle which it decides. In litigation, analogy is a dangerous form of argument.

However, the most inexorable consequence flows from the rule that negligence is irrelevant to nuisance. It gives the complainer two strings to his bow. Either you were negligent in letting the thing cause me damage, or if you were not, it was a nuisance, is how he can put it. And he can sometimes put it all the more powerfully because the simple facts are very persuasive.

'Nothing could be simpler than the facts in this appeal; nothing more far-reaching than the discussion of the fundamental legal principles to which it has given rise.'

Lord Macmillan, Read v. J. Lyons & Co. (1947) A.C. 146.

Miss Read was a munitions inspector at Lyons' factory and was injured by an explosion.

'She said high explosive shells are "dangerous things" and the respondents knew it,'

was Lord Simonds' summary of her case. Now, a 'Dangerous Thing' is practically as much of an enigma as a Reasonable Man. The law with relation to liability for it is a development of the law of nuisance or negligence or of neither, flowing from a decision reported as *Rylands v. Fletcher (1868) L.R. 3 H.L. 330.* (It is gamesmanship of a high order to call it Fletcher and Rylands. It shows you know that in those days the appellant's name was put first, but that it has been altered because people got confused.)

It was Mr Rylands and his associates who needed a reservoir for their mill. They engaged a competent engineer and workmen to build it. During excavations, they found old vertical mineshafts and carefully filled them up. Nevertheless the water ran out of the reservoir through them and flooded Mr Fletcher's mines. It was not like Mr Pickles' case because although Rylands and Co. were doing as they were entitled to do on their own land, the water 'escaped' beyond their boundaries.

If the case had been heard today there is quite a good chance that the independent contractors would have been found negligent for not blocking off the mineshafts properly. But Lord Blackburn held it to be the Common Law that if for his own purposes a man brings something on to his land which is likely to do damage if it escapes, he does it at his peril and is liable for all the natural consequences of the escape. It is irrelevant whether he was at fault or blameless for the escape. The foundation of the rule is the tag *sic utere tuo ut alienam non laedas*—do as you like with your own so long as you do not damage other people.

Now whilst they are perfectly willing to make anyone liable if they think that he should pay, the judges in England regard their job as saying what the law is. They extend it only in so far as it is necessary for the expression of principle in the case with which they are concerned. And principle does not demand that wrongs should be multiplied unless the facts of new cases accord with earlier principles. And so Miss Read lost her action against Lyons. The House of Lords said that the explosion was not an escape because she was on Lyons' property when she was injured. Presumably if you are blown up just outside the factory, you or your relatives can recover damages, but not if you are inside when it blows up, or in other words, 'Abandon hope all ye that enter here.'

Read v. *Lyons* has been interpreted by some people as meaning that damages for personal injuries cannot be recovered in an action depending on *Rylands* v. *Fletcher*, but this is not so. What is clear is that occupiers of land can get such damages. The real point is whether it is a strict liability for nuisance, or for a kind of indefensible negligence in controlling 'Dangerous Things'. The class of such things is wide: a bit of rusty wire swallowed by a cow (*Firth* v. *Bowling Iron Co. 3 C.P.D. 254*); projecting branches of a yew tree eaten by a horse which was poisoned. (*Crowhurst* v. *Amersham Burial Board 4 Ex. D. 5.*) It was very nearly possible to find out if this case would stand up today. Three horses ate a great deal of yew in a case last year, but unfortunately for the legal theorists they did not die.

'Strict' liability can be imposed by Act of Parliament. It was a natural extension of the doctrine *res ipsa loquitur*. 'If that phrase had not been in Latin, no one would have called it a principle', said Lord Shaw in *Ballard* v. *North British Railway* (*1923*) *S.C. H.L. 43*. It means simply that 'the thing speaks for itself'. Its modern power is dependent on three cases decided between 1863 and 1871. Mr Byrne was walking past a flour dealer's warehouse when a sack of flour fell out of the loft on to him (*Byrne* v. *Boadle 33 L.J. Ex. 13*); Customs Officer Scott was similarly struck by a sack of sugar (*Scott* v. *St Katherines Dock* (*3 H. & C. 596*); and a brick from a railway bridge fell on Mr Kearney (*L.R. 6 Q.B. 759*). These instances of the operation of the law of gravity were imported into the Common

Law and deemed to be evidence of negligence. But they raised only a rebuttable presumption. If the person from whose premises they dropped could show that he was not in any way negligent, he could escape liability. Professor Fleming (*Law of Torts, 3rd Edn. 1965*) has pointed out that this actually is more effective than the strict liability doctrine. That has so many exceptions by reason of the ways Dangerous Things have been defined, and the requirement that the use of the land has to be 'non-natural' and that there has to be an 'escape' that, as the Law Commission has said, it 'seldom forms the basis of a successful claim in the courts'.

Now since 1966 we have become accustomed to the Law Commission taking problems apart and publishing learned analyses with 'suggested' Draft Bills by which the law can be improved. Parliament has gratefully nodded to all of these and it looked until 1970 as if the Rylands Rule would be next. The Commission had a sort of juristic Summit Conference at All Souls, and discussed their difficulty in recommending reform. It is therefore not without a spiteful sense of satisfaction that one records that Rylands and Fletcher has beaten the Law Commission. Their programme did not allow them to consider the effect on the law of personal injuries and they could not therefore recommend any overall reform. Accordingly they have left it as it is 'complex, uncertain and inconsistent in principle'. They closed ranks over speculation that they could not agree what the law was, let alone what it should be.

Where we shall look for relief now is anyone's guess. For as long ago as 1951 in *4. Current Legal Problems*, Professor Goodhart showed that in the American cases of strict liability the principle had been analysed as one of allocating the risk of liability to the person who created an unusual peril. Consequently, he should be liable for harm 'even though the immediate cause was an Act of God'.

No doubt there was healthy academic dissension among the Commissioners. But one cannot blame them for declining to legislate for the supernatural.

The impact of *Read* v. *Lyons* shows how pusillanimous is a high-explosive device when compared with a law, which is mere words. In his judgment, Lord Justice Scott showed that the law is concerned with arts.

Lord Justice Bowen, perhaps the most brilliant of the 19th Century Common Lawyers, observed that the law:

> '*does not consider that what a man writes on paper is like a gun or other dangerous instrument*'.
>
> *Le Lievre v. Gould (1893) 1 Q.B. at p. 501.*

Accordingly the surveyor in that case, was not liable for an inaccurate statement made merely carelessly. Fraudulent words were the stuff of the ancient wrong of deceit. But in the case which comes nearest to defining 'fraud'—*Derry* v. *Peek*, the Law Lords put such impossibly heavy burden of proof on the victims of the company promoters that virtual licence to defraud was created.

Parliament had to pass the *Directors' Liability Act* (now part of the *Companies Act*) to make directors responsible for the glowing prospectuses by which they parted gullible spectators from their fortunes.

Right up to 1964 there was considered to be no legal liability for a merely negligent wrong statement or 'innocent misrepresentation'. When it came, however, it was not the urgent legislation of reforming Parliamentarians but the Law Lords, who made it. Well, they did not so much make it as discover that it had been there all the time. The early 1960s was an Age of Discovery in the House of Lords with the rediscovery of *Unlawful Intimidation, and Conspiracies to Corrupt Public Morals* all being resurrected from the obscurity in which they had slumbered for centuries.

Once the Law Lords held in *Hedley Byrne & Co.* v. *Heller & Partners (1964) A.C. 465*, that a bank could have been liable for causing an advertising agency to give large credit to a company on the strength of a Bank Reference, Parliament enthusiastically enacted the Law Commission's *Misrepresentation Act, 1967*. The reception of these new doctrines was mixed, but many of the reformers who welcomed them overlooked two things.

The bank escaped liability on the reference because—as banks always do—they had given it 'without responsibility'.

Damages can be recovered by someone who enters into a contract in reliance on an innocent misrepresentation—*Misrepresentation Act, 1967*. However, liability can be escaped if the person who made the statement 'had reasonable ground to believe and did believe up to the time of making the contract that the facts represented were true'—*S. 2 (1)*.

A lawyer who was on his way to a remote magistrates' court in the Essex marshes asked a British Railways servant at Liverpool Street station where he should change trains. He was told Southend; which was wrong. When he got there, he found that not only was there no connection from there but that if he retraced his journey to the junction it would take a very long time to get to his destination. He therefore went by taxi at a cost of £5. When he claimed that £5 back from British Rail they denied liability, but he issued a summons in the Marylebone County Court (covering the district where British Rail resides) and they settled him up.

It is rather a pity that it did not go to judgment and appeal to the Court of Appeal and the House of Lords. The breed of lawyer who sues railway companies really died with Victoria, and the one who

337

demanded a special train for an excursion because he had a ticket but the train left early, had to pay the whole hire of the replacement. No doubt British Rail have already altered their terms and conditions upon which tickets are issued to exclude liability for misinformation by railway staff whose geography has not kept pace with the Commission's closure programme. They are very lively on points like this.

In *Thompson* v. *L.M.S.* *(1930)* *1 K.B. 41* the plaintiff was a lady who was injured whilst on a railway journey. Her ticket was obtained for her by her niece, and bore the words 'Excursion. For conditions, see back'. There were no detailed conditions on the back, but there was a statement that the ticket was subject to the conditions of the time tables and excursion bills. In the time tables, which cost sixpence, was a notice disclaiming liability for injuries. All this information remained outside the plaintiff's knowledge, however, because she could not read.

The Court of Appeal held that she was bound by the exclusion clause, nevertheless. Illiteracy is a misfortune, not a privilege. No doubt all the day-trippers who bought tickets read them avidly and immediately purchased time tables as well. This is not a valueless digression into the law of contract. The wise man nowadays bears in mind that his tortious liabilities and his contractual ones might be equally onerous. We might all soon walk round with little plastic notices on our hats disclaiming liability for everything we do. The attitude 'couldn't care less' could well become 'Won't be liable if I am careless'. It can work. In *Bennett* v. *Tugwell* (*The Times*, 9th February, 1971) Mr Bennett claimed damages for injuries suffered whilst a passenger in Mr Tugwell's car, and his claim was valued at £1,000. Mr Tugwell frankly admitted that his driving was negligent. His defence was conducted by his insurers, who felt constrained to point out that there was on the dashboard of the car a notice which Mr Bennett had often seen:

'*Passengers travelling in this vehicle do so at their own risk*'.

Said Mr Justice Ackner:

'*It is of course no part of my function to pass moral judgment upon insurance companies who choose to accept premiums against passenger liability and then, when a passenger is injured, seek to assert that the passenger has voluntarily accepted the very risk in respect of which the insurance company has been happily accepting premiums from the owner of the car.*

'*If I had such a duty, and if I thought that the insurance company was taking this point not in order to get this important point of principle decided, but also to avoid payment of this relatively small sum to the injured party, my criticism of such behaviour would indeed be stringent.'*

It is clear that it is possible to exclude not only liabilities flowing from breach of contract, but also some tortious liabilities, by announcing that you will not be responsible. Why then, it might be asked, do not the newspapers and publishers and the BBC and the ITA simply keep giving notice that they will not be liable for any libels, slanders, breaches of copyright and other wrongs which might be incidental to their ordinary transactions? In order to answer that, the curious nature of the law must be examined. It will reveal that Lord Justice Bowen was wrong. The pen can do a great deal more damage than a sword. And the law comes down quite severely on unwise words and pictures. The great advantage of mounting processes of law on what people say and write is, of course, that most people talk and write about things much more than they actually do anything. When James II demanded that the clergy read the Declaration of Indulgence suspending the anti-Papist laws, Archbishop Sancroft and his six suffragans only asked him please to excuse them. But they were thrown into the Tower and prosecuted. The begging petition was described as a seditious libel.

Even the venal and bullying judges headed by Chief Justice Scroggs thought that a bit steep, but they left it to the jury, who acquitted, and the celebrations plainly amounted to James' notice to quit. It is from such stirring episodes that our great tradition of 'free speech' stems. In truth, it is a freedom to risk being punished for every word you say or write. And I mean 'punished', not just 'sued' or 'made to pay damages'. For although criminal applications of libel (seditious, blasphemous, obscene and merely defamatory) invented by the Star Chamber were the most common cases, civil actions for damages for libel have occurred since 1670. The plaintiff in the first case was, as usual with litigious innovation, a lawyer. He was a barrister called King, who claimed to have been 'damnified in his good name and profession' by Sir Edward Lake saying that a document he drafted was 'stuffed with illegal assertions, ineptitudes and imperfections and clogged with gross ignorances, absurdities and solecisms'. As the Americans still do, he demanded a specific sum of damages—£5,000. He only got £150—the kind of reduction which until lately was the fate of husbands who claimed damages against co-respondents for seducing their wives.

But the importance of the case lies in what Sir Matthew Hale, the Chief Justice of the Common Pleas, said in judgment:

'Although such general words spoken once, without writing or publishing them, would not be actionable; yet here, they being

339

King v. Lake (Hardres, 470).

All that was being done in giving damages was adapting a crime to give compensation to the private citizen whose direct interests could be damaged. It had happened earlier with the wrong of trespass. It was punished as a crime when it resulted in assault or murder or property damage. And damages were given for the private injury. Because of what Hale had said in *King* v. *Lake*, lawyers began to allege in defamation claims that the defendant 'falsely and maliciously published of the Plaintiff' the words or things complained of. They still do. And they go on to say that the said words exposed him to public odium, hatred, ridicule and contempt. One would have thought that it would be necessary for plaintiffs to call into the witness box large numbers of people who could describe the odium, hatred, ridicule and contempt. Whilst libel claimants often do produce friends like that, they are not essential.

But even though words be not libellous the law long recognised that false words which injured someone's property, or trade, should be compensated for. Usually the wrong would have to be tainted with fraud, but mere use of someone else's words can be restrained in the case of infringement of copyright.

What is essentially done here is to protect one's brainchildren in the same way that one's reputation is protected.

> *'Good name in man or woman dear My Lord,*
> *Is the immortal jewel of their souls.'*

Maitland tells us that a good reputation was a defence to a charge of crime in the Middle Ages. So it is today. The evidence has to be cogent indeed before a policeman will risk his promotion and pension on besmirching a pillar of society. Skeletons in cupboards can destroy reputations but they cannot make copyrights.

In *Cummins* v. *Bond (1927) 1 Ch. 167* Mr Justice Eve had to decide the question whether a psychic medium or the journalist who transcribed what 'came through' from her, owned the copyright jointly or whether she was solely entitled as author.

The 'onlie begetter' was agreed to be 'an individual who has been dead and buried for some 1900 years'. It would seem that he and the medium should be jointly entitled to the copyright, said the judge but:

> '*inasmuch as I do not feel myself competent to make any declaration in his favour, and recognising as I do that I have no jurisdiction extending to the sphere in which he moves,*'

he confined himself to the people whom Parliament might have had in mind when passing the *Copyright Act, 1911*.

He therefore adjudged that the copyright belonged to the medium, to whose 'peculiar ability to reproduce in archaic English matter communicated to her in some unknown tongue we owe the production of these documents'.

When someone damages another by taking the fruits of his labours on by injuring him in his body, his trade or his reputation, the court must reduce all or any of those to money. Lord Diplock has said that to compensate an injury to reputation in money is the 'scale of values of the duel', when it is considered that the damages awarded for libels are often multiples of those awarded for lost limbs. The rate at which the person injured in a road crash or industrial accident—or his widowed or orphaned dependants—are compensated depends on comparison of the loss by insurance officials and judges, with similar cases for several years past.

If someone is injured and cannot work, his usual wage is the rate at which he will be able to claim conpensation for lost earnings from the person who injured him. He need give credit only for half the Industrial Injury Benefit he receives (for the first five years of injury) and no credit at all for his sick pay from any special source. It is common for a man to get more when he is sick or injured than when he is working, if the wages are paid during absence. But often they are not and have to be claimed against the person who caused the injury, either the employer or some stranger. There is a convention that the rate of wages is calculated by averaging the previous 26 weeks actual payments. The amount of lost wages should invariably be agreed beforehand in the event of litigation. Most judges cannot divide an award by two when they find someone half to blame for an accident. They invariably suggest that 'someone can work it out'. The leading counsel refer it to the juniors, and they refer it to the solicitors, who refer it from their clerks. The clerks on each side get different answers from each other, and both get different answers from the Associate, who decides to enter judgment for his answer anyway.

Lawyers are no worse than anyone else in these matters. Factory workers who know how much they actually get each week are rare. They usually state their wages gross but the inroads made by PAYE, Social Security and pension fund payments reduce these sums considerably. But the basic principle of the law of damages (which must be kept completely distinct from all its other principles) is that a person who has suffered a loss should be compensated only for what he has actually lost. In *British Transport Commission* v. *Gourley* in the House of Lords in 1956, Lord Goddard said of the question whether a person should be paid his whole earnings as compensation for loss of a job or his earnings after tax, 'It is remarkable how little authority there is on this subject . . . The question is whether taxation is or is not too remote to be taken into account.'

Anyone that remote from taxation (the Standard Rate of Income Tax is currently 40 per cent, having been reduced for 1971) is singularly fortunate. '. . . to say that a taxpayer has the benefit of his full income is, in my opinion, to be out of touch with reality', he declared of self employed people who pay tax the year after earning the money.

'Damages which have to be paid for personal injuries are not punitive, still less are they a reward.'

And yet, money received under insurance policies for injuries is not deducted from the compensation payable by a tortfeasor (*Bradburn* v. *Great Western Railway* [*1874*] *L.R. 10. Ex. 1*). The distinction is clear, not everyone insures, but everyone has to pay tax. Consequently, damages for actual loss of pay are calculated on the take-home pay, not the gross.

The valuation of personal injuries in terms of suffering apart from actual loss of earnings is a most difficult art. It has been turned into a legal matter by the sheer industry of the profession in deploying arguments about it, with the result that it is perfectly impossible to state with any certainty, what a court will award in any particular case. An engineer union branch secretary some years ago was settling broken arms for £250 a go. That approach would have had most solicitors racing up to Chancery Lane to organise resistance in case of a deluge of professional negligence suits.

A perfectly straightforward simple fracture in a 21-year-old labourer in perfect health, earning normal wages and unmarried and mending in five weeks off work without sequellae might very well have been valued at the time in the region of £250 having regard to the hazards of litigation. No doubt there are many such cases at any given moment. But to reduce them to a common job lot is downright unethical, practically as bad as a cash register in your office and giving trading stamps with your advice.

Anyone who practised much in one particular county court at that time might have noticed in the senior judge there a distressing propensity to value broken arms at £250 a go. But at least he wrapped it up in a few well chosen words, and he had the 'special damages' which always included a few odd coppers to add variety to what would otherwise have been tiresomely uniform decisions.

The principle is, you see, that if Yehudi Menuhin broke his arm, the great value of the loss, being impossible, and yet important, would have to be appealed to the House of Lords upon every point of principle. And the theory is that every one else gets the same individual attention.

342

There has to be considered the Pain and Suffering. They have always seemed to me to be the same thing, but no doubt someone will mount a couple of appeals on the distinction between them. Then there is the question whether the effects are permanent or temporary, and if temporary, for exactly how long are they endured. Then there is Loss of Future Earnings; Changed Position in the Labour Market; Loss of the Amenities of Life; Loss of Expectation of Life; Changed Personality.

But not the change in the value of money. This is quite amazing. Since the whole purpose of damages is to place the injured person in that position so far as money can, in which he would have been but for the happening of the injury, one would have thought that inflation was relevant. But upon the most modern authorities, the best thing to do if you are going to injure someone is to do it before the price goes up. The principle is apparently that when you injure someone you pay for it at the going rate. Anyone unwise enough to get himself maimed some years ago when money was worth less has only himself to blame. He should, it seems, take care of inflation either by wise investment or by having another accident.

Generally speaking, an employer is not liable to strangers for the torts of his non-servants. How far he is liable for the dishonesty of his servants was tightened up considerably in 1965 when a lady sent her mink stole to be cleaned. She did not send it to the defendants herself, but the trader to whom she delivered it sent it, to be cleaned by them, and one of their employees stole it. As Lord Denning explained ([*1965*] *3 W.L.R. 276*): it was the old law that a man was liable for his servant's dishonesty depended on whether the servant was acting for his own benefit or his master's. In *Lloyd* v. *Grace, Smith & Co.* (*1912*) *A.C. 716* a Liverpool solicitor's clerk—employed by a reputable firm—induced a client to transfer a mortgage to him by lying to her about the nature of the assignment deed. There he used it to obtain and make away with every penny her husband had left her. Although the firm was innocent, it was held liable to her. Although it was not within his actual authority to steal, it was within his ostensible authority to do business with a client.

This has been traced back in the Common Law as far as *Hern* v. *Nicholls* (*1700*) *1 Salkeld 289* where Chief Justice Holt said:

> '*Seeing somebody must be a loser by this deceit, it is more reason that he that employs should be a loser than a stranger*'.

The problem of the stolen stole was when does a fraud of a servant, for his own benefit stop being in the course of his employment? Lord Denning instanced a garage mechanic taking a car, which was in at his place of employment for repair, either for a drunken joyride or stealing it. Suppose he runs into someone. If he had authority to drive the car, say to take it back to the owner, or to road test it, he would be in the course of his employment and so the owner of the car could recover against his employer, because of the duty of care of the car created by the repairing contract. But the employers would owe no duty to the unfortunate person he ran over. So far as he was concerned, the mechanic was not in the course of his employment. But that was changed by the Court of Appeal, and the fur cleaners were held liable for the value of the fur stolen by their workman. However, if an employer brings to the attention of someone with whom he contracts a provision saying that he will not be liable for thefts by his employees, he can escape liability—*Southcote's Case (1601)*.

Employers therefore sometimes feel that they should operate security systems, and their security staff are sometimes instructed to search employees. If the employees have agreed to this by incorporation of say a Works Rule Book into the contract of employment, or some other specific agreement to submit to a search, this is lawful. In the absence of any such contractual term, and without the consent of the employee on the occasion, to search an employee would be an assault and battery for which he or she could complain to the Justices and have the employer fined, and also the person who made the search, and a trespass to the person for which damages may be recovered. They would not be if it was merely a common assault contrary to *S. 42* of the *Offences Against the Person Act, 1861* for *S. 45* precludes that. But if it was an aggravated assault—against a girl by a man for instance, or an assault which occasioned actual bodily harm, damages could be awarded.

The employee is under no obligation not to work in his spare time, but if deliberately and secretly he does things in his spare time to profit himself which would damage his employer's business he will be restrained by injunction and made to pay damages. But as the name of the leading case, *Hivac Ltd.* v. *Park Royal Scientific Instruments Ltd. (1946) Ch. 169*, shows, the kind of employment which would lead to such things would be that requiring specialised knowledge. It is, however, only actionable if confidential information is given away to competitors.

There is in every contract of employment, an implied condition that the worker will keep confidential his employer's 'trade secrets'. This is not so dramatic a field as Industrial Espionage, proper. Exactly what a trade secret is is hard to say. The employee is perfectly entitled to use his skill and experience, probably because he cannot help it.

He must not tell other people confidential methods of work used by his employer, details of business relationships, plans, the financial position. It appears to be suggested in *Merryweather* v. *Moore*

(*1892*) *Ch. 518* that if the employee memorises information he cannot be called to account, but this no doubt merely recognises the difficulty of proving that memorised information was wrongly used later. The milkman who asked customers to change to him next day when he would no longer be employed by Wessex Dairies ([*1935*] *2 K.B. 80*), and the employee who copied out the names and addresses of the firm's customers before leaving ([*1895*] *2 Q.B. 315*), could not really wonder at being held liable.

'Size Eight Hats' often make particular contracts with their employers about the ownership of inventions and copyrights. The copyright in a work made by an employee belongs to the employer (*Copyright Act, 1956 s. 4*) unless of course, it is a work commissioned by someone from the employer, in which case it belongs to the person commissioning. The copyright in a work for a magazine or newspaper, except for the right of publication in such papers, belongs to the employee.

If an employee makes an invention, the employer owns it if the employee's job is such as to make such inventions. Inventions are things, or processes for making things. The Theory of Relativity could not be patented, though it might be the subject of copyright, so far as the form in which it was expressed was concerned. Einstein would have understood this, perhaps, because he worked as a Patent Examiner. Employees often find that seemingly great discoveries are not worth patenting. On the other hand 'know how' which cannot be patented because it is not inventive but merely a clever way of doing something can be very valuable. Disposing of the employer's 'know how' is a serious Breach of Confidence, and precisely the sort of thing protected by the Law of Trade Secrets, which is much more dramatic than a list of customers for a milk round. *S. 56* of the *Patents Act, 1949*, however, enables the ownership of an invention to be apportioned between an employer and an employee, but only where they have agreed to share it.

Very few such disputes are heard. The modest rewards of the Suggestion Box or bonus scheme are more attractive to the ordinary worker. The fruits of victory are not all that sweet and the costs are likely to be great—win or lose.

Nil Sine Labore

'Legislation is unable to prevent the necessary working of the laws of political economy.'
Charles Oman in *A History of England.*

EVERYONE, says the 23rd Article of the Universal Declaration of Human Rights, has the right to work, to free choice of employment, just and favourable conditions of work and to protection against unemployment.

If one were to put that together with 'Where there is a right, there is a remedy' (*Coke Upon Littleton, 197*) and Chief Justice Holt's declaration in *Ashby* v. *White* (*1704*) *2 Lord Raymond 938* that

> *'every man that is injured ought to have his recompense'*,

it would follow that English law recognised the Right to Work. Of course, it does not. Indirectly, it recognises the concomitant duty to work which is not at all the same thing, for though rights may beget duties, it by no means follows that the converse applies.

It may very well be objected that the Universal Declaration is part of International Law, and so it is. But International Law is only part of English Law in so far as the English Law does not provide to the contrary. It might be contended—and indeed a powerful political rump do—that English Law is less than perfect in this regard.

Should the point reluctantly be conceded, an immediate retort presents itself. English Law has now a Right Not to Work.

The peculiar genius of British statesmanship has always been to achieve political superiority by appealing to the lower instincts, if not the Lower Orders. *Section 128* of the *Industrial Relations Act, 1971*, is a master-stroke.

> *'No court shall . . . compel any employee to do any work or to attend at any place for the purpose of doing any work.'*

Add this to the classification of persons liable to be paid unemployment benefit in *Section 1 of the National Insurance Act* of 1965 who are:

persons gainfully employed in employment in Great Britain . . .
under a contract of service; self-employed persons . . . who are
not employed persons; and non-employed persons, that is to say,
persons who are neither employed nor self-employed persons'.

To get unemployment benefit, someone must show that he belongs to the category of 'employed persons' and that 50 contributions have been paid by or credited to him in the previous year, and that at least 26 of those have been paid since becoming insured. That entitles him to the full rate. If he has the 26, but not the 50, he gets a reduced rate. He may also qualify for the Earnings Related Supplement. It is, however, plain that the Right Not to Work does not carry with it an automatic right to unemployment pay.

People who are determined to assert this right cannot fall back on Social Security themselves, but the strikers are subsidised by benefits of £4.60 for a wife, £1.70 for a child and up to £3 per week for rent.

A person who is out of work because of an Industrial Injury gets benefit provided it arose 'out of and in the Course of his employment'. This phrase was employed for the first time in the *Workmen's Compensation Act, 1909,* at the insistence of a Cabinet Minister obsessed by the notion that it would have to be operated by ordinary people in factories and offices, and should therefore be absolutely clear to anyone. At the last count the list of reported cases about its meaning occupied 38 pages of the standard legal digest.

Anyone who thinks it has no further application because Workmen's Compensation was done away with in 1947 is gravely mistaken. It was adjudicated on in a 1971 case. The Common Law would not let such a simple doctrine of universal application as 'course of the unemployment' escape it, and it is the foundation of most of the accident litigation which still takes up most of the working time of the High Court and the County Courts (and which the abolition of Workmen's Compensation was meant to abolish as well). A worker cannot get compensation generally speaking unless he was injured in the course of his employment.

A worker can be disentitled to Industrial Injury Benefit for misconduct, because no one is employed to misconduct himself. Exactly what amounts to misconduct sometimes is a difficult question of fact. As Lord Denning put it in *R.* v. *Industrial Injuries Commissioner, ex parte Amalgamated Engineering Union (1966) 2 Q.B. 31*:

'What is the position when a man overstays his tea-break? . . .
Even if it is done negligently or disobediently, it does not auto-
matically take him outside the course of his employment . . . only
. . . when he is doing something of a different kind from anything
he was employed to do'.

Similar considerations apply to Sickness Benefit. But disqualification does not apply where

'the incapacity is due to venereal disease, or, in the case of a woman who is not a wife, or, being a wife, is separated from her husband, to pregnancy'.

It is clear that the law of the Welfare State though not different in essentials from the old law, does differ in important details. Quite apart from the details of the cases, the circumstances in which they arose are material to be considered. It may now arise only theoretically, but not so long ago it was usual to dismiss a woman servant if she became pregnant.

Upon looking into legal texts dealing with the Law of Master and Servant, there might have been discovered some justification for this in law, on the authority of cases like that brought by the Crown against the Inhabitants of Brampton in 1777 (*Cald. Mag. Cas. 11*). But they were concerned with which parish ratepayers had to support a pauper under the Elizabethan Poor Law, and the validity of the dismissal was relevant in that context. Since a pregnant woman has difficulties in performing manual work, the pregnancy might not have been legal 'misconduct' at all (though no doubt a great many people thought it was), but merely inability to perform her contract.

Whilst the changes in many aspects of the Law of Employment are more apparent than real, it must be appreciated that the existence of a separate body of law covering work is only a modern notion. If any English learning negatives Maine's statement about society moving from status to contract it is the Master and Servant law.

Status dominates the Law of Employment now overlaid with the Law of Redundancy, and that of Industrial Relations.

However much the first may in fact contribute to the poor quality of the latter, they have one great distinction. *S. 22* of the *Redundancy Payments Act, 1965*, disqualifies people who have lost employment by reason of a trade dispute at their place of employment from unemployment benefit, except for people 'not participating in or financing' the dispute.

'Trade dispute' means any dispute between employers and employees, or employees and employees, connected with employment, or terms and conditions of it, whether of those employed by that employer or not—*Section 22 (6) National Insurance Act, 1965*. It therefore applies equally to locked out workers as well as strikers. If there was a Right to Work, lock outs would be illegal. Parliament in *The Industrial Relations Act, 1971* has therefore very wisely refrained from providing one. This is not merely an expression to the effect that what the British Working Man has never had he will not miss. For it is extremely doubtful whether he wants a Right to Work. What he appears to want is a Right Not to Work When it Suits Him.

For a long time now, workers have been asserting this right without troubling about the legal implications. This Right to Strike is not to be found in any law book. A strike may or may not be a breach of contract. A termination of a contract by proper notice is not a breach.

Until the *Contracts of Employment Act, 1963* came into force on the 6th July, 1964, a great many hourly paid workers could be sacked on payment of their wages up to and including the current hour, whether or not they had committed serious misconduct. But by requiring minimum notice of a week for a worker employed for at least six months, a fundamental change was wrought in strike law, which was totally unappreciated at the time. The statute also imposed on a worker the duty to give a week's notice to his employer.

A strike on notice shorter than a week, such as the immediate down tools and walk out, whether or not accompanied by bell-ringing in the Dagenham tradition, was therefore a breach of contract by any worker who had been employed for six months, but not by those who had just started working there. Had any such provision or doctrine of the Common Law existed in 1895, a great deal of our history might have been very different. There might have been a Right to Work. The case was one based on the ancient crime of conspiracy.

The *Ordinacio de Conspiratoribus* of 1305 was directed at those who 'breathe together' to plot false legal action against other people. Its direct descendant, the *Statutum de Conspiratoribus*, is to be found in the *Statutes of Uncertain Time*. Parliament in 1351 passed what Charles Oman called in 1910 'the foolish Statute of Labourers', by which the Justices of the Peace were given power to fix wages, a sort of mediaeval Prices and Incomes Policy.

It cannot be claimed for the Statute of Labourers that it was an unqualified success but from time to time in the next five centuries Justices of the Peace exercised their undoubted rights to fix wages. As late as 1811 the Justices for Kent exercised their equally undoubted right not to fix the rates when requested by the journeymen millers of their county. For while they could do so, they did not have to do so. The virtue of this system as an economic regulator was obvious. If, as was frequently the case, the Justices were the employers, or favoured the employers, and wished a wage fixed, then they could fix it. If they did not wish a wage fixed, then the Justices would not fix one.

The *Statute 5 Eliz. 1 c. 4* also enabled this rate fixing to be done, and provided as well that 'general hirings' of workmen should be for a year. If an employer sacked a man he had to pay 40s forfeit unless he had good cause. If the workman left without cause he had to go to prison or go back to work for his master. In 1854, some 3,000 work-people were imprisoned under the *Act 4 Geo. IV c. 34*, passed in 1823, by which a servant could be arrested and imprisoned for three months for breaking his or her contract. This measure had been rendered necessary by the irresponsibility of the working classes after the wage-fixing statutes were repealed in 1813 by *53 Geo. III c. 40*, which left the Industrial Revolution open to Freedom of Contract.

The exigencies of the Napoleonic Wars were extremely serious for the economy. The feeding and equipping of the armies caused rents and prices to rise and the natural escalation of wages would no doubt have kept the Justices busy fixing new rates had not the employers and workers both shown that disinclination for legal bargains which manifests itself to this day. This may have been because of the *Combination Acts* enacted by the administration of Pitt the Younger. The preamble to the 1799 Act read:

'*Whereas great numbers of journeymen, manufacturers and work-men in various parts of this Kingdom have by unlawful meetings and combinations endeavoured to obtain advance of their wages and to effectuate other illegal purposes, and the laws at present in force against such unlawful conduct have been found to be in-adequate to the suppression thereof . . .*'

But it was not tough enough and it was replaced by another Act a year later which made it crystal clear that the bosses as well were not to combine or agree with other people to raise wages. It is only fair to say that they did their very best to obey, to such good effect that no employer was ever punished under them, which is more than the workers can say for themselves. The Combination Acts were repealed in 1824, but the Lower Orders did not appreciate their freedom and started throwing their weight about, and so the Combination Laws had to be restored and amended in 1825.

The right of combination was limited to people employed by the same undertaking or at the same place of work, and to the questions of hours, and wages. This was the foundation for the unappreciated doctrine which made a bunch of unofficial strikers, or a local branch of a national union a 'trade union' in law. Some 'professional' and 'staff associations' were also trades unions, because they regulated wages and working conditions, though they did not thank you for mentioning it. So, too, were employers' federations which regulated wages and conditions. The 1825 Act also made threats and violence in the promotion of strikes illegal, which was not necessary because they were criminal offences anyway.

Agreeing to strike was strictly not a legal wrong, civil or criminal.

351

However, the Star Chamber had made 'breathing together' into the powerful misdemeanour of conspiracy which is probably used more nowadays in the fight against crime than ever before. Serjeant Hawkins in his *Pleas of the Crown* (*1716*) defined it as the agreement of two or more people to do any unlawful act or to do any lawful act by unlawful means. The crime is complete when the agreement is made. No modern improvement has been found necessary, for the willingness of juries to accept that there is no smoke without fire is exceeded only by the eagerness of judges to do so. Even so, it was some time before it was commonly used to suppress trade union activity.

The Tolpuddle Martyrs were transported after conviction under the *Unlawful Oaths Act, 1797* and the *Unlawful Societies Act, 1799*.

The real troubles of trades union inspired strikers began with the *Molestation of Workmen Act, 1858*, which made picketing legal. In 1867, some tailors were convicted of conspiring to impoverish Henry Poole, the Prince of Wales's tailor, by striking in support of efforts to break a lock-out at other tailoring shops. A man called Druitt and some of his mates were alleged to have intimidated some blacklegs.

Baron Bramwell directed the jury that even though the pickets were only doing their duty, if it had 'a deterring effect' on ordinary people.

'By exposing them to have their motions watched, and to encounter black looks, that would not be permitted by the law of the land.'

It may have been appreciated that making black looks a crime was laying it on too thick, and in 1871 a Trades Union Act was passed which made members of them no longer liable to prosecution for conspiracy or any other offence simply because their combination was 'in restraint of trade'. But it also made unenforceable, by Section 4, agreements concerning the conditions on which they should be employed, and internal and inter-union agreements. Nevertheless, it made strikes legal—for any strike was a restraint of trade. It is a little surprising therefore that the very next Act passed by Parliament, which came into force on the same day, the *Criminal Law Amendment Act, 1871*, aligned the unlawful behaviour of strikers with breaches of the Peace. It was consequently difficult to know what was legal. Among the first successful prosecutions were those of seven women picketers imprisoned for jeering at a strike-breaker. This was quickly followed by the imprisonment of some gasworks stokers for threatening a strike to get one of them reinstated after sacking. The coercion was a conspiracy, but much of the discussion was about the illegality of agreements to break contracts.

Now the distinction which lawyers have long made between the employed person and the 'independent contractor' is that one makes a contract 'of service' whilst the latter contracts 'for services'. The distinction is a vitally important one, the limits of which remain undefined. In 1852, the *prima donna* Johanna Wagner came here to sing at Her Majesty's Theatre which was managed by Mr Lumley. According to the contract she was not to sing elsewhere during her stay. But the manager of the Royal Italian Opera, Covent Garden, induced her not to perform at all for Mr Lumley, who sued them both. These classic actions dominate the law of employment today. In the action against Miss Wagner, Lord St Leonards said:

> '*It is true that I have not the means of compelling her to sing, but she has no cause of complaint if I compel her to abstain.*'
>
> **(1852) 1 D.M. & G. 604.**

Thus was crystallised the Common Law doctrine that a contract to perform personal services can never be specifically enforced—though, of course, damages for refusing to perform it will be awarded. Now it might appear that those unfortunate labourers who were imprisoned at this very time for breaking their contracts were being forced to work. But of course they were not, for two reasons. They had the clear choice of continuing in their employments or going to prison—if they were lucky and the job was still open. And they, of course, were not on contracts 'for services' but 'of service'. They had the status of servants, not independent contractors.

The basis of the *Lumley* v. *Wagner* doctrine is that to force a human being to work is slavery. *Section 128* of the *Industrial Relations Act, 1971*, protects a worker from compulsion to work as well as from compulsion to take part in industrial action. However, in the action *Lumley* v. *Gye (1853) 2 E. & B. 216* it was held that inducing the breach of any kind of contract was an actionable wrong. The basis for this decision was *Winsmore* v. *Greenbank (1745) Willes Reports 577*, which made it tort to entice away or harbour a man's wife—who after all was a valuable servant. This action, the old books stress, is wholly independent of any sexually immoral factors. The last such action was heard—and failed—in late 1971 and enticement has now been abolished. However, the ghost still walks, for *Winsmore* v. *Greenbank* was the basis of *Lumley* v. *Gye*.

> '*He who maliciously procures a damage to another by violation of his right ought to be made to indemnify; and that whether he procures an actionable wrong or a breach of contract,*'

said Mr Justice Erle, who later became Chief Justice and whose view prevailed. But Mr Justice Coleridge, who also later became a Chief Justice, dissented strongly:

> '*To draw a line between advice, persuasion, enticement, and procurement, is practically impossible in a court of justice.*'

That does not stop people from trying.

These cases support a confusing variety of decisions affecting not only employment law but the relations between trades unions and employers, and the transactions of commercial concerns in competition with each other, and having nothing to do with contracts of employment. If there is a basic principle underlying the English law of tort, Chief Justice Erle's words might be it. Lord Haldane said in *Jasperson* v. *Dominion Tobacco Co.* (*1923*) A.C. 709:

> '*What was laid down long ago in* Lumley *v.* Gye *reaches all wrongful acts done intentionally to damage a particular individual, and actually damaging him.*'

The great difficulty it has left to us at the present is to determine what is 'wrongful'. Several of the earliest cases of Intentional Wrong involved frightening ducks away from decoy ponds, and so ruining the trade of the decoyman. The combination of these cases and the old seduction and enticement cases are the foundation of the most important laws of our modern industrial society.

In 1895 the Glengall Iron Co. was carrying out repairs on the *Sam Weller* in the Regent Dock, Millwall. Mr Flood and his mate Mr Taylor were shipwrights—craftsmen who then did and still do the woodwork in the building and repair of ships. They belonged to a little union called the Shipwright's Provident Union. At that time the Independent Society of Boilermakers and Iron and Steel Shipbuilders had not extended to organise the Structural Steelworkers, but it was a big union. Forty of its members were carrying out the ironwork on the *Sam Weller*. It came to the notice of their official Mr Allen that Mr Flood and Mr Taylor had previously worked for a different employer and had carried out metal work as well as woodwork. And demarcation was as strong a prejudice then as in the Fifties.

Mr Allen told the Glengall Iron Co. that unless Flood and Taylor were sacked, the boilermakers would strike. They were sacked on the spot.

Mr Justice Kennedy tried their claims with a jury which he directed that there was no conspiracy, intimidation or coercion, and no breach of contract. For the hourly-paid men need neither give nor receive notice. The boilermakers were free to leave; Flood and Taylor were free to leave; and the Glengall Iron Co. was free to ask them to leave. The jury awarded each plaintiff £20 damages because Mr Allen had maliciously induced the employers not only to sack them, but not to re-employ them. The Court of Appeal upheld the decision, following *Lumley* v. *Gye*.

The Boilermakers' Union official appealed to the House of Lords. Six Law Lords heard arguments. They called in ten more judges to hear it re-argued. But they, of course, could not cast votes in the House of Lords, which is how the decisions of this highest court in the land are made. Nine Law Lords voted six to three to allow the appeal. But of a total of twenty judges who considered the case only eight were in favour of the union official who finally won.

'Everything depends on the nature of the act, whether it is wrongful or not,'

said Lord Herschell.

'There is not much help to be found in the earlier cases . . . not even . . . the great case about frightening ducks in a decoy, whatever the true explanation of that decision may be,'

said Lord Macnaghten.

Lord Shand pointed out that the boilermakers were quite entitled to resolve not to carry on working for the Glengall Iron Co. If that were so, they must be perfectly entitled to tell the company so. They made no threat to do anything but to exercise their rights.

Lord Morris dissented. The plaintiffs were only day-labourers, he conceded, but with a 'certainty of their employment being continued *de die in diem* for a considerable time'.

They referred to the opinions written for their guidance by the judges. The great Mr Justice Cave had posed the question:

'If a cook says to her master "Discharge the butler or I leave you" is that actionable? With submission I say that it is, if the master does discharge the butler in consequence.

'. . . Allen's motive was not to secure the work they were then doing . . . but to punish Flood and Taylor for what they had previously done.'

All those who found for the Union official had to say that his motive was irrelevant. The boilermakers were only exercising their legal rights, like Mr Pickles of Bradford.

Three years later the House of Lords had to consider a similar case from Ulster, which had been tried there by a jury before their decision in *Allen* v. *Flood* was made. Mr Quinn was an official of the Belfast Journeymen Butchers' and Assistants' Association. Mr Leathem was a flesher at Lisburn, whose workers were not in the Union, but he was willing that they should join and was prepared to pay their dues. But the Union officials said the men must walk the streets. They wanted their jobs for existing members. Leathem refused to sack his men and so the officials told their members at Munce's that Leathem's meat was 'black'. Munce perfectly lawfully cancelled his order to Leathem. The jury called this a malicious conspiracy to induce Munce and his workers not to deal with Leathem, and awarded £200 damages.

Lord Shand said that the vital distinction between this case and *Allen* v. *Flood* could be stated in a sentence. Allen was promoting his own trade interest, which he was entitled to do even though it injured his competitors (the shipwrights). But the Journeymen Butchers were injuring Mr Leathem in his trade.

It can certainly be stated in one sentence that Flood and Taylor were employees and Leathem was an employer. But no judge has ever spoken the sentence.

Soon after the case, in the Appeal Cases, for 1901, comes that of the *Taff Vale Railway* v. *Amalgamated Society of Railway Servants* (*p. 426*), holding that a trades union in its corporate capacity could be held liable for the wrongs of its officers which caused loss.

> '*Then came the blow of the Taff Vale decision in 1901, whence much of our recent political history takes its origin*,' wrote G. M. Trevelyan. '*The Judges once more undid the work of former Parliaments and destroyed by a legal decision the rights that trades unions had held for a generation under Gladstone's Trades Union Act of 1871 . . .*
>
> '*Trades unions durst not, under peril of losing all their funds in damages, take any strike action to raise wages or to prevent the lowering of wages.*'

> **Illustrated History of England P. 700.**

The Liberals restored the position with the *Trades Disputes Act*, *1906*—to get the balance of power on their side from the first Parliamentary Labour Party of any size. Section 3 provided that an act should not be actionable 'on the ground only that' it induced someone to break a contract of employment or interfered with someone's business. Section 4 made any trades union immune from actions for torts, whether the members were workmen or masters, and the members and officials were personally protected as well.

How, it might be wondered, could the Crofter Hand Woven Harris Tweed Co. hope to succeed against Mr Veitch in 1940? Their cloth was woven by the crofters on the island of Lewis, but the yarn was imported from the mainland and was not sold under the Harris Tweed trade mark. The mill workers were in the Transport and General Worker's Union and so were the dockers at Stornoway who handled the exports. The union officials made common cause with the mill-owners and blacked the cloth made from the cheaper yarn of the pursuers, so that there was no dispute between masters and servants. But it was claimed to be a conspiracy to injure the pursuers.

'A perfectly lawful strike may aim at dislocating the employer's business for the moment but its real object is to secure better wages or conditions for the workers. The true contrast is, I think, between the case where the object is the legitimate benefit of the combiners and the case where the object is deliberate damage without any such just cause.'

Lord Wright *(1942) A.C. 435.*

And so a conspiracy to strike and cause damage to an employer could not be prevented or compensated for by legal action. Or could it?

In 1958, Mr Douglas Rookes, a highly skilled draughtsman at London Airport, had been a member of the Association of Engineering and Shipbuilding Draughtsmen. But he came into dispute with the union and left. Now the union had an agreement with his employers, the British Overseas Airways Corporation. It made BOAC a 'closed shop', and provided that there should be no lock-outs and no strikes.

This is one of the only two reported cases in English law where the collective agreement was actually incorporated by express reference in the contract of employment. (The other involves a National Coal Board worker.) After Mr Rookes left the union there was a meeting at which the defendants spoke to their colleagues, and BOAC were told that the draughtsmen would strike unless Mr Rookes was dismissed from the design office, which was done. He sued his colleagues and one of the union's officials and in 1961 a jury awarded him £7,500 exemplary damages. The Court of Appeal reversed this decision holding that 'intimidation'—which was the wrong alleged to be the 'wrongful act' could only be committed by threats of violence, and was not committed by a threat to break contracts.

This, of course, seemed to go back to the *Molestation of Workmen Act, 1859*, or possibly the *Criminal Law Amendment Act, 1871*. Anyway, Mr Gerald Gardiner, QC, who led for the union men, said there was no such tort as intimidation, and even if there was, union officials were protected by the 1906 Act. In the cliché most often employed in upholding Acts of Parliament, he told the Court of Appeal that the decision would 'drive a coach and four horses' through the Act unless it was reversed and they obliged. Mr Rookes took it to the Lords and won.

'So long as the defendant only threatens to do what he has a legal right to do he is on safe ground,'

said Lord Reid.

However, threatening a breach of contract was equally effective though 'subtler' than a threat of violence. Lord Devlin was even clearer about the violence of the threat:

> '*Metaphorically speaking, a club has been used. It does not matter to the plaintiff what the club is made of—whether it is a physical club or an economic club, a tortious club or an otherwise illegal club.*'

So there was a tort of 'intimidation'. But what about the 1906 Act?

> '*In my judgment, it is clear that Section 3 does not protect inducement of breach of contract where that is brought about by intimidation or other illegal means,*'

said Lord Reid.

Apart from that, however, the union men claimed the protection of Section 1 of the 1906 Act, protecting 'an agreement or combination by two or more persons in contemplation of a trade dispute'. But their Lordships held that 'intimidation' could be committed by a single person and so the protection did not apply.

Precisely where this case differs from *Allen* v. *Flood* is obvious. It had the result of the true majority of the opinions given sixty-five years before. But it led to some curious results.

The Donovan Commission on the Trades Unions reported in 1968 (*Cmnd. 3623*). It pointed out that if one person alone threatened an unlawful act, say the breach of his own contract, he would not be protected by *s. 1* of the *1906 Act*. But if a lot of people got together and threatened it, they would. By the time that came out, however, the *Trade Disputes Act, 1965* had been passed. It provided that if a person threatened in furtherance of a trade dispute that a contract of employment (his own or someone else's) would be broken, or that he would induce someone to break such a contract he could not be sued.

This was the position in 1965 when Jack Stratford controlled two companies. J. T. Stratford & Son Ltd. hired out barges and repaired them. It employed no lightermen. Bowker & King Ltd. operated motor barges, its bargemen belonging to the Watermen, Lightermen, Tugmen and Bargemen's Union and to the Transport and General Workers' Union. Although both unions had previously negotiated jointly with Bowker & King, the Transport Union made an agreement with it, without notice to the Watermen's Union, which thereupon 'blacked' Stratford & Sons hired barges. The company was said to be losing £1,000 per week and it applied for an interlocutory injunction against the ban.

> '*There does not appear to be even a trade dispute in contemplation of which the defendants can be said to have acted,*'

said Lord Radcliffe.

Preventing the barge hirers from using Stratford's barges was within *Lumley* v. *Gye*, said Lord Reid. Even the 1965 Act did not protect inter-union disputes.

The Right to Work does not have to be synonymous with the Right to be Employed—which is really what inducement of breach of contract of service offends against. In Lord Davey's speech in *Allen* v. *Flood* this passage, still perfectly good law:

> '*An employer may refuse to employ for the most mistaken, capricious, malicious or morally reprehensible motives that can be conceived, but the workman has no right of action against him.*
>
> '*A man has no right to be employed by any particular employer, and has no right to any particular employment if it depends on the will of another.*'

Section 22 (1) of the *Industrial Relations Act, 1971* provides that every employee has a right not to be 'unfairly dismissed'. The employer has to justify with substantial reasons or pay compensation which is 'just and equitable' up to a maximum of two years' pay or £4,160 whichever is less.

Section 5 (2) (b) makes it an unfair industrial practice and liable to similar penalties to 'discriminate against' or to penalise a worker for exercising the rights given by the first part of the Section. These are:

> (a) *the right to be a member of such trades union as he may chose.*
>
> (b) *the right to be a member of no trades union or to refuse to belong to a particular union.*

The Act provides for the approval of closed shops and the creation of 'agency shops'. Conscientious objectors to paying union dues can be made to contribute to charity. By *s. 17 (b)* unless a worker is 'specially exempted' he loses his right not to belong to a union, and the employer does not dismiss him unfairly if he sacks him for refusing to join.

Far from these being a Right to Work the Closed Shop is a means for the union to restrict it—so long as the union is registered under the Industrial Relations Act. Employers are bound not to refuse to employ someone on grounds of colour, race or origin, by the *Race Relations Act, 1968, s. 3*. The Government can force large employers to find jobs for a few disabled people and the Dock Labour Board can force a registered employer to accepted allocation of a particular registered dockworker.

But the Boilermakers' Case had finally been copied by Parliament —the minority cannot win (even though it took a minority decision to uphold the big union).

359

The general rule therefore remains: no one can force anyone else to contract with him. Recognising this essential principle, a great many people insist on being self-employed. There is an opinion not without foundation that much 'labour-only sub-contracting' (described in the construction industry as 'The Lump') is intended to avoid liability of employers for National Insurance contributions, redundancy pay, vicarious liability for torts by employees, and the insurance they are compelled to carry against it, Industrial Training Levies, and collection of PAYE, among other liabilities. But workers find it attractive, and organisations exist to operate the system. Labour Force Ltd. was held not to be an employer (*[1970] 2 All E.R. 220*) and so not liable to pay £12,000 Training Levy in respect of the 50,000 workers on its books. Self-employed 'labour-only sub-contractors' are as much liable to pay National Insurance and Income Tax as the rest of us, of course. But considerable economies can be effected by fairly frequent changes of residence.

It therefore sometimes assumes great importance to determine exactly what relationship exists between an employer and his worker. The *Truck Act* of *1831* confined the benefits of legal compulsion to be paid in coin of the realm (instead of trading coupons) to 'artificers'—and although the Payment of Wages Act, 1960 allows workers to agree to be paid by cheque, cash is still the favoured method—for which payroll bandits are duly grateful. Artificers were turned into ordinary 'workmen' by the *Truck Act (Amendment) Act, 1887*, and they were defined in the *Employers and Workmen Act, 1875* as those engaged in manual labour, on contracts of service or 'personally to execute any work or labour'. This of course, would include the men operating The Lump, although 'manual labour' has been taken to mean the expenditure of considerable muscular power, and a railway worker and a hairdresser have both been ruled not to be manual workers. A stoker was held not to be covered by the term—but he was a domestic worker in a hospital and 'domestic servants' were excluded.

When the Industrial Court was set up by the 1919 Act, 'workman' was extended to clerical workers, and the term has in cases under special provisions included school teachers and local government officers. The *Industrial Relations Act, 1971* distinguishes between 'workers' and 'employees' who are the people covered by both the *Contracts of Employment Act, 1963* and the *Redundancy Payments Act, 1965*, and who get the protection against 'unfair dismissal'.

An employee is 'an individual who has entered into or works under a contract of employment', but not a policeman or a special constable. 'A worker' is 'a person who works or normally seeks to work' under such a contract or:

'any other contract whereby he undertakes to perform personally any work or services for another party to the contract who is not a professional client of his'.

Compensation for unfair dismissal under the Act therefore depends on what exactly is a 'contract of employment'. This is defined by *s. 167* of the Act as:

'a contract of service or of apprenticeship . . . express or implied'.

Which leaves it up to the Common Law to say whether a contract is one 'of service' just like it had to be before the Act was passed. Lord Denning said it is often easy to recognise a contract of service when you see it but difficult to say where the difference lies.

'A ship's master, a chauffeur and a reporter on the staff of a news-paper are all employed under contracts of service; but a ship's pilot, a taxi-man and a newspaper contributor are employed under a contract for services.'

> **Stevenson, Jordan & Harrison v. Macdonald (1952) 1 T.L.R. 101.**

Lord Justice Bowen, in *Donovan* v. *Laing, Wharton & Down Construction Syndicate Ltd. (1893) 1 Q.B. 629*, had enunciated a test of 'control'. An employer could either control the men he employed himself in their work, or he could put them under the control of someone he contracted with. Actual control of the job made them servants. The one who gives the orders is the master.

In *Mersey Docks and Harbour Board* v. *Coggins & Griffiths (Liverpool) Ltd. (1947) A.C. 1*, the Board employed Mr Francis Newall as a crane driver. He and his crane were hired for some work by a firm of stevedores, and he negligently injured someone. Who should pay the damages naturally turned upon who was his employer, for their insurers would have to pay. He was naturally asked in the course of his evidence who gave him his orders:

'I take no orders from anybody.'

That answer put the problem in the House of Lords, because it undermined completely the legal test of 'control' by which a contract of service was distinguished from a contract for services, as then understood. Lord Simonds felt no difficulty over the true relation:

'It was a sturdy answer which meant that he was a skilled man and knew his job, and would carry it out in his own way. Yet ultimately he would decline to carry it out in the appellants' way at his peril for in their hands lay the only sanction, the power of dismissal.'

Thus a servant is a worker over whom the employer has the

Right of the Sack. But if he exercises it, without 'substantial reason', he will have to pay compensation to the employee.

That makes no inconsistency in legal logic. A right is no less a right because it has to be paid for.

What's In A Name?

*The result in a libel case depends upon whether or
not the jury likes the Plaintiff. If they do, he gets
a verdict, otherwise not.*

A. G. Hays in *Harvard Law Review*, 1945.

WHEN Sir Valentine Holmes, QC, was at the height of his career, a
solicitor took Bud Flanagan and Chesney Allen to him for advice.
A provincial newspaper critic had censured them in a review for
appearing in the same show as some act which outraged his moral
sense. The comedians, of course, had no control over whom the
management put on the same bill. They had nothing to do with the
other turn.

Holmes advised them that they had been defamed in the notice,
and were bound to win an action. Bud Flanagan was too old a
punter to believe in anything so like a racing certainty, and pointed
out that there was nothing sure about a jury's verdict. What if
some of the jurors did not like the Crazy Gang? But Holmes had no
fears. They must win.

> *'Well, all right, Sir Holmes, if you say so. But I'll tell you some-
> thing. If you win this case for us, we're going to bring Nervo
> and Knox to you. The perisher did not even mention them.'*

This Rule in Flanagan and Allen might be traced to the dictum
of Miss Mae West to a reporter:

> *'Say something nice about me if you can;
> Say something bad about me if you must;
> But for God's sake say something about me.'*

Mr Justice Milmo, a most distinguished member of the Defamation Bar before his elevation, explained to a jury soon after that
Defamation is like an elephant. You know it when you see it but it is
hard to describe. This, with all deference, is a misdirection. Analogy
is always a dangerous form of argument, and it may be that its
employment led the judge into the error. Few people have much
difficulty recognising an elephant, even though they might not be
very good at describing it. The point in most defamation cases
which are contested, however, is that the defamation is not recognisable by anybody except the witnesses called by the plaintiff.

Why then do people bring such actions? In most cases the reason is money. To be libelled can be a blessing in disguise. The net cash expectation can be better than a Treble Chance win. Opening the appeal of the newspapers in the cases brought by Rubber Improvement Ltd. and its director, Mr John Lewis, Mr Neville Faulks, QC (now Mr Justice Faulks), told the court that the verdicts of successive juries in 1962 had brought to the company and Mr Lewis a total of £217,000 tax free.

'That was not the verdict,' remarked the court. 'No, but it is the law', replied counsel. It still is. It is not the law that juries must award large sums in damages against publishers, but they do it. This is probably because the newspapers particularly are always bragging about giving cars away. Magazines are always offering glamorous prizes such as holidays for two on Canvey Island, or more southerly seasides. Jurors therefore treat them as big spenders who would be affronted at having to write a cheque for less than four figures.

The only real protection anyone has against being sued for libel or slander is that the *Legal Aid and Advice Act, 1949* does not permit Legal Aid to be given for such actions—either to bring them or to defend them. They cannot be brought in County Courts, either (though they can be and sometimes are transferred to them). Since a solicitor whom a defamation victim instructed to take action would have to do it in the High Court, he would usually ask for a substantial sum on account of the costs.

He might do it out of generosity or for a speculative fee, of course, but it would have to be a pretty concrete case before most solicitors would do that for a stranger. The law undoubtedly favours plaintiffs to a most unjust degree, but the chances of success in a particular case might be poor.

Harold Loughans might have been supposed to have a good chance of success in his action against *The People* in 1963. It had published the memoirs of J. D. Casswell QC who had defended, often successfully, no fewer than 40 people accused of murder in the hanging days. When Loughans was tried, charged with murdering Mrs Rose Robinson at Portsmouth, in 1944, the first jury disagreed and the second acquitted him. But, he said, the articles made him out to be the murderer. This was one case in which 'Josh' Casswell had prosecuted, not defended.

Loughans had confessed to killing Mrs Robinson in a struggle while burgling her beershop. His own counsel told the jury he was a 'confirmed liar', and there was put forward an alibi. And three unimpeachable witnesses testified that on the night in question he was with them in the underground station at Warren Street in London, which was used as an air raid shelter.

However, the alibi did not cover the period between 12.30 am and 5.15 am on the night of the murder, and a test drive from Warren Street to Portsmouth showed that the trip could be done comfortably in the time. The Judge, Mr Justice Cassels refused to permit this evidence to be given in the second trial because it had not been available in the first. But it was permitted in the libel action, which Mr Loughans lost.

He later confessed.

The trouble with claims such as that is that they are usually brought by people who cannot pay the costs when they lose. It consequently costs the defendant a large sum to employ solicitors and counsel and gather the proof he needs, and he cannot get it back. A lot of unscrupulous people realise this and make black-mailing claims in defence of their reputations. In its conspicuous fairness, the law assumes until the person who spoke or wrote the defamation proves otherwise, that he (or she) is guilty until he proves himself innocent. The foundation of this rule is lost in antiquity.

It is supposed to be founded on the logic of the defendant being the accuser.

> *'Who steals my purse steals trash . . .*
> *But he that filches from me my good name*
> *Steals that which not enriches him*
> *And makes me poor indeed.'*

> *Othello. Act 3 Sc. 3.*

This is a most noble sentiment, but rarely does the question in a libel suit amount to high drama. The cases which have made the law what it is have been more ludicrous than chivalrous. The first thing a plaintiff has to do is to show that the slander, if spoken, or libel, if written, drawn, sculpted, or shown by photograph, was about him. It might have been thought that Mr Artemus Jones, the well-known barrister on the Wales and Chester Circuit would have no difficulty in proving that the article in the *Sunday Chronicle*, Manchester, in July, 1908, applied to him.

It was supposed to be about the social side of the motor races at Dieppe.

> ' *"Whist! There is Artemus Jones with a woman who is not his wife, who must be, you know—the other thing!"* . . . *Who would suppose, by his goings on, that he was a churchwarden at Peckham?'*

The *Chronicle*'s Paris reporter, who wrote the piece, had never heard of Artemus Jones. Nor had the editor. The proprietor, Edward Hulton, had. Fifteen years and more earlier, Jones was a sub-editor on that very paper. When he left for London, to work in the Parliamentary Press Gallery for *The Daily Telegraph*, Mr Hulton gave him a letter of recommendation.

Newspaper proprietors quite often find out what is in their papers only after they have been published. All those earnest political people who complain so much about the Press Barons manipulating information know as well as anyone else that they do not actually write the copy and set the type. Mr Hulton, however, concluded that no harm had been done, for no one would connect Artemus Jones with the totally fictitious Peckham churchwarden. The judge at the Manchester Assizes was Mr Justice Channell and he said it did not matter whether there was any intention to refer to Jones or not. He was awarded £1,750 damages—quite a big award for those days.

The witnesses who said that they associated the plaintiff with the article were not his brother barristers who were alleged to have teased him about it. But they included some of the people who had known him since his boyhood as the son of a Denbigh stonemason, born Thomas Jones.

Now if there is a Welsh name which confers no distinction at all upon its owner it is Tom Jones. At about his confirmation time, in order to add lustre to an otherwise bald and inconspicuous cognomination, Tom and his father decided that he should become known to the world as Thomas Artemus Jones. When he became a reporter in London he signed his pieces, 'T.A.J.', and when called to the Bar he was known as Thomas Artemus Jones. Why he chose 'Artemus' as his distinction has never been explained.

This was another of the cases Rufus Isaacs KC lost so magnificently. Everyone in the world called Artemus Jones could not sue the *Sunday Chronicle*, he protested. If that was permitted, every time there was a true story about a Bill Jones or a Tom Smith committing murder, all the other Bill Joneses or Tom Smiths could bring libel actions against any paper that printed them. There had to be something which showed which Tom Smith was intended.

In the Court of Appeal, the Chief Justice, Lord Alverstone, agreed with the trial judge that it was entirely up to the jury whether the libel referred to Artemus or not. We shall never know how much weight they gave to his former association with the *Sunday Chronicle* —though his counsel accepted that the writer and the editor were totally unaware of his existence. Lord Justice Fletcher Moulton said that he could not understand how anyone of any intelligence could think that a name like that was not fictitious—as indeed the real Tom Jones's was—and that an inadvertent libel was no more possible in English law than 'an honest fraud'.

On principle, no doubt he was right. Sir Valentine Holmes KC wrote 40 years later that this case was wrong in principle but curiously enough the question had never before been decided by the House of Lords. When they dealt with it, they all seemed to support the judgment in the Court of Appeal of Lord Justice Farwell.

He had decided for Artemus, but by analogy with negligence, and the company fraud case of *Derry* v. *Peek*. He said Hultons were reckless, adding:

> '*If the libel was true of another person and honestly aimed at and intended for him . . . the plaintiff has no cause of action, although all his friends may fit the cap on him.*'

The speeches in the House of Lords really accepted this doctrine, and consequently should have accepted also what both Farwell and Fletcher Moulton had insisted on, that no action could be brought where a libel was true of someone else, otherwise no paper would ever dare print a story true of someone in case someone of the same name should sue over it.

Which is just what happened in the Case of the Camberwell Bigamist. The *Daily Express* had a little story in 1938 which said that Harold Newstead, a 30-year-old 'Camberwell man' liked having two wives at once, and it had got him nine months. There was a Harold Newstead, a ladies' hairdresser of that locality. When his witnesses read the story they were so upset that they rang him up, it was said. Then, remarked the judge, they knew he was not doing nine months.

The jury, on the Farwell line, were asked to say whether the *Express* was negligent or reckless in not describing the bigamist more clearly. They replied that it was negligent but not reckless. The damages they assessed at a farthing. The Court of Appeal, again divided, held that negligence was irrelevant and the unjust absurdity recognised in Artemus Jones's case came to pass. A libel which was true of one man could be sued upon by another.

Mr Newstead, so far as is known, did not bring a new trial although one was ordered, even though Lord Justice McKinnon disagreed with the order.

> '*Twelve reasonable people have assessed the Plaintiff's possible damages at one farthing. And on the facts proved I cannot conceive that any twelve reasonable people would arrive at a larger figure.*'

He was against permitting another trial so that Mr Newstead could perhaps get his farthing.

> '*For I think we sit here to administer justice, and not to supervise a game of forensic dialectics.*'

The dialectics have not stopped there.

The House of Lords decided the case of *Morgan* v. *Odhams Press* in July, 1971. There, the witnesses for the plaintiff said that they had seen him out and about with a girl a couple of weeks before *The Sun* published a story about her. She was identified as a girl who had given information to the police about a dog-doping conspiracy. The story said that 'last week' she had been kidnapped by the gang, and held in a house at Finchley. They had therefore assumed that the plaintiff was connected with the gang.

It might have been more logical—and what are dialectics but logic?—to assume that since they saw her with him a couple of weeks before quite freely dining in a restaurant and walking about the street, that he had not kidnapped her a week later. But, said Lord Reid (*1917*) *2 All E.R. p. 1163*:

> '*If we are to . . . take the ordinary man as our guide then we must accept a certain amount of loose thinking.*'

With due deference, the Ordinary Man gave Mr Newstead one farthing damages. It was Law Lords and Lord Justices of Appeal who brought in the loose thinking.

Lord Morris said that the ordinary readers did not read sensational articles with cautious and critical analytical care. Artemus Jones, he pointed out, succeeded though he was not a churchwarden and did not live at Peckham. This appeared to justify him in ruling that Mr Morgan was properly identified with the libel even though he did not live in a house at Finchley but in a flat at Cricklewood.

The Court of Appeal had ruled that the libel could not refer to the plaintiff because his witnesses had not identified him from the newspaper article but from other circumstances. But by three to two, the Law Lords held that the story could properly refer to him. Thus by one vote the House of Lords has achieved the revolution that a libel which does not itself identify a plaintiff can libel him.

It is established by Artemus Jones's case that the libeller can be unaware of his victim's existence, and have no intention to refer. Consequently, anyone who can fit a libel upon himself can make it expensive for any publisher.

Much support for this proposition is drawn from *Cassidy* v. *Daily Mirror*, in 1929. The libel there was a picture caption. In page 1175 of the *All England Law Reports Vol. 2 of 1971*, Lord Guest is reported as saying that the caption described the man in the picture as 'Mr Cassidy'.

It did not. It described him as Mr. Corrigan—the name under which this former General in the Mexican Army was known. His real name was Cassidy. But his society name was what appeared in the paper. And that makes it more surprising that his wife, from whom he was separated, successfully sued the paper. For the caption announced the engagement of the racehorse owner to the girl in the picture with him. His wife claimed that because of that her friends—who knew Corrigan visited her at her shop—thought that he was free to marry and that therefore she was not really his wife. And those ladies came forward and described how disappointed they were in their friend and she got £500 damages, which she kept in the Court of Appeal, even though it was divided. Lord Justice Greer was moved to remark how careful he would have to be about describing people whom he thought to be bachelors as such.

The high point of these dialectics was the action by Mrs Hough, the wife of a boxer called Frank Hough, against the *Daily Express*. They had a story about his curly-headed wife who watched all his fights—but she was not his wife. His real wife's witnesses had to admit that they were not misled for they danced at the wedding. Mrs Hough, however, kept her 50 guineas damages, because the Court of Appeal thought other people might have been misled.

'I see nothing wrong with these decisions', said Lord Reid, in *Morgan's Case, p. 1162.*

It being fairly easy to get yourself identified as the victim of a libel —perhaps by changing your name in good time to be libelled—it remains then to be seen whether the words injure your reputation.

If they injure you but they are not 'defamatory' you can only recover damages if they are false and maliciously published. Malice means a wrong motive.

How wrong the motive has to be is an esoteric judgment rather similar to the determination whether words are 'defamatory'. Animal similarities are again helpful. Mr Reddaway called his excellent hair belting 'Camel Hair belting' and impressed on it the likeness of a camel. By this means he distinguished a common commercial substance from 'Yak belting' and 'Crocodile belting'. His former employee, Mr Banham, commenced business on his own account and started to call it 'Camel Hair belting' using it in the merely descriptive sense because the hair from which he made it was called in the trade camel hair! Mr Reddaway sued him for this and when the action was well under way it occurred to an expert witness to find out exactly what kind of hair it was that they used. So he went to the Manchester Zoo and helped himself to a sample from a camel and it was thus discovered that the stuff was indeed camel's hair. The Court of Appeal held therefore that Mr Banham was perfectly entitled to describe truthfully the material he sold. But the House of Lords, notwithstanding the truthfulness of the description, restrained him.

'*Neither Banham nor anybody else is entitled to steal Reddaway's trade under colour of imparting accurate and possibly interesting information,*'

369

said Lord Macnaghten (*1896*) *A.C. 199.*

This is not a manifestation of Moores' epigram 'The greater the truth the worse the libel'.

A libel is a personal action for a wrong. The right dies with the victim. But the Draconian severity of the law of libel causes it to be pressed into service in order to get damages where it would be difficult to prove damage, which must be done in the 'actions on the case for words'.

> '*There are no words so plain that they may not be published with reference to such circumstances and to such persons knowing those circumstances as to convey a meaning very different from that which would be understood from the same words used under different circumstances,*'

said Lord Blackburn in *Capital & Counties Bank Ltd.* v. *Hewtry* (*1882*) *7 App. Cas. 741.*

The defendant Brewers had a row with a bank manager and instructed their managers and tenants that they would not accept any cheques drawn on the Bank. When the word got round there was a run on the Bank which nearly ruined it. The Law Lords held that it was not a libel; even though it caused a great deal of damage.

However:

> '*That an action will lie for written or oral falsehoods, not actionable* per se *nor even defamatory, where they are maliciously published, where they are calculated in the ordinary course of things to produce and where they do produce, actual damages, is established law,*'

said the court in *Ratcliff* v. *Evans* (*1892*) *2 Q.B. C p. 527.*

This is just the 'intentional wrong' doctrine in another guise. To conspire to damage a man, induce his contractors not to work for him is an actionable wrong. And yet the damaging words often fail to be visited by damages—even though the *Defamation Act, 1952* does away with the necessity for proof of actual damage where the words refer to the plaintiff in his office, profession, trade or calling.

In *Mawe* v. *Pygott* (*1869*) *Ir. R. 4 C.L. 54*, an Irish priest failed in a claim over words which said he was an informer. This would destroy his reputation among criminals, he said. The judge agreed but added:

> '*The very circumstances which will make a person be regarded with disfavour by the criminal classes will raise his character in the estimation of right-thinking men.*'

The 'right-thinking man' is therefore an Irish import but he was pressed into service by Lord Atkin in *Sim* v. *Stretch* (*1936*) *52 T.L.R. 669.*

> *'That juries should be free to award damages for injuries to reputation is one of the safeguards of liberty. But the protection is undermined when exhibitions of bad manners or discourtesy are placed on the same level as attacks on character and are treated as actionable wrongs.'*

That case was remarkable for its pettiness. The plaintiff claimed to have been libelled after the defendant had enticed away a treasure of a parlourmaid and sent a telegram saying:

> *'Edith has resumed her service with us today. Please send her possessions and the money you borrowed, also her wages.'*

The publication lay in the necessity for the Post Office staff to read the telegram in transmission. Three judges thought it was defamatory to say that the plaintiff borrowed money from a servant. This pettifogging dispute thus went to the House of Lords, and the claim was dimissed. But it enabled the highest judicial approval to be given to the 'right-thinking man' approach.

This case should not be confused with the unsuccessful attempt by Alistair Sim, the actor, to restrain Heinz from using his voice in a television advertisement (*1959*) *1 All. E.R. 547.*

That was a claim founded on the not very legal sounding tort called 'passing-off'. It is a cousin to the 'trade libel' as 'injurious' or 'malicious falsehood' is sometimes called. In a 'trade libel' the wrong-doer directly attacks a competitor. In 'passing-off' he takes the competitor's trade by appearing to be the competitor. It is quite common for a 'trade libel' to be an ordinary libel or a malicious falsehood and not *per se* defamatory.

Mere extravagant puffing of one's own product, and all the 'bests' and 'better thans' are not, however, actionable under English law, although this field of law is much more active on the Continent and Market membership might well see a change here.

> *'Comparison—yes; but Disparagement—no'*,

said Lord Justice Hodson (*Cellactite and British Ucallite* v. *Robertson, The Times* 23rd July, 1957)

It has to be so for otherwise:

> *'the courts of law would be turned into a machinery for advertising rival productions by obtaining a judicial determination which of the two was the better'*,
>
> **Lord Herschell in *White* v. *Mellin* (1895) A.C. 154.**

Attacking another's product is also called 'slander of goods'. And a butcher, baker or candlestick maker stood a better chance in our grandfather's days of getting a judgment for that than many a person with more social status. For ordinary slander would not command a verdict unless either damage was proved or the victim was injured 'in the way of his profession'—rigidly considered

> '*Some of the cases can hardly fail to excite surprise:*
> '*a clergyman having failed to obtain redress for the imputation of adultery; and a schoolmistress having been declared incompetent to maintain an action for a charge of prostitution*',

said Lord Denman in (*1834*) *2 Ad E.*

In 1892 the *Slander of Women Act* made any slur on a woman's chastity actionable without proof of damage—as it was, of course, if written. But even in 1916 the Law Lords would not accept that

> '*adultery, profligacy, immoral conduct or the like*'.
>
> **(1916) 2 A.C. 499.**

slandered a man unless they affected his business conduct, though of course, if written or depicted they libelled him.

As long ago as *Dr Sibthorpe's Case* (*1628*) *1 Roll. Abr. 76*, it was actionable 'to impute incontinence to a clergyman who is beneficed'. In 1857 it was held equally dastardly to imply that a clergyman misappropriated the Sacrament money (*Highmore* v. *Countess of Harrington 3 C.B.N.S. 142*). Ignorance of the law in barristers and solicitors is naturally actionable—the very first civil action for libel was one such (*King* v. *Lake* [*1672*] *2 Vent 28*) and even before then it was held slanderous (*Bankes* v. *Allen* [*1616*] *1 Rolles Abr. 54*). 'Quack', defames a doctor (*Allen* v. *Eaton* [*1630*] *1 Rolles Abr. 54*).

> '*To say of a physician that he had debauched a lady patient would be actionable* per se. *But to say that he had committed adultery or was the defendant in an action of criminal conversation or was of general immoral behaviour would not be actionable* per se.'
>
> **Jones v. Jones (1916) 1 K.B. 360.**

That was rather odd because criminal conversation had been abolished in favour of divorce for nearly 60 years by then. But of course, doctors were then being struck off as now for philandering with patients but not for other inconstancies. Charges of incompetence among professionals and short weight and insolvency among tradesmen are the foundations of this protection of trading reputation.

And here the law of trade competition meets the law of defamation properly. If a man tries to take away another's trading reputation he can be restrained or cast in damages. And so he can by cashing in on the goodwill. This is called 'passing-off' his business as the plaintiff's—like the camel hair belting case. Even though the description was true.

The criminal law of false trade descriptions can be invoked here but the injunction and damages are used most between traders. They want compensation. They can only get it when the advertising or get-up or way of carrying on business is such that there must be every chance of confusion and so loss of trade. The characteristics they claim for their trade must therefore be distinctive and not merely descriptive. In the Spanish Champagne Case there had been an unsuccessful prosecution of the defendants for labelling their sparkling wine as *Spanish Champagne.*

The august Champagne Houses of that district round Espernay in France claimed an injunction. Sir Milner Holland QC, the counsel for the defendants, argued with that confident expertise for which he was celebrated, that the champagne process was merely double fermentation—used for cider and perry and other wines. There was nothing special about it.

'Why then do your clients want to use it?' asked Mr Justice Danckwerts (*Bollinger* v. *Costa Brava Wine Co.*). They lost.

That was a bit unusual, for geographical descriptions are usually not considered distinctive—but descriptive.

In order to save traders having to prove damage to goodwill, and therefore to establish goodwill, they often register trade marks and so can easily restrain infringements of their marks. But the purposes for which marks are registered are restrictively construed, and a mark will not be registered if it is merely descriptive. It must be distinctive.

When Mr Perky invented and patented a machine for making 'shredded or filamentous cereal foods' it was some time before the product caught on but from about 1926 *Shredded Wheat* was a household word. However in litigation in England, Canada and USA in the Thirties the manufacturers failed to restrain the Kellogg Company from the use of the words for it was merely descriptive. It is now, of course, highly distinctive of a particular product.

The law is much more jealous of the name of a business.

It was no doubt the simple coincidence that his parents admired the Prince Consort which led them 'by felicity at the font' according to a Lord Justice to christen the infant who grew up into the musical Mr Hall 'Albert Edward'.

On reaching man's estate he organised and led a small band of musicians which he called 'the Albert Hall Orchestra'. Unquestionably deriving their title from the same source, the Corporation of the Hall of Arts and Sciences, who owned and managed the neo-Gothic rotunda opposite the Victoria Memorial, claimed an injunction restraining Mr Hall from using that description, even though they had no orchestra of their own. The action failed for the law of England does not mind what anyone calls himself or herself, so long as it is not for a fraudulent purpose (*Corporation of the Hall of Arts and Sciences* v. *Hall* [*1934*] *56 T.L.R. 518*).

After Lord and Lady Cowley were divorced, the court refused to restrain her from using the title of Lady Cowley (*1901*) *A.C. 450*. Had it been a fraudulent 'holding out' the court would have interfered. A suit for Jactitation of Marriage can be brought to restrain someone from holding himself or herself as one's spouse, or even a libel or slander action if it infers that they are not legally married when they are. While, therefore, there is a right in every free-born Briton to call himself what he likes—though there is no way known to the law to change a Baptismal name or forename—(*Re Parrot* (*1946*) *Ch. 183*)—it is a right which can cause a great deal of trouble. It caused litigation between father and son over 'Burgess's Essence of Anchovies'. Like Mr Hall, Mr Burgess Junior was vindicated. The honest use of one's own name is perfectly lawful even though it affords a distinct trade advantage.

> '*All the Queen's subjects have a right if they will to manufacture and sell pickles and sauces,*'

said Lord Justice Knight Bruce (*1853*) *3 De. G.M. & G.*

Miss Ann Summers who opened the first Sex Shop has discovered that this simple principle of the law can degenerate into complexity. When people start to trade through limited companies, life usually does become very complicated. Having been a member of Ann Summers Ltd., she found that the members of that company objected strongly to her trading as 'Ann Summers'.

The law generally leaves it to people who want to complain about other people's names to get on with it themselves. The Legislature has interfered very little. *The Geneva Conventions Act, 1957*, prohibits the employment of Red Cross and a few connected titles, and the *Chartered Associations* (*Protection of Names and Uniforms Act*) *1936*, prohibits the unauthorised use of Scout, Guide, British Legion, Royal Life Saving, and Order of St John. *The Charities Act, 1960 s. 31* (*2*) requires the permission of the Charity Commissioners for the use of the phrase 'common good' but the main restriction is that in *s. 17* of the *Companies Act, 1948*

> '*No company shall be registered by a name which in the opinion of the Board of Trade is undesirable.*'

There is no caucus of little men sitting on Millbank choosing names for their euphony. Such skill and taste as is expended thereon is that of the 'onlie begetters' of the fledgeling company. All the Registrar does is to refuse names which are too much like existing names, and those which hint at connections with Royalty. Similar considerations are exercised under the *Registration of Business Names Act, 1916*, in respect of unincorporated firms and sole traders using names other than their very own. But the Registrar will permit registration of names so very similar that lawsuits over the confusion of businesses and goods are quite common, especially when the businesses are located so far apart that confusion would not occur to the Registrar but does to the business men.

It is a proposition as safe as any other in our law that no copyright protection will be given to a name. (A design protection is not really the same thing.) The reason is that it is difficult to call a name an original literary work, which is what copyright protects—e.g. William Hill's Fixed Odds Football Coupon (*[1964] 1 W.L.R.*). A few words strung together does not usually take much working out. A pool coupon, on the other hand, is the cornerstone of a multi-million pound business.

'Way back in the 15th Century the weavers and miners from Europe who came here under the King's protection were given *literae patentes*—'open letters'—from him telling all men that they were entitled to work and take the profit from some enterprise for ten or twenty years. All these grants of privileges were designed to enable the native British to become skilful in these crafts. By the time the young Elizabeth took the throne trade was well enough developed for Cecil to sell her on the policy of Monopoly, which very effectively ensured the Royal rake-off. Cecil did rather well out of it too, and so did Francis Bacon. There were basically three kinds. The biggest deals were the creation of corporations by charter, as boroughs had been incorporated for centuries. Patents granted monopolies of particular branches of trade or manufacture. Nowadays they are confined to inventions, and they are sealed by the Patent Office Controller under the authority of Act of Parliament. They can only be granted for ways and means of making things or doing work upon things. The great majority of them are pretty useless. They are not granted unless they are novel and provide something more original than just an intelligent development of an old way of doing something. In that respect they depend on ideas.

Copyright, on the other hand, which protects the fruits of a person's brainwork, does not protect ideas at all. Anyone can pinch anyone else's ideas so long as he does not express them in the way the originator did. The right to restrain piracy is therefore a virtual monopoly.

Once having received a monopoly from Elizabeth, it by no means followed that the patentee had 'a licence to print money' as Lord Thomson described the statutory monopoly of commercial television in its golden days. She was much more interested in selling franchises than in protecting those she had already sold. The Great Case of Monopolies (*D'Arcy* v. *Allein* (*1610*)) established the plaintiff's monopoly in respect of playing cards. But public policy reared its head in the next few years and in 1623 Parliament enacted the *Statute of Monopolies* which made unlawful the monopolies created by merchants who cornered the market in any trade. It might be thought that this conflicted in principle with the grant of prerogative monopolies by the Crown to individuals, and so it did. But with that *sang froid* which always has characterised the 'people with a stake in the country' no one took any notice of the statute except to repeal it in 1789.

Modern patents are sealed by authority of Act of Parliament. Einstein was a Patent Examiner and in civilised nations all over the world learned men labour in libraries looking up specifications of patents to find out whether they are real 'inventions' or whether there is 'prior art' from which they are mere developments and so not entitled to protection. The result is that it can take several years to get a patent for an invention. Quite often the technologists have improved on the device during that time and the competitors have worked out something of their own which is just as useful but does not infringe the patent.

There was not long ago patent action in London about silos. The patentees called a professor as an expert witness and he told Mr Justice Lloyd-Jacob the history of silage-making. The early silos, he said, were often railway sleepers with a chain round.

'Why was the chain there?' asked Counsel. 'You must tell My Lord so that it is on the record.' The professor thought. Finally he said 'To stop the sleepers falling down'.

> '*I should not have thought it required a Fellow of the Royal Society to tell me that,*'

said the judge.

He was followed into the witness box by a farmer who explained that he had made silage, man and boy, simply by putting layers of crop and molasses in a space formed by some walls in his yard. Cross-examined on behalf of the patentee, he was asked what was the main disadvantage of his silo. He could at first think of none, but eventually agreed that the walls were not portable.

> '*You therefore cannot get your silo to where your stock are, can you?*' *demanded Counsel in a brilliant exposition of the main feature of the invention.*

> '*No,*' *admitted the farmer.* '*But all my beasts can walk to the silo.*'

Sometimes the details of an invention are kept secret. The court goes into chambers and the witnesses are permitted to conceal some of the best bits of testimony. But since the production of a whole factory and the jobs of the workers and the capital of the business might well depend on the result of the action, these are pretty tough struggles.

Sometimes they are also fought on the wrongful use of confidential information. The Vice-Chancellor Sir John Pennycrick sat in his court for several days in 1964 surrounded by brassieres of all shapes and sizes. He was deciding the case of *Peter Pan Manufacturing Corporation* v. *Corsets Silhouette Ltd.* (*1964*) *1 W.L.R. 96.* The confidential nature of the 'know how' for making certain brassieres was established. How does one define 'know how' in a legal document?

> '*A person who has obtained information in confidence is not allowed to use it as a springboard for activities detrimental to the person who made the confidential communication—and a springboard it remains even when all the features have been published or can be ascertained by actual inspection by any member of the public,*'

declared Mr Justice Roxburgh in *Terrapin Ltd.* v. *Builders Supply Co.* (*Hayes*) *Ltd.* (*1967*) *R.P.C. 375.*

The basis of this branch of the law can be found in an action actually brought by the Prince Consort to restrain a man called Strange from publishing some etchings made by Victoria and Albert as a hobby ((*1849*) *1 M. & G. 25*). That was how *lese majeste* gave birth to breach of confidence, and the case was followed in an action by Margaret, Duchess of Argyll against the Duke (*1967*) *Ch. 302* to restrain publication of details of personal matters and conduct while they were married to each other.

Mr Brian Walden MP is following in the path of others who wish to see enacted a Right of Privacy. The virtues claimed for some such law are that people should not be disturbed in the enjoyment of their private life by publicity, or by having confidences revealed.

The confidences already have some protection. Some of the earlier demands for a law to punish industrial espionage pointed out that no offence was committed by someone who photographed, but did not remove, a confidential document. The idea seemed to be to legislate against that and against the importunities of door-to-door salesmen and journalists. Most people can order unwelcome callers away from their doors but cannot prevent the publication of pictures and stories about them—though if they are libellous they can do so.

Copyright law has been invoked to try to prevent such disclosures. Mr Fraser the public relations consultant of the Greek Colonels' regime failed to prevent the *Sunday Times* from quoting from his report to his employers, even though it was undoubtedly his copyright work (*Fraser* v. *Evans* [*1969*] *1 Q.B. 349*).

If a libel suit or a breach of copyright is proved and there was an invasion of privacy the damages will probably be large but the breach of privacy itself will not be grounds for damages without the other.

Cyril Tolley, the amateur golf champion, sued Fry's the chocolate people in 1929 over one of their advertisements. It showed a caricature of him with a bar of chocolate sticking out of his hip pocket. He got £1,000 damages on the argument that it was a libel, reflecting on his amateur status because it made it appear that he profited from advertising. The Court of Appeal held that the advertisement was incapable of a defamatory meaning. Lord Justice Scrutton dissented:

> '*I do not know if a judge is allowed to know of the Duchess who made an income by vowing that:*
>> *Her complexion derived its perfection from somebody's soap which it doesn't.*'

W. S. Gilbert.

But the House of Lords said the advertisement was capable of a defamatory meaning. Eminent lawyers have argued that *Tolley* v. *Fry [1931] A.C. 333)* is the beginning of a Right of Privacy in English law. Hardly, but it shows that when the court can turn something it does not like into a libel, it will.

The attractions of preventing undesired publications of things of which the plaintiff can claim the copyright are more apparent than real. Marie Corelli failed to prevent a tea shop proprietor selling postcards of her home to the trippers who came to gawp (*Corelli* v. *Gray (1913) 29 T.L.R. 570*).

He that trades upon another's name might well filch the trade as well, and enrich himself considerably. On the other hand anyone fortunate enough to be libelled by a wealthy newspaper might end up rich indeed.

However 'Uncle Mac' the Children's Hour personality, failed to restrain the use of his name on the packets of Uncle Mac's Puffed Wheat, because the cereal firm had no common activity with the BBC. This seems curiously obtuse of the law. One would have thought that the description of Lord Macnaghten in the Camel Hair Belting case would cover it.

> '*The whole merit of that description, its one virtue for Banham's purposes, was its duplicity.*'

Names are rarely protected by copyright. When they are expressed as a trade mark they have the protection of registration and infringements are actionable. But there is seldom enough work or originality in a name to make it attract copyright.

Mr Justice Peterson's (1916) comment that 'What is worth copying is *prima facie* worth protecting', is honoured strongly nowadays. But the protection of William Hill's Fixed Odds coupon is the protection of the business expertise which goes into working out the commercial correctness of offering particular bets. The coupon, said Lord Greene was, 'the very instrument of their trade'. This is how the protection was afforded to it as a 'literary or artistic work'—though the *Copyright Act, 1956* includes among them 'compilations'. To protect the trade of the plaintiff this and the *Registered Designs Act, 1949* do not demand artistry in conception or execution of the work.

Said Lord Justice Megaw in *Amp. Incorporated* v. *Utilux Property Ltd. (1970) R.P.C.*:

> *'Courts of law should not be made arbiters on matters of aesthetic taste.'*

To use a name to steal trade is 'passing-off'. But so powerful is the freedom of British enterprise that not even the intention to deceive will lead to restraint if there is no great likelihood of deception. In other ways the intention to injure the trade of the competitor can be carried into powerful execution without offending any known principle of the law. Whilst trading reputation and good-will are protected, so is competition. Restraints on trade always have been anathematical to the Common Law.

The Elizabethan monopoly law was recognised as supporting the notion, even if it was sacrificed on the altar of expediency. When a couple of stage coach operators agreed not to compete, a Georgian judge refused to recognise it as a commercial conspiracy to damage other coaching firms. It was merely a sensible accommodation to prevent cut-throat competition which could ruin them both.

On the other hand when the China Tea suppliers combined to slash the freight rates in 1890 and excluded the plaintiffs from their club it was attacked as a conspiracy of unfair competition (*Mogul Steamship Co.* v. *McGregor, Gow and Co. (1892) A.C. 25*).

> *'What is unfair that is neither forcible nor fraudulent?'*

asked Lord Bramwell.

The Law Lords were careful to explain that there was no personal malice or ill-will towards the plaintiffs. The defendants just wanted to lure them out of the trade. If incidentally it drove them into bankruptcy, that was too bad. But it was not and is not illegal.

In *Ratcliff* v. *Evans (1892) 2 Q.B. 524* some Master Boilermakers, showing that same propensity for litigious innovation which the journeymen boilermakers emulated a few years later, falsely and maliciously published in a newspaper that their competitor had ceased business, and so caused his trade to decline. That was going just too far, and they were made liable in damages for malicious falsehood.

But when Nordenfelt, the arms magnate, freely entered into a covenant not to carry on this profession of weapon maker anywhere for a long period, the House of Lords held that he was not bound by it because it was an unreasonable restraint of trade (*Nordenfelt* v. *Maxim-Nordenfelt Guns and Ammunition Co.* [*1894*] *A.C. 535*). The world was getting smaller and to deny an arms magnate anywhere to trade was intolerable.

In *Kreglinger* v. *The New Patagonia Meat Co.* (*1914*) *A.C. 25*, a mortgage condition binding a company to sell its sheepskins to a lender of money even after the loan was repaid was similarly held repugnant.

Already in America the *Sherman Act* of 1890 had provided penalties and government remedies for monopolies and restraints of trade by restrictive practice. The *Clayton Act* of 1914 was aimed at mergers and combines designed to eliminate competition. European countries were beginning to want controls on 'Cartels'. A Cartel registered with and approved by Government was desirable. Other monopolies were outlawed.

In 1914 Lord Haldane was saying in *Seddon* v. *North Western Salt Co.*:

> '*Unquestionably, the combination was to regulate supply and keep up prices. But an ill-regulated supply and unremunerative prices may in point of fact be disadvantageous to the public . . . drive manufacturers out of business, lower wages, cause unemployment . . .*'

Trade and politics were marching hand in hand, and the law blessed the union. For the law is life, said Lord Simonds in *Gilmour* v. *Coats* (*1949*) *A.C. 426*.

An Account Of Stewardship

'*A trust is its weakest point.*'
O. Henry in *The Gentle Grafter.*

THOUGH THE BASIC problems of economic law raised in the disputes
of boilermakers remain unresolved, the credit for establishing the
essential principle of corporation law must go to a bootmaker.
The law long recognised 'corporations sole'—such as bishops.
Such institutions do not die, nor even fade away. There was no
reason to wind them up, for until the last century some of them
were indeed thriving concerns. The Durham Bishopric had an
income of some £136,000 per annum before the reorganisation of
the ecclesiastical finances which put them in to the hands of the
Commissioners. But of course, the bishops who had been given
vast resources so that they could afford to keep the Scots at bay
were not the real owners of that wealth. They were Trustees. The
idea of a formal legal owner of property being bound by law to
manage it not for his own benefit originated with the Franciscans
in the 12th Century. Their vow of poverty forbade them to own the
building in which they prayed and sheltered. Their property was
thus owned for them by others, though it may well have been bought
with alms given to the friars.

At the time, the Royal revenues consisted largely in collecting
taxes on the deaths of wealthy subjects or exacting similar taxes
called fines from orphans of wealthy parents when they married or
took up their inheritances. Local lords could also levy taxes in this
way. If the land was legally owned by trustees, the ownership could
be changed to avoid what the *Estate Duty Act, 1894 s. 2* so belatedly
described as 'passing on death'. Consequently the mediaeval tax
dodge has survived to the present day—somewhat circumscribed,
but nevertheless retaining most of its essential advantages.

Even now it is not settled by the House of Lords who actually
'owns' trust property in every case and for every purpose. The true
principle seems to be that enunciated in *Schalit* v. *Joseph Nadler
Ltd.* (*1933*) 2 K.B. 79, a judgment of Mr Justice Goddard—as he was
even that long ago; not even a Chancery judge. He said that the

right of a beneficiary to the rent of a trust property was

> '*not to the rent, but to an account of the profits from the trustee*'.

That does not in any way conflict with the Law Lords' decision in *Baker* (*Inspector of Taxes*) v. *Archer-Shee* (*1927*) *A.C. 844*. Lady Archer-Shee was beneficiary under the will of her father, an American. 'Does the income of a trust fund "belong" to the beneficiary?' asked Viscount Sumner, forensically, and he gave the same answer as Lord Goddard gave six years later. That, however, was the position under the ordinary, long-standing law of England, and not under the *Income Tax Act, 1918*. Although the trust estate 'belonged' to the Trustees, she could compel them to account to her and so was 'entitled to' the income under 'income tax law'—and had to pay tax.

Said Lord Loreburn:

> '*If such a property is not taxable it results that a person residing here (whether a British subject or not) can be creating a foreign trust of stocks and shares and accumulating or spending the income abroad, can escape taxation upon that income.*'

And however pleasant that might be it cannot be done by a resident here, which is, of course, why so many people exile themselves.

Not that a trust is not a good way to save tax.* The rate of Estate Duty on estates between £80,000 and £150,000 is 65 per cent. Over £750,000 it is 85 per cent. If a testator leaves his estate to his widow absolutely, she will pay that duty. When she dies the appropriate duty will be paid on what she has left—which may well be more than she took if it is wisely invested for a few years. But if the testator left it in trust to his wife for life and thereafter to his children the duty would be paid only on his death and not that of the widow. Because the Trustees would inherit by it 'passing on' his death, and would still own it when the widow died so that it would not pass on her death.

The taxing statutes have been more successful than Henry VIII in trust-busting. In 1535 he introduced no fewer than three Bills to rid the nation of the abuses of 'uses' as trusts were called, just as Richard III had done.

> '*Costs and grievous vexations daily grow among the king's subjects,*'

lamented one of his Acts.

---

* Three years later, by showing that American law was different, the Archer-Shees won a similar tax claim.

It was not, however, the subjects that felt the draught. It was the Kings. Henry's Statute of Uses

> '*was forced upon an extremely unwilling Parliament by an extremely strong-willed King. It was very unpopular and was one of the excuses, if not one of the causes, of the Great Catholic Rebellion known as the Pilgrimage of Grace*'.

Maitland, *Equity, P. 35.*

That led, of course, to the *Wills Act, 1540* which gave more freedom of leaving land by will.

The *Statute of Uses* was repealed in 1925. The complicated wording of the deeds of transfer of land was such that its effect was avoided for centuries by adding three words to a conveyance deed. It was knowing the three words and where to put them that earned lawyers their fees.

'Equity' is perhaps the most misunderstood word in the language. It is the system of legal rules by which trusts are enforced. There is no trace of it in Criminal Law for a Trustee who fraudulently converts the trust property to his own use is liable to be imprisoned for seven years. What the civil courts hope to do is to compel trustees to administer trust assets properly before they run off with them or even if they do not. One of the oldest maxims of the Chancery is that 'Equity acts in person'. That simply means that if a Trustee does not do as the court orders it can lock him up for contempt.

There were many corporations formed for trading under Royal patents of monopoly, like the East India Company and the Hudson Bay Company, and just like Bishops they were corporations having a separate legal personality to the corporators. The popularity of company promotion led of course to the South Sea Bubble Company being floated in 1711 by Act of Parliament to buy the National Debt and sell interest producing stock to the contributors. But the South Sea Company had to bribe the Bank of England to set the deal up and bankrupted itself, causing a financial scandal which the Government—which had largely caused the trouble—sought to overcome by passing the *Bubble Act*, in 1720.

Section 18 declared illegal and void joint stock companies which tended 'to the common grievance, prejudice and inconvenience of His Majesty's subjects'.

The East India Company was exempted and survives today. Until the Bubble Act was repealed in 1825, merchants got used to organising their businesses with Trust Deeds. The advantages were that 'shares' of the same amount each in the joint stock could be held by shareholders who were equitable owners of the business and so the ordinary shareholder today is called an equity shareholder.

He is, however, nothing of the kind. A company is a separate legal person entirely owing its existence to Act of Parliament; and has been since William Gladstone as President of the Board of Trade invented Statutory Companies in 1845. A shareholder is liable to pay the face value of his share on its issue or when called upon. That share he can sell to anyone else eligible. By owning enough shares he can make the company do as he wishes. If he owns too few, he is powerless. If the company cannot pay its creditors they can get what is left shared equally in a winding-up.

They all have permanent notice of this instability because the word 'Limited' appears after the name of the company on the plate outside its Registered Office and on all its stationery and documents. Lord Bramwell, the Victorian judge who thought of putting 'Limited' behind company names was so pleased with himself that he even suggested that the word should be engraved on his grave stone. The idea is that anyone about to do business with a limited company is perfectly free to check up with the Registrar of Companies to find out if the capital and property of the company is large or small, or mortgaged and that the company has power under its Memorandum of Association to take part in the transaction.

This is a valuable legal protection, no doubt, but comparatively few people are aware even now that in 1964 the Registrar of Companies moved from Bush House in the Strand to Companies House in the City Road. Even if you make a search of the company's file there it will not reveal the current balance on the banking accounts of the company. (It quite likely will not even have the last few annual returns.)

It is frequently said in court that a company with £100 authorised capital and two £1 shares issued for cash might well have £10,000 in the bank. By the same token, since 1960, at least three companies with issued capital of over £1,000,000 have been compulsorily wound-up with deficiencies far outweighing their assets. Appreciating this, very few people bother to go to the City Road to find out just what the companies they deal with are worth, and of course, no bank manager would dream of revealing the state of a client's account without permission or the compulsion of an order under the *Bankers' Books Evidence Act, 1879.* The actual protection afforded to the public is therefore indeed 'Limited'.

The *Companies Act, 1967,* has provided for the accounts of all limited companies to be available to the public, but it is of little assistance to the man who has lost a great deal of money by dealing with an insolvent company to find out afterwards that a lot of other people have been 'tucked up' as well. And though the *Companies Act, 1948 s. 147 (i)* requires that the accounts shall show 'a true and fair view' of the company's financial position, very few people understand them even when they do, even though double entry book-keeping and balancing have been known to us since Lombard Street was built 600 years ago.

The great majority of companies are operated by people alone or with a few others in what would be a partnership if the enterprise was not owned by the company. Partnerships often hold their property in trust, but perhaps more often, the partners themselves own the property and allow the other partners to use it. Not all partnerships own the property and share the profits or the work equally. There is, of course, no technical reason why several limited companies should not be partners, nor why they should not carry on business under a Registered Business Name, different from that of any of the companies. Such a business name, of course, would not have 'Limited' behind it and no one dealing with it would be alerted to make inquiries in the City Road.

Sir Oscar Hobson, the doyen of city editors, used to say that economics was basically a simple subject. That could also be said of the English Law connected with it. A scheme for the re-organisation of the capital of some great company and its subsidiaries and the victims of its latest take-overs and mergers is a daunting document, which only an esoteric coterie of expert lawyers and accountants can comprehend.

The principles of the matter are succinctly expressed however in *Section 1* of the *Partnership Act, 1890*.

> '*Partnership is the relation which subsists between persons carrying on a business in common with a view of profit.*'

A 'business' might be defined as anything not illegal. Letting flats does not turn premises into 'business premises' though, of course, it is a business. The main necessity for defining the term is in connection with tax.

Lady Zia Wernher owned a racing stable which she ran as a hobby. She also owned a stud farm, which was a business. She was held liable for tax purposes to bring into the stud farm as a receipt the market value of five horses which she transferred from the business to the hobby (*Sharkey* v. *Werhner* [*1956*] *A.C. 58*).

There is nothing generally to stop a trader selling stock in trade at a loss to save tax. But where 'associated persons' sell property for less than strangers would have paid, the market value of the subject matter is used in computing profits or losses for tax purposes. But this only affects transactions which are part of the real trade of the person concerned.

While in Berlin on cinema business, Mr Rutledge had the opportunity of buying a million toilet rolls for £1,000. As soon as he came home he sold them for £10,000. The court leapt to the conclusion that he must have intended to resell the toilet paper when he bought it. The transaction was therefore 'an adventure in the nature of trade' and the profit was taxable (*1929*) *14 T.C.*

But the fact that an asset may be sold later for a profit does not turn its purchase into a trading venture, even if it is intended as an investment. But, of course, the Capital Gains Tax will apply to real estate, not owner-occupied and most other assets. If the main object of a company is to hold investments, as distinct from dealing in property it still pays tax on profits made by buying and selling property.

Section 1 of the *Partnership Act* also provides that a company is not a partnership. This is not simply because many people who have shares in companies never see a profit. This is because companies have after several centuries of development been refined to the stage where they can make a great deal of profit even when they lose money—for some people.

The real reason for the decline of business partnerships and the proliferation of companies was quite simply that the Victorians who ran the Workshop of the World had no intention of having it spoilt by too many chiefs leading not enough Indians. The mere fact that widows in Cheltenham had put their all into a company was no reason for letting them have any say in the business.

It is not essentially the limitation of liability which causes this, though that has often turned out to be the 'engine of fraud' which it was feared it would become when it was being enacted during the early Victorian railway boom. It was the fact that legally a company is entirely separate from the people who belong to it. This was, of course, the foundation of the pretended corporations at the time of the South Sea Bubble. But the Victorians found it hard to accept that merely by registering a company with the Board of Trade you brought a new person into the world.

When Mr Salomon the bootmaker converted his business into a limited company he charged the company £39,000 for it. It hardly mattered that the company had not the money to pay for it. It was an over-valuation anyway. He took 20,000 £1 shares issued as fully paid up, and six of his family took one £1 each for cash—to make up the seven members then required. And Mr Salomon took a debenture, which is a loan as distinct from a share, which mortgaged the business to him personally for £10,000 of the balance of the price. For the company could borrow from him.

When the company went broke, there was enough left to pay Mr Salomon's debenture, but nothing for the trade creditors. They were—as ordinary creditors usually are—'unsecured', having no mortage on the company's possessions. They did not appreciate this, and they persuaded the Court of Appeal that Mr Salomon's company was a sham, a mere front for him and so he should indemnify it against its trading debts—an anology with Equity. But the Law Lords declared that far from the company being Mr Salomon's agent, he, as director, was its agent.

Nowadays, of course, when bailiffs call on used-car lots and similar businesses to distrain on the possessions of individual entrepreneurs they find either that the goods the creditor believed to belong to the director belong to the company (£100 authorised; £2 issued) or conversely that the assets believed to belong to the company belong to the members personally.

If there is one rule enforced more strictly than most in the English courts it is that whoever chooses to allege that some person—real or artificial—has been fraudulent, he must allege with great particularity just what was fraudulent and prove it well and truly by convincing evidence. And the person accused in a civil or criminal court will be afforded every opportunity to defend himself—during which meantime the carcase of the enterprise can be picked bare and the beneficiaries can disappear.

Apparently poor old Salomon had actually mortgaged his debenture and tried to save the business and he lost everything as well. But like so many other unconscious litigants, he established a principle, which has enriched many people and impoverished more, but without which we could not run our modern society.

Professor L. C. B. Gower, in *Principles of Modern Company Law* (a topic not renowned for entertainment) said that 'Many of the most fundamental and salutary principles were worked out by the courts with little or no help from the statutes'. As befits one of the first of the Law Commissioners, that sentence exhibits comprehension of the true state of affairs denied to those unfamiliar with that recondite discipline. What actually happened when Joint Stock Companies were permitted to operate with limited liability was appalling confusion. A great dispute over the duties of stock jobbers was litigated in both the Chancery and the Common Law Courts. Both originally came to the same conclusion, but when the verdicts were appealed, the two appellate courts disagreed, since when businessmen have for the most part avoided taking the public trafficking of shares to any court so far as possible, and the Stock Exchange is internally policed like a mediaeval gild.

Not so long after that, the courts were able to expose the machinations of company promotors in the case about Olympia:

> '*They issue a prospectus representing that they had agreed to purchase the property for a sum largely in excess of the amount which they had, in fact, to pay. On the faith of this prospectus they collect subscriptions from a confiding and credulous public. And then comes the last act. Secretly and therefore dishonestly, they*

out into their own pockets the difference between the real and the pretended price. After a brief career the company is ordered to be wound up . . .'

Gluckstein v. Barnes (1900) A.C. 240.

Lord Macnaghten wondered why only Mr Gluckstein had been sued by the liquidator and for only a part of the secret profit. That was his good fortune, but he insisted that if he was liable at all—and he contended that he could not be—his co-directors ought to be made liable as well.

'I cannot think that this is a case in which any indulgence ought to be shown to Mr Gluckstein. He may or may not be able to recover a contribution from those who joined him in defrauding the company. He can bring an action at law if he likes. If he hesitates to take that course, or takes it and fails, then his only remedy lies in an appeal to that sense of honour which is popularly supposed to exist among robbers of a humbler type.'

It is hardly to be wondered at that businessmen did not want their transactions misconstrued like that. Public Policy was the great juristic theme then, and *laissez faire* still governed political economy. And had not the great Sir George Jessel himself, when Master of the Rolls, set the seal of approval on freedom of contract?

'You are not to extend arbitrarily those rules which say that a given contract is void as being against public policy because if there is one thing more than another public policy requires it is that men of full age and competent understanding shall have the utmost liberty of contracting and that their contracts when freely and voluntarily entered into shall be held sacred and shall be enforced by courts of justice.'

Printing & Numerical Registering Co. v. Sampson (1875) L.R. 19 Equity 462.

The formation of a company is only a contract. A contract is only a legally binding agreement. A contractor has only himself to blame if he gets caught. The legal magic by which it begets an artificial person which will obey its Svengalis is, however, subject to the totally natural restraint of the Rule in *Foss* v. *Harbottle*.

Of this rule, Professor Gower was able to write in 1957 that he thought he understood it. It can, of course, be stated with the utmost simplicity as was done in *MacDougal* v. *Gardiner* (1875) 1 Ch. D. 13.

'If the thing complained of is a thing which, in substance, the majority of the company are entitled to do, or if something has been done irregularly which the majority of the company are entitled to do legally, there can be no use having litigation about it, the ultimate end of which is that a meeting has to be called and the majority gets its wishes.'

The trouble with the Rule in *Foss* v. *Harbottle* is that it does not end there. Unhappily it does not apply to protect the majority and their leaders when what they are up to is against the law—the ordinary law. Nor does it enable them to do by simple counting of heads things which under the Memorandum or Articles of Association have to be done by special votes—such as altering the Articles.

Imagine for instance an insolvent football club of which a bevy of public spirited local businessmen become directors. They are bound to have among them someone on the local planning committee and someone else who is an estate developer, as builders are now described. Selling the ground for development would usually only be profitable if that common provision that on a winding-up surplus capital shall be distributed to all the shareholders was out of the way. All the holders of one share each would become suspicious if they were asked to sell their shares for their par value. What has to be gone in for, of course—for efficient management—is a New Share Structure. One is at once in the terminology of take-over bids. Quite early in the history of limited companies, the courts set out to find ways of clipping the wings of high fliers in company management, and the real difficulty of the Rule in *Foss* v. *Harbottle* is the result. The Rule is relaxed when it is 'in the interests of justice' so to do. Exactly when that occurs is extremely difficult to define. It can broadly be said to be when the judge has seen through the scheme.

As might be expected, the Rule rather prevents minority shareholders from resisting the majority. However, when the 'real' complainant is the company itself—that helpless creature whose earthly existence is only as a file at Companies House—a single shareholder can sue the majority and ask the court to enforce the Memorandum of Association and the Articles. This will be done if the majority are doing something illegal or outside the powers conferred on the company by its constitution. When the controllers of the *News Chronicle* wanted to devote the price received from the sale to pensions for former staff a shareholder prevented them in this way. There was nothing in the Memorandum and Articles giving power for the company to pay pensions.

But the responsibilities which the Rule enforces are those which are owed to the company, not to the minority personally. In *Percival* v. *Wright* (1902) 2 Ch. 421 the directors bought the shares of other members without letting on that they had arranged to sell the company's business for a good price. The court saw nothing wrong in that. The directors owed their duty of disclosure to the company, not to the shareholders personally. This decision has been judicially criticised, but the rescuing directors in our football club situation can take heart from it. It is really what Sir George Jessel meant by 'men of full age and competent understanding'. Those words are capable, of course, and are widely understood to mean that all except infants and lunatics are free to contract.

Both the Cohen and Jenkins Committees on Company Law have attacked the law which allows directors and controllers of companies to diddle the shareholders so long as they do not diddle the company. It may be stopped by legislation along the lines of the American law. *Section 20* of the *Companies Act, 1948* which provides that the Memorandum and Articles bind the company and each member as if he or she had signed them, does not make a contract between each of the members, but many contracts between each member and the company.

The minority member of a company might seem to have very few rights, and this is of course a direct result of the democratic majority control by which companies are administered. That does not stop them trying, as the Arderne Cinemas saga shows. Mr Greenhalgh bought into Arderne Cinemas Limited when it was hard up. It had been controlled by the Mallard family, but Mr Greenhalgh assumed control. Apart from that control, the deal involved an agreement by the Mallards to vote with him. In the first lawsuit the Mallards contended that this deal was void. The argument was that to place such a limitation on directors prevented them from doing their duty to the company. A sort of public policy, Foss and Harbottle reasoning. They lost. So they transferred their shares to other people who had not promised to vote with Greenhalgh. He lost. That left him without voting control but able to prevent special resolutions being passed. In the fourth action, the Mallards managed to divide up the ten shilling shares into floriners, and thus increase their supporters' holdings to a large enough number to pass special resolutions. Mr Greenhalgh lost again. He therefore sued them for conspiracy to injure him, and lost again, on the usual rock which wrecks conspiracy suits, that the Mallards were wronging him to protect their own interests and so were entitled to do it. Mr Greenhalgh actually had two tries at this, both of which he lost, but the Mallards decided to pull out, having had an offer of six shillings for the two-shilling shares they controlled—in spite of ten years of litigation over control of the concern.

This offer involved selling the shares to Mr Sol Sheckman, who was not a member, and therefore permission to sell was required from a meeting if the rule about offering shares to existing shareholders was not to be broken. The Mallards got their special majority, and Mr Greenhalgh brought his eighth action claiming that the resolutions were a fraud on the minority, i.e. himself. He lost that, too. Sir Raymond Evershed MR (as he then was) said that the special resolution could be impeached if its effect was to discriminate between the majority and minority shareholders so that the former got an advantage of which the latter were deprived. It would seem that that was precisely what Mr Greenhalgh was complaining about. But his view was coloured by the fact that he had lost control. The sale to Mr Sheckman did not make any difference between the majority and minority as shareholders. This must have been no comfort at all to Mr Greenhalgh, even though his shares had become more valuable.

Section 210 of the *Companies Act, 1948* provides that any member of the company who considers that it is being conducted oppressively as regards him (or quite often, her) can petition the court to wind-up the company or force the other members to buy his shares at a proper value or make any other order which would be just. *Foss* v. *Harbottle* does not apply to this jurisdiction, in which there have been only a few contested cases in the past decade. For Mr Greenhalgh it would have been quite useless, of course. He did not want to get out of the company. He could have managed that without any difficulty. He wanted to control a company whose value trebled in spite of its troubles.

There is often expressed the opinion that a Securities and Exchange Commission is required to govern company affairs overall in this country. America has one, and that does not prevent it from being the archetypal private enterprise economy. The objection to Government interference seems to be that directors are subject to stringent legal safeguards, like trustees.

> *'I can see but little resemblance between the duties of a director and the duties of a trustee,'*

said Mr Justice Romer in *Re City Equitable Fire Insurance Co.*

They have, he conceded, a fiduciary relationship. But this, of course, is owed to the company, not the shareholders. *Rule 30* of the *1972 City Code on Takeovers and Mergers* forbids anyone who takes part in merger discussions to deal in the shares of the concern doing the take over or the one being taken over until after the bid is announced.

But if two brothers are in business together as equal shareholders in a substantial family company, and one dies leaving his widow and children his shares, the surviving brother is under no duty to consider their personal advantage when he continues running the company. So long as the company itself is benefited he can run it to their disadvantage so far as the Memorandum and Articles permit him to do so. This constitution governs every action of a company—and consequently its controller.

He may treat employees very badly and the widow may object. When the *News Chronicle* and *The Star* 'died' in 1960 the controlling shareholders wanted to pay £1,925,000 of the price paid by Lord Rothermere's Associated Newspapers to the employees. But a shareholder procured an injunction against it (*Parke* v. *Daily News Ltd.* [*1962*] *Ch. 927*). The argument was that in modern times a company has a duty to its workers:

'*In my judgment such is not the law,*'

said Mr Justice Plowman.

He was following one of the celebrated railway cases.

'*The directors of the company might send down all the porters at a railway station to have tea in the country at the expense of the company. Why should they not? It is for the directors to judge . . .*

'*The law does not say that there are to be no cakes and ale, but that there are to be no cakes and ale except such as are required for the benefit of the company . . .*

'*Charity has no business to sit at boards of directors* qua *charity,*'

said Lord Justice Bowen in *Hutton* v. *West Cork Railway Co.* (*1883*) *23 Ch. D. 654.*

Had there been power to grant pensions in the company's Articles of Association, the directors could have done it. If the company was continuing the business and so gaining the advantage of good industrial relations by doing so, they could have done it. But not simply to do the decent thing.

The separate identity of companies established by Salomon's case made it worthwhile for quite small businesses to incorporate. When in 1909 the membership of private companies (which did not offer shares to the public) was reduced to two, and there was no need to reveal the balance sheets nor to distribute the profits, the company ousted the trust as a favourite tax dodge. Even the Perpetuities Rule could be avoided. A family company could own investments and property. The members could live in the property cheaply and draw modest incomes from the company to keep their tax liabilities down. The company could accumulate the surplus income but not distribute it. By capitalising it, it could turn into capital and at a convenient time a capital distribution could be made which would not be taxed in the hands of the members.

After all, as Lord Macnaghten pointed out:

'*The Income Tax, if I may be pardoned for saying so, is a tax upon income.*'

L.C.C. v. Attorney-General (1901) A.C. 26.

At 6d in the £1 it was—to us—hardly worth bothering about although they regarded it as an unconscionable curse in those days. Surtax, a mere deferred payment of Income Tax at a higher rate, was not known. The point of the remark was that it only bit on income—not capital.

Lord Justice Lindley had said of company accounts:

> '*There is nothing at all in the Act about how dividends are to be paid, nor how profits are to be reckoned. All that is left, and very judiciously and properly left, to the commercial world.*'
>
> ### Lee v. Neuchatel Asphalte Co. (1889) 41 Ch. D. 1.

That is not quite the modern law. The 1948 Act requires that distinction be made between fixed and current assets.

The main legislative battle of this century has been to draft taxing statutes which plugged the holes in the dykes through which Private Enterprise drained the Exchequer. Where the profits of a company were not distributed, they were 'deemed' to have been distributed in taxable manner. But companies are still used for tax dodging even though in 1965 the Income Tax and Profits Tax were replaced so far as companies were concerned with Corporation Tax, which is expressly on profits and capital gains. The real value of trading through a limited company was not very great for many small businesses, when that change occurred. The working director might be paying as he earned and the expenses of professional accountancy might have swallowed up the saving made by the company.

Personally, or through a company, losses can be offset against profits. But companies can utilise these reliefs better than real persons. A subsidiary company can pay income to its parent without deducting tax, and assets can be transferred between companies in a group without paying Capital Gains Tax. Thus the losses of one company in a group can be employed to relieve another company from heavy tax. But, of course, in order to bring companies with tax losses into a group to utilise them, they have to be bought. It is one way of paying something for less than nothing.

One of the most overworked citations in the books is Lord Tomlin's:

> '*Every man is entitled if he can to order his affairs so as that the tax attaching under the appropriate Acts is less than it otherwise would be. If he succeeds in ordering them so as to secure this result, then, however unappreciative the Commissioners of Inland Revenue or his fellow taxpayers may be of his ingenuity, he cannot be compelled to pay an increased tax.*'
>
> ### Inland Revenue Commissioners v. Duke of Westminster (1936) A.C. 1.

Apart from during and just after the war, when tax paying was regarded judicially as a patriotic duty and ingenuity as Black

Marketeering, that attitude persists. Judges, after all, pay tax.

But now there is a wider aspect to it. International concerns are made up of companies in several countries. Their turnover and income collectively are much greater than the revenues and budgets of many countries which are 'Sovereign States' in International Law. They can bring so much into an economy that governments are pleased to have them. They can have their 'residence' where the tax laws are best. They can put their processing plant near the raw materials. They can put up their noisome nuisance-making factories where the planning and anti-pollution laws are lax or non-existent, e.g. Africa. This is objected to very firmly by the Leftist economists. It is evasion of democratic control, they say.

But the essence of companies is the evasion of democratic control. Does the ICI shareholder individually say what the company shall do?

Whoever controls the company can make it do what he likes, so long as it is capable of that deed. The German Date Coffee Co. was formed to exploit a process for making coffee from dates, but the venture was unsuccessful. The shareholders were successful in their petition to wind it up because its substratum had disappeared (*1882, 20 Ch. D.*). Edwardian draughtsmen accordingly expended considerable labour on Objects Clauses in Memoranda of Association, and in spite of liberal interpretation policies in the courts these tend still to give companies power to do just about everything— though Jon Beauforte (London) Limited, a 'rag trade' concern overlooked that its objects did not include the manufacture of veneered panels. The suppliers could not therefore get paid by the liquidator because the Company had no power to make veneered panels ((*1953) Ch. 131*). Only one supplier was *intra vires*, but history does not record whether he had taken the precaution of looking up the memorandum at Bush House.

Lord Justice Harman considered that 'an object to do every mortal thing you want' is legally impossible (*1969, 2 W.L.R.*) even though everything *reasonably* (there it is again) incidental to carrying on the *intra vires* activities will be impliedly *intra vires*. An object to

> '*carry on any other trade or business whatsoever which can, in the opinion of the Board of Directors be advantageously carried on by the company in connection with or ancillary to any of the above businesses*'.

was approved by the Court of Appeal in *Bell Houses Ltd.* v. *City Wall Properties Ltd.* (*1966) 2 Q.B. 6 56*. It is firmly in the tradition of directors being bosses. And Trustees are not bosses. The beneficiaries of full age can demand that trust property be transferred to them. But shareholders cannot; for the company is the owner.

If the shareholders have enough votes to sack a director he needs skill and diligence sufficient to retain their confidence or he will be sacked, but the beneficiaries cannot sack a trustee. Lord Blanesburgh said in *Bell* v. *Lever Brothers Ltd.* (*1932*) *A.C.* that there was nothing to stop a director of a company becoming a director of a rival. Lord Denning disagreed in a 1959 case—but what else happens in a take-over or merger?

By *Section 199* of the 1948 Act a director directly or indirectly interested in a contract or proposed contract with the company must declare his interest at a Board meeting under pain of £100 fine. And they are accountable to the company for any inequitable 'secret profits'. But so long as they are pretty candid with each other, and thereby the company, they are quite entitled to make other profits from their position.

In *Regal (Hastings) Ltd.* v. *Gulliver* (*1942*) *1 All E.R.* a subsidiary company was formed to lease two cinemas, the idea being to make a chain of three with the company's own cinema and sell the whole as a going concern. The directors needed £5,000 cash for the subsidiary business but the company only had £2,000 and the directors and their friends took up the other 3,000 £1 shares (which they later sold, with their holdings in the original company, for £2 16s each). But the new owners of the old company made it sue the former directors to recover this profit on the subsidiary's shares.

The result would be that the purchasers, by accusing the directors of 'secret profit' cut the price they had paid for the cinemas by £1 16s a share.

The ridiculous part is that since those former directors were controllers they could without doubt have ratified what they did under the Rule in *Foss* v. *Harbottle*. But it had never dawned on them to go through the formality of doing so. The House of Lords held them liable because their profit resulted from using special knowledge they possessed as directors. However, since the chairman had not subscribed but only found other people to do so, he had no secret profit to pay back. The Solicitor for the company, who was not a director, had owned shares and made the profit. Since he advised the chairman on the transaction the result was that the company got a cheap cinema chain for the benefit of the new shareholders at the expense of the people who helped out the old directors—and the director and the lawyer who arranged it not only escaped liability but the latter made a profit. Ever since, Accountants and Secretaries have worshipped Mammon by writing up minutes of meetings and pasting them into Minute Books—whatever was said or done at 'meetings'.

By a curious oversight the proposition that dividends must be paid out of income, not capital, appeared in the *Companies Clauses*

Act, 1845 s. 121, and so was applied to the earliest companies set up by Act of Parliament, but it has not been legislated for since. It is put into most Articles of Association because judges have several times said it is the law. Why Parliament dropped it is unknown. Dividends cannot be paid if to do so would make the company insolvent. But if it is, it may well be sold for the sake of its tax losses. Should the price amount to a profit, the members can pay themselves a dividend.

Much was heard a few years ago of 'dividend-stripping'. Lord Denning explained how it was done in *Griffiths* v. *J. P. Harrison (Watford) Ltd. (1963) A.C. 1*, the first but not the last time that the Law Lords had to contend with this ingenuity of the tax lawyer. Tax consultancy is highly skilled. But it is not a profession nor a trade. Mr Currie who carried on 'The Income Taxpayer's Appeal Agency' claimed exemption from excess profit and duty because he was carrying on a profession. The Commissioners had found as a fact that he was not. Lord Herndale said that the Act under which the matter came was vague and left a good deal to be desired from the standpoint of composition and grammar, and he did not know whether it was possible to give a positive answer to the question whether carrying on a trade was a matter of fact a law (*1921, 2 K.B. 332*). In the dividend stripping case it appeared that tax dodging, whilst not professional, was not trading either. I think it is an art. Oddly enough, none of the Schedules to the Income Taxes Acts provide for profits of arts. They commercialise everything, and no doubt tax consultants pay tax on the profits of their 'business'.

However, the question whether tax-dodging is a trade is the fundamental one in dividend-stripping. What had happened was simply that Harrisons made a loss of £13,585. They closed their business down, and changed (by resolution in a company meeting) their Articles of Association. This was necessary so that they could deal in shares. Then they bought Claiborne Ltd. This had also ceased trading but was 'pregnant with dividend' according to Lord Denning. It had made £28,912 profit—and paid tax of £13,010 out of that. The value of the dividend-money was £15,901 19s 3d. Harrisons bought the shares for £16,900—with borrowed money. When they owned them they distributed the dividend of £15,901 19s 3d to their members, sold the shares for £1,000, and paid back the £15,900 which they had borrowed—leaving a profit to themselves of £1 19s 3d. It seems a lot of trouble for a little profit. But tax had been paid on the Claiborne profits, and there had been a loss on the sale of the Claiborne shares by Harrisons in their newly-authorised share dealing.

Harrisons' losses were therefore:

Old business	*£13,585*
Claiborne Shares cost £16,900, sold for £1,000	*£15,900*
	£29,485
The Claiborne total dividend was a similar sum	*£28,912*

The Harrison losses slightly exceeded the Claiborne profits.

Consequently they could claim repayment from the Revenue of the tax already paid on the Claiborne profits—£13,010, i.e. nearly all their loss on the old business.

The necessities were losses—which they had; and some profits on which tax had already been paid against which to set them. However, the losses had to be trade losses. Harrisons contended naturally enough that the loss on the Claiborne shares was in the new Harrisons capacity of share-dealing. This, they suggested, was trading. Lots of people trade in shares. The Revenue saw it not as trading at all but as 'dividend-stripping'. That must be a trade, they said—what else is it? What characteristic of a trade does it lack? Lord Denning rejoined with what detail must it have to be a trade?

> *'Take a gang of burglars. Are they engaged in trade or in an adventure in the nature of trade? They have an organisation. They spend money on equipment. They acquire goods by their efforts. They sell the goods. They make a profit. What detail is lacking in their adventure? You may say it lacks legality, but it has been held that legality is not an essential characteristic of a trade.'*

It did not help to ask how it fell short of being a trade. It was just burglary and not a trade and this was just dividend-stripping and not a trade. That view did not prevail. By three to two the Law Lords held that the Commissioners were entitled to decide as a fact that the losses enabling Harrisons to reclaim the tax already paid on the Claiborne profits were sustained in trade.

As a result various modifications to the tax laws were attempted and various other ways were worked out to get tax back from profits by finding losses to set against them. But not all reforms were for the Revenue's advantage. The *Finance Act, 1965 Section 61 (1)* enabled a predecessor company which stopped trading to have its trade treated as being in its ownership even though it had been continued by a successor company if more than threequarters of the business belonged to the same people. There were time limits, but the combination of this and the carrying forward of losses under *Section 58* of the 1965 Act enabled the 'forward stripping' techniques to be successfully exploited. Provisions designed to stop this were enacted in the *Finance Act, 1969 s. 30*—as one would expect under an enthusiastic Socialist Government—which had, of course, created the facilities for the tax dodge in the first place.

One of the essential characteristics of revenue law seems to be that the details are minutely defined in order to make actual administration efficient whilst the principles have to be left vague because if they were closely defined, dodging would be simplified. The absence of definition of 'trade' is an example. If there was one, people would so organise their enterprises as not to amount to 'trade'. Mr J. D. Casswell QC in his memoirs recalled acting for 'an elderly and impecunious burglar' who had been assessed to tax on £3,000 of his wife's 'earnings'. With some such decision as the Harrisons case to cite it could have been contended that those 'earnings' were not the profits of a trade—though trafficking in stolen goods involves selling. But that negative definition of burglary was enunciated so that the taxpayer should be at a disadvantage— not to enable burglars to resist tax claims.

Even when a very candid disclosure of a course of dealing imposes the stigma of dishonesty upon some part of it the law does not always manage to exact its toll. This is nowhere better illustrated than in the saga of *Peter Buchanan Ltd.* v. *McVey* in *(1955) A.C.* at *page 516*. Since the Appeal cases are the reports of the decisions of the House of Lords and the Privy Council it might be appreciated that the inclusion therein of a judgment of a puisne judge of Northern Ireland is an honour. Mr Justice Kingsmill Moore had decided the case in July, 1950, and, said Lord Keith 'This admirable judgment somehow escaped the notice of the reporters'.

It turned on the fact that although the company—entirely owned by Mr James McVey—had made small losses in 1937–40, and even smaller profits in 1941–4 it had considerable liquid assets—stocks of whisky bought for some £19,000, but in 1944 worth (conservatively) £300,000. The judge remarked that sober thinkers considered that retroactive legislation like the *Finance Act, 1943* was ethically and politically immoral.

> '*The Defendant was emphatically of this opinion, though indigna-tion, more than the niceties of political ethics, seems to have been his motive force.*'

For the sake of £155,000 he bent his ingenuity to defeating the Revenue because he strongly felt that they had no moral claim to the money. And he mortgaged all the whisky to a bank to secure advances of money. He then drew on the funds so secured and put them into a bank in Northern Ireland, leaving just £3,212 11s to satisfy all the creditors except the Revenue. They put Sir Andrew Macharg in as liquidator because he was 'a financial Sherlock Holmes' and he brought in Scotland—the domicil and residence of the Company—an action for the recovery of the tax. The contention was of course, that it was the company's money and even though

Mr McVey owned the shares and could distribute the company's property to himself, he had to settle the company's liabilities first—including the Excess profits tax made retrospective by the 1943 Act. The liquidator got judgment in Scotland but by then Mr McVey was in Northern Ireland. So was the money.

They sued him in Northern Ireland. Mr Justice Kingsmill Moore ruled that the disposal of the whisky was a fraud on the Scottish Revenue and therefore not 'honest' according to Scottish Law.

But there was a rule of conflict of laws established for two centuries that

'*In a British Court we cannot take notice of the Revenue laws of a foreign State*'.

And since the whole object of revenue's proceedings in winding up the company in Scotland was to collect a Revenue debt, for a foreign state—Scotland—their Irish claim failed.

You Can't Take It With You

'If it is trite learning that the thought of man is not triable, for the devil himself knows not the thought of man.'

Chief Justice Brian (1478) Y.B. 17 Edw. IV.

THAT LAWYERS make more money out of home-made wills than from drafting wills themselves is an article of faith. It is, however, incapable of proof for the precise amount of injustice, unhappiness and perplexity, to say nothing of downright misery, caused by testamentary dispositions is incapable of proof or estimation. Thousands of wills are never found. The temptation to suppress an inconvenient testament must be great sometimes, and fraudulent destruction of a will was punishable with life imprisonment under the 29th section of the *Larceny Act, 1861*. With characteristic lenity, the Permissive Parliament reduced this to seven years in the *Theft Act, 1968 s. 20*.

There must be other thousands of wills which could lead to disputes, but the relatives do not bother. Having a will drawn by a lawyer should save the elementary mistakes which ordinary people make, and which make their wills invalid. However, the will of Doctor Tristram, one of the original authors of the standard work on the law of Probate—the validity of wills—was not properly executed. The will of Lord Chancellor St Leonards was lost. Judges and eminent barristers have proved equally incompetent with other testators, but one seldom hears of a solicitor's will being upset. Their families are too sensible to publicise the firm's incompetence and waste their patrimony in litigation costs.

This necessity for witnesses to 'attest' (i.e. prove the testator signed) a will in the presence of the testator originated ages ago. The witnesses need not sign in the presence of each other, only in the presence of the testator after he has acknowledged that he has signed the will. (This has to be done at the foot or end—a provision the courts interpret liberally.)

Anglo-Saxons used to speak their last wishes, writing not being common. In the 9th Century, Archbishop Egbert of York advised clerics witnessing dispositions to take a friend:

> '*So that in the mouth of two or three witnesses every word may be established for perchance the avarice of the kinsfolk of the dead would contradict what was said by the clergy.*'

So many people tried to get right with God by making gifts to the Church, or particular abbots, bishops or priests that it was not surprising that they assumed legal power over testamentary dispositions. Many gifts were made to ecclesiastics on conditions that the dependents of the deceased received certain benefits. A bishop's cross on the 'landbook' was proof that he was entitled to the land and observing the wishes of the Testator. Who could argue? The sealing of probates—proven-true wills—by the consent of the interested parties or after trial and proof in the ecclesiastical court continued until 1857, when it was transferred to the Court of Probate. Most Probate Registries are still in cathedral towns. It is still possible to find among old property deeds grants of probate with their big wax seals on.

The two witnesses were required by the *Wills Act, 1837*, still the main statute governing wills. But much of the work of lawyers is of a more practical nature than interpretation of statutes and precedents. The ordinary solicitor in the High Street is used to relatives charging breathlessly into his office claiming that Auntie Daisy had helped herself to the canteen of cutlery, saying that Mother had always meant her to have it. The heinousness is exacerbated by the fact that Mother is not yet cold.

The wise man first looks at the copy will on his file, or the original if he has it, to see if Auntie Daisy is an executor. They are entitled to 'gather in the estate' and they have a year to do it. She is technically entitled to take possession of the spoons—though not of course to keep them unless they are left to her by will, or she takes under intestacy law, or she takes them as a *donatio mortis causa*.

In large families, the other relatives are ransacking the house whilst the indignant few are at the solicitor's office. All the lawyers do is to get in touch with the executors and tell them to get all the loot back. Whether they do or not is largely their affair, for the resultant vendetta, seldom lead to costly litigation.

Testamentary law has only lately been given over to one branch of the court system. Probate used to be done by the same judges who tried divorce and shipwreck cases. The reason was the origins of all in Civil and Ecclesiastical Law—not mordant analogy. This involves the technical requirements for validity, all designed to secure that the paper is indeed a testamentary instrument. The effect of the valid instrument was in the hands of the Chancery Court.

A will can be formally perfect but so uncertain or unintelligible that the property has to pass as if there was no will. And since a will speaks from death whenever it was written, it sometimes fails to dispose of property because the Testator has not got it. 'My freehold house No. 19 Acacia Avenue' would not pass his next abode, say No. 49 Mornington Gardens, just because he had sold the first and moved to the second. 'My freehold house' would pass whichever he lived in at his death. The possibility of either or both kinds of proceeding looms over every will. Probate can be disputed because an obviously formally valid will is alleged to be a forgery or the Testator lacked capacity by reason of insanity or undue influence. These allegations are often threatened, but seldom litigated.

The principal role of interpretation of any legal document is to give to the words used their 'plain, ordinary meaning'. The number of plain ordinary meanings a sentence can bear is unappreciated until some relatives hear what it is. A Testator left all his 'money' to a beneficiary and it transpired that most of his wealth was not in cash. For two hundred years the courts had construed 'money' as meaning 'cash'. This is fairly reasonable. A bank balance is often thought of as money, but it is not. You cannot have back the notes and coins you paid in. It is a right to be paid by the bank. Stocks and shares and insurance payments are similarly often thought of as 'money' but they are not.

The House of Lords decided that that particular Testator intended all his wealth to go to that beneficiary.

> '*I anticipate with satisfaction that henceforth the group of ghosts who . . . wait on the other side of the Styx to receive the judicial personages who have misconstrued their wills will be considerably diminished,*'

said Lord Atkin (*Perrin* v. *Morgan* (*1943*) *A.C. 399*).

That is the meaning of a word. The meaning can be clear beyond peradventure on its face, but its effectual meaning can be obscured. Consider the simple bequest, 'to my nephew, William'.

It is very easy to have more than one nephew called William. It would be less common to have two called Peregrine, but still perfectly possible. In a leading case the Testator had two nephews called Arthur, but the court held that he actually meant neither of them, but a third Arthur, the illegitimate son of his sister, who had married a legitimate neice, and was therefore in a sense a nephew (*Re. Jackson, Beattie* v. *Murphy* (*1933*) *Ch. 237*).

In the ordinary way, the court does not allow evidence to be given to explain the meaning of a document. To do so is not interpreting the paper itself, but trying the claims of people who put forward arguments, usually those 'avaricious kinsfolk'. Lord Justice James said that a judge should place himself, so to speak, in the Testator's armchair and consider the circumstances by which he was surrounded when he made his will, to arrive at his intention. And the rule has existed a long time. Bacon said that:

'ambiguens patens *is never holpen by averment; but if it is* ambiguens latens *then it is otherwise'.*

Modern judges treat cases where several people have the same name at latent ambiguities. But they are not ambiguities at all. The Testator has simply not identified the one he means.

'When there is doubt on the face of the instrument, the law admits no extrinsic evidence to explain it,'

said Chief Justice Tindal in *Saunderson* v. *Piper* (*1839*) *5 Bing˙ N.C. 425.*

The evidence was allowed in the case of the three Arthurs because one was illegitimate. Had the two legitimate Arthurs been the only claimants, the court could not have allowed evidence to resolve it and there would have been an intestacy. But because there was an Arthur who was not a nephew, evidence was received, and he took under the words 'to my nephew Arthur'.

This kind of case must be distinguished from:

'. . . *those unsatisfactory cases in which the Court is called upon to say what a Testator meant, when it is perfectly clear that he did not know what he meant himself.'*

Lord Chancellor Cranworth, *Dormer* **v.** *Phillips (1855) 4 De G.M. & G. 855.*

All the court could do, added Lord Cranworth, was to construe the words actually used. Certain terms of art and technical expressions have over the centuries become so hallowed that a testator using them can be fairly sure that his estate will be distributed and enjoyed according to his wishes—so long as the law has not been altered between the making of the will and putting it into effect.

The real problem in making a will is that very few people manage to forecast accurately what will be the state of their circumstances and those of their beneficiaries when they die. A testatrix a few years ago left blanks beside all her beneficiaries' names in her will because she was clearly uncertain how much to leave to each. The argument that each should receive an equal share failed as it was bound to do. The court cannot make a will for the deceased. It can sometimes help out the relatives as it did a few years ago when a husband died with his wife in a disaster. The ordinary presumption that the younger died last was discounted for that would have resulted in the wife inheriting the husband's estate for an instant of time and passing it as well as her own to her successors.

When people make mutual wills leaving their estates to each other, the survivor cannot revoke his or her will after the first dies. The other beneficiaries' claims are protected by the contract of making the mutual wills and a trust is thereby established. Such contracts are the only way of making a will irrevocable, and they do not really do so. If one party secretly revokes, the other is no longer bound to stick to the bargain. But if the survivor remains in ignorance, the trust binds the other estate. Apart from such transactions, a testator can make as many wills as he likes up to the moment of his death, so long as each is signed at the end and witnessed by two witnesses. The latest document in date to deal with a piece of property is the one which effectively disposes of it.

The appallingly complex law of trusts is deceptively simple in its application to wills. Lord Justice Lindley in *Re. Williams (1897) 2 Ch. 12* pointed out that trusts are really nothing except confidences reposed by one person in another and enforceable in a court administering the system of Equity. Any words can be used to create a trust so long as the words used are clear enough to impose the obligations. Then he held that certain bequests 'to my wife Lucy . . . in the fullest confidence that she will carry out my wishes' were not sufficiently clear in that case.

A trust does not have to be declared in a will to attach to a gift. It can be 'secret'. If completely secret, of course it cannot be effective. A man may give a valuable property to his old friend. If he had told him that he would do so, but that he was to make a home there for the Testator's mistress, the beneficiary could be held to the trust, if anyone else who knew about it gave evidence to that effect and was believed. If the beneficiary was never told, but after he inherited, some document or letter was found supporting that condition of affairs, a problem could arise. The document would be inadmissible in evidence to qualify the will, because, not being executed, and attested it would be no testamentary document. On the other hand, if the mistress or someone else swore that the Testator had told her or him of the second trust, the document could be admitted to corroborate this allegation. By artful extensions of reasoning, inheritance disputes can thus be built up. Even when the property is not very valuable, people still feel encouraged to litigate, because the costs are often ordered to be paid out of the estate, and so the loser has the satisfaction of seeing the winner's inheritance depleted or even lost entirely in lawyers' fees.

When wills of land became possible in 1540 the great process of tying up land in families became pretty efficient. A husband took his wife's land and in a few generations vast estates could be put together by a few wills. The old rule was that land descended to the heir-at-law—the eldest son or nearest successive male relative except where local custom provided otherwise.

It was abolished by the *Administration of Estates Act, 1925 s. 45.*

The principal beneficiary now is the widow. The *Intestates' Estates Act, 1952* created a scheme of inheritance where there was no effective will, or where property was not disposed of by will. It was worked out after the examination of thousands of wills filed at the Principal Probate Registry at Somerset House. The idea was to research the usual scheme of disposition by the average man.

In 1938 the average man was in the habit of leaving his wife out of his will and leaving his riches to his mistress. Accordingly, Parliament passed the *Inheritance (Family Provision) Act, 1938* to enable a wife or other dependant to order reasonable provision out of an estate if the court is of opinion that reasonable provision was not made for the maintenance of that dependant. In case the 1952 Act had not provided well enough for wives, they were allowed to make claims in respect of intestacies. In 1958 the right to claim such provision was extended to divorced spouses who had not remarried.

On an intestacy, the spouse gets the whole estate absolutely if it is under £8,750. Above that the spouse gets the personal effects, motor car, furniture and the first £8,750 out of the rest of the estate. The remainder is halved. One 'moiety' goes to the children absolutely. The spouse has a life interest in the other moiety, i.e. has the income from it when invested, but cannot touch the capital. When the spouse dies, it descends to the children. If there are no children the spouse takes everything up to £30,000 absolutely and half the balance. The deceased parents get the other half of the balance. Unmarried people's parents take first. If the parents are dead, the brothers and sisters take. Half-brothers and half-sisters or their children are next in line, then grandparents and uncles and aunts. Remotest legal 'next of kin' are half-blood uncles and aunts or their children representing their shares.

If there are no relatives, the Crown takes the estate as *bona vacantia*. People to whom the deceased owed some sort of moral duty sometimes get *ex gratia* grants from the Crown when it inherits. In *Law Reform Now* published in 1963, a group of Labour lawyers criticised and suggested changes in the law. The complaint about the Inheritance Act was that it could be avoided relatively easily by making covenants to transfer property, conferring the benefit of insurance policies on people other than spouses and making settlements on trust. The courts should, they contended, have power to over-ride all such things to provide for dependants. But these expedients are really giving things away in life rather than disposing of an estate on death. The remedy of the deserted wife, for example, is to claim a settled provision.

They also complain that it is unjust that a surviving spouse not living with the intestate when he dies should take the first slice of the estate. They wanted it changed so that the inheritance was lost if the couple were not living together. That seems tough on deserted spouses. They are the people who are disinherited by wills and that is why the Inheritance Act was passed. It was regarded as a very un-English provision when it was enacted. It now covers the deceased's wife or husband, a daughter who has not been married, or is incapable by reason of physical or mental incapacity of maintaining herself, sons under 21, or incapable of maintaining themselves, and the surviving 'spouse' under a void marriage. The children can be adopted, or illegitimate or unborn at the time of the death.

In 1833, a husband was empowered to cut off his wife's right to dower from his estate, and from then until 1938 an Englishman could do as he wished on death, not only with his own, but also with the property he had got from his wife.

He was not entirely free for that century, for the *Finance Act, 1894* by *Section 1*, introduced Estate Duty levied:

> '*upon the principal value . . . of all property, real or personal, settled or not settled, which passes on the death of a person*'.

The next section listed property which was 'deemed to pass' on death. Thus began that great struggle in which 'the legislature has often been worsted by the skill, determination and resourcefulness of its opponents of whom the present appellant has not been the least successful' as Lord Green said in *Lord Howard de Walden* v. *Inland Revenue Commissioners (1942) 1 K.B. 389.*

The Death Duties properly so-called are no longer in existence. Nor is the Legacy Duty by which the beneficiary had to share his good fortune with the rest of the taxpayers. Tory bright sparks have come to feel in the euphoric period after the 1972 Budget that Estate Duty is unkind and they suggest that beneficiaries ought to pay rather than the estate. The idea is new, again.

The great advantage of Estate Duty is that when the death is registered and probate or Letters of Administration granted by the court, the Revenue can put the bite on the personal representatives and take their cut before distribution. This circumstance has been responsible for a great deal of charity, simply to spite the taxman. The best ways to do it are well known. It no longer excites comment when some distinguished judge is recorded in the wills column of *The Times* as having left only a couple of hundred pounds.

It has been well said that anyone can save Estate Duty if he will undertake to die before the next Budget, but there is a little more to it than that. A gift of one's wealth during one's lifetime is 'aggregable' for this tax unless it was made more than seven years before death.

Only five years' survival was necessary until Mr Wilson started to get the economy going again in 1965.

An Estate Duty dodge put out every now and then by some bright newspaper columnist comes up with the idea of a testator in settled expectation of death libelling the person he wishes to make his heir and paying substantial damages to him, free of duty. The idea has been in tax books for at least 25 years, and might well lead to a prosecution of the 'heir' for a conspiracy to defraud the Revenue. If anyone has ever done it, there has been no publicity, and very wisely.

Of course, it is perfectly possible to insure one's life and provide that the insurance money shall never be part of one's estate, but go straight to someone else on your death. By *Section 11* of the *Married Women's Property Act, 1882* if either husband or wife insures his or her life and expresses the policy to be for the benefit of the spouse or their children, the life assured's creditors cannot get at the policy even if he is bankrupt and they get all the policy moneys when he dies. Where property has been settled on trust and one of the spouses has died and Estate Duty has been paid, the settled property is exempt from duty on the death of the spouse who survived.

If people own property as 'joint tenants' but not if they own as 'tenants in common' the survivor becomes the sole owner immediately upon the death of the other joint tenant. Thus the deceased's share of the property never goes into his estate. Contrary to popular belief, however, this does not prevent Estate Duty being levied on the value of the half share of a deceased spouse. If both spouses contribute to a joint bank account, they are entitled to it in proportion to their contributions. But since the *Married Women's Property Act, 1964*, if it contains money for expenses of the matrimonial home, in the absence of an agreement to the contrary it is deemed to belong to them in equal shares. Thus half would be considered to be the husband's for Estate Duty purposes. If, however, the wife points out that what is left in the account is her contribution, it will not go into the husband's estate. The husband can make the same objection on his wife's death.

This does not affect people whose estate is under £15,000 but nowadays houses are so valuable that they are often put into joint names in case of Estate Duty becoming payable. Then if the marriage breaks down, the wife can get up to a half share without having paid a penny towards it. It can of course be argued that though jointly owned, it is not owned in equal shares. But the plea that it is a prospective tax dodge in case the marriage works out is hardly likely to get express legal sympathy, however the court might in fact regard it.

The judicial attitude to tax avoidance varies with the times.

During and just after the War it was regarded as akin to sabotage. Now it is widely accepted that a person has a duty to manage his wealth so that he can benefit his dependants as fully as possible. That means tax-saving as much as personal thrift. Since the *Variation of Trusts Act, 1958*, the Chancery Division has had power to approve arrangements made between beneficiaries for varying or revoking trusts, even where some are prevented by the terms of the trust instruments or wills from giving consent. These variations are often employed to re-arrange the settlements so that Estate Duty will be avoided. Parliament therefore provides ways in which the Exchequer can be legitimately deprived of its expectations.

In the result, a growth industry has developed by which insurance and investment can be coupled with wise charity and skilled legal drafting to preserve for one's loved ones the fruits of one's labours. Unless your fortune is large, the cost of the expertise might outweigh the saving in tax. An ordinary man's will would be drafted by a solicitor for about a fiver. Something more complicated might cost twenty pounds.

A Bencher of Lincoln's Inn was indignant to learn that the will of a wealthy man was to be disputed, no doubt because he had worked hard for his large fee. But the solicitor calmed him a little by telling him that it was not the will which counsel had so expertly drawn that was being disputed. The client had torn that up after spending hundreds of pounds on having it made, and made one for himself on a form bought from a stationer—in Scotland where the law and the form are different.

A country solicitor was scornful of the large fees paid to counsel and accountants for their advice over tax-avoidance schemes. He boasted that in his office they had drafted a millionaire's will and charged him only 25 guineas. The revenue dispute ended up in the House of Lords at rather greater expense.

Against such a background is it surprising that Mr Jarman, the original author of the great book upon the law of wills, which bears his name still, died intestate?

Epilogue

THE YOUNG science of jurimetrics involves the reduction of legal problems into their components to be fed into computers for solution. Reasonable computers might replace judges and magistrates quite soon.

Judges qualify for pensions, of course, and lay magistrates can always devote themselves to Ratepayers' Associations. But what is to become of the redundant lawyers?

They have surely deserved better than to be automated out of existence. In Henry Tudor's time, a man whose annual income was under 40 shillings could get free legal aid. The right was not well used because an Elizabethan statute provided that if a person who sued *in forma pauperis* lost, 'he shall be punished with whipping and pillory'.

By 1729, Parliament was regulating attorneys' fees. Is all this to be forgotten when for each vacancy as a law computer programmer, there is a queue of down-at-heel Silks, and solicitors with screwdrivers are taking night classes in electronics? Dick the Butcher was kinder when he suggested, 'Let's kill all the lawyers'.

The profession will regenerate itself by drawing upon its essential strength. The lawyers will plead the bad cases which the computers throw out. They will prove to the Court of Appeal and the House of Lords that the computer was wrong.

Thousands of right-thinking people will be delivered from the tyranny of 1984 upon payment of proper, cost-effective fees to some Artful Pleader.

411

NOTES

NOTES